Money
Meltdown

Money Meltdown

Restoring Order to the Global Currency System

JUDY SHELTON

THE FREE PRESS
A Division of Macmillan, Inc.
NEW YORK

Maxwell Macmillan Canada
TORONTO

Maxwell Macmillan International
NEW YORK   OXFORD   SINGAPORE   SYDNEY

The Free Press
A Division of Macmillan, Inc.
866 Third Avenue, New York, N.Y. 10022

Maxwell Macmillan Canada, Inc.
1200 Eglinton Avenue East
Suite 200
Don Mills, Ontario M3C 3N1

Macmillan, Inc. is part of the Maxwell Communication Group of Companies

Printed in the United States of America

printing number

1 2 3 4 5 6 7 8 9 10

Library of Congress Cataloging-in-Publication Data

Shelton, Judy.
  Money meltdown: restoring order to the global currency system/
Judy Shelton.
    p. cm.
  Includes index.
  ISBN 0-02-929112-7
  1. International finance. I. Title.
HG3881.S513 1994
332'.042—dc20   93-48786
                                                      CIP

Grateful acknowledgment is given to the publishers for permission to reprint excerpts from the following works:

The International Monetary Fund, 1945-65: Twenty Years of International Monetary Coopera-tion. Volume I: *Chronicle.* Volume III: *Documents.* By J. Keith Horsefield, et al. Inter-national Monetary Fund, Washington, D.C., 1969.

From *Changing Fortunes* by Paul Volcker and Toyoo Gyohten. Copyright © 1992 by Paul Volcker and Toyoo Gyohten. Reprinted by permission of Times Books, a division of Random House, Inc.

Adapted from "Monetary Policy for the 1980s" by Milton Friedman in *To Promote Prosperi-ty*, edited by John H. Moore, with the permission of the publisher, Hoover Institution Press. Copyright © 1984 by the Board of Trustees of the Leland Stanford Junior Uni-versity. (Quoted in *The Search for Stable Money* by James A. Dorn and Anna I. Schwartz, University of Chicago Press, 1987.)

"Toward a Free-Market Monetary System" by Friedrich A. Hayek, *Libertarian Studies* 3, no. 1 (1979). (Reprinted in *The Search for Stable Money* by Dorn and Schwartz.)

"Competing Currencies" by Roland Vaubel, *Cato Journal* 5 (Winter 1986). (Reprinted in *The Search for Stable Money* by Dorn and Schwartz.)

The Case for Gold: A Minority Report of the U.S. Gold Commission by Ron Paul and Lewis Lehrman, Cato Institute, Washington, D.C., 1982.

"The Dangers of a Quick Fix" by Michael Prowse, *Financial Times*, February 27–28, 1993.

"Let's Fall in Love with Falling Currencies" by Anatole Kaletsky, *The Times* (London), June 30, 1993, © Times Newspapers Ltd. 1993.

"Fix What Broke," *Wall Street Journal*, July 11, 1984; "President Salinas on Mexico's Econ-omy," *Wall Street Journal*, April 4, 1990; "Foreign Travels, Foreign-Exchange Travails" by Herbert Stein, *Wall Street Journal*, August 27, 1990; "75%: Why Sweden Acted," *Wall Street Journal*, September 11, 1992; "Remembering the Fifteenth of August" by Herbert Stein, *Wall Street Journal*, August 14, 1981. Reprinted with permission of the Wall Street Journal © 1993 Dow Jones & Company, Inc. All rights reserved.

"Europe's Monetary Day of Reckoning " by Paul Krugman, *CEO/International Strategies* IV, no. III (May/June 1992).

"A British Official, Stirring Outcry, Says German Are Taking Over" by Sheila Rule, *New York Times*, July 13, 1990. Copyright © 1990 by The New York Times Company. Reprinted by permission.

"Private Money: An Idea Whose Time Has Come" by Richard W. Rahn, *Cato Journal* 9, no. 2 (Fall 1989).

"The Classical Gold Standard as a Spontaneous Order" by Giulio M. Gallarotti, paper pre-sented at the Cato Institute Seventh Annual Monetary Conference, Washington, D.C., February 23–24, 1989. Reprinted by permission of Giulio M. Gallarotti.

To my husband G. L.

Contents

Introduction:
Losing the Dream

The end of the Cold War. The dawning of a new era of international cooperation and peaceful global trade. For one brief shining moment—somewhere between when Boris Yeltsin defiantly stared down communism from astride a tank and when Europe's currencies fell into turmoil while Americans watched from afar and scratched their heads—it almost seemed possible to attain the dream.

Instead of devoting massive chunks of economic output to military preparedness, nations would be able to concentrate on improving the living standards of their citizens. Humankind had seemingly changed the main venue of competition; superpower status would be defined in terms of economic and financial prowess, not the ability to intimidate with weapons of destruction. All nations would be eligible to peacefully pursue their own best economic interests in the global marketplace. The only requirement was that every government should embrace the doctrine of free trade. Then the world would be able to benefit fully from the energized output of newly released sources of productivity, both human and material, as formerly communist nations joined in the promise of democracy and free markets.

It was a nice dream, one full of hope and human yearning for peace and prosperity. It was based, perhaps naively, on the premise that there existed a fundamental willingness to permit all participants to take advantage of an open global trading system. Economic competitors—in the classic American tradition of fair play—would all abide by the same rules. Governments would seek to remove existing trade barriers and refrain from erecting new ones. The dream envisioned a global economy where the guiding principle was to provide opportunity and the reinforcing message was that competence counts.

In some ways, political developments in the early 1990s were just catching up to what the global entrepreneurs had long since discovered; capital carries no flag and profits know no borders. Governments could encourage business growth with low taxes and a stable financial environment, or they could drive away investment by punishing economic success and engaging in dubious fiscal strategies. They could strive to maintain sound monetary policies so that capital resources would flow to their optimal economic use, wherever that might be in the world. Or they could seek to capture any possible temporary advantage by manipulating currencies and intervening in credit markets.

By late summer 1992 it was becoming clear that the vision of an open global marketplace offering equal access and governed by universal rules was being distorted by a breakdown in international monetary relations. Instead of moving to build on the concept of an expanding world economy that had received such momentum with the dissolution of the Soviet Union, the governments of the leading Western industrialized nations seemed suddenly caught up in their own domestic worries to the exclusion of their trading partners' concerns or the needs of the rest of the world. Money, the language of international business and the foundation for global commerce, was losing its facility to communicate price signals across borders as exchange rates fluctuated irrationally. Worse, currencies were becoming economic weapons to be used by self-seeking governments, insidious instruments of protectionism.

CURRENCY CHAOS

The breakdown began in Europe as the scenario for currency union abruptly began to unravel with Denmark's rejection in June 1992 of the Maastricht Treaty, which sought to bring about European political and monetary union. For years there had been slow but inexorable progress toward the realization of a single European currency. The goal was clear enough: to eliminate the uncertainty and accompanying cost of exchange rate risk when conducting cross-border business and thus to enhance the benefits of a single European market. But now there was squabbling over whether the rewards of monetary union would be worth the price—if the price was submission to the dictates of the German Bundesbank.

For all the prior agreement about the need for economic convergence and stable monetary relations, for all the detailed reports and timetables devised to resolve any final obstacles that might derail the process of European monetary unity, the fundamental question had yet to be answered: What happens when national domestic priorities demand financial remedies that deviate from the conditions required to preserve international monetary stability? If the theorists and "Eurocrats" had ascertained the proper response, they had not yet successfully persuaded the politicians. Or else the politicians were just finding it too difficult to explain to their constituents, especially the unemployed ones, that it was more important to emulate Germany's high interest rates than to stimulate a domestic business recovery.

Tensions were rising across Europe as the apparent impasse over Germany's determination to run an anti-inflationary monetary policy, even at the cost of sentencing its neighbors to continuing recession, was throwing the whole issue of European unity into question. In France, public support for a single European currency was dropping precipitously; a survey indicated that the percentage of French voters planning to vote in favor of the Maastricht Treaty dropped from 68 percent in May to 59 percent in June.[1] The referendum ultimately passed in September, but only by a razor-thin 51 percent margin, prompting frenzied re-examination of the prospects for monetary union and inducing gloomy pessimism about the future of the New Europe.

In the meantime, Americans were caught in the throes of an election year and the heightened political atmosphere associated with the race for the White House. Concerns about the falling dollar—which was declining to record lows against the world's other leading currencies—tended to be relegated to the business section of newspapers. Even after world stock markets plunged on July 20 and some thirteen central banks felt compelled to intervene forcefully in the exchange markets to support the sinking dollar, the average American paid little notice. Indeed, the U.S. treasury secretary, Nicholas Brady, said he didn't care about the dollar's decline, prompting *The Economist* to observe: "This smacks of negligence. As a reserve currency, the dollar is supposed to be a reliable store of value, yet successive American governments have failed to help it fulfil this role."[2]

By late August, though, it was becoming difficult to ignore the message of a skidding dollar that would leave the U.S. currency at its lowest point in more than forty years.[3] The day after President Bush addressed the Republican convention in Houston and laid out his program for U.S. economic recovery, the dollar plummeted against the deutsche mark, despite concerted intervention efforts by the U.S. Federal Reserve, Germany's Bundesbank, and other European central banks. Financial analysts attributed the dollar blowout to Bush's lackluster agenda for a second term. According to Patrick Harverson writing in the *Financial Times*, the response of the foreign exchange markets to Bush's convention speech "was the equivalent of a big raspberry."[4]

Still, American headlines did not start echoing their European counterparts with exclamations of "currency crisis" and "monetary turmoil" until mid-September 1992. Then, suddenly, Europe's exchange rate bedlam and the apparent collapse of its monetary system was seen to hold frightening implications for the entire global economy; nervous Americans began to realize that their own interests were at stake. "What happens today in Bonn affects tomorrow the daily life of Bangor and Baton Rouge," observed Jodie T. Allen in the *Washington Post*.[5] What was happening in Germany was that the Bundesbank was persisting in maintaining high interest rates to stave off inflationary pressures associated with the massive cost of German unification. Since the deutsche mark serves as the anchor currency for the European monetary system, Germany's neighbors found themselves likewise forced to maintain high interest rates to keep their currencies aligned with the deutsche mark. But high interest rates were the last thing their economies needed; Britain was looking dismally on its third year of recession. Something had to give.

Once Europe's currency markets started to erupt on September 16, which would come to be called Black Wednesday, pandemonium quickly ensued. Britain desperately tried to pump up its currency by raising one of its key interest rates from 10 percent to 12 percent, only to watch the pound sink still further. Within hours, the Bank of England announced that interest rates would be raised yet higher, to 15 percent. But defending the value of the pound proved to be a futile exercise. By day's end, Britain retreated in defeat and withdrew from the European monetary system.[6]

Italy's lira and Sweden's krona had also come under attack as exchange rates fluctuated erratically; the Italian government spent large sums selling marks to buoy up the value of the lira, which had already been devalued 7 percent the prior weekend. Sweden—not yet a member of the European Community but hoping to bring its finances into line—pushed its base lending rate to a stratospheric 500 percent.[7] In the face of intensive speculative selling, though, even such high interest rates proved insufficient to maintain the value of the krona, and Sweden was forced to abandon its efforts.[8]

After the crisis had played out, the currency carnage was tabulated both in terms of the vast sums expended by central banks trying to defend their national monies and the changed profile of what had seemed to be a fairly stolid European exchange rate mechanism. In the denouement of the monetary turmoil as it had unfolded by April 1993, only Germany and the Netherlands had emerged with their currencies unscathed; Denmark, France, and Belgium remained in the system with their currencies "blooded but essentially unbowed," as Peter Marsh of the *Financial Times* put it, while Ireland, Spain, and Portugal had clung to their positions within the system only by succumbing to devaluation. Britain and Italy had been pushed out.[9]

After such devastation, it was only natural that the victims would begin to search for the villains behind the currency debacle. The first choice was Speculators. According to a report issued by the Bank for International Settlements—the central bankers' central bank—the nature of foreign exchange dealing had been fundamentally altered by the huge new amounts of money flowing into the international currency markets. Between 1989 and 1992, turnover in foreign exchange increased 42 percent to an estimated $880 billion per business day.[10] Much of that money was coming from investment fund and pension fund managers who were engaging in currency transactions to make profits, not to finance trade.

And make profits they did. The Quantum Group of investment funds run by George Soros bet $10 billion on the German deutsche mark against the British pound and the Italian lira during the September debacle and earned some $2 billion in profits within a few weeks, according to an account in *The New York Times*.[11] Against such sums, even the seemingly unlimited resources of central banks start to look vulnerable to "market" forces. An assault by speculators on the French franc at the beginning of January 1993 required a counterattack by the French and German central banks to prop up the franc at an estimated cost of $50 billion.[12] These are not mere accounting entries on the books of central banks, but real sums representing the depletion of a government's financial resources. After the Bank of England had engaged in its doomed attempt to rescue the pound, it was criticized in a banking periodical for wasting money in an activity that was essentially as if Britain's chancellor of the Exchequer "had personally thrown entire hospitals and schools into the sea all afternoon."[13]

Sensitive to such criticism, governments have begun to take a harder line against the speculators, attempting to portray them as profit-motivated opportunists whose interests clash against the higher aims of government. "The speculators will not win," declared French President François Mitterrand in January 1993. "They will be forced to pay because the political will exists to hold the line against them."[14] Denmark's economy minister Marianne Jelved likewise insisted in February 1993 that the government would not waver in its support for the krone and warned speculators: "It will be expensive not to listen to what I am saying."[15] Currency traders tend not to be impressed by such statements, however, as they can recall similar staunch declarations by British officials just before the pound fell.[16]

It seems useless, not to mention embarrassing, for governments to take out their frustration over currency chaos on the speculators who are only seeking to capitalize on market opportunities to benefit from exchange rate movements. For French Finance Minister Michael Sapin to declare speculative attacks on the franc "irrational" because France's economic condition is relatively good is to beg the important questions.[17] Is the current system, where the value of a nation's money is determined more by the frenzied activities of exchange market players than by any objective standard, a rational approach to international monetary relations? Does it provide a proper foundation for an open world economy dedicated to free trade? Sapin's veiled threat to punish the currency mavens—"During the French Revolution such speculators were known as *agioteurs*, and they were beheaded"[18]—can be ascribed to his supreme frustration.

Much more damaging insinuations, though, have been directed by leading European government officials at unnamed "Anglo-Saxon" forces that might be deliberately aligning to prevent the creation of a European currency that could pose a rival to the dollar. "I am not among those who see plots everywhere. It's not at all my temperament," said former French Prime Minister Raymond Barre in February 1993. "But I really think there is a will in a certain number of economic and financial circles not to promote—in fact to do everything to prevent—the creation of European monetary and economic union, and in consequence to blow up the European monetary system."[19]

The theme of a plot to sabotage Europe's dream of a single currency has also been picked up by Chancellor Helmut Kohl of Germany and Jacques Delors, president of the European Commission.[20] While no hard evidence has been found to support the notion that the United States and Britain are secretly attempting to derail plans for European monetary unity, the allegation is nevertheless disturbing. At a time when the world should be moving toward fulfilling the promise of a truly global economy, such accusations belie the lofty rhetoric about international financial cooperation in the post-Cold War years. Instead of working together to establish ground rules for sound monetary relations to support open world trade, nations are viewing their neighbors with suspicion and seem more concerned about protecting their own narrow interests. "It seems everyone has taken their hands off the steering wheel and forgotten about the idea of coordination," notes financier and scholar Jeffrey E. Garten. "Despite all the talk of a global economy, governments have become inward looking."[21]

RETREAT TO PROTECTIONISM

Nowhere has the trend toward rivalry among trade partners become more pronounced than in the relationship between Japan and the United States. While both sides outwardly hail the "mature" and "business-like" approach that characterizes the nature of trade discussions that are riveted on Japan's continuing large trade surplus with the United States, it is apparent that inner tensions are driving the negotiations. The United States, under the leadership of President Clinton, is serious about reducing the trade imbalance and intends to pursue policies that will achieve "measurable results" even if they violate the philosophical doctrine of free trade.[22] Responding to Japanese assertions that the United States should avoid resorting to actions such as raising tariffs or attempting to manage trade, U.S. Trade Representative Mickey Kantor commented: "I'm not interested in theology."[23]

Such disregard for free trade principles in favor of boosting U.S. competitiveness through strong government intervention apparently extends to manipulating the dollar–yen exchange rate if deemed necessary. At a joint news conference with Japanese Prime Minister Ki-ichi Miyazawa in April 1993, Clinton said the rise in the yen was "number one" on a list of the "things working today which may give us more results" in shrinking the United States' huge trade deficit with Japan.[24] Clinton's remark sparked a record-smashing surge in the yen and heightened fears among Japanese officials and industrialists that Washington was deliberately pushing the currency higher to give U.S. companies a price advantage against Japanese-made products.[25]

Only a few months earlier at a televised economic conference held in Little Rock, the capital of his home state of Arkansas, Clinton had expressed a quite different view. "I'm for a strong dollar," he declared during a debate on exchange rate policy.[26] But the commitment of the Clinton administration to that approach came into question early in its reign when Treasury Secretary Lloyd Bentsen told reporters in February 1993 at the National Press Club in Washington: "I'd like to see a stronger yen."[27]

For its part, Japan cannot help but recognize that it is being extorted. U.S. efforts to curb its trade surplus by depreciating the dollar against the yen might seem the lesser evil when compared to more overt acts of protectionism that give full expression to anti-Japanese sentiment. Yet the impact on Japanese industry is substantial—and potentially very damaging to U.S.–Japan relations, both economic and political. While U.S. officials view adjustments in the dollar–yen exchange rate as a costless way to reduce trade pressures, Japanese producers are showing signs of hysteria at the return of the dreaded *endaka*, or high yen. Industry executives warn that the yen's rapid rise causes their goods to become more expensive in foreign markets and undermines their ability to compete internationally. Tokyo's afternoon tabloids offer a less subtle analysis with headlines that scream out: "Yen Shock."[28]

Ironically, the strong yen policy is likely to produce results opposite from those desired by U.S. trade and finance officials. Japanese business executives see export sales and profits dropping off at a time when Japan's economic performance is already sluggish. Isao Yonekura, vice-chairman of Keidanren, Japan's most influential big business group, points out that the rising yen "could throw cold water on the Japanese economy" just when the Clinton administration wants a strong recovery so that consumer demand for U.S. imports will increase.[29]

Adding insult to injury, visiting government officials from the Clinton administration advised their counterparts in Tokyo in April 1993 that the best way to stimulate Japan's economy was to proceed with a huge program of public spending. According to a *Wall Street Journal* account, Japan's policy makers listened politely, but after the Americans had left, they rolled their eyes. "Our feeling is, 'Thank you very much but please mind your own business. Don't you think there are enough problems with America's budget without telling us what's wrong with ours?' "[30]

Tempers are flaring around the world as nations batten down the economic hatches and governments accuse each other of promoting domestic monetary and financial priorities at the expense of working toward greater global coordination and cooperation. At one point in September 1992, desperate to convince the head of the German central bank that interest rates needed to be lowered to cure recessionary ills throughout Europe, Britain's Chancellor of the Exchequer Norman Lamont reportedly banged his fist on the table and shouted: "Twelve finance ministers are all sitting here demanding that you lower your interest rates. Why don't you do it?"[31] The sixty-eight-year-old president of the Bundesbank, Dr. Helmut Schlesinger, was visibly shaken. But his German colleagues were supportive, reiterating that the Bundesbank had but one mandate: To insure a sound German money supply.[32]

The scene was equally tense a few months later when the Irish government criticized its European partners for not helping it avoid a devaluation of its currency. Ireland's Finance Minister Bertie Ahern made it clear in January 1993 that he resented the absence of assistance from richer countries. "We wanted multilateral aid, from the Bundesbank. But the Germans helped the French. There is not equal help for all members, for a small country."[33] By August 1993, even the French would feel abandoned by the Germans.

Britain's Prime Minister John Major effectively summed up the new mindset, aimed away from international monetary stability in favor of domestic economic and political concerns, with his earlier declaration during a boisterous parliamentary debate: "Just as the interests of France and Germany come first for them, so should the interests of Britain come first for us."[34]

None of these developments offer much comfort to the newest members of the group, the nations of Central and Eastern Europe. In April 1993 they were confronted with a one-month blanket ban by the European Community (EC) against their exports of live animals, meat, milk, and dairy products. The ban was imposed, ostensibly, to suppress the spread of foot-and-mouth disease to Western Europe. But according to the *Financial Times*, East European governments doubted the EC's good faith and suspected that the decision was motivated by agricultural protectionism.[35] Retaliation came swiftly; within a week, Bulgaria joined with the Czech Republic, Poland, and Hungary in banning imports and the transit of livestock, meat, and dairy products from the European Community. Sir Leon Brittan, the EC trade minister, was clearly anguished by developments, and he decried the ostensible necessity for protecting Western companies from newly privatized Eastern enterprises. "This approach is as disloyal to our Eastern European partners as it is to the facts," he lamented.[36]

The cruelest blow of all to those struggling East European nations newly freed from the communist yoke was conveyed by EC recommendations urging them to rebuild trade ties between themselves and the former Soviet Union.[37] East European countries balk at the suggestion, not just because of political sensibilities, but for economic reasons as well. East–East trade is simply inferior to East–West trade, explained Geza Jeszenszky, Hungary's foreign minister, because of the lower quality of goods.[38] Also, it is difficult to make a convincing case that Russia and other former Soviet republics constitute exciting new market opportunities; these nations are in no position to go on a spending spree for imported goods with their own economies wracked by monetary chaos and financial devastation.

GLOBAL CONFLICT

If the potential for tragedy were not so great, it would be easy to wryly attribute the breakdown in orderly currency relations around the world to the emergence of humankind's baser political instincts and resignedly accept the notion that we are slated for a new round of beggar-thy-neighbor exchange rate policies. Certainly this century has witnessed previous times when nations confronted with domestic economic difficulties have retreated into protectionism and abandoned their commitment to international free trade. In the 1930s, concern over massive unemployment drove governments to take measures to promote demand by manipulating exchange rates in favor of domestically produced goods. Through a series of competitive devaluations, nations sought to undercut each others' ability to sell their products in world markets. Instead of raising global demand and employment levels, however, the exercise led to a downward spiral of increasingly isolationist economic policies that in turn fostered greater political tensions. The combination of global stagnation and short-sighted monetary nationalism set the stage for World War II.

But in this nuclear age can we afford to accept the inevitability of a scenario that has led to such misery and destruction in the past? Shouldn't we take evasive actions to halt the process that begins with currency turmoil and protectionist exchange rate policies and ends with political confrontation and the possibility of military conflict? The current disarray in international monetary relations must be replaced by a new global currency order; the national resentments sparked by exchange rate warfare must be cooled. Money meltdown is a warning sign that nationalistic economic policies are threatening to dissolve the trade and financial relationships that undergird a peaceful world community. Just as the melting of a nuclear reactor core that is left uncontrolled by inadequate efforts to cool the fuel elements can result in a disastrous leakage of radiation into the air, so too can an inadequate response to a meltdown in monetary arrangements lead to serious economic damage and release political hostilities that poison the global atmosphere of peaceful coexistence.

Can the syndrome be interrupted to prevent a catastrophic outcome? Does there exist sufficient foresight and leadership within the global community to thwart the historical pattern and recast it into an agenda for achieving a sound international monetary system to maximize global prosperity? By virtue of its experience and destiny, the United States is called on to rise to the challenge of bringing order to international currency relations. It has met that challenge in the past; references to the Bretton Woods system that prevailed after World War II rarely fail to mention the vital role of the United States in imparting monetary stability to global trade and financial relations in the postwar years. It is a laudable legacy and a tribute to America's belief in free markets and economic opportunity for all nations.

Such an exalted heritage contrasts sharply, however, with U.S. policies today, which seek to undercut the competitive efforts of foreign producers through exchange rate manipulation. When officials in the White House—including President Clinton—inject politics into the world's currency markets, openly advocating a sharp rise in the yen to reduce Japan's trade surplus, it makes a mockery of the concept of a level playing field. Is it possible to pursue an overall trade policy based on fairness while reserving the right to change the unit of measurement—that is, the relative values of currencies—when one government deems it economically desirable or politically expedient?

What kind of message does it send to Latin America when the United States comes so close to rejecting a free trade agreement with its neighbor, Mexico? A strong peso has enabled Mexico to lower inflation from triple digits to a single digit and has provided the monetary platform for dynamic economic growth. But if efforts to carry out free trade are frustrated, undermining the confidence of foreign investors and spurring capital flight, it could trigger a devaluation of the peso and derail Mexico's economic hopes.[39]

How, too, can the global community respond appropriately to the looming presence of China? Its huge economy is expanding at growth rates of 13 percent, and China is eager to take its place in the world trading system. Unless the world adopts an economic attitude that welcomes newcomers to the international marketplace and sees their participation as a means to raise aggregate living standards, rather than as a threat to domestic industry and employment, a zero-sum mentality will reign. Nothing fuels economic nationalism and protectionist retaliation more than the misguided assumption that one nation's economic rise spells another nation's decline.

Much is at stake, then, in recognizing the warning signs of impending global conflict as spelled out in the international currency markets. Now is not the time to nurse petty economic grievances or indulge in loose rhetoric aimed at intimidating trade partners. Now is the time to absorb the sobering lessons of history and stake out a new monetary order to accommodate the needs and aspirations of an anxious global economy.

1
The Legacy of
Bretton Woods

E ven as World War II raged, two economists, John Maynard
Keynes and Harry Dexter White, directed their considerable intellectual prowess toward a single momentous objective: How to structure a new world economic order based on
international cooperation. The crux of the challenge was to set up
a global monetary system to serve the needs of a postwar world re-
covering from devastation. Given that the outcome of the war was
not yet assured, the timing for such an endeavor was both hopeful
and fateful. Allied forces would land in Normandy on June 6,
1944, less than four weeks before the opening day of the international monetary conference at Bretton Woods, New Hampshire.

Keynes, a British subject, was already a legend at the time he
was tapped to lay out designs for a postwar financial system. He
had written *The General Theory of Employment, Interest and Money*
in 1936. Sweeping in its philosophical implications, the *General
Theory* was a tirade against laissez-faire economic principles and a
pitch for activist fiscal policy on the part of governments. Keynes
advocated massive public spending programs to counteract down-

15

turns in the economy, which were caused, he contended, by insufficient demand for goods and services by households and businesses. Keynes's solution to private sector inadequacies was economic intervention by government.

White, an American expert on international finance with degrees from Columbia, Stanford, and Harvard, had his own ideas for structuring a postwar monetary order. White was a firm believer that stable domestic and international prices were a prerequisite for economic order and that stable exchange rates among national currencies were necessary to promote foreign trade and global prosperity. White wanted to reduce the ability of individual governments to impose exchange controls and other barriers that inhibited trade. Instead, he envisioned an international banking institution charged with the authority to stabilize exchange rates so as to encourage the most productive use of international capital.

Both Keynes and White were drawn to the idea of establishing supranational agencies to manage economic and financial affairs at the global level. National sovereignty would be partially surrendered to these organizations for the sake of achieving the greater good of stable international exchange rates. While Keynes wanted to ensure that individual governments could manipulate their own domestic economies in accordance with his theories about fiscal activism, he recognized the importance of orderly global arrangements to stimulate international trade. White's main concern was to prevent the chaotic consequences of multiple currencies growing at different rates and to avoid the harmful effects of competitive depreciations. As a monetary expert at the U.S. Treasury, he had assisted several Latin American countries to establish formal currency stabilization arrangements with the United States.

Both men also favored the idea of a universal currency of sorts, a global monetary unit that would transcend the vagaries of individual national monies. Keynes wanted to call his international currency "bancor" (derived from the French words for bank and gold) and use it as a bookkeeping money for the purpose of settling international balances. Bancor would be defined in terms of gold, but the conversion rate would not necessarily remain unalterably fixed. Countries would be able to obtain bancor in exchange for gold; they would not be able to obtain gold in exchange for bancor.

White's concept of an international currency, which he christened "unitas," was more definitively linked to gold. As a global monetary unit of account, the unitas would consist of 137½ grains of fine gold (equal to ten dollars). White proposed to set up an international fund consisting of gold, national currencies, and other securities that could be used to stabilize monetary relations among contributing countries. The value of each nation's currency would be established in terms of unitas, and the accounts of the fund would likewise be kept and published in terms of unitas.

Despite their mutual admiration for global institutions and the notion of a world currency, Keynes and White did not always get along well personally. This friction was due in some measure to differences in their respective British and American cultural backgrounds. Keynes accused White of writing in "Cherokee" as opposed to his own "Christian English." He complained that White was "over-bearing" and did not have "the faintest conception of how to behave or observe the rules of civilized intercourse." For his part, White found Keynes insufferably arrogant and referred to him sarcastically as "your Royal Highness."[1]

Still, personality clashes between the two primary architects of the Bretton Woods system did not preclude them from working closely together to lay the foundation for the postwar international economic order. Both Keynes and White were motivated by a humanitarian desire to prevent the kind of financial stresses and economic dislocations that might lead to future wars. Both believed that it was possible to shape the world through sheer human determination and intellectual effort. By establishing global monetary mechanisms and organizations, imposing in their power and resources, they sought to create optimal conditions for achieving world prosperity and world peace.

In short, Keynes and White were convinced that international economic cooperation would provide a new foundation of hope for a world all too prone to violence. "If we can continue," Keynes observed, "this nightmare will be over. The brotherhood of man will have become more than a phrase."[2]

KEYNES'S VISION

Finely honed during his student days at Cambridge, Keynes's combination of brilliance, charm, and cynical wit greatly enhanced his ability to communicate ideas. He had a tremendous talent for turning scholarly insights into logical arguments; these in turn provided the basis for public policy initiatives. Although Keynes seemed to possess an innate sense of elitism and preferred to socialize with more sophisticated members of society, he took great pains to express his views in terms that made sense to common people. For example, propounding his theory that a dwindling economy should spend its way out of recession, he wrote in *The Listener*:

> When anyone cuts down expenditure, whether as an individual or a town council or a Government Department, next morning someone for sure finds that his income has been cut off, and that is not the end of the story. The fellow who wakes up to find that his income is reduced or that he is thrown out of work . . . is compelled in his turn to cut down his expenditure, whether he wants to or not. . . . Once the rot has started, it is most difficult to stop.[3]

Unlike some scholars, Keynes was not at all reluctant to dispense his economic views outside the halls of academe. He often submitted articles to popular magazines such as *Redbook* or opinion weeklies such as *The New Republic*; indeed, between 1919 and 1938 he wrote fifty-three pieces for the *The New Republic*.[4] Whether he was dashing off newsy observations for general consumption or crafting articles with scholarly rigor for the prestigious *Economic Journal*, which he edited for over three decades, Keynes managed to calibrate the tone of his text to his intended audience. He appealed directly to his readers' sensibilities, carefully geared his message to what he deemed the appropriate level of intellect, and always strived to persuade as he informed.

Keynes's ability to move easily from professorial jargon to everyday language figured keenly in his efforts to influence politicians and shape public policy. When political leaders ignored his recommendations—for example, concerning excessive German reparations after World War I—Keynes retaliated by writing polemical essays and arranging for their immediate publication.

He could be brutal in his indictments of the world's most powerful leaders, and he did not hesitate to charge them with lack of foresight or intelligence. For Keynes, human values were more compelling than sterile economic analyses; they provided the starting point for resolving the world's most pressing problems. By starting literary backfires of vehement public opinion, Keynes ensured that his views received attention at the highest political levels.

In contrast to his impressive mental powers, Keynes considered himself physically unattractive, an opinion that apparently was justified. According to an assistant master at Eton, where Keynes received his early education, he was "distinctly ugly at first sight, with lips projecting and seeming to push up the well-formed nose and strong brows in slightly simian fashion."[5] But Keynes did not let his shortcomings in this area dampen his appreciation for beautiful objects and intensely personal relationships. In keeping with the philosophy of the Bloomsbury set, an elite group of gifted intellectuals with whom he associated, Keynes affirmed that one's primary goals in life should be "love, the creation and enjoyment of aesthetic experience, and the pursuit of knowledge."[6] Keynes was homosexual, which posed little problem to the anti-Victorian Bloomsbury group; at age forty-two, however, he married the Russian ballerina Lydia Lopokova.

Although Keynes was devoted to the cultured world of art and theater, he departed sharply from the attitude of his Bloomsbury compatriots in a most significant way: he did not share their disdain for the world of action. On the contrary, Keynes's interpretation of aesthetic achievement was actively to utilize his vibrant intellect to improve the human condition. He saw himself as a unique individual who could change the course of economic thought, a catalyst poised at the center of "one of those uncommon junctures of human affairs where we can be saved by the solution of an intellectual problem, and in no other way."[7]

Transcending Orthodoxy

Keynes had respect for the classical body of economic knowledge to which he had been exposed at Cambridge; he was particularly influenced by the teachings of his mentor, Alfred Marshall. He absorbed the arguments and mathematical formulas that framed such fundamental works as Marshall's *Principles of Economics* and used them as the basis of his own intellectual foundation for explaining how the world works.

But Keynes had the unique ability to go beyond the elegant equations and verbiage, to grasp the essence of the argument, and to discover some new twist, some new insight that would enliven the theoretical text into a directive for human action. Even as he was back at Cambridge teaching economics, following a brief stint in government after graduation, Keynes was beginning to venture beyond the classical tradition in his interpretation of real world relationships. Describing Keynes's first major book, *Indian Currency and Finance*, biographer Roy Harrod wrote:

> It is the work of a theorist, giving practical application to those esoteric monetary principles which Marshall had expounded and Keynes was explaining in Cambridge classrooms, and at the same time it showed an outstanding gift for penetrating the secrets of how institutions actually work.[8]

Why did Keynes choose to write about the Indian currency situation? It was his first opportunity to apply scholarly analysis to real world circumstances. After leaving Cambridge, Keynes did not get the position he was seeking when he applied to work for the government; he had wanted to receive an appointment at the Treasury but instead was assigned to the India Office in London. On its own merits, the job was not particularly challenging for Keynes. Among his early tasks was to make shipping arrangements for ten young bulls to Bombay.[9] But even if Keynes found the administrative duties somewhat tedious, he was intrigued by India's developing monetary and financial system. He observed that, as it was moving toward establishing a traditional gold standard, India was in the meantime operating according to a hybrid system where paper claims on gold were redeemed for export purposes but were not part of the nation's internal currency mechanism. Keynes decided that this "gold-exchange standard" was better than a full-fledged gold standard because it permitted India to link its paper currency to sterling without having to engage in "the needless accumulation of the precious metals."[10]

Keynes thought that paper money was not only much more efficient than gold coin but was also more flexible, allowing the volume of currency to be temporarily expanded to accommodate seasonal demands of trade. Rather than having every nation maintain reserves in gold to back its currency, Keynes believed it made more sense for India and other countries to guarantee convertibility of their money into sterling, which functioned as an international currency, and keep reserves in London in the form of sterling balances on which they were paid interest. Keynes advocated the use of "a cheap local currency artificially maintained at par with the international currency or standard of value (whatever that may ultimately turn out to be)" as an attractive alternative to the gold standard and "the ideal currency of the future."[11]

With the advent of World War I, Keynes left Cambridge once more and went back into government service. This time he made it to the Treasury where he had ample opportunity to turn his attention to the political side of financial and economic questions. Indeed, by the end of the war his talents in analyzing policy options and writing position papers had propelled him to the top ranks of the department and provided him a strong forum for influencing government decisions. When Keynes, then aged thirty-five, was sent to the peace conference in Versailles following the armistice, he was designated senior representative of the Treasury and was authorized to represent the views of the chancellor of the Exchequer.

At the conference, Keynes was appalled at what he considered the excessively punitive financial measures that were being assessed against Germany. He was upset that the leaders of the Allied nations—President Woodrow Wilson of the United States, French Premier Georges Clemenceau, British Prime Minister Lloyd George, and Italian Premier Vittoria Orlando—seemed unable to comprehend that in demanding such high reparations from their defeated and humiliated enemy, they were destroying Germany's ability to regenerate and become economically productive in the future. Keynes observed:

> The entrepreneur and the inventor will not contrive, the trader and
> the shopkeeper will not save, the labourer will not toil, if the fruits

of their industry are set aside, not for the benefit of their children, their old age, their pride, or their position, but for the enjoyment of a foreign conqueror.[12]

Keynes felt that Germany's ill-fated future would end up having negative repercussions for its neighbors and the entire region; rather than destroying the German economy, Keynes asserted, the Allied leaders should be endeavoring to restore it as a safeguard against political instability throughout the whole of Europe. The remedies offered by Keynes were much less harsh toward Germany and much more oriented toward rebuilding Europe's economy. Keynes proposed to (1) set reparations within Germany's capacity to pay, (2) waive the United Kingdom's claim on such reparations and cancel interallied war indebtedness, and (3) provide an international loan to meet Europe's immediate requirements for reconstruction funds. But to no avail. According to Keynes:

> The Council of Four paid no attention to these issues, being preoccupied with others—Clemenceau to crush the economic life of his enemy, Lloyd George to do a deal and bring home something which would pass muster for a week, the President to do nothing that was not just and right. It is an extraordinary fact that the fundamental economic problem of a Europe starving and disintegrating before their eyes was the one question in which it was impossible to arouse the interest of the Four. Reparation was their main excursion into the economic field, and they settled it as a problem of theology, of politics, of electoral chicane, from every point of view except that of the economic future of the states whose destiny they were handling.[13]

Keynes resigned his Treasury position in June 1919 to protest the accepted terms of the treaty and within months churned out a scathingly critical book, *The Economic Consequences of the Peace.* It created an international sensation, broke book sale records in England and the United States, and elevated Keynes to new heights of recognition in public policy circles.

Ensconced at Cambridge once again after the war, Keynes continued to ponder and lecture, accumulating the insights and arguments that would ultimately find their way into *The General Theory of Employment, Interest and Money*. Keynes was not satisfied with prevailing explanations of the factors leading to economic depression, nor did he accept orthodox prescriptions calling for patience and perseverance as the price of economic recovery. Keynes instead sought to mesh his own theories about the relationship among key financial variables with his proposals for government-directed stimulation of the economy. He felt certain that there was a fundamental error in the traditional economic literature, which stipulated that demand equals supply in a self-regulating capitalist economic system and that savings and investment are perfectly equilibrated by the rate of interest. He was not willing to totally dismiss the classical approach, but he was intent on discovering what his predecessors had overlooked in their zeal to pursue theory at the expense of reality. "A large part of the established body of economic doctrine I cannot but accept as broadly correct," Keynes wrote. "For me, therefore, it is impossible to rest until I can put my finger on the flaw in . . . the orthodox reasoning."[14]

The flaw, according to Keynes, turned out to be that prices are not as flexible in reality as they are in theory. Prices are "sticky" downward; that is, they don't automatically go down in the face of decreased demand. The price of labor was especially prone to stickiness to the extent that unions and long-term contracts protected workers' salaries from declining, even in the midst of a recession. Keynes noted, too, that business investment was not necessarily equal to household savings. Sometimes investment came in too low for reasons that had more to do with psychology than mathematical tautologies. Because business investment was a major component of the total demand for goods and services, a glut of savings would result whenever business investment was not high enough to compensate for inadequate consumption by households.

Keynes had a solution. If a capitalist economy could not protect itself from imbalances between demand and supply, which could lead to a recessionary spiral of falling demand and supply, then the government should come to the rescue and spend money to stimulate recovery. "The object is to start the ball rolling," Keynes wrote in a 1933 letter to President Roosevelt.[15] Facing a recession, the government should not hesitate to run a budget deficit. When conditions became more prosperous, the government could count on achieving a budget surplus. Over the course of the business cycle, revenues and expenditures would even out and the budget would be balanced. The key to counteracting negative economic tendencies, then, was to have the public sector exercise fiscal flexibility as necessary to make up for the temporary market failings of the private sector.

Global Application

Over the course of his career, Keynes had come up with three essential propositions that greatly influenced his thinking on structuring a new international economic order to reign after World War II. First, based on his early familiarity with India's monetary situation, Keynes had concluded that a gold exchange standard was more efficient than a classical gold standard. Second, as the result of his experience at the Paris Peace Conference, he was convinced that sweeping multilateral initiatives and extensive financial cooperation were necessary to assist crippled economies and promote political stability. Finally, Keynes believed that governments should act as counterweights within their domestic economies by spending money when private demand failed to meet aggregate output.

How could these broad conclusions be drawn into a logically coherent, intellectually consistent paradigm that would frame his vision for global economic, financial, and monetary order in the postwar world? As author Anthony Sampson explains, Keynes was first approached to take up that challenge in November 1940 by Harold Nicolson, who was then working for the British Ministry of Information. Nicolson asked Keynes to respond to Nazi proposals on the radio calling for a New Order; for inspiration, he furnished some German broadcasts promising to abolish the role of gold in the contemplated postwar financial system along with a derogatory response from the British government. Keynes replied frankly that he did not much care for the gold standard either and that "about three quarters of the German broadcasts would be quite excellent if the name of Great Britain were substituted for Germany or the Axis."[16]

When Keynes, who was serving as honorary advisor to the British Treasury, was asked once more in 1941, this time by Britain's ambassador to Washington, Lord Halifax, to start thinking about how to build a new world economic order that would foster international trade, he began in earnest to formulate his own design. He had been working on a lend-lease agreement to provide Britain with defense aid from the United States, but had come to the conclusion that bilateral agreements were not the answer to the larger question of how to channel capital from wealthy countries to needy countries. Keynes turned his attention to elaborating a "truly international plan" for global financial cooperation.[17]

Building on his earlier proposals for setting up efficient monetary mechanisms, Keynes elaborated on his concept for a supranational bank; it would be a central bank for central banks. In Keynes's imagined system, the central banks of nations throughout the world would maintain accounts at this ultimate central bank, or International Clearing Union (as he came to call it), in the same way that commercial banks maintain accounts with their own country's central bank. Nations would settle their exchange balances with one another at some predetermined par value defined in terms of an international currency; after first wanting to call the currency grammor, Keynes settled on bancor. (In his critique of the draft plans of Keynes and White, Professor Jacob Viner ventured the term "mondor.") Keynes proposed that exchange rates be fixed in terms of bancor and that bancor be valued in gold. For Keynes, such a system would constitute the application on a global scale of his earlier recommendations, in keeping with his assertion that a gold exchange standard was superior to the classical gold standard.

Keynes's other main concern in devising a global economic plan was that the new system should be aimed at eliminating huge financial gaps between rich and poor nations. Keynes was especially sympathetic toward countries that had suffered great damage from the war, including his own, and he felt that wealthy countries had an inherent obligation to provide financial assistance for reasons of morality as well as economic self-interest. The aim of the new system should be to channel capital from creditor countries to debtor countries, Keynes argued, and in doing so, to promote increased international trade. The essence of the scheme, as Keynes explained in a letter to the governor of the Bank of England, was simple:

> It is the extension to the international field of the essential principles of *banking* by which, when one chap wants to leave his resources idle, those resources are not therefore withdrawn from circulation but are made available to another chap who is prepared to use them—and to make this possible without the former losing his liquidity and his right to employ his own resources as soon as he chooses to do so.[18]

One rather distinct variance from normal banking practice, however, was that Keynes's International Clearing Union would charge interest on both credit and debit balances. In that way, well-off countries would be induced not to hoard their wealth but to circulate it around the world. Under Keynes's plan, interest charges would be assessed against creditors as a "significant indication that the System looks on excessive credit balances with as critical an eye as on excessive debit balances, each being, indeed, the inevitable concomitant of the other."[19]

Shades of the *General Theory* can be discerned in this attitude. Keynes had long argued that it was society's savers who inflicted the most economic harm by reducing aggregate demand. Forcing them to pay interest on their savings would be a way to change their behavior and spend more on consumption. But by advocating stimulative spending while at the same time striving to establish a stable international monetary mechanism, Keynes was beginning to construct an intellectual conundrum. How would it be possible to promote global price stability and fixed exchange rates without impinging on an individual country's ability to pursue aggressive fiscal policies? How could a government deliberately run a budget deficit to stave off domestic recession, as recommended by Keynes, without having its currency devalued as the result of heavy government borrowing and increased inflationary expectations?

The key, in accordance with traditional Keynesian reasoning, was flexibility. Keynes wanted to give his envisioned world central bank considerable authority in determining exchange rates and was prepared to grant it vast disciplinary powers over its members. This new global institution would have broad discretion when it came to telling members how they were to conduct their monetary and financial affairs. The International Clearing Union would even reserve the right to change the value of the bancor relative to gold if its governing board deemed it useful; the very definition of the value of the international monetary unit would not be beyond the reach of the authorities empowered to manage the union. Member countries, too, would be able to make adjustments in their exchange rates as long as the governing board granted them permission to do so. Decisions could be changed on the basis of new information; rules would be tempered by collective wisdom and discretionary judgment. Indeed, Keynes suggested that during the five years after the inception of the system, the governing board should "give special consideration to appeals for adjustments in the exchange-value of a national currency on the ground of unforeseen circumstances."[20]

In short, Keynes wanted it both ways. The need to preserve international monetary stability should not get in the way of expansionist domestic policies. "There should be the least possible interference with internal national policies," he wrote in the preface to his April 1943 draft proposal, "and the plan should not wander from the international terrain."[21] Still, it was clear that some degree of national monetary sovereignty would have to be sacrificed if the plan were to work. The basic objective in setting up an International Clearing Union, after all, was to avoid the chaos of exchange rate manipulations that had characterized the interwar period.

Keynes was keenly aware of the need to establish an orderly system for handling balance of payments adjustments among trading nations, and he was eager to start the global rebuilding process. While Keynes knew that achieving international monetary stability demanded that member nations surrender the right to define their currency's rate of exchange to a supernational organization, he also understood it was a sensitive issue and sought to reassure governments they would still retain some control over their monetary fate. In any case, he was thoroughly convinced that global economic cooperation was vital for the preservation of peace. "A greater readiness to accept supernational arrangements must be required in the post-war world than hitherto,"

Keynes asserted. In his view, the proposal for an International Clearing Union was nothing less than a call for global "financial disarmament."[22]

WHITE'S BLUEPRINT

Compared to Keynes, who had a tendency to wax poetic in his proposals for international economic cooperation, Harry Dexter White was all business. When White's boss, U.S. Secretary of the Treasury Henry Morgenthau, asked him to prepare a paper outlining the possibilities for coordinated monetary arrangements among the United States and its allies, White responded quickly with a crisp, comprehensive proposal.

Morgenthau made the request to his subordinate on December 14, 1941, one week after the attack on Pearl Harbor. What Morgenthau had in mind, according to J. Keith Horsefield, who wrote the history of the International Monetary Fund, was the establishment of a stabilization fund to help provide monetary assistance to the Allies during the war and to hamper the enemy. Ideally, the fund would serve as the basis for setting up a postwar international monetary system and might evolve into some kind of "international currency."[23]

Just over two weeks later, White submitted a report entitled "Suggested Program for Inter-Allied Monetary and Bank Action." The objectives of the program, as laid out by White, were:

(1) To provide the means, the instrument, and the procedure to stabilize foreign exchange rates and strengthen the monetary systems of the Allied countries.

(2) To establish an agency with means and powers adequate to provide the capital necessary:

(a) to aid in the economic reconstruction of the Allied countries;

(b) to facilitate a rapid and smooth transition from a war-time economy to a peace-time economy in the Allied countries;

(c) to supply short-term capital necessary to increase the volume of foreign trade—where such capital is not available at reasonable rates from private sources.[24]

A study in efficiency, the analysis was detailed and to the point. White felt, however, that stabilizing the international monetary system and supplying cheap loans to Allied countries were two different tasks. While a special multilateral bank could be set up to take care of the latter, White noted, "monetary stabilization is a highly specialized function calling for a special structure, special personnel, and special organization."[25] White suggested that two separate institutions would therefore be required: (1) an Inter-Allied Bank and (2) an Inter-Allied Stabilization Fund.

The reaction to White's proposal was positive. Morgenthau was impressed and began laying the political groundwork for introducing what he sensed might well become a monumental international project. In April 1942, after some revisions and refinements, White's paper was circulated under the title "Preliminary Draft Proposal for a United Nations Stabilization Fund and a Bank for Reconstruction and Development of the United and Associated Nations." Among the primary purposes of the stabilization fund, White emphasized, was the need to stabilize foreign exchange rates among the United Nations countries and to encourage the flow of productive capital. He also wanted to promote sound note issuing and credit practices among the United Nations countries and to reduce barriers to foreign trade.[26]

That White was particularly committed to the importance of stable exchange rates is evident in his analysis of the worldwide benefits that could be attained. His arguments, reproduced below, still ring with clarity and logic:

> The advantages of obtaining stable exchange rates are patent. The maintenance of stable exchange rates means the elimination of exchange risk in international economic and financial transactions. The cost of conducting foreign trade is thereby reduced, and capital flows much more easily to the country where it yields the greatest return because both short-term and long-term investments are greatly hampered by the probability of loss from exchange depreciation. As the expectation of continued stability in foreign exchange rates is strengthened there is also more chance of avoiding the disrupting effects of flights of capital and of inflation.[27]

White felt strongly that the stability of price levels was an important economic goal at home, as well as a vital social and political objective worldwide. "Wide swings in price levels," he stated, "are one of the destructive elements in domestic as well as international trade." White clearly recognized the connection between internal and external monetary policies and hoped the establishment of an international stabilization fund would exert a healthy influence in reducing price fluctuations within individual countries.[28]

In attempting to convince the United States and its allies that his proposals should be adopted, White did not hesitate to employ what was obviously the most compelling argument of the day. He suggested that serious discussion of these ideas would help win the war. In his April 1942 draft, White argued that the countries struggling against the Axis powers needed inspiration to spur them to victory; they needed to have a vision of a better world that would offer them a more prosperous existence in the future:

> It has been frequently suggested, and with much cogency, that the task of securing the defeat of the Axis powers would be made easier if the victims of aggression, actual and potential, could have more assurance that a victory by the United Nations will not mean in the economic sphere, a mere return to the pre-war pattern of every-country-for-itself, or inevitable depression, of possible widespread economic chaos with the weaker nations succumbing first under the law-of-the-jungle that characterized international economic practices of the pre-war decade. That assurance must be given now. The people of the anti-Axis powers must be encouraged to feel themselves on solid international ground, they must be given to understand that a United Nations victory will not usher in another two decades of economic uneasiness, bickering, ferment, and disruption. They must be assured that something will be done in the sphere of international economic relations that is new, that is powerful enough and comprehensive enough to give expectation of successfully filling a world need. They must have assurance that methods and resources are being prepared to provide them with capital to help them rebuild their devastated areas, reconstruct their war-distorted economies, and help free them from the strangulating grasp of lost markets and depleted reserves. Finally, they must have assurance that the United States does not intend to desert the war-worn and impoverished nations after the war is won, but proposes to help them in the long and difficult task of economic reconstruction. To help them, not primarily for altruistic motives, but from recognition of the truth that prosperity, like peace, is indi-

visible. To give that assurance now is to unify and encourage the anti-Axis forces, to greatly strengthen their will and effort to win.[29]

For all his technical expertise and highly analytical skills, White was driven by very human yearnings for a more compassionate international economic system. Like Keynes, he believed that formalized global cooperation was the key to preserving the peace and saving humankind. "Just as the failure to develop an effective League of Nations has made possible two devastating wars within one generation," White observed, "so the absence of a high degree of economic collaboration among the leading nations will, during the coming decade, inevitably result in economic warfare that will be but the prelude and instigator of military warfare on an even vaster scale."[30]

In some ways, White seemed the consummate social liberal with his vision of global cooperation and his skepticism that unregulated commerce could be wholly relied on to distribute global resources in an equitable and orderly manner. Yet White also embraced certain notions of financial conservatism that would please the most fiscally prudent hearts. As a condition for membership in the proposed fund, for example, White decreed that a country must agree "not to adopt any monetary or general price measure or policy" that would bring about "sooner or later a serious disequilibrium in the balance of payments."[31] Unlike Keynes, White acknowledged that domestic monetary and fiscal policies had to be reconciled with the goal of stable exchange rates.

White also stipulated that countries should not be eligible for membership in the fund unless they agreed to embark on a program to reduce existing trade barriers such as import duties, import quotas, or administrative devices; in addition, they should make a determined effort to avoid any future increases in tariffs or the implementation of other trade obstacles. White also included the exhortation that members should agree "not to subsidize—directly or indirectly—the exportation of any commodity or services to member countries." Members should not permit defaults on the foreign obligations of governments, White declared, and he suggested that half of the initial cash payment made by countries to join the fund should consist of gold.[32]

All of these decrees, however, could be bypassed by appealing directly to the board of directors of the fund for consent. As much as White disapproved of unhealthy monetary and financial policies on the part of individual countries, and as much as he resented selfish trade practices—"one is tempted to list 'mercantilism' or its more expressive heir 'protectionism' as 'World Enemy No. 1,' in the economic sphere"—he wanted the fund to assume a sort of patriarchal role over its members through the ability to grant or withhold special approval for erring nations.[33] In this respect, White was in agreement with Keynes.

The chief task of the fund, reflecting White's economic philosophy, would be to establish stable exchange rates to provide the necessary solid monetary foundation for increased international trade and capital flows. An elaborate set of rules would determine the constancy of currency values with respect to gold and to each other. The ultimate integrity of the system would rely not on rules, however, but on the discretion of the fund. White, like Keynes, put a great deal of faith in the fund's ability to perceive when a member country's economy suffered from "fundamental disequilibrium" and to discern the appropriate corrective course of action. In White's own words:

> What this matter boils down to is that the Fund should have the authority to determine whether the transactions causing a balance to turn unfavorable include transactions which the Fund would judge "illegitimate" under the circumstances. There are times when some types of capital outflow for some countries would be considered "legitimate," whereas the same type for other countries or even for the same country under different circumstances would be regarded as "illegitimate." There might also be instances in which all types of capital outflows for a given country might be considered "illegitimate," whereas for another country, all types might be considered "legitimate." No generalization can be made without all the circumstances being given. It is necessary only that the Fund have authority to make the decision on this matter and, as explained later, that the Fund have the authority to obtain the kind of information that would enable it to make an intelligent decision.[34]

The fund, then, would have final authority in determining the appropriate trade-off between allowing individual nations to pursue their domestic financial agendas while preserving the soundness of the international monetary system. White was well aware that some governments were apt to balk at the idea that the legitimacy of their budgetary or financial decisions should be subject to evaluation by a supernational organization. He concedes in the introduction to his April 1942 draft proposal that "some of the powers and requirements included in the outline of the Fund and the Bank will not survive discussion, prejudice and fear of departure from the usual." He admits that certain aspects of his plan might be regarded as "going too far toward 'internationalism'" and would perhaps not survive the test of political reality.[35]

However, White's answer was not to compromise the powers attributed to the envisioned global organizations but to strengthen them. In designing the fund, complemented by a Bank for Reconstruction and Development, to facilitate international economic collaboration, White was deliberately seeking to go beyond prior attempts to coordinate financial relations on a bilateral or regional basis. "It will be at once apparent that the resources, powers and requirements for membership, accorded both agencies go far beyond the usual attributes of monetary stabilization and of banking," White stated. "They must if they are to be the stepping stone from shortsighted disastrous economic nationalism to intelligent international collaboration."[36]

BUREAUCRATIC NIGHTMARE

On May 16, 1942, the introduction from White's plan was sent to President Franklin Delano Roosevelt from the Treasury. Secretary Morgenthau included a memorandum suggesting that White's proposal constituted an effective answer to the Germans and their talk about establishing a New Order in Europe and Asia. Morgenthau thought it would be useful to set up an international conference to discuss the plan for a Stabilization Fund. Along with a proposed agenda for such a conference, he also included a draft invitation letter and a suggested guest list of foreign finance ministers who should be asked to attend.[37]

As Horsefield recounts in his chronicle of the IMF's origins, an answer from the president was received the same day. Roosevelt asked for input from other agencies and departments, specifically the State Department, the Board of Economic Warfare, and the Export-Import Bank. He also urged Morgenthau to obtain the opinions of Secretary of State Cordell Hull and Under-Secretary of State Sumner Welles. After doing so, and after the interdepartmental studies were completed, Morgenthau was to bring up the matter of a conference again.[38]

In the bureaucratic scheme of things, this start seemed propitious—although urging further study in consultation with other governmental bodies might not be seen as the embodiment of White's spirited call for action. ("Timidity will not serve," he had written in the introduction of his plan.[39]) White had emphasized that the long-term effectiveness of his proposed fund and bank would depend on the extent to which "boldness and vision" were displayed at the outset in getting the two institutions established.

White's proposal was essentially the work of a single author, a pure vision of his own design, an elaborate conception of what he wished to accomplish. But from the moment the draft was submitted to the White House, it was subject to compromise from all sides. Other departments within the U.S. government attempted to insert their own ideas. Keynes's proposals would have to be accommodated. Representatives to the Bretton Woods Conference would seek to safeguard the positions of their own countries and to preserve whatever advantages they thought they could maintain within the world trade system. Finally, the U.S. Congress would promote the interests of bankers and businessmen under the guise of looking out for U.S. financial and economic interests.

Following the president's instructions, an Interdepartmental Committee was established to review White's plan and make suggestions for improving it. Members of the committee sought to include some of the features that had surfaced in rival plans that were being circulated within the U.S. government; in particular, they thought they should consider the version being offered by the Federal Reserve Board. The committee also felt it wise to incorporate some of the suggestions put forth by representatives of other countries who had seen copies of White's draft and had expressed their concern about U.S. dominance within the proposed system.

The Federal Reserve Board's plan focused strongly on the matter of gold; it decreed that the fund contributions of member countries should be made entirely in gold, even if it meant that up to one-half or even three-fourths of a country's entire gold reserve would be held by the fund. Under the Federal Reserve Board's approach, all countries would be prohibited from buying gold except from the fund, and they would be obliged to sell gold only to the fund. Each member country would be able to purchase foreign exchange from the fund only up to the amount of its original contribution plus the value of any extra gold it had sold to the fund.[40]

The U.S. Treasury was not enamored with the Fed's approach, largely because of its concern over the negative results of creating such a monopoly on gold dealings. Moreover, based on initial discussions with foreign representatives, Treasury officials feared that the Fed's requirements would be off-putting to potential member countries, especially the less wealthy ones. Belgium, Bolivia, Czechoslovakia, France, and Norway had already suggested that the proportion of gold required for initial membership was too high, and the Philippines had argued that no country should have to part with more than 20 percent of its own gold and dollar balances. Canada argued that a country should be able to pay up to 85 percent of the membership quota in its own currency. Cuba wanted to know why it couldn't pay part of the quota in silver.[41]

As various countries were consulted about the proposed fund, they expressed increasing concern over the question of how "fixed" the fixed exchange rates would be and whether they would have any real voting influence over fund decisions relating to exchange rates. They were also disturbed about the details of the proposed voting system to be used by the fund. Australia, Belgium, and Norway complained that the United States would have an effective veto by virtue of the size of its quota and the voting rights it would retain. Brazil suggested that the number of votes granted to a country should not be based on its monetary contribution, but rather on its population. China thought it would be appropriate to take into account the sacrifices a country had endured during the war. Mexico sided with Cuba in calling for a simple majority vote among members, rather than a weighted voting system based on contributed quotas, and cited the importance of respecting a member's "dignity."[42]

In the meantime, a copy of Keynes's plan for an International Clearing Union had been delivered to White's superior, Secretary Morgenthau, and a careful comparison was being undertaken at the Treasury. Members of the Interdepartmental Committee wanted to know what the two proposals had in common and where they differed. Both Keynes's International Clearing Union and White's Stabilization Fund sought to create an international monetary mechanism to be administered by a supernational organization; that much was clear. But the differences between the plans were significant, reflecting the different relative financial positions of the United Kingdom and the United States at the time, not to mention the different perspectives of the individual authors.

Keynes was much more inclined to grant member countries the right to expand their domestic economies and, if need be, even to employ trade restrictions and make exchange rate adjustments in the process without being unduly restricted by external requirements for international financial stability. White, as noted earlier, was much less willing to accommodate expansionary domestic programs that served the short-term economic interests of individual countries at the expense of their trade partners, caused prices to vary worldwide, and ultimately distorted international capital flows.

White was not advocating a hands-off approach to international economics; indeed, he thought unbridled trade permitted governments to engage in cut-throat competition to gain unfair advantages that ultimately led to inefficient economic dislocations and dangerous political rivalries. What White wanted to do was to make individual governments subject to a higher authority, a global institution that could more or less force them to operate in accordance with the collective wisdom of the international trading community. In White's plan, if 80 percent of members believed a country was engaging in domestic economic practices that could lead to serious balance-of-payments problems, the fund would express its official disapproval to the offending government and take appropriate measures.

Keynes, on the other hand, did not wish to look too closely at these potential conflicts between domestic economic priorities and international financial obligations. He ventured the opinion that "it may be better not to attempt to settle too much beforehand" and recommended that such matters, should they arise in the future, be subject to arbitration by a central authority endowed with (not surprisingly) considerable discretion. Keynes understood the appeal of rigid standards and automatic discipline. He ended up putting his faith, however, in the wisdom and reasonableness of men. "If rule prevails, the scheme can be made more water-tight theoretically," Keynes admitted. "But if discretion prevails, it may work better in practice."[43]

Despite his penchant for flexibility, though, Keynes was insistent when it came to structuring an exalted role for the United States and the United Kingdom in managing his envisioned International Clearing Union. He wanted them to jointly exert substantial control over international financial and monetary developments. Under the Keynes plan, the United States and the United Kingdom together would be in a position to out-vote the rest of the members on key issues. As an additional testimonial to the special status of the United Kingdom and the United States as founding members, London and Washington would alternately play host for meetings of the union's management. The head office of the organization, Keynes suggested, should be located in London.

White's approach was much more populist in spirit. Although wealthier countries would be able to exert more influence in most areas because their financial contributions were greater, key questions on exchange rate changes would be decided by a simple majority of the members: one country, one vote. Given the dominant position that the United States held as the world's largest creditor at the time, White's willingness to sacrifice power was an extraordinary act of noblesse oblige. He recognized it as such, but felt that the United States should have no more ability than any other country to gain trade advantages by manipulating its money supply or exploiting its financial strength against its neighbors. "Unless nations are willing to sacrifice some of their power to take unilateral action in matters of international economic relations," White stated, "there is very little hope of any significant international cooperation—let alone collaboration."[44]

One lingering point of contention in the discussions leading up to the Bretton Woods conference was the matter of an international currency and its proper functions. Keynes thought his version of a special currency, bancor, should be created ad hoc by the International Clearing Union as necessary to make balance-of-payments adjustments and that its supply should be capable of deliberate expansion or contraction to offset deflationary or inflationary tendencies in world demand. White, by stipulating two-way convertibility between the unitas and gold, and by requiring that the fund maintain a 100 percent gold reserve against unitas deposits, was effectively advocating a more fixed relationship between gold and the global money supply. Indeed, Britain's chancellor of the Exchequer pointed out that White's concept for the unitas was not much different from the classical gold standard.[45] Keynes' bancor, as noted earlier, could be purchased with gold but could not be redeemed in gold.

Throughout all the deliberations and discussions, there were many instances where lofty intellectual arguments gave way to more down-to-earth, practical considerations. For example, Norway thought the unitas should be worth only two dollars instead of ten. Moreover, Norway preferred the name bancor over the word unitas because the latter was pronounced differently in different countries.[46]

An International Conference

On May 25, 1944, two years after Secretary Morgenthau had sent the introduction of White's plan to President Roosevelt, invitations were dispatched to forty-four governments by the Secretary of State to attend an international conference "for the purpose of formulating definite proposals for an International Monetary Fund and possibly a Bank for Reconstruction and Development."[47] The conference would be held at the Mount Washington Hotel, located in the resort area of Bretton Woods, New Hampshire, starting on July 1, 1944.

To ensure that the conference, which was scheduled to be over by July 19, would accomplish its objectives in an efficient manner, a preliminary meeting was set up in Atlantic City for June 15 (exigencies of the war would delay the arrival of many European delegates until June 24) to lay out the specific issues that would be decided at Bretton Woods. The group that came to participate in the advance session was composed of representatives from the United States, the United Kingdom, and fifteen other countries: Australia, Belgium, Brazil, Canada, Chile, China, Cuba, Czechoslovakia, France, Greece, India, Mexico, the Netherlands, Norway, and the Soviet Union.

White, who chaired the preliminary meeting, had hoped to resolve a number of issues to avoid burdening the Bretton Woods conference with tedious details on relatively unimportant matters. He also had hoped to reconcile remaining differences between the United States and the United Kingdom involving more fundamental points about the relative priority of fund decisions over national economic interests. But White ran into stiff resistance from the British delegation, as evidenced by these revealing comments taken from a memorandum he sent to Secretary Morgenthau, dated June 25:

1. The British want to increase the flexibility and ease of alterations of exchange rates. We think we should not budge one bit.

2. They are advocating changes in the direction of making the resort to the resources of the Fund much more automatic and a matter of right as compared with our view that the resort to the resources of the Fund is always conditional upon the taking of measures for correcting the situation and always in a sense that they are implicit or explicit of the Fund.

3. They strenuously object to what we call "deterrent charges" on those who utilize the Fund. These deterrent charges are in effect interest rates which increase progressively with the amount purchased from the Fund by any one country and likewise increase the longer the period before which they are repurchased. . . . We

regard this as an important feature in our proposal and it looks as though the American delegation will be in for a nasty fight on this matter at the conference.

4. The British are going to back the small countries in their demands for larger quotas, particularly Australia, and are going also to back India's demand that it be accorded an equivalent position with that of China.

5. There also appears on the horizon a technical fight on what constitutes gold holdings and offsets and a large number of other technical points of complex though minor character. We hope that most of these minor and technical points will be ironed out before the conference so that the delegates will be free to handle the larger issues.[48]

In short, the United Kingdom wanted the fund to absorb, rather than prevent, distortions to the international monetary system caused by domestic economic policies. Reflecting Keynes's views, the British delegation sought more elasticity in exchange rates and wanted no sanctions against sovereign borrowing. They resisted White's insistence on monetary stability versus a more expansionary bias and effectively took the side of economically backward debtor nations. India was quick to second the British position by suggesting that the objectives of the fund should be enlarged to include "assisting in the fuller utilization of the resources of economically underdeveloped countries."[49] Australia expressed a Keynesian attitude as well, complaining that the designated purposes of the fund placed "too little emphasis on the promotion and maintenance of high levels of employment, and too much emphasis on the promotion of exchange stability and on shortening the duration and lessening the degree of disequilibrium in international balances of payments."[50]

The preliminary meeting in Atlantic City crystallized rather than resolved differences. By the time the delegates began making their way to the resort at Bretton Woods to join representatives from another twenty-seven countries, some seventy additional amendments had been put forward to be resolved. Keynes wanted to delete what he considered minor amendments and begin the full-scale conference with a streamlined version of the proposed statement for establishing a fund based on U.S. and British drafts. He was overruled by lawyers from the U.S. delegation, though, who believed that in the interest of fairness a comprehensive draft including all the proposed amendments had to be made available to the Bretton Woods delegates.[51]

The Mount Washington Hotel, meanwhile, was starting to overflow with the arriving delegates, many of whom chose to bring along their technical experts. More than three times the original number expected had shown up—some 730 people in all—forcing the management to make frantic arrangements to place them at neighboring hotels. Although a formal structure for the meetings had been laid out in advance, specifying work to be allocated to different committees under the leadership of Secretary Morgenthau, the sheer size of the group in attendance and the complexity of the various issues involved evoked a sense of chaos and political intensity among the Bretton Woods participants. White was named chairman of the commission on the fund; Keynes was named chairman of the commission on the bank. As described by Keynes:

> It is as though . . . one had to accomplish the preliminary work of many interdepartmental and Cabinet committees, the job of the . . . draftsmen, and the passage . . . of two intricate legislative measures of large dimensions, all this carried on in committees and commissions numbering anything up to 200 persons in rooms with bad acoustics, shouting microphones, many of those present . . . with an imperfect knowledge of English, each wanting to get something on the record which would look well in the press down at home, and . . . the Russians only understanding what was afoot with the utmost difficulty. . . . We have all of us worked every minute of our waking hours . . . all of us . . . are all in.[52]

Keynes's reference to the difficulties of "the Russians" was telling inasmuch as the Soviet delegation had indeed made its presence known, registering numerous complaints over the proposed fund and voicing constant suspicions about U.S. motives. The Union of Soviet Socialist Republics was particularly unhappy with its assessed quota; it wanted more voting power but at the same time wanted to make a smaller financial contribution. The Soviets also brought up a novel point concerning the fund's control over exchange rates. Because the ruble was not convertible into other currencies, they argued, and therefore had no international significance, the Soviet government should be free to change this rate without the approval of the fund.[53] Delegates from the U.S.S.R. were concerned, too, about having to provide data to the fund about their country's financial condition, especially with respect to its gold holdings and money supply. At one point, the Bretton Woods conference was suspended for twenty-four hours to permit the Soviet delegation to obtain specific authority from Moscow to release certain information.[54]

How to assess the proper quota for each country posed a tricky question from the start. To address it in a seemingly objective way, a formula was devised by Professor Raymond Mikesell, then at the U.S. Treasury, for calculating individual quotas based on a country's level of international trade and exchange reserves. White had provided some general guidance about what kinds of results should be achieved through the formula. Given that the United States did not want the total quotas to exceed $8.5 billion, the formula should put the United States in first place with a quota of about $2.5 billion, the United Kingdom in second place with about half that amount, with the Soviet Union coming in third, and China fourth.[55]

Quantitative assessments, however, would remain vulnerable to political influence. Going into the Bretton Woods conference, the figures derived by the U.S. Treasury formula specifically recommended quotas of $2,929 million for the United States, $1,275 million for the United Kingdom and its colonies, $763 million for the U.S.S.R., and $350 million for China. By the time the Committee on Quotas finished reviewing and discussing the suggested figures at Bretton Woods, the amounts had been significantly adjusted. The United States' quota was reduced to $2,750 million; the United Kingdom's quota was raised to $1,300 million; the U.S.S.R.'s quota was dramatically increased to $1,200 million; China's quota was likewise considerably increased to $550 million.[56]

The Committee on Quotas was chaired by Fred Vinson, who was the vice-chairman of the U.S. delegation (and would succeed

Morgenthau as U.S. Secretary of the Treasury in 1945). Vinson reported to the conference that the formula "had to be discarded" because it relied on statistics over particular periods that were not necessarily fair to all countries. A member of the French delegation to Bretton Woods, Professor Robert Mosse, subsequently wrote that quotas were established more or less arbitrarily by the United States in a series of deals.[57]

The United States may have lost some ground in terms of its quota and voting influence, but it won the day in deciding where the headquarters for both the fund and the bank would be physically located: Washington. Besides having the world's largest economy, the United States was putting up by far the most money at the outset, so that not even the United Kingdom was in a position to strongly resist. In terms of staffing these offices, however, less wealthy participants pushed for a more egalitarian approach. India entered a proposal that "due regard shall be paid to the fair representation of the nationals of member countries." That idea was watered down in committee to the general notion that personnel should be "recruited on as wide a geographical base as is possible" with the stipulation that obtaining the "highest standards of efficiency and of technical competence" would be of paramount importance.[58]

Even relatively trivial matters consumed considerable time at Bretton Woods. Delegates were issued over 500 documents filling some 1,200 printed pages; the need to make translations caused proceedings to bog down yet further. By the scheduled July 19 deadline for ending the conference, the work of the delegates was not nearly complete. A set of definitive proposals regarding the establishment and operation of the fund and bank had still not been finalized. (One of the biggest negotiating challenges, as it turned out, was to convince the hotel management to extend room privileges for another three days by postponing incoming guests and cancelling some reservations outright.)

Finally, after exhausting activity and frenzied meetings lasting into the small hours of the morning, a document embodying the official Articles of Agreement of the International Monetary Fund was ready for signing by the representatives on July 22, 1944. The document contained a number of ambiguities, "some intended and others not," as noted by the chairman of the Drafting Committee, Louis Rasminsky of Canada.[59] In all, some thirty-one articles, addressing everything from the fund's role in making capital transfers to obtaining special tax exemptions for nonlocal fund employees, were laid out.

The varying influences of Keynes and White alternate throughout Article I, which lists the original six purposes of the International Monetary Fund:

(i)   To promote international monetary cooperation through a permanent institution which provides the machinery for consultation and collaboration on international monetary problems.

(ii) To facilitate the expansion and balanced growth of international trade, and to contribute thereby to the promotion and maintenance of high levels of employment and real income and to the development of the productive resources of all members as primary objectives of economic policy.

(iii) To promote exchange stability, to maintain orderly exchange arrangements among members, and to avoid competitive exchange depreciation.

(iv) To assist in the establishment of a multilateral system of payments in respect of current transactions between members and in the elimination of foreign exchange restrictions which hamper the growth of world trade.

(v)   To give confidence to members by making the Fund's resources available to them under adequate safeguards, thus providing them with opportunity to correct maladjustments in their balance of payments without resorting to measures destructive of national or international prosperity.

(vi) In accordance with the above, to shorten the duration and lessen the degree of disequilibrium in the international balances of payments of members.[60]

A fundamental conflict still existed between the Keynesian emphasis on promoting high employment and real income versus White's focus on international monetary stability and his desire to avoid competitive exchange rate manipulations. At one point in the deliberations, Keynes had been asked by the U.S. delegation if "the British recognized that in joining the Fund they were accepting some obligation to modify their domestic policy in the light of its international effects on stability?" Keynes replied that they did—but at their own discretion.[61]

A seeming contradiction in terms had made it into the final charter for the International Monetary Fund. White would later explain that the compromise that had been achieved would provide a "stable, if moderately flexible" system of exchange rates. He compared it to the sway of the Empire State Building, with flexibility deliberately built into the design to prevent its destruction.[62] Another version of the compromise, offered by Keynes's biographer Harrod, was that "Keynes and White agreed that it was desirable to have a fixed rate of exchange in the short run, with flexibility in the long run."[63]

In any case, the representatives of the various delegations to the Bretton Woods conference signed off on the Articles of Agreement as presented. They were ready to go home and present the document to their individual governments for ratification. The agreement would come into force only if nations representing 65 percent of the total quotas allotted had signed it by December 31, 1945. On signing, each government was required to deposit one-hundredth of 1 percent of its own quota in gold or U.S. dollars to meet the administrative expenses of the fund.

Aftermath

The period of denouement following the Bretton Woods conference had a decidedly less heady feeling about it than the process leading up to the agreement. Basically, it involved a series of appeals to the various governments to condone the ideological objectives of the fund and commit themselves to abiding by its rules and regulations. The delicate question of monetary sovereignty was raised again and again, and each time it touched off new concerns and vociferous debate.

The U.S. Bretton Woods Agreements Act, which authorized acceptance of the fund's Articles of Agreement by the United States, ran into stiff opposition in both the House and the Senate. To satisfy members of Congress, certain political concessions had to be made concerning the relationship of U.S. monetary policy to the operations of the fund. Congress wanted to assert more influence over the fund's ability to make decisions and issue policy directives that would obligate U.S. financial resources. A National Advisory Council on International Monetary and Financial Problems was set up to provide "guidance" to the U.S. representatives at the fund and the bank; its members would be the Secretary of the Treasury, the Secretary of State, the Secretary of Commerce, the chairman of the Board of Governors of the Federal Reserve System, and the chairman of the Board of Trustees of the Export-Import Bank. The council would be asked to provide recommendations to the president as to whether or not the United States should give its approval to any act of the fund requiring such consent.

That Congress had strong reservations about the fund was also made clear by the fact that this council was expected to provide special reports every two years giving its appraisal of "the extent to which the operations and policies of the Fund and the Bank have served, and in the future may be expected to serve, the interests of the United States and the world in promoting sound international economic cooperation and furthering world security."[64]

For all its initial support and instrumental role in bringing the whole plan to fruition, the United States seemed eager to be the first to point out the fund's failings. But the successful lobbying efforts of two members of the Senate and two members of the House who had served as delegates to Bretton Woods, along with two more House members who had been technical advisers on the fund, succeeded in bringing about passage of the act.[65] It was approved by President Harry S. Truman on July 31, 1945 (President Roosevelt had died on April 12 of a cerebral hemorrhage).

The United Kingdom had an even more difficult time reconciling its concerns about belonging to the fund. Lend-lease aid from the United States would not be forthcoming after September 1, 1945. The United Kingdom was desperately in debt and fearful of subjecting itself to the financial obligations engendered in the fund agreement without having some assurance that additional loans could be secured. In the meantime, Prime Minister Winston Churchill had been defeated in July and the new British government was not yet familiar with the issues involved in the Bretton

Woods agreement. Keynes found himself in the middle of stressful negotiations as time was running out for approving the Articles of Agreement. He delivered an impassioned speech before Parliament in which he connected the need for the United Kingdom to sign on to the fund as a condition for receiving the benefits of a newly negotiated Anglo-American Financial Agreement that would provide $3.75 in emergency loans on generous terms. Parliament finally approved both measures in December 1945.

Many other countries likewise held out to the very end to sign the agreement for the fund. By December 18, only eleven were ready to do so, although another eight were close to making the necessary legislative decisions. Nevertheless, the U.S. State Department felt sufficiently confident to schedule a formal ceremony for December 27 to hail the official establishment of the fund. Their belief that the arrangements worked out at Bretton Woods would come into force proved justified; on the appointed day, representatives of twenty-nine countries were present to sign the agreement and the total quotas amounted to $7,079.5 million—well over the 65 percent required.[66]

There was, however, one very notable absence among all the represented nations. The Soviet Union, which early on had shown keen interest in the objectives of the fund and the bank and had actively taken part in the Bretton Woods conference, opted not to sign the agreement. After all the wrangling over quotas and the provision of sensitive monetary information, the Soviet representatives conveyed to U.S. officials the curt message that Moscow needed more time to consider the agreement. The deadline was allowed to expire.

Given the powerful role that the Soviet Union had been slated to play in the fund—the U.S.S.R. would have had only slightly less voting influence than the United Kingdom—it seems somewhat ironic in retrospect that Soviet leader Joseph Stalin spurned such an opportunity to influence global economic and financial affairs. The designated position of the Soviet Union after the Bretton Woods conference was so favorable, in fact, that it might be seen to support allegations against White, who would later be accused of having collaborated with the communists. White came under the scrutiny of the FBI for his suspected cooperation with Soviet agents and the matter was brought to the attention of President Truman. Earlier, it had been expected that White would become the first managing director of the fund; Truman's reservations in early 1946, however, decreed that White only be named one of several executive directors and be surrounded by carefully screened assistants.[67]

Whittaker Chambers, in his book *Witness*, asserts that White regularly provided original documents to the communist underground, as well as longhand memos covering work going on in the Treasury Department.[68] "He was perfectly willing to meet me secretly," according to Chambers, who was a member of the communist apparatus at the time.[69] Chambers states that in 1937, as a contribution to the Soviet government, White wanted to offer a plan of his own authorship for reforming the Soviet monetary system. The idea was transmitted to Moscow, "which reacted with enthusiasm to the idea of having its monetary affairs 'controlled' gratis by an expert of the United States Treasury Department," according to Chambers.[70]

White was called before the House Committee on Un-American Activities, chaired by Congressman Richard Nixon, in 1948 to refute charges that he had cooperated with the communists. White sweepingly denied Chambers's accusations and "skirmished brilliantly with the Committee, turning their questions with ridicule and high indignation," as described in *Witness*.[71] A few days later, White died of a heart attack. A document in longhand, written by White, later surfaced as crucial evidence of White's willingness to provide information about Treasury Department matters to communists. Nixon read White's memo, obtained from Chambers, into the congressional record following the conviction of Alger Hiss.[72]

From such grandiose objectives for structuring a new world economic order to such an ignominious personal ending is the stuff of human tragedy born of intellectual hubris. White had wanted to bring about international monetary equilibrium through the establishment of an authoritative supernational institution controlled by technical experts and visionaries such as himself; White's mistake, it would seem, can be traced to his pretension that any organizational entity embued with such power and directed by humans could ever be immune from the influence of personal politics, including his own.

It was a lesson Keynes had already learned. At the inaugural meeting for the fund and the bank held in Savannah, Georgia, in 1946, Keynes warned that the "Bretton Woods twins" were becoming too politicized and were in danger of irrevocably compromising their economic mission to benefit humankind. Keynes had found himself losing control over the fate of the organizations he had personally helped to design to bring his economic vision for the world to reality. He had been overruled on key issues—he had argued that if the fund had to be located in the United States, it should at least be in New York rather than Washington—and he was disappointed that White would not be named managing director.[73] Keynes felt personally pressured by Britain's dependence on U.S. financial assistance. The ongoing mental exhaustion was beginning to severely affect his physical health. On the train back to Washington from Savannah, Keynes had a heart attack; six weeks later he died.

Both Keynes and White, it can be said, met their demise in the birth of the organizations they had created through the force of their ideas. Both men had thought it possible to change human destiny through deliberate engineering, social and economic. As Keynes observed in his memoirs, "civilization was a thin and precarious crust erected by the personality and the will of a very few, and only maintained by rules and conventions skillfully put across and guilefully preserved."[74] Keynes and White clearly saw themselves as members of that illustrious few, and accordingly, they directed their efforts toward preserving civilization in the terms best suited to their expertise: by empowering global institutions to control monetary relations and to redistribute the world's financial resources.

GREAT EXPECTATIONS

Starting March 1, 1947, the International Monetary Fund officially commenced operations. The International Bank for Reconstruction and Development, later to be called the World Bank, was not yet in a position to make extensive loans, so several member countries opted instead to obtain financial assistance by drawing down their accounts at the fund for a total of $631 million during the first year-and-a-half after resources were made available.[75] Even if the global economy was flailing, though, the growth in the personnel lists of the two new institutions was booming. Despite Keynes's earlier observation that he could not conceive how there would be enough work on the board for "15 highly qualified monetary experts," the staff had grown to 403 people representing some twenty-nine countries by April 30, 1948.[76] In just over a year, the institutions had outgrown their Washington headquarters at 1818 H Street and the fund began renting extra office space in an adjoining building.[77]

If the number of employees had swelled, though, the importance of the Bretton Woods institutions had not. Neither politicians nor the press seemed to appreciate just exactly what the fund was supposed to accomplish. It was seen as some kind of technical financial branch of the U.S. government rather than as a global organization. Camille Gutt of Belgium, the fund's first managing director, observed that the problem was due in large measure to inadequate public relations: "We did not explain enough to the technicians, governments, central banks, universities—we did not explain enough to the public at large." On the other hand, the fund was "bristling with technicalities," he confessed, and was indeed "very difficult to explain."[78]

Then, too, the romanticized mission of the fund was being supplanted by the more dramatic Marshall Plan. Compared to the program laid out by U.S. Secretary of State George Marshall, which would supply a generous $13 billion in financial capital to help rebuild war-torn Western Europe, the resources of the fund were relatively limited. Moreover, the board of the fund tended to lecture to member countries that drawings were supposed to be used only to settle temporary balance-of-payments deficits. Such a stingy attitude seemed at odds with the universal brotherhood ideology that had been promoted at Bretton Woods. The old message was fast being replaced by a new strategy wherein economic assets would be used for purposes of political self-interest. Investment in Western Europe was being touted as the best tactical weapon for staving off the spread of communism in Europe.

So while the fund attempted to focus attention on the evils of inflation and monetary disequilibrium, General George Marshall was grabbing headlines with his dire warnings about a weakened Europe's vulnerability to exploitation by totalitarian forces. In his speech at Harvard on June 5, 1947, Marshall called for the United States to provide massive assistance in conjunction with a program undertaken by the Europeans themselves to adopt market-oriented policies aimed at fortifying their domestic economies. "Our policy is not directed against any country or doctrine," Marshall insisted, "but against hunger, poverty, desperation and chaos."[79]

The Soviet Union, feeling the threat behind the growing ideological gap with the West, didn't see the plan that way and promptly rejected the proposal for countries on the east side of the Iron Curtain. (Churchill had made his famous speech at Fulton, Missouri, the prior year.) In April 1947, an article by George Kennan, an adviser to Marshall at the State Department, had appeared in *Foreign Affairs* under the pseudonym X; in it, Kennan stressed the need for "containment" of the Soviet Union. Soviet leaders sensed that in providing financial capital, the United States intended to impose its own free market values on Europe and thus strengthen capitalism's hold across the Atlantic.

To a great extent, that assessment was correct. The United States did want to help Western Europe improve its economic productivity, not only to serve as a buffer against communism, but also to create markets for American goods. A newly reconstructed Europe would be a primary trading partner for the United States. As the success of the Marshall Plan became increasingly apparent, leftist critics in France began to denounce it as a scheme by American big business, working arm-in-arm with the government, to build a "Bankers' Europe."[80] The emphasis of the Marshall Plan from the beginning, it was true, was to implement in Europe the conservative domestic economic policies that served U.S. industry so well. About half of the members of the Harriman Committee, which effectively wrote the Marshall Plan legislation, were also members of influential business associations and no doubt recognized the payoff to private sector interests when government policies foster investment and economic reconstruction.

Despite the inevitable conflict inherent in any "private-public partnership," the Marshall Plan went a long way toward promoting free market values by calling for less regulatory interference so that private capital could go to work in Europe.[81] Like the Bretton Woods agreement, the Marshall Plan advocated stable currencies and exchange rates and sought reductions in trade barriers. It also pushed for balanced budgets and took the position that financial integration in Western Europe could best be achieved if all countries agreed to exercise domestic fiscal prudence; if each country put its own house in order by implementing responsible economic policies, the task of coordinating international relations would be relatively straightforward and prosperity would be quickly forthcoming. The Marshall Plan, in short, eclipsed the impact of Bretton Woods because it backed up its commitment to price stability and expanded international trade with directed financial assistance and a definitive plan to revitalize the economies of Western Europe.

Not that the fund entirely dropped out of the international monetary and financial picture. During the immediate postwar years, it continued to refine its articles and attempted to determine in what capacity it could appropriately respond to the financial requests of member countries. But fund leaders persisted in stressing the disciplinary role of the institution over its mandate for international cooperation, thus undercutting the vision of its founders with an attitude that came across as irritatingly petty. Countries that sought to draw down funds were lectured about their laxity in monetary matters and sternly urged to exercise more financial restraint. Sometimes member countries were denied access to funds on the basis that they were "using the resources of the Fund in a manner contrary to the purposes of the Fund."[82]

Delayed Impact

As the fund struggled to rise above its obsession with rules, regulations, and punitive actions, the underlying set of laws governing international monetary stability inherent in White's original blueprint slowly began to assert its own influence on global trade. At the heart of the Bretton Woods agreement, beneath all the rhetoric about promoting high levels of employment and real income, was the solid reality that the U.S. dollar was technically worth a specified amount of gold. As the result of a January 1934 proclamation by President Roosevelt, a dollar was equal to 1/35 ounce of gold; 35 dollars was equal to one ounce of gold. The U.S. government was thus obligated to maintain a stable relationship between gold and the value of its currency—at least, for international purposes. (Private citizens had been ordered in April 1933 to deliver their monetary gold holdings to the Federal Reserve.) Recognition of this commitment was encapsulated in the U.S. government's promise to freely convert dollars into gold, or gold into dollars, at the established rate when so requested by any foreign central bank in the Bretton Woods system.

Because the Bretton Woods agreement permitted member countries to declare the par value of their currencies in terms of either gold or the dollar, there effectively could be no distinction between these two forms of international money. So long as the U.S. dollar was truly "as good as gold," because of the convertibility privilege, other countries did not need to hoard gold to serve as reserve backing for their own currencies. It was enough to maintain a fixed exchange rate with the dollar to ensure the integrity of their own money.

The discipline of the classical gold standard of the pre-1914 period had largely been reinstated, but with key refinements that ostensibly made it more efficient and less vulnerable to the disrupting effects of temporary imbalances. Dollars functioned as paper claims on gold that could be redeemed for settling payments among trading partners. Keynes's earliest proposals for setting up a gold exchange standard on a global basis, based on his analysis of India's currency system, had thus effectively been implemented. The irony, though, was that the link between the dollar and gold would turn out to be a key factor in promoting global economic growth, despite Keynes's implicit desire to insulate domestic economies from the fiscal restraint necessary to maintain fixed exchange rates. The stabilizing influence of the Bretton Woods system would finally kick in—but for unintended reasons. The connection between the dollar and gold would provide the monetary foundation for increased international trade as producers around the world realized that their profits would not fall victim to competitive currency devaluations. The U.S. dollar was solidly anchored to gold, other countries' currencies were pegged to the dollar at fixed exchange rates, and the resulting elimination of currency risk would serve as a tremendous boon to international trade and economic growth around the world.

Still, the fund continued to take a back seat to other programs for nearly the whole first decade of its existence. The catalyst for activating the gold–dollar connection as the basis for international monetary stability was the European Payments Union (EPU), put into effect to carry out the objectives of the Marshall Plan. Starting with an initial fund of $350 million in September 1950, the United States set up a financial clearing union for Europe to manage the monetary aspects of trade, not so much between European countries and the United States, but among the European countries themselves. The U.S. dollar served as the official unit of account for settling payments associated with imports and exports within Western Europe.

Instead of continued internecine warfare among the European currencies, with each country still resorting to devaluations to gain temporary trade advantages, there was now a single currency available to all. Goods and services could be valued consistently across borders in terms of the dollar, fostering intra-European trade on the basis of genuine comparative advantage versus artificial currency effects. Where multilateral trade earlier had been stifled for lack of an equitable and workable payments mechanism, it now began to flourish. Convinced that a solid currency existed for tabulating the appropriate payments arising from transactions among European countries, governments began to dismantle the quota and tariff restrictions they had erected to protect themselves from their neighbors' monetary machinations.

The EPU was administered not by the fund, which logically should have been entrusted with the task of managing a payments clearing union, but rather by the Bank for International Settlements in Basle, Switzerland. In essence, the EPU represented a limited version, encompassing Western Europe and anchored by the United States, of what the fund sought to do on a broader world scale. The EPU used the dollar as its international reserve currency rather than some abstract concept of a bancor or unitas. Private producers had a reliable money for denominating trade transactions, central banks had a reserve currency for clearing international payments, and trading nations had a stable unit of account and a monetary standard of value.

Golden Age

With the dollar stabilizing price levels around the world, productivity began to soar in the 1950s. International trade flourished as restrictions were steadily reduced. Governments still maintained the right to exercise fiscal policies in accordance with their own perception of domestic priorities, but they did not have carte blanche to indulge in financial or economic fixes that ultimately would put pressure on currency exchange rates. With the dollar providing outside monetary discipline, governments were forced to act responsibly in implementing economic policies for their nations. For the most part, they did so, and the 1950s marked an extraordinarily successful economic era characterized by stable prices, high productivity, and free trade.

Different governments pursued economic growth in different ways that reflected their own national values and traditions, as well as current political trends.[83] Great Britain, for example, had gone through a period of determined nationalization under the Labour Party during the mid-1940s. An expansion of social services had ensued and sweeping new programs were implemented to attain the government-proclaimed goal of full employment. Great Britain had seemingly embraced the Keynesian philosophy of running budget deficits as necessary, with social goals outranking fiscal discipline at every political turn.

Yet the solid foundation of stable international money, in conjunction with the financial incentives of the Marshall Plan, spurred increasing calls from both business and labor interests for a less pronounced government role in the economy. A backlash developed against the welfare state policies that had been imposed at the close of the war. By 1951 the Conservative Party, under the leadership of Churchill (at the age of seventy-seven), had returned to power with a renewed sense of commitment to market-oriented economic solutions, a zeal for free trade policies, and a mandate to restore world confidence in the British pound.

Government intervention grew less onerous in Britain as Conservatives pushed their agenda for the separation of private enterprise and state planning actions. They believed that fiscal policy should be tempered by a concern for the damaging effects of inflation and looked to the discipline of monetary stability to provide an overlay of order and regulated growth. The Conservatives accepted the regulatory aspect of a global monetary mechanism as the master control of economic activity and embraced the anti-inflation stance engendered in convertibility. In short, the existence of an external form of monetary order gave them the confidence to pursue internal strategies based on free market values that would ultimately help Britain shrug off the structural rigidities that had impeded growth in the immediate postwar years.

France, even more than Great Britain, had succumbed to the idea of running the economy by government decree by the time World War II was drawing to a close. The government that came into power in 1944 consisted largely of socialists and communists; continuing the conversion process started during the war, it supported the state-directed management of economic forces and the broad nationalization of industry. A new Ministry of the National Economy was created and charged with determining the overall direction of the economy.[84] Those who advocated long-term planning on such a grand scale, however, found their efforts foiled by lackluster productivity and high inflation.

In the meantime, the Marshall Plan was beginning to exert its influence in the direction of more conservative economic policies. Jean Monnet, who would become known as the French architect of the Common Market in Europe, began advocating a less rigid approach to national economic planning. He preferred to encourage certain selected industries, such as high-tech electronics, by providing capital rather than micromanaging their development. The availability of Marshall Plan funds permitted the French government to pursue Monnet's approach for "soft targeting" its pet industrial objectives with financial assistance. In return, though, Marshall Plan officials "asked the French to control private credits, restrain wages and prices, reduce government borrowing, and put state-owned enterprises on a self-supporting basis."[85] This bargain was a form of bribery, but the French government accepted the terms and the nation became the beneficiary. France's inflation rate dropped from over 30 percent during the 1940s to just over 5 percent in the 1950s; productivity took off at the same time and exceeded annual growth rates of 5 percent during the mid-1950s.[86] The stimulus toward greater market competition engendered in the Marshall Plan and the ability to tap into a stable international monetary mechanism helped moved France into an era of impressive economic growth unaccompanied by debilitating inflation.

Elsewhere in Europe, Germany was in the throes of anti-Nazi, antitotalitarian political sentiment after the war. The banking and financial system was in shambles and the money supply was out of control. But Ludwig Erhard, Germany's first postwar Minister of Economics (who would be elected chancellor in 1963) introduced a new philosophy of free market principles that restricted government intervention to the minimal functions of insuring open competition and guarding against the formation of monopolies. The rest would be handled by private incentive and newly unleashed productive forces. A supply-side approach emphasizing tax reduction and sound money would be the new economic creed and the key to Germany's spectacular economic recovery.[87]

Under Erhard, the virtually worthless reichsmark was replaced in June 1948 by a new currency, the deutsche mark. The impact of the change on the German economy was immediate and astonishing. According to Henry Wallich, who was serving with the U.S. military government in Germany at the time (and who would later oversee U.S. monetary policy as a Federal Reserve Board governor), the monetary reform "transformed the German scene from one day to the next." The day after the new currency was introduced, Wallich observed, goods began to appear in the stores once again, money resumed its normal function, and the black and grey markets reverted to a minor role. "The spirit of the country changed overnight," he noted.[88]

Japan, unlike Germany, could not wholly abandon its industrial and banking structures to the forces of private competition, nor could it entirely forsake its interventionist tendencies. Instead, Japan pursued its own version of conservative domestic economic policies using more rigid government controls. Tempered by the Japanese tradition of close cooperation between commerce, banking, and government, fiscal prudence was enforced by powerful industrial blocks working in tandem with government, rather than by private entrepreneurial interests. Japan tailored its domestic economy to encourage savings, which in turn made substantial internal sources of financial capital available to Japanese banks. These banks were then used by the government, not only to control the money supply, but also to steer investment into industrial facilities that would increase Japan's manufacturing capabilities.

The high levels of savings that prevailed in Japan in the postwar years would normally lead, according to Keynesian theory, to reduced consumer demand. Ultimately there would be a decline in national income and a contraction of the economy. But Japan found salvation by exporting its goods to foreign markets, particularly the United States. Japan protected its internal economy from outside competition while exploiting the free trade policies of other countries.

Having access to U.S. markets permitted Japan to practice self-indulgent domestic economic policies in the sense that it could build up private savings without having to resort to exchange rate adjustments to fend off competition from the outside world. So while Japan enjoyed the benefits of sound monetary and fiscal policies in the 1950s, it did not choose to engage in more liberalized trade policies such as those being pursued in Europe. As Henry Nau suggests, this stance was partly because of Japan's cultural sense of vulnerability due to its island economy and partly because Japan was excluded from the competitive pressures arising from the process of regional trade integration taking place in Europe.[89]

Thus, there can be little question that the sound money environment that reigned in the postwar years contributed to the impressive economic performance of both the victors and the vanquished and enabled the world to begin reconstructing an industrial base that would raise living standards to new heights for the generations that followed. By the time the EPU was dismantled in late 1958, the use of the dollar as an international currency was firmly entrenched. At that point, the fund was finally able to grasp the baton and take over its original assigned duties for maintaining international monetary stability.

During the next decade, stable domestic prices and expanded international trade resulted in extremely high rates of economic growth for the countries hardest hit by the war. For Britain, France, Germany, and Japan, all taken together, the yearly growth in real domestic gross product from 1947 to 1967 averaged 6.4 percent. The rate of inflation for these same four countries during the same period averaged 3.7 percent. Even though policy makers generally were attempting to avoid the Keynesian preoccupation with obtaining full employment, these countries managed to enjoy gratifyingly high levels of employment as a side benefit of economic growth; they averaged only 2 percent unemployment during that same time period.[90]

Throughout this twenty-year period following the war, the United States served as the stabilizing force for the world's currency system and rose to predominance as a financial and economic power. While some American economists would later complain that the dollar's role as the world's key currency put an untenable burden on domestic economic policy making, it appears that responsibility for anchoring international monetary arrangements exerted a healthy influence on the U.S. economy as well. From 1947 to 1967, the annual growth in the U.S. gross domestic product averaged a very respectable 3.6 percent. During the same period, the U.S. consumer price index rose an average of only 2.6 percent a year. Unemployment in the United States during this interval averaged 4.7 percent.[91]

All of this achievement was possible because the stable monetary and financial conditions that prevailed encouraged optimal use of capital and maximum development of the factors production. The existence of a rational international currency system provided an incentive for producers to manufacture goods not just for domestic consumption, but for export to other nations; as international trade expanded, so too did global levels of economic production and prosperity.

By virtue of its promise to maintain convertibility between gold and dollars, the United States was charged with ensuring that the international economic and financial order functioned efficiently, predictably, and fairly. Other countries were willing to stake the value of their currencies and the well-being of their economies on the continued integrity of the dollar because they trusted the U.S. government to honor its commitment to keep the dollar anchored to gold. While U.S. citizens could not redeem dollars for gold, the fact that foreign central banks could—and that foreign goods competed openly against American products—kept price levels remarkably stable, not only in the United States but throughout the world.

In short, the fixed exchange rate system that came into being as the result of the arrangements worked out at Bretton Woods set the stage for a golden age of robust trade and unprecedented global prosperity. The period from 1947 to 1967, often referred to as the "Bretton Woods era," marked the emergence of a new world economic order based on solid money and increasingly free competition in the international marketplace. Given the intentions and sympathies of Keynes and White, it might be argued that the rules-based system of fixed exchange rates that came to characterize the Bretton Woods approach—with its reliance on convertibility between the dollar and gold—was not exactly in keeping with the more exalted visions of its founders, who favored flexibility and organizational "discretion." But there can be no denying that the global economic order that developed in the years following the adoption of the Bretton Woods agreement worked—and much to the world's benefit. As the *Wall Street Journal* noted some forty years after the Bretton Woods conference took place, the discipline of the international monetary system hammered out during those three weeks of intense activity in July 1944 helped bring about "a generation of economic progress and order the likes of which the world had seen seldom before and never since."[92]

2

The Fall from Grace

For some two decades following the end of World War II, the global community had a universal currency at its disposal: the U.S. dollar was king. Prices were stable, investment returns provided meaningful signals about the optimal use of financial capital, and international trade was unencumbered by the distorting effects of monetary manipulation across borders. Global prosperity seemed to stem from the fact that the most economically and militarily powerful nation in the world had responsibility for keeping the international currency system running smoothly. That the United States should provide the monetary foundation for the world's postwar economic order seemed entirely appropriate.

For the United States, though, the pride in being the world's dominant economic power and serving as its monetary anchor was beginning to give way to a feeling of being put upon for having to exercise constraint in domestic fiscal policy in order to ensure price stability for the rest of the world. The dollar had become entrenched as the world's undisputed key currency; other currencies derived their value as a function of being pegged to the dollar, which meant the United States was effectively dictating monetary policy for the global economy. But was that a privilege or a burden?

No one could argue that the price stability achieved through the gold-linked dollar system had not provided benefits for the U.S. economy as well. Prices in the United States had increased more than 100 percent during its four-year engagement in World War II (not untypical for wartime periods); yet with the dollar playing a key role in a rational international currency system, U.S. prices increased by just 2 percent during the years of the Korean War from 1950 to 1953.[1] It finally seemed possible to have a dynamic, growing economy, even during wartime, without being plagued by inflation.

But price stability as an objective in itself was not accorded a great deal of scholarly respect once it was attained. By 1960 the conservative domestic economic policies that had emphasized balanced budgets and price stability were starting to come under attack within the academic community. Government intervention in the economy was still largely frowned upon by private business; it was the free market-oriented approach that was given credit for launching the strong recovery after the war. But for a generation of academics who had now come of age, a rebirth of Keynesian fervor called for more powerful fiscal initiatives by government as part of a new liberalism aimed at achieving even higher growth rates and increased levels of employment. Leading economists such as Paul Samuelson and Abba Lerner embraced the veracity of the Phillips Curve as a representation of the relationship between inflation and employment. It was up to the government, they argued, to choose the optimal trade-off between the two variables and then take the appropriate fiscal action—either stimulate demand with government spending or slow it down with higher taxes—so as to fine tune the economy toward reaching the targeted point on the curve.[2]

Along with this faith in the government's ability to manage economic levers and the accompanying zeal for more activist fiscal policies came a disdain for the U.S. role as international keeper of the currency. Why should the United States sacrifice its own best economic interests to provide monetary stability for the rest of the world? Proponents of the Keynesian view resented the imposition of budgetary spending constraints and high interest rates to keep the money supply tight at a time when they felt growth should be encouraged with stimulative government spending and easier money. It was not that U.S. growth rates had been bad during the 1950s, but Europe and Japan had been growing much faster.[3] There was even concern that the United States might begin to fall behind the Soviet Union in terms of economic output if Washington did not take deliberate steps to stimulate domestic expansion. If these measures meant running a deficit in the domestic budget, so be it.

In any case, the Keynesians argued, the United States would be better off to concentrate on its own domestic priorities than to worry about preserving a fixed exchange rate system for the rest of the world. And in a classic example of strange bedfellows, the Keynesians gained support before the end of the 1960s from a most unlikely intellectual source. Members of the emerging group of monetarist economists associated with the Chicago School—led by Milton Friedman—likewise argued that the prevailing system of fixed exchange rates imposed unacceptable constraints on the United States' ability to address its domestic economic concerns. Harry Johnson, a University of Chicago professor who would go on to promote the monetarist viewpoint at the London School of Economics, suggested that flexible rates were necessary to "allow each country to pursue the mixture of unemployment and price trend objectives it prefers."[4] For both the Keynesians and the monetarists, the dollar's central position in the fixed exchange rate system as decreed under Bretton Woods was a monetary straitjacket that should be thrown off in favor of national macroeconomic autonomy.

GUNS AND BUTTER

The academic arguments for abandoning the fixed rate system, emanating from both the Keynesian and monetarist camps, had to be sifted through the political grinding mill before becoming official U.S. government policy. In the early 1960s, finance officials at the Treasury and the Federal Reserve still clung to the doctrine of conservatism in monetary and fiscal matters. There was no sense of resigned acceptance about running budget deficits; indeed, there was such zealousness for achieving balanced budgets that occasionally even a budget surplus was obtained (for years 1956, 1957, and 1960).[5] Social goals, such as reducing unemployment or increasing transfer payments, were considered secondary to the fundamental task of demonstrating fiscal responsibility and maintaining the integrity of the U.S. dollar at home and abroad.

President John F. Kennedy found himself besieged with conflicting economic advice from government officials who held more traditional views about fiscal restraint versus the Keynesian disciples who were anxious to transform academic charts into U.S. economic policy. Kennedy respected Robert Roosa, the monetary expert who had managed currency relations with foreign central banks at the Federal Reserve Bank of New York and who later became Treasury Under-Secretary for Monetary Affairs in the Kennedy administration. Roosa believed that the primacy of the dollar in the international monetary system had to be upheld as a matter of national integrity; he thought it imperative to defend the dollar's value and soundness in terms of the $35 gold convertibility price. As former Chairman of the Federal Reserve Board Paul Volcker recounts, Kennedy's people were paying attention to Roosa's advice on international monetary issues even before the presidential election. After a member of the Kennedy campaign staff consulted Roosa, Kennedy made the statement the following day: "If elected, I shall not devalue the dollar."[6]

At the same time, Roosa was open to the idea of enlisting the help of other countries to assist the United States in carrying out its duty to guarantee international monetary stability. At the Treasury, he proposed that U.S. allies cooperate to provide "peripheral support" for the dollar by pooling their gold reserves and selling as necessary to neutralize speculative jumps in the price of gold. Responsibility could be shared; it could not be shrugged off. As Volcker describes it, the Treasury "was in no mood for radical experimentation" at the beginning of the 1960s. "It was foursquare for the Bretton Woods system, for the sanctity of the $35 gold price, and for fixed exchange rates."[7]

More liberal Keynesian thinkers, though, such as Walter Heller (chairman of Kennedy's Council of Economic Advisers) and John Kenneth Galbraith (whose 1958 book *The Affluent Society* had garnered much attention), were ready to discount the glories of being the key currency country in their eagerness to maximize the performance of the domestic economy. Heady with the notion that it was possible to have it all—full employment, social programs, tax cuts—they moved ahead with a "New Frontier" program characterized by direct government manipulation of key economic variables. In early 1963, Kennedy approved a program calling for a massive cut in taxes to put more spending power in the hands of consumers and thus spur the economy. His untimely death later that year did not mean that his program likewise met its demise. Quite the contrary occurred. President Lyndon Johnson pushed the tax bill through the following year and went even further with increased government spending than Kennedy had anticipated. Under Johnson, a slew of programs aimed at achieving near utopian social goals were created and liberally funded. The United States would fulfil its destiny as the "Great Society" that had conquered poverty, illiteracy, and urban blight. Medical care and retirement security would be made available to everyone through the largesse of the federal government.

The plan came close to being realized by the mid-1960s as social benefits ballooned while the economy prospered and the financial system remained fundamentally sound. Unemployment was low, inflation was low, plus the United States was running a gratifyingly high trade surplus. Government expenditures were high, but the strain on the budget had not yet worked its way through the monetary system and the inevitable inflationary pressures were not yet being felt. All that would change, however, after 1965 with the escalation of the Vietnam War and the increase in military spending under President Johnson.

Costs of War

If Johnson had been willing to impose new taxes to offset the rise in government expenditures, or if he had been willing to cut federal spending on social programs in recognition of the high costs of war, it might have been possible to continue to pursue the ideal of balanced budgets and stable prices. But Johnson had embraced the spending side of the Keynesian formula without acknowledging that surplus years were part of the same approach; over the course of an average business cycle, deficits and surpluses were supposed to net out. Instead, the mentality that it was all right to run a budget deficit persisted to the exclusion of the notion that the shortfall must eventually be covered by a surplus. Deficit spending was deemed useful in itself because it enabled the federal government to stimulate the economy with directed fiscal inputs and target key economic growth areas such as construction and housing. Why not continue to run budget deficits indefinitely, year in, year out?

Whatever academic justification could be offered for accepting chronic budget deficits, it served Johnson's political preferences inasmuch as he did not want to confront voters directly with the notion that a financial trade-off was involved. The Vietnam War was costing American taxpayers a great deal of money at a time when the U.S. government was already spending huge amounts to support a liberal agenda of social programs. It wasn't clear that the nation would support an escalation in the war; asking them to pay for it out of their own pockets would exacerbate the backlash of political resistance. Johnson was not willing to frame the decision in such stark terms. Rather than focusing on the financial sacrifice required of the American people to pursue their nation's military objectives in Vietnam, he delayed the immediate impact of the spending decision by financing the budget deficit through increased government borrowing.

"We tried to finance the Vietnam War and the Great Society programs without a tax increase," admits Charles L. Schultze, Johnson's budget director at the time, "and clearly that started us on our course of inflation."[8] Not that this dilemma was new. Political leaders always have tended to take the view that in time of war the nation must do whatever is necessary to succeed, and the financial repercussions can be dealt with later. Johnson was only following the pattern that had been adhered to by his predecessors: Lincoln during the Civil War, when inflation in the Union from 1861 to 1865 was 117 percent; Wilson during World War I, when prices rose from 1917 to 1918 by 126 percent; and Roosevelt during World War II, when prices rose from 1941 to 1945 by 108 percent.[9]

While it is one thing to delay the costs of war until a future time when circumstances are not so pressing, it is another to hide the costs of war indefinitely by financing them with government borrowing—that is, by expanding the money supply. In the former case, it makes sense to impose a special "war tax" after hostilities have ceased to cover the additional expenditure necessitated by the war effort. (Congress did enact an income tax surcharge in 1968, but it was insufficient to redress the earlier financial damage.) In the latter case, the government opts to avoid explicitly acknowledging the additional expenditure connected with an active military conflict. Not daring to ask its citizens to pay for war with higher taxes, it instead borrows the money by issuing Treasury bills and bonds. These government obligations are purchased by individuals and commercial banks, and the funds are then injected back into the economy through government spending. Because the interest rate on Treasury securities is determined on an auction basis, the government is always assured of being able to sell its entire offering; through the bid-and-ask process, the market will set the interest rate to whatever level is required to satisfy private investors. If market reaction to government obligations seems less than enthusiastic, though, the Treasury may coerce the Federal Reserve to buy government bonds for its own account. In either case, the money supply is expanded as the government takes on additional future financial liabilities to cover present spending for consumption.

Politicians may feel entirely comfortable with the option of deficit financing; central bankers, as a rule, do not. Marriner Eccles, a banker from Utah who was appointed Federal Reserve Board chairman in 1934 under Roosevelt, because increasingly uncomfortable with the financial practices of the government at the time of World War II. He was upset with the assumption that the Federal Reserve would passively absorb excess government spending, accommodate profligate fiscal policies by injecting more money into the system, and thus inflict higher prices on the population. Eccles argued vehemently that war should be financed from the savings of consumers rather than the artificial expansion of money. He urged Roosevelt to borrow less and tax more.[10]

Eccles's concern was that expanding the money supply indefinitely to cover deficit spending would ultimately lead to serious inflation—the bane of central bankers. Ironically, Eccles once had been a leading advocate of Keynesian economics. His own observations about the need for government spending to spur the economy in slack periods preceded publication of the *General Theory* by several years.[11] But the practice of financing a budget deficit through borrowing, rather than taxing, went against his sound money instincts. "There is no limit to the amount of money that can be created by the banking system," Eccles explained, "but there are limits to our productive facilities and our labor supply, which can be only slowly increased and which at present are being used to near capacity."[12]

Fortunately, the high inflation associated with wartime spending tends to drop off once a nation's economy reverts to a more normal civilian footing. Soldiers are transformed back into productive workers whose jobs and incomes then begin to generate tax revenues for the government. At the same time, military spending dramatically decreases. Although the price tag for the war may still remain outstanding, the budget comes closer to being in balance on a current basis. Meanwhile, the newly invigorated economy begins to grow its way into the expanded money supply. At least, that process has taken place during the postwar periods following prior U.S. military engagements.

But the Vietnam War did not conform to the United States' earlier pattern of experience in terms of its economic and financial fallout. Military spending was no longer a temporary do-or-die effort required in time of war. Instead, it had become a permanent part of the U.S. budget. A massive part. And the all-encompassing social programs initiated in pursuit of the vision of a great society had so mushroomed in size that they were likewise consuming a huge portion of the budget. U.S. fiscal policy had turned into a Keynesian nightmare: government spending could be increased at the volition of political leaders, but it could never be cut. The trade-off would not be between guns and butter; elected officials would deliver both. The only option related to how the resulting deficit would be financed—with higher future taxes or inflation. Political considerations entered into the decision once again. Americans might grumble about inflation, but taxes were something they would vote against.

By late 1968, as newly elected President Richard Nixon was preparing to enter the White House, inflation in the United States was approaching 6 percent a year. William McChesney Martin, who had served as chairman of the Federal Reserve Board for almost two decades, sought to resist the inflationary pressures by aggressively tightening credit in 1969. Nixon was not pleased with the resulting recession, which he felt reflected badly on his administration. Though he was forced to wait until Martin's term expired in 1970, Nixon eagerly replaced him with Arthur Burns on January 31, 1970. Two weeks later, at the next meeting of the Federal Open Market Committee, Burns argued that the weakness of the economy called for a substantial easing of credit.[13]

Conditions for higher prices were now firmly embedded in both the fiscal and monetary processes. Nixon had not started the inflation; Johnson could take responsibility for that. But Johnson could also pin some of the blame on Kennedy for initially getting the United States involved in Vietnam, for fostering grandiose social welfare programs, and for legitimizing Keynesian economics as official government policy. By the time Nixon made the proclamation "We're all Keynesians now" in 1971 it was becoming clear that a permanent departure from the original doctrine had set up conditions for a financial fiasco. The rationale for running a countercyclical budget to neutralize negative trends in the economy was fine in theory, but it was not politically workable. Like wages, government spending tends to be sticky downward. And when chronic budget deficits are financed through government borrowing, the inevitable result is domestic inflation.

THE ALMIGHTY DOLLAR

The United States had turned away from the fiscal orthodoxy of balanced budgets in favor of providing constant stimulus to the domestic economy in the form of government spending. The decision had been largely blessed by the academic community and eagerly embraced by politicians, who were only too happy to reap the rewards that came from having been released from traditional budgetary restraint. Voters could have it all, courtesy of their elected representatives in Washington: a strong defense, broad spending for social welfare, and low taxes.

Conservative financial doctrine had been replaced by the dangerously seductive appeal of deficit spending and a more "sophisticated" approach to monetary policy that downplayed the importance of the link between dollars and gold. The money supply was something that could be managed by officials to conform with domestic economic policy objectives.

But if Washington and academia were rejoicing in the United States' new fiscal freedom, the rest of the world was not. Inflation in the United States was becoming a serious problem; at 6 percent annually, the price level doubles in only a dozen years. And while it would seem bad enough to inflict such price distortions on the American public, the damage went much further. Not only Americans, but citizens in every other nation that had signed on to the Bretton Woods system were affected by an unwarranted increase in the supply of U.S. dollars. Because these other participating member nations were obliged by the Bretton Woods agreement to keep their currencies linked to the dollar at fixed exchange rates, they had little choice but to absorb the excess dollars as if nothing had changed since the days when U.S. officials were concerned about balancing the domestic budget.

But clearly something had changed. The United States had become addicted to deficit spending as the government sought to finance the Vietnam War abroad while increasing living standards at home. The federal budget deficit for 1971 was over $24 billion; the prior year it had been less than $12 billion.[14] From January to August of 1971, M1, the monetary aggregate that served as a primary measure of changes in the money supply, grew at an annual rate of 10.8 percent, more than twice the rate of increase during the preceding year.[15] Nixon was understandably anxious to get the economy moving after the downturn that started in 1969 and continued through 1970, and he believed that generous fiscal policy and lower interest rates would bring about a recovery. He was right; but U.S. expansionary monetary policies, aimed at producing an economic boom, were taken at the expense of its allies and the cause of international monetary stability.

A rupture between the role of the dollar within the U.S. economy and the role of the dollar as the anchor for the international monetary system under Bretton Woods had been developing for some time. Foreign observers, such as French economist Jacques Rueff, had long warned that U.S. preoccupation with domestic economic priorities would eventually compromise Washington's willingness to keep the value of the dollar stable. Rumors had begun circulating as early as the beginning of the 1960s that a dollar devaluation was imminent because U.S. gold holdings were shrinking relative to the amount of dollars accumulating in the hands of foreigners. If foreign central banks opted to exercise their right to trade dollars for gold at the rate of $35 per ounce of gold, U.S. reserves might be depleted altogether—something the U.S. government could hardly permit and still expect to retain its role at the center of the international monetary system. Even if American citizens had been weaned away from gold–dollar convertibility, participating Bretton Woods member countries still had the right to choose gold over dollars. Their motivation to do so posed a conundrum that was as much psychological as financial; as long as U.S. gold holdings covered U.S. dollar liabilities held abroad, foreigners were willing to hold dollars. But as the ratio was squeezed, the urge to exchange dollars for gold grew more pressing. The more gold reserves were drawn down, the faster the requests accelerated to convert dollars into gold.

The dilemma for foreign governments and their central banks was that they did not actually want to exchange the dollars for gold; to the extent that they were technically interchangeable in value they preferred to keep dollars as a convenient surrogate for gold. It was easier, obviously, to handle paper claims than to retrieve, transport, and store gold. One could not earn interest on gold bars—indeed, it cost money to store them and protect them—whereas dollars could be invested in U.S. Treasury obligations or deposited in banks where they would generate interest income. Foreign central banks, too, were reluctant to put too much pressure on the Bretton Woods arrangements that provided the underpinning for the continued stability of their own currencies.

No one wanted to be responsible for destroying the international monetary system.

Presumably there was a limit to what foreign governments could be expected to tolerate for the sake of preserving the illusion of the Bretton Woods agreement. It had become clear that the United States was more interested in accommodating its own fiscal follies with loose money than it was in upholding its responsibilities as the key currency issuer for the rest of the world. But foreign governments found their ability to complain was substantially muffled by the sheer dominance of the greenback in world trade; practically speaking, there was no alternative to the dollar. Although the British pound sterling, by virtue of its earlier role as monetary anchor, might have been seen to function as a secondary reserve currency, it was no substitute in reality. The U.S. dollar had successfully displaced it as the universal currency, the common denominator for international transactions.

So foreign central banks were inclined to abide by the Bretton Woods agreement and take the necessary actions to maintain the value of their own currencies relative to the dollar, even when the value of the dollar was obviously being diluted through the expansive monetary policies undertaken by the Federal Reserve. The foreign central banks had little recourse but to keep buying dollars with their own currencies, despite the fact that the excess supply of dollars in the world was diminishing their underlying value. As domestic inflation in the United States continued to rise, the prices of foreign goods became relatively more attractive and Americans started purchasing more imported products. These were paid for with cheaper U.S. dollars, which foreign recipients would then exchange for their own national money. As foreign central banks were deluged with requests to take in dollars and dole out local currency at the fixed exchange rate, they were forced to issue excess amounts of the national money. Essentially, foreign countries found themselves having to eat U.S. inflation by swallowing up the excess dollars that flowed overseas.

To further complicate matters, many of the dollars finding their way to Europe and other foreign destinations were not being exchanged for the local currency, but were being held abroad as dollars. These "Eurodollars" wreaked havoc with U.S. money supply calculations because they were not subject to the normal controls used by the Federal Reserve to restrict the growth of money. Banks in Europe and elsewhere had begun accepting deposits in the form of dollars and then making dollar-denominated loans to businesses and governments on the basis of those deposits. Dollars created outside the United States were not officially part of the domestic money supply, but they could easily be transferred to banks located within U.S. borders. To the extent such flows occurred, the U.S. money supply expanded, further inciting inflation and exacerbating the pressure on foreign central banks to keep their own currencies aligned with an increasingly overvalued dollar—overvalued in the sense that, given the rapidly growing supply of dollars in the world, each dollar was worth less in terms of other currencies than it had been earlier, and worth decidedly less in terms of the implicit value of gold.

But the United States government was still obligated to pay the designated price for gold as established under the terms of the Bretton Woods agreement. Because an ounce of gold had to be surrendered for every 35 dollars presented by a foreign central bank, and because 35 dollars had come to be worth less in terms of existing stockpiles of gold as more dollars were created—domestically through the expansive policies of the Federal Reserve and internationally through Eurodollar loans—a rift between the official price of gold and its market price was bound to develop.

As early as 1960, a sudden heightened demand for gold in private markets sent the price soaring to $40 an ounce in London and Zurich, even though the price was presumably limited to the dollar–gold convertibility rate, which was five dollars lower. To monetary experts, such a gap was inconceivable. As Volcker recounts:

> I remember very well sitting in my Chase Manhatten office when somebody came in and excitedly said, "The gold price is forty dollars." I said, "That can't be, you mean thirty-five dollars and forty cents." Even that would have been unprecedented, so we checked the news ticker. My visitor had it right, and even if the implications were not well understood, it created a sense of uncertainty and concern, which quickly reached Kennedy's political entourage.[16]

The intense speculative move on gold had been sparked, according to Robert Kuttner, by a casual response made by Kennedy to a reporter's question implying that the Democrats might consider devaluation of the dollar.[17] At that point Roosa was consulted and Kennedy quickly offered the public affirmation that he would defend the dollar's "present value and soundness." The damage to confidence, however, had already been incurred. Moreover, the price differential for gold suggested obvious arbitrage opportunities. Foreign central banks could potentially buy gold from the United States at the official price using their accumulated dollar reserves and then sell it for the higher private market price.

To ward off temptation and to maintain the viability of the Bretton Woods system, which served their own needs, the United States in conjunction with the European Common Market nations—Belgium, West Germany, Italy, France, the Netherlands, and Luxembourg—plus Britain and Switzerland agreed in early 1961 to carry out Roosa's proposal to pool their gold reserves to jointly combat increases in the private market price of gold. They formed a syndicate to sell gold to the public through the London market in whatever quantities were required to prevent its free market price from exceeding the official price of $35 an ounce. By countering market forces, the central banks succeeded in keeping the market price roughly equivalent to the official convertibility rate. At least, for a few years. But the upward pressure on the dollar price of gold would continue so long as the supply of dollars continued to grow at an unwarranted pace. Although the consortium of central banks was technically committed to buy or sell gold as necessary to keep the price stabilized, the overriding pressure was in the direction of having to sell gold.

By 1967 the concerted strategy for defeating the market was becoming untenable. What had happened to the United States in terms of the steady draining of its gold reserves was now happening to the entire syndicate of central banks acting together to stabilize the price of gold. The syndicate had to sacrifice nearly $2 billion worth of gold to the cause of preserving the value of the dollar in 1967 alone.[18] In March 1968, the volume of turnover in the London gold market rose precipitously from 30 tons a day in the first week of March, to 100 tons on March 8, to 225 tons on March 14.[19] The syndicate decided it was a lost cause and terminated the arrangement.

But just because its members found it too draining to reconcile the free market price of gold with the official dollar–gold convertibility ratio did not mean they were ready to give up on the Bretton Woods agreement. Instead, they opted to explicitly recognize the two distinct prices and take advantage of the fact that only foreign governments and their central banks, not private citizens, had the right to redeem dollars for gold at the cheaper rate. A two-tier system, under which central banks agreed to buy and sell gold strictly among themselves, leaving the free market price to be determined by the forces of supply and demand among private citizens, replaced the gold pool scheme.

The two-tier approach, however, only illustrated how far the United States had drifted from its mandate to maintain the soundness of the dollar for the sake of preserving international monetary stability. The adoption of a two-tier system represented the final attempt to put form over substance by insisting on a nominal convertibility rate that was no longer validated by underlying U.S. fiscal and monetary policies.

Abuse of Privilege

Arguments had been put forward at various points since the inception of Bretton Woods agreement to take the focus off the gold–dollar convertibility rate by moving toward a multilateral key currency system. Instead of relying on a monopoly issuer, the United States, to supply the world's key currency, why not have a group of the most powerful industrial nations together establish a supplemental reserve currency and exercise collective responsibility for international monetary stability? Professor Robert Triffin, a Belgian economist and Yale University professor, was one of the first to perceive that having the U.S. dollar serve as a global currency was incompatible with carrying out domestic monetary policies geared toward achieving the fiscal and economic objectives of the United States. In his 1960 book *Gold and the Dollar Crisis*, he had identified a fundamental contradiction in the Bretton Woods system. As the volume of global trade and investment increased, the world would require more dollars to finance its growth. The United States would thus have to run a balance of payments deficit to furnish the necessary liquidity. The greater the deficit, though, the more foreign confidence in the dollar would be undermined. To mitigate pressure on the dollar and the United States, Triffin urged that, in the spirit of the earlier concepts proposed by Keynes and White, a new genuinely international currency unit be created.

But the United States was not necessarily anxious to give up the advantages of being the keeper of the world's currency, even though it had ceased to be diligent about the accompanying responsibilities. As the sole key currency issuer, it enjoyed a position of economic and financial hegemony that seemed perfectly in keeping with its dominant role in exerting global political and military influence. U.S. money was valued throughout the world, and even if foreign governments and central banks weren't particularly happy with it, international investors continued to seek it and use it. Dollars were the language of international trade because the United States was the guardian of international peace.

France, though, was especially resentful of the preeminent role of the United States in the global monetary system and aggressively pushed for a multilateral approach. Charles de Gaulle was convinced that the United States held a privileged position that effectively exempted it from the rules of international exchange to which other countries were forced to submit. He felt the United States took advantage of its unique position and abused it by printing its own currency to cover external debts rather than having to pay for balance of payments deficits in foreign currencies or gold. Going back to a gold standard would be better, according to de Gaulle, than continuing to be victimized by U.S. monetary excesses.[20] Asked how to reform the current system so that it would be truly international and not bear the stamp of any one country in particular, de Gaulle made the statement at a press conference in February 1965:

Actually, it is difficult to envision in this regard any other criterion, any other standard than gold. Yes, gold, which does not change in nature, which can be made into either bars, ingots, or coins, which has no nationality, which is considered, in all places and all times, the immutable and fiduciary value par excellence. Furthermore, despite all that it was possible to imagine, say, write or do in the midst of major events, it is a fact that even today no currency has any value except by direct or indirect relation to gold, real or supposed. Doubtless, no one would think of dictating to any country how to manage its domestic affairs. But the supreme law, the golden rule . . . is the duty to balance, from one monetary area to another, by effective inflows and outflows of gold, the balance of payments resulting from their exchanges.[21]

While France may have been the most vociferous in its criticism, practically all the European nations were expressing some kind of disapproval toward the United States concerning abuse of its role as key currency issuer. Europe kept pressing for a multilateralization of the Bretton Woods system, ideally by designating a new international reserve unit, as suggested by Triffin, that would provide a new foundation for international monetary stability not contingent upon the behavior of a single dominant nation. The other option, of course, was to devalue the dollar in relationship to gold and thus explicitly acknowledge the depreciation that had taken place as the result of profligate U.S. fiscal and monetary actions.

The United States at first resisted both of these options. To challenge the exclusivity of the dollar by setting up a competitive key currency would not only entail a loss of face, it would also mean losing the advantages associated with controlling the world's financial liquidity. U.S. officials had reservations about empowering the International Monetary Fund to issue its own reserve currency, a proposal under discussion in the mid-1960s, because they saw such a move as potentially displacing the dollar's central role in international trade. Nor did they want to change the original convertibility rate for foreign central banks of 35 dollars for one ounce of gold. To raise the number of dollars required to purchase an ounce of gold would not only be an admission of having diluted the value of the dollar, it would also be inflationary. Even if U.S.

practices had indeed been inflationary, the United States did not want to tamper with the illusion of monetary discipline inherent in the status quo link to gold.

West Germany, unlike France and its other European neighbors, more or less acquiesced to the monetary preferences of the United States and accepted U.S. military protection with the resigned understanding that having to absorb a certain amount of U.S. inflation was part of the price. Succumbing to pressure from the U.S. Treasury, West Germany agreed in March 1967 to forgo its right to exchange dollars for gold; as far as the Bundesbank was concerned, the dollar was inconvertible. The West German government was well aware that the United States was reneging on its commitment to perform its duties as the world's monetary anchor, but it did not want to press the issue. With U.S. troops actively protecting German citizens, and with U.S. taxpayers footing a large part of the defense bill, West Germany's government could hardly complain.[22]

But West Germany was unique in its passivity toward the dollar and in its initial acceptance of U.S. monetary policies. For the most part, Europe had begun to feel like a dumping ground for the residual effects of U.S. inflation. European leaders resented the situation, but felt helpless to do anything about it. They could appeal to U.S. Treasury officials, they could complain about the accumulated dollars in their central banks, they could chastise the United States for drifting away from its mandate to preserve the stability of the international monetary system. But they could not abandon the dollar. Their own currencies were tied solidly to the dollar through the fixed exchange rate system, and there was no alternative key currency. As Jelle Zijlstra, a Dutch banker who would later become the head of the Bank for International Settlements, expressed it: "When we left the pound, we could go to the dollar. But where could we go from the dollar? To the moon?"[23]

Citing the need for prudent "contingency planning" in case the Bretton Woods system became seriously threatened, a feeble attempt to institute an international monetary unit was launched with an agreement at the 1967 annual IMF meeting to begin creating Special Drawing Rights. These SDRs were effectively bookkeeping entries representing deposit accounts at the IMF; they were originally defined in terms of gold (by mid-1974 they would be valued as a basket of major currencies), they functioned as money for settling balances between individual central banks, and they permitted countries with reserve shortages to meet payment obligations to other countries. They were not put into use until 1970, following a period of heavy debate among IMF members, who had qualms about introducing this new "paper gold." In theory, the idea made sense. At least, the new reserve currency would not be dependent on the integrity of a single issuer but rather subject to cooperative control—if one accepts the notion that the IMF represents an international consensus of views. But it soon became obvious that SDRs could pose no serious challenge to the dollar. They were an artificial creation, a financial figment of the IMF's mind, and never came into contact with private individuals carrying out their daily economic activities. Central banks used them, but international traders continued to rely on the dollar.

Nixon's Choice

U.S. postwar economic policies, at home and abroad, had reached full fruition by the time Nixon assumed the presidency in 1969. The United States' former enemies, Germany and Japan, were thriving economic powers in their own right and had been fully restored to the community of friendly nations. The array of domestic programs that had been adopted in the United States demonstrated a social conscience of impressive scale for a capitalist country. It was very gratifying in many ways, a vindication of American resolve and a testimony to American compassion.

Problems with the dollar and complaints from foreign central banks might have been relegated to the arcane world of international economic and monetary specialists for a few more years had they not been stimulated by Nixon's preference for lower interest rates and looser money early in his administration. Or had they not involved something as fundamental and emotionally charged as gold. The expansionary monetary policies put into effect by Burns immediately after becoming Federal Reserve chairman in 1970 soon had repercussions in foreign markets. Cheaper dollars flew across the Atlantic to buy European goods. At the same time, interest rates in Europe were higher than in the United States, causing short-term capital to flow into foreign bank accounts. Strong demand to change dollars into European currencies such as deutsche marks and Swiss francs put additional pressure on exchange rates. European central banks were forced to buy the dollars being thrust at them in order to keep their own currencies from appreciating above the limits imposed by the fixed rate Bretton Woods system.

At the end of January 1971, foreign central bank holdings of U.S. dollars had reached a historic high of $20 billion. Fear that the U.S. Treasury would not be able to cover its obligations in gold, should it be asked to, caused a sudden acceleration in the rush to convert dollars into other currencies. A near-panic mentality to dump the dollar took hold throughout the world, and foreign central banks were the receptacles. During a period of just four months, until the end of May 1971, another $12 billion in U.S. dollars was taken in by foreign central banks. Official claims against the gold reserves of the United States now stood at $32 billion.[24] Yet the gold reserves were not nearly equal to that amount; they could only cover about one third of the foreign central bank claims.

The situation had clearly reached the crisis point. What could Nixon do? If he had chosen to take sweeping measures earlier to reform the role of the dollar in the international monetary system or to reconcile domestic economic policy with the responsibilities of a key currency country, the run on U.S. gold reserves perhaps could have been staved off. The United States had earlier accepted the burden of being the provider of the world's reserve currency, the so-called "nth country" at the heart of an international gold exchange standard. Indeed, it had long resisted attempts to divvy up those duties or to designate a rival key currency, instead preferring to consume the perquisites of hegemonic influence over global trade.

Now the United States was being asked to prove that its currency was truly as good as gold. Such demands, coming from allies who had benefited from U.S. economic largesse in the postwar era, were viewed not only as a threat—they were an insult.

John Connally, whom Nixon had selected as his Treasury secretary in December 1970, did not like to see the United States being intimidated by lesser nations. "Foreigners are out to screw us," he reportedly said. "Our job is to screw them first."[25] Connally believed that the United States was not the cause of international monetary problems, but was rather the victim. Other nations were guilty of protectionism and unfair trade practices. They took advantage of the United States' traditional commitment to free trade. Connally felt little obligation to alter fiscal and monetary policies that were in his country's best interests just to appease these foreign ingrates.

In August 1971, America's gold stock dropped below $10 billion, a key psychological level.[26] Foreign governments knew that to insist on redemption of their accumulated dollar balances in gold would be to finally force the collapse of the Bretton Woods system. But they also felt the U.S. government should face up to its global responsibilities and take steps to resolve the international monetary crisis and initiate meaningful reform. They wanted to put the United States on notice by at least suggesting that they might turn in their dollars for gold.

Nixon and Connally, along with Burns, Herbert Stein (who would become chairman of Nixon's Council of Economic Advisers), and Paul Volcker (who was Treasury Under-Secretary for Monetary Affairs at the time) assembled at Camp David to confront the impending problem of foreign gold redemption and to devise a strategy for heading off an embarrassing financial catastrophe. On the Sunday evening of August 15, 1971, that strategy was announced: the United States would no longer permit foreign governments or central banks to redeem U.S. dollars in gold.

Shocking as that decision may have been to the rest of the world, it did not receive primary attention in the United States. Besides closing the gold window, Nixon announced that the government was going to impose wage and price controls to fight inflation. In addition, a 10 percent surcharge would be assessed on imports. Dubbed the New Economic Policy, the program's ostensible purpose was to brake inflationary trends by freezing incomes and prices and by stemming the inflow of cheap foreign goods. There was, however, very little new about it. Mostly the program represented a combination of tired strategies for alleviating the symptoms of inflation rather than confronting the underlying reasons for economic distress.

The inflation could be traced to the classic formula of excessive government spending and accommodative monetary policy. Imports had become relatively cheap because the diluted dollar distorted the comparative prices of competing foreign goods against American-produced goods. Not only did the new domestic program fail to address the United States' fundamental fiscal and monetary problems, it absolved the U.S. government from responsibility for manipulating the spending power of its citizens and for abusing its position of international leadership in the Bretton Woods system.

The architects of Nixon's plan saw things differently, though. Reminiscing ten years after the Camp David decision to suspend gold payments, Stein asserted that the American public was not indignant, nor was the rest of the world stunned:

> In fact, the gold window was already closed before Mr. Nixon declared it closed in 1971. That is, the major central banks of the world knew with a high probability that if they asked us for gold they would not get it, simply because we didn't have enough. When the British came in that August and asked for $3 billion of gold they were only checking whether that generally held belief was correct. The question at Camp David was whether to acknowledge the existing state of affairs or to try to postpone that acknowledgment in the hope that the condition would change.
>
> Even though acknowledging that the window was closed does not, in this perspective, seem such a historic step, the people at Camp David that weekend did consider that they were cutting the dollar's last link to gold, with the possibly serious effects economically and politically. The issue did not appear in the conventional terms of sticking to the gold standard and fighting inflation versus abandoning the gold standard and tolerating inflation.
>
> Insofar as there was a connection, closing the gold window did not permit less anti-inflationary action but required more anti-inflationary action. There were people, at home and abroad, who regarded our link to gold as an anchor against runaway inflation in the United States. If we were to cut loose from that anchor we would have to offer them some assurance, which was one reason for packaging the closing of the gold window with the price-wage freeze.

For some of the participants in the August 1971 meeting the choice was not gold versus inflation but was gold versus free markets. One must remember that in the summer of 1971 the country was going through one of its spasms of hysteria about the balance of payments, the balance of trade, and, particularly, competition from Japan Inc. This anxiety was stimulating demands for quotas or higher tariffs on imports and for retaining the controls on capital flows that President Nixon had promised to remove. Cutting loose from gold was a way of defusing these demands for restraints on trade and capital movements by increasing the possibility for achieving international adjustment through changes in the dollar exchange rate.

When President Nixon decided to declare that the gold window was closed he knew that there might be serious political repercussions. But these repercussions did not appear. For a great many people closing the gold window was welcomed as a declaration of national economic independence. A much larger number didn't care. There was no more sign of a deep-seated loyalty to gold in 1971 than there had been on any of the other occasions when the government took steps to dilute the role of gold.

This says nothing about whether the action on gold in 1971 was correct. I believe it was wise, but that is another story. The experience of 1971 does suggest that it is unrealistic to think that the gold standard will present governments with an unequivocal choice between inflation and adherence to gold which governments will be forced to make in favor of gold because the public has a strong emotional attachment to it.[27]

According to Stein, Nixon was more concerned about the public's strong attachment to their favorite television entertainment; Nixon was reluctant to announce his New Economic Policy on Sunday night after he and his advisers emerged from Camp David because he did not want to annoy millions of citizens by preempting the show "Bonanza."[28]

Whether the Bretton Woods system had effectively already been in disarray, whether the link between the dollar and gold had been severed for all intents and purposes, the announcement by Nixon on August 15, 1971, was the official death knell for the international monetary order that had arisen at the close of World War II and that had governed international trade and payments during the intervening years. The system had been cut loose—cut free, many would insist—and other nations no longer had the dollar to kick around anymore.

On the day immediately following Nixon's announcement, Connally reportedly turned to his advisers with the open question: "What do we do next?"[29] And if there was any lingering sense of U.S. stewardship for international monetary stability subsequent to Nixon's decision to end Bretton Woods, Volcker suggests, it was dispelled by Connally's cavalier attitude toward U.S. allies. "The dollar may be our currency," Connally said, "but it's your problem."[30]

INTO THE VOID

For the next nineteen months, until March 1973, there were several piecemeal attempts to patch together some kind of fixed rate system out of the remnants of Bretton Woods. The first serious effort occurred in December 1971, just a few months after the Camp David decision, when the major currency countries decided to reinstate a fixed rate system. This system would represent the changed status of the dollar and would be based on much more flexible arrangements. Called the Smithsonian Agreement, this new system permitted currencies to fluctuate up to 2.25 percent on either side of the established fixed rate before central banks were required to start intervening to bring them back to par—that is, to their "central rates." (The Bretton Woods system had allowed just a 1 percent deviation before action was required.) In addition, under the new system, the dollar was devalued by about 8 percent; now it took 38 dollars to buy an ounce of gold. However, the United States let it be known that it would not be willing to defend the new rate with either its gold or foreign currency reserves, so the whole arrangement was rendered somewhat moot. Allies were welcome to fix their currencies to the dollar, but the dollar would not have its former credibility.

Nevertheless, the Smithsonian Agreement was announced with great fanfare by Nixon, who hailed it as "the most significant monetary agreement in the history of the world."[31] Other nations saw it less as an agreement than a unilateral action by the United States that showed little concern for the economic welfare of allied industrial nations. For Japan, the decision to cut the dollar loose from gold had already come to be known as the "Nixon Shock" and had caused economic turmoil and a sharp fall in the stock market index; the Smithsonian Agreement did little to calm Japanese anxieties about monetary relations with its major trade partners.[32]

In any case, the agreement didn't last much longer than a year. Britain's Conservative Prime Minister, Edward Heath, decided to float the pound in June 1972 in the face of speculative pressure. Then there was a run on dollars in January 1973 when the Italian lira was devalued. Italians quickly dumped liras for dollars and then turned around and exchanged dollars for Swiss francs. After a few intense days, Switzerland's central bank refused to continue intervening to try to stabilize the exchange rate with the dollar and instead allowed the Swiss franc to float. Soon dollars were being abandoned all over Europe as investors rushed to exchange them for deutsche marks or yen, which were still fixed relative to the dollar. Asserting that the dollar was obviously not being priced realistically in international currency markets, the United States imposed another devaluation on February 12, 1973, this time reducing its value by 11 percent. Now an ounce of gold was officially worth $42.22.

Within weeks, even that price did not hold. The private market price of gold was approaching $90—more than twice the official price. On March 12, 1973, as pressure to dump dollars in anticipation of yet another devaluation caused continued instability in currency markets, all links between the dollar and gold were officially abandoned in the Brussels Agreement. The value of the dollar would be determined by the actions of traders and would fluctuate with the ebb and tide of supply and demand. The era of fixed rates was over. Now currencies would float.

Even though it had long since been clear that the solid value of the dollar, based on its link to gold, could not be maintained in the face of chronic budget deficits and inflationary monetary policies, and even though many economists, starting with Triffin, had long predicted the rupture of Bretton Woods, its final demise still produced a sense of disorientation among government finance officials and central bankers. Volcker, who had provided much of the technical analysis and intellectual rationale at Camp David for closing the gold window, still clung to the idea that the former system could be resurrected, albeit in a significantly revised form. "We had to have a breathing space," he explained, "but I looked hopefully for a reconstruction of the orderly system."[33] It did not happen. What was initially looked upon as a temporary period of adjustment, an opportunity to fix what had gone wrong with Bretton Woods, increasingly came to represent the permanent state of affairs as floating currencies became the norm.

The days of an orderly global currency system were gone. For most academic economists serving on university faculties, it was none too soon. Stanford's Professor Ronald McKinnon notes that despite the unusually rapid growth and unparalleled price stability experienced by the industrial world under the old system of fixed exchange rates, when the system came under pressure at the beginning of the 1970s, "there was virtually no organized intellectual defense of the existing monetary order!"[34] Over the prior decade, the idea of adjustable rates as opposed to fixed rates had attained much more scholarly respectability as the basis for international currency relations. Leading monetary experts such as Robert Solomon, who headed the international division of the Federal Reserve, began to join the chorus of academics and practitioners in openly questioning the virtues of fixed exchange rates. Flexibility was coming to be seen as the key desirable trait for a global currency system; the prevailing opinion among scholars, along with international bankers and businessmen—and, increasingly, politicians—was that smaller, more frequent changes in exchange rates would be less disruptive overall than larger, infrequent changes. And if smaller, frequent changes made for better international monetary relations, why not go all the way and have continuously adjusted rates—that is, a floating rate system? In theory, such a system made perfect sense. It was the free market approach to international exchange rates. Currencies would compete against each other in the world market.

When Milton Friedman first suggested the notion in the early 1950s that permitting flexible rates might provide a viable way to deal with the changing values of national currencies, his voice was almost alone among economists. By his own assessment, probably not more than five percent of the specialists on monetary and international trade issues would have supported the idea of substantially greater exchange rate flexibility at the time.[35] As IMF historian Margaret Garritsen de Vries notes, fund officials, along with most central bankers, felt strongly that fixed exchange rates provided the necessary firm foundation for international trade and capital movements, while fluctuating rates engendered great uncertainties and, hence, increased costs. The other benefit of fixed rates was that they forced the world's most powerful industrialized nations to integrate their economic policies and cooperate with each other to fight inflation.[36]

Indeed, among more traditional government finance officials, there was almost a deep-seated moral indignation against the idea of floating rates. As Paul H. Douglas, both an economist and a senator who was drawn to the case for flexibility, described it:

> For years I have urged the Federal Reserve, the Treasury, and our representatives on the IMF to consider the flexible exchange rates, and I have been deeply disappointed by their refusal even to consider or study the matter. It has been an automatic reaction and, to tell the truth, I have not been able to generate any real argument. It has been a sort of tropismatic response, even below the level of instinct.[37]

But some two decades after Friedman first wrote about the advantages of flexible exchange rates, the general consensus largely had come around to his way of thinking. By Volcker's reckoning, "a half or even two-thirds of the academic community were in favor [of floating] and so were some people on Capitol Hill and in the Administration."[38] Friedman had provided theoretical backing for an alternative that began to look increasingly attractive as the old system fell apart. Instead of sacrificing domestic monetary stability for the sake of redressing international imbalances, Friedman argued that the Federal Reserve should concentrate on supplying the right amount of money at home and let the currency markets decide what the dollar was worth abroad. To illustrate his approach, Friedman invoked the analogy of a circus clown who, instead of bringing his stool over to the piano, would practically break his back pushing the piano over to the stool. Why should governments distort their own domestic economies to solve balance-of-payments problems?[39]

If exchange rates absorbed all the impact of trade imbalances between nations, domestic policy could proceed unperturbed. The idea was that U.S. currency would grow relatively more expensive (if it appreciated) or less expensive (if it depreciated) for other countries and U.S. exports and imports would be affected accordingly. That is, the fluctuating dollar would automatically bring exports and imports into balance by making their prices more or less attractive to their intended buyers. The ideological appeal of an invisible hand governing the exchange rates between currencies seemed far preferable to the awkward responses of central banks to every currency crisis.

Recycling Money

But the big impact of floating rates turned out to be not so much on traded goods, but rather on international capital flows. Financial flows increasingly came to dwarf the level of internationally traded goods. Moreover, there was an important timing factor: capital could be moved quickly via electronic transfer as opposed to trade in goods, which usually took place over a period of weeks or months. Over and above the huge amounts of money being shifted daily to take advantage of short-term interest rates around the world, too, were the speculative capital placements seeking to take advantage of pure currency arbitrage opportunities. In short, the financial effects of capital moving around the world would have vastly more impact on currency exchange rates than traditional economic variables involving relative labor costs or other comparative advantage. The looked-for balance between imports and exports would be lost in the currency shuffle.

One of the first global tests of the new floating rate regime took place in October 1973 when the oil-producing nations banded together to drastically increase the world price of oil. Egypt and Syria had invaded Israel; to punish the United States for supporting Israel, Arab petroleum producers decided to use the "oil weapon."[40] The Organization of Petroleum Exporting Countries

(OPEC) succeeded in forming a cartel that dictated the levels of production its members could engage in, thus limiting the world supply of oil and putting its producers in a position to set their own price. The price of oil was doubled in October 1973 and doubled again two months later.[41]

Although the OPEC move was sparked by political tensions, there were underlying economic and financial reasons for the Arabs' move as well. Oil was priced in dollars. With the dollar floating, the only real value behind U.S. currency was the inherent integrity of Washington's monetary policy. It was becoming obvious that too many dollars were being printed to paper over domestic fiscal indulgences. Thus the petroleum producers had every incentive to fight back by demanding more dollars in exchange for their nonrenewable commodity. They would demand many more dollars, as it turned out. The world, and particularly the United States, was very dependent on Middle Eastern oil and would pay practically whatever it was forced to pay. The OPEC countries received an extra $80 billion over the year because of the price hikes on exported oil.[42]

Now it remained to be seen whether the new floating rate regime that had arisen in the void left by the dissolution of the Bretton Woods fixed rate system would be able to handle the huge sums of money accumulating in Arab hands. Using up the money by paying for imports was out of the question; there was far more money than could be spent, even after paying for all the luxuries desired by members of the royal families and other well-to-do Arabs who had a connection to the oil bonanza. Improvements in national infrastructure were initiated; but again, the payments from oil were building up far too quickly to be spent, even on grandiose projects. The Arabs knew, too, that the money might not flow forever and that it was important to save the windfall earnings that were being accumulated at the moment.

Wealthy personages in the Middle East had long been dependent on their savvy Western investment advisers to safeguard their financial interests by investing the money prudently. The Koran specifically forbids collecting interest on loaned money, so it was necessary to couch the financial transactions in terms of receiving service charges or commissions for making money available. However the interest was calculated, though, it was made payable to the source of the funds, the Arabs. And the bulk of it went into Western banks, primarily in London, New York, and Zurich.

Bankers are normally gleeful at receiving deposited funds, because it enables them to expand lending, collect interest on loans, and raise the amount that accrues to them in profits as determined by the net spread—that is, the difference between the cost of the deposits and the return on the loans. But the formula depends on being able to channel the deposited funds into good loans. During the mid-1970s, a time when Arab money was pouring in, most of the industrial countries were experiencing a recession, one caused largely by the fact that sky-high oil prices had put a damper on their economic productivity. Demand for loans was depressed in the United States and Western Europe. Developing countries in Latin America, meanwhile, were desperate for imports, even though they lacked funds to pay for them. As a matter of survival, they were willing to go into debt. But where could they borrow the money? Not directly from the OPEC nations, which were not willing to make such risky loans. But the international bankers who were playing the role of middlemen—and collecting fees in the process—soon turned their attention to Latin America and other third world regions.

As Darrell Delamaide explains in *Debt Shock*, big international banks found themselves recycling the oil dollars around the world. A tremendous imbalance had been created in the wake of the decision to quadruple the oil price. OPEC nations were building up huge balance-of-payments surpluses while their customers were incurring equally massive balance-of-payments deficits. International banks directed the monetary traffic by tallying up assets for the OPEC countries in the form of deposits on their books and recording liabilities on the part of importing countries in the form of debts. Industrialized countries sought to ameliorate their economic straits by exporting goods to developing countries, and thanks to the zealous lending practices of Western banks, these poorer nations found adequate financing. The developed countries thus shifted a large part of their deficits to the developing countries.[43]

The dollars on both sides of the transaction were worth decidedly less than they had been a few years before when rates were fixed, but their intrinsic value did not seem so important. The absolute levels in nominal terms were still astounding. As Delamaide relates:

> In the period 1974–79 alone . . . the OPEC countries ran a balance-of-payments surplus of about $220 billion. The twenty industrialized countries grouped together in the OECD registered a deficit of $100 billion, keeping to round numbers. The non-oil-producing developing countries, called NOPECs by some, ran a deficit of $150 billion in the six-year period.[44]

To put such vast sums into perspective, *The Economist* offered helpful calculations suggesting that the two richest oil-producing nations, Saudi Arabia and Kuwait, would be able to buy up IBM in seven months, Exxon in four months, and the Bank of America in sixteen days.[45]

Gyrating Dollar

What was the impact of a floating dollar during all this period of monetary redistribution around the world? Floating rates had set the dollar free, but free to do what? To lose its integrity, to decline in value? To the extent that the oil shock was a reflection of outrage among petroleum-producing countries at the drop in the dollar's purchasing power since the late 1960s, the United States was beginning to pay the price for past profligacy. With so many dollars having been exported to Europe, however, and with so many existing in the form of Eurodollars on foreign soil, it was impossible to control their numbers even if the Federal Reserve had the resolve to do so. The dollar was no longer the world's key currency officially, but it still reigned as the most dominant and accepted currency. People attributed qualities to it that it no longer possessed, perhaps out of habit or sentiment. Or merely wishful thinking.

In any case, the world continued to use the dollar. Because the dollar's value had been significantly diluted by U.S. monetary policy, the major industrial countries found themselves suffering unprecedented levels of inflation from 1973 through the end of the decade. In the mid-1970s, the deepest worldwide recession since the 1930s took place, and with it came a new phenomenon called "stagflation," in which rising prices coexisted with high unemployment in industrial countries.[46] The price of gold soared—it touched $450 an ounce in September 1979—and the new floating rate approach, which was supposed to use flexibility to deliver stability among the major currency exchange rates, instead brought about fluctuations that far surpassed those that had occurred under the Bretton Woods system.

Indeed, the objectives of the old system were all but abandoned under floating rates. The U.S. perspective on international economic and monetary cooperation collapsed into the every-country-for-itself attitude that Harry Dexter White had been so determined to avoid in the era following World War II. Floating rates did, indeed, free the United States from its obligation to provide a stable anchor for the international monetary system, but there was nothing magic about removing fiscal and monetary discipline. The more dollars issued, the less each one was worth unless its issuance was matched by a corresponding increase in economic productivity that justified the creation of new dollars. Unfortunately, sufficient productivity gains were not realized. Yet, irrationally, the world continued to look toward the dollar to serve as the lodestar of monetary value. To the extent that Western Europe and Japan remained financially dependent on the dollar, they were confronted with the same stagflation problems that were besetting the U.S. economy.

In 1975, in the midst of global recession, cries to restore some kind of formal international monetary system reached the point where the governments of the most powerful industrial nations felt compelled to reevaluate the situation. There were mixed opinions about how floating rates had performed during the interval after the dollar–gold link had been dismantled. U.S. monetary authorities stressed that floating rates had been useful; they pointed out that any system of fixed exchange rates would probably have fallen apart in response to the stresses caused by the oil price hike in 1973.[47] They pointed to the historically high inflation rates, as well as the global recession, as economic circumstances that would have ruined a fixed rate system, not as the consequences of a floating rate system. From the U.S. government point of view, floating rates had gotten them off the hook for a slew of calamitous economic and monetary developments.

Monetary authorities from most of the European Community nations, particularly France, would have none of that argument. As Garritsen explains, they held "diametrically opposite views":

> They argued that floating rates themselves might be a source of the inflation that was already a worrisome problem and might quicken the transmission of inflation from one country to another. They argued also that floating exchange rates were not bringing about as much adjustment in countries' balances of payments as might have been expected and, indeed, might not be doing much beyond compensating for the differences in their rates of inflation. Most important, in their view, fixed exchange rates ought to be an immediate major objective for all countries. Since countries had to defend fixed rates by adhering to strict monetary and fiscal policies, it was only with fixed rates that inflation could be controlled. And stable prices were essential for a stable international monetary system.[48]

In November 1975, the heads of state of the major industrial nations met at Rambouillet Castle in France to discuss the prospects for international monetary reform. It was the first of what would become ritual annual economic summits, high-visibility meetings among Western world leaders aimed at coordinating policies to foster international monetary stability and free trade. President Gerald Ford could not match the experience and background of three of his counterparts—Helmut Schmidt of West Germany, Valéry Giscard d'Estaing of France, and James Callaghan of Britain—who had all served as their countries' finance ministers.[49] Nevertheless, the proponents of floating rates at the Rambouillet summit, mostly Americans, squared off against the proponents of fixed rates, mostly French. The U.S. delegation conveyed the United States' sense of having been snake-bit by the Bretton Woods experience and the pressures of being the key currency country. Since the world had somehow muddled through with floating rates, why not continue to allow this approach to evolve as the basis for global monetary relations?

What emerged from the Rambouillet meeting was an uneasy consensus that floating rates were useful in some ways, but that guidelines were needed to prevent international chaos among currencies. Rather than specify exact rules or reinstitute fixed rates, perhaps the major industrial nations could informally assess their mutual economic problems and begin to work together to resolve them. No structured framework, no definitive obligations would be imposed. An expression of goodwill and a vague commitment to seek international cooperation were all the requirements deemed necessary. In short, the new approach toward floating exchange rates with its emphasis on the need for close collaboration to achieve "orderly underlying economic and financial conditions" was hardly a solution to the world's monetary problem. As Volcker observed, it "did not offer any real guidance as to how the requisite cooperation would be achieved."[50]

The gyrating dollar had meanwhile turned foreign trade into a game of currency speculation. There were brief periods during the mid-1970s when the Federal Reserve ostensibly was prepared to take actions to reassert control once more over the dollar and to impose some kind of discipline on the issuance of U.S. money. Ford's "Whip Inflation Now" (WIN) strategy provided the appropriate rhetoric, if not any actual solution. (Louis Rukeyser quips that the Ford administration's war against inflation was fought entirely with WIN buttons.[51]) But such feeble efforts were swamped by the sins of the past. Too many dollars had made their way overseas, too many Eurodollar accounts had been established. To make matters worse, the U.S. budget deficit in 1975 was $75.4 billion, a figure that exceeded the cumulative total deficits under Nixon for the prior five years.[52] The dollar was a runaway currency, and the overriding trend toward the end of the decade was in the direction of an increasingly lower value. The U.S. government was aware of the state of its currency but acted helpless to prevent it, and was perhaps even relieved that floating rates had somehow absolved it of responsibility for monetary stability.

What floating rates had done, though, was clarify the cause-and-effect relationship between government fiscal decisions and the integrity of government-supplied money. With gold convertibility no longer a protective device to shield money from the consequences of political actions, fiscal initiatives became a determining factor in currency exchange markets. Moving to floating rates did not relieve U.S. legislators of their responsibility to make prudent spending decisions, nor did it insulate the domestic economy from the monetary consequences of financing budget deficits; it only allowed users of currency to appraise the value of national monies and decide how much it was worth to them to utilize a particular currency. To the degree that the dollar was still popular as a medium of exchange for international transactions, the discount for decreasing quality was not as heavy as it would have been otherwise. But the dollar was also a hot potato that people at times wanted to pass on quickly to avoid getting burned.

Despite its own penchant for easy money, the U.S. government under President Jimmy Carter took the attitude that the United States was bearing more than its share of the costs of recovery from the collapse of fixed exchange rates and the oil shock. At the London economic summit in 1977, Carter pressed Germany's Chancellor Schmidt and Japan's Prime Minister Takeo Fukuda to assist the United States by running budget deficits in their own countries and by raising the value of their currencies to take pressure off the dollar.[53] "As a triple locomotive," Robert Kuttner explains, "the world's three most powerful economies together would pull the world out of recession."[54]

But compounding the fiscal and monetary errors of the United States only seemed to exacerbate the decline of the dollar, which hit an all-time low against the yen and the deutsche mark in 1978. Concerted intervention efforts by central banks did little to prevent the free fall; by the end of October, the dollar had lost nearly a quarter of its value from the beginning of the year.[55] Moreover, the United States' trade partners now had to pay the price for excessive public spending and expansionary monetary policies. In Germany's case, that meant higher inflation. Schmidt later complained that the locomotive strategy was a mistake, that Germany had succumbed to international pressures against its own better economic instincts and in violation of its dedication to sound money.[56] Japan's view of the strategy, as recounted by Toyoo Gyohten, was hardly more complimentary:

One way we know that policies have become discredited is that they become easy targets of jokes. In financial circles at that time, there was a joke about three locomotives. One locomotive simply didn't run; that was Germany. The second locomotive ran, but it ran in the wrong direction; that was Japan, which grew by increasing its exports instead of its domestic demand. The third locomotive also ran, but it polluted the air; that was the American locomotive, burning too much oil and leaving a trail of dollars behind.[57]

Certainly the part about burning too much oil was true. The United States was extremely vulnerable to the inflationary impact of the second oil shock in 1979, when the price per barrel of crude Arabian light was raised to $18, some 40 percent higher than the 1978 price. And the trail of dollars could be traced to the accommodative monetary policies of the Federal Reserve under G. William Miller, who in turn could claim that he had inherited the inflationary consequences of mistakes made by Burns that caused excessive money growth in late 1976 and 1977.[58]

In any case, the consumer inflation rate in the United States topped 13 percent in 1979, the highest rate since the 1940s. Money markets around the world were panicking, and U.S. allies were confused and resentful. Paul Volcker was pressed into service in July as chairman of the Federal Reserve and was quickly exposed to the wrath of the international financial community. At a fall 1979 conference in Belgrade, as Kuttner relates:

Volcker faced dire warnings from his fellow central bankers and from commercial bankers that the global financial system was on the verge of collapse. There was mounting anger that the United States under Carter and Miller no longer understood its international obligations or took them seriously.[59]

But what were the international obligations of the United States on monetary policy? Did it have any? More important, what were the obligations of the U.S. government domestically on monetary policy? Did American citizens have any right to expect that their money would hold its value from year to year? Volcker sensed the severity of the crisis of the dollar, both at home and abroad, and quickly took actions to fight inflation—at any cost. On October 6 he revealed a startling change in the Federal Reserve's approach to monetary policy: From now on it would act in accordance with the monetarist dictum that you can control the money supply or you can control interest rates, but you cannot control both. The Federal Reserve would concentrate on controlling the money supply; interest rates would go wherever the financial markets carried them.

Where they carried the rates was up. Way up. The commercial bank prime lending rate reached the shocking level of 15.25 percent in early February 1980; the monthly inflation rate was nearly as high at 14.9 percent.[60] The price of gold in the meantime had skyrocketed to $850 an ounce since the October 6 announcement.[61] The psychological game of monetary chicken had begun, and it was now a matter of seeing how close Federal Reserve officials would be willing to brush with financial disaster before providing interest rate relief. The gross national product contracted by nearly 10 percent in the second quarter,[62] and the bank prime lending rate hit a record 21.5 percent by Christmas 1980[63] as the Federal Reserve doggedly stuck to its policy of focusing on the money supply, grappling to control money growth while interest rates and inflation figures seesawed. Though the resulting economic price was wrenching in terms of lost sales, lost production, and lost jobs, the tight money policies pursued by Volcker eventually wrung inflation out of the U.S. domestic economy. The U.S. consumer inflation rate retreated to 8.85 percent in 1981 and dropped to 3.89 percent in 1982.[64]

As early as midsummer 1980, though, the severe actions undertaken by the Fed were having an effect on the dollar's value in international money markets. The dollar finally began to stabilize against foreign currencies and then started slowly to ascend as world demand for dollar-denominated financial instruments steadily rose. Investors were impressed by the resolve being demonstrated by the Federal Reserve governors to rein in domestic inflation. But they were even more impressed with the high yields that could be obtained by purchasing U.S. Treasury securities or private capital offerings. Dollar-denominated assets had the special appeal of offering dual financial returns; not only were U.S. nominal interest rates high, there was also the potential for exchange rate appreciation as global capital poured into the strengthening dollar.[65]

Who could have guessed that, so soon after U.S. allies were accusing Washington of grossly neglecting its international responsibilities by permitting the dollar to sink to such lows in currency markets, the dollar would rise to such highs that global trade and capital flows would be severely distorted? And its allies again accused the U.S. government of grossly neglecting its international responsibilities. This time the complaint was that the jackknifing dollar made it difficult to have reliable trade relations with the United States and virtually impossible to engage in meaningful business planning. France took the position that the problem wasn't trade per se: "The real problem is the erratic variation of the currencies."[66]

No one could argue that the dollar had provided any kind of meaningful standard of value for comparing goods and services across global markets. In late February 1985, the dollar was worth 263 yen and 3.44 deutsche marks. According to IMF calculations, that meant the dollar had appreciated 67 percent over the average level in 1980.[67] No wonder foreign governments complained about the lack of U.S. leadership in the international monetary sphere; the dollar was a roller-coaster currency whose value was up for grabs as investors and speculators chased high interest returns and exchange rate profits. Moreover, the combination of large budget deficits and tight monetary policy carried out under President Ronald Reagan caused foreign investment funds to flow into the United States to such an extent that much of the rest of the world was starved for capital. The United States quickly became the world's largest debtor nation, relying on the kindness of strangers to fund its borrowing requirements as government spending continued to outpace the growth in revenues.

During the early Reagan years, the operating philosophy toward the dollar in international currency markets was that its value should be determined by private supply and demand; central bank intervention to influence exchange rates was frowned upon by Treasury Secretary Donald Regan and Under-Secretary for Monetary Affairs Beryl Sprinkel. But when the U.S. trade deficit went over $100 billion in 1984 for the first time, and U.S. manufacturers and agricultural interests felt the squeeze of competition in world markets because of the strong dollar, domestic political pressures came to bear on Washington. American business had been hurt by high interest rates and cheap imports. Both Democrats and Republicans were now openly questioning whether a floating exchange rate system was compatible with free and open markets for traded goods. Senator John Danforth called on Congress to focus on the connection between trade and monetary relations. "No trade policy can work," he noted, "if the exchange rate problem is not resolved."[68] Senator Lloyd Bentsen, who would later serve as Treasury Secretary in the Clinton administration, was highly critical of the Reagan administration for its "blatant disregard" of exchange rate movements. He urged a more coordinated exchange rate policy among trading partners based on a system of currency target zones, if not fixed rates: "We have to find something between the excess rigidity of the Bretton Woods system and the excess gyrations we're seeing now."[69]

Unfortunately, the request for something in between Bretton Woods and floating rates yielded the oxymoronic "managed float" policy pursued by James A. Baker III (who replaced Regan as Treasury Secretary in January 1985) and his deputy, Richard Darman. Striving to head off overtly protectionist legislation against Japan and other competitors, while at the same time calming the fears of American exporters and other victims of the strong dollar, Baker and Darman engineered a plan to bring down the value of the dollar in international currency markets through an orchestrated intervention effort carried out by the central banks of the United States, Japan, Germany, the United Kingdom, and France. The strategy culminated in the Plaza Agreement of September 1985, which did little to address the fundamental economic, financial, or monetary policies being followed by the participating nations; it did, however, set the stage for coordinated central bank activities in global money markets to drive down the dollar. Or, in language more in keeping with official communiqué style, to bring about "some further orderly appreciation of the main non-dollar currencies against the dollar."[70]

If the success of the Plaza accord is judged by the steep descent in the dollar's value as measured against other major currencies in the ensuing months, there can be no denying that the plan worked. By January 1986, the dollar was worth 25 percent less than it had been worth one year earlier.[71] But Baker and Darman soon realized that in attempting to manage exchange rates through the brute strength of joint central bank buying and selling activities in world currency markets, they had a tiger by the tail. The dollar refused to stabilize at the level considered appropriate by government finance officials, instead continuing to drop like a stone against foreign currencies. By March 1986, U.S. allies were beginning to panic that the Baker-Darman monetary cure would prove worse than the disease. According to Gyohten, "arguments were raging in Japan that the Plaza accord had been a mistake or even a failure, because it had started an unstoppable, uncontrollable fall of the dollar, or in other words, an uncontrollable rise of the yen."[72]

In February 1987, just seventeen months after the Plaza Agreement, Baker and Darman found it necessary to launch another coordinated effort by central banks to manipulate the value of the dollar in world currency markets through collusive actions. This time the goal was not to drive down the dollar, but rather to prevent its further decline. Stressing his preference for "consultation and cooperation" over automaticity during meetings held in Paris at the Louvre, Darman urged the other members of the Group of Five industrial nations to support an arrangement whereby each country would attempt to keep rates within a range of plus or minus 2.5 percent from the prevailing rates of 1.8250 deutsche marks and 153.50 yen to the dollar.[73] However, no specific actions were laid out and no firm commitments were obtained with regard to what each nation was expected to do toward achieving that end.

Not surprisingly, the ambiguous Louvre accord did little to stem the dollar's fall and stabilize its value against other major currencies. After a brief rise in March, it began to fall once more as central bank officials bickered among themselves over whose government was spending sufficiently large amounts to intervene to defend existing exchange rates as per the understanding. A disastrous stock market crash occurred some six months later on October 17, 1987, and newly installed Federal Reserve Board Chairman Alan Greenspan was compelled to pump in money to keep brokerage houses solvent.[74] In early 1988, the dollar slipped to 1.56 deutsche marks and 120 yen—new record lows.[75]

But then the dollar mysteriously began to recover once again, showing "surprising bullishness" starting in late spring 1988 and continuing through July 1989.[76] The dollar's appreciation was so impressive during the summer of 1988, when it reached 1.90 deutsche marks and 135 yen, that rumors were fueled of an international conspiracy to buoy up the U.S. currency to help elect George Bush as the nation's forty-first president. Baker dismissed such charges as "ridiculous."[77] And, indeed, if foreign central banks were conspiring to strengthen the dollar to somehow assure a Bush victory in the 1988 presidential election, their efforts did not pan out nearly so successfully four years later. The dollar plummeted to historic lows against the deutsche mark (1.3990) in August and against the yen (118.60) in September 1992. Unless, of course, they were working to defeat Bush.

But political intrigue aside, what are the economic implications of such fluctuations in the value of the dollar against the currencies of the United States' trading partners? How is it possible to reconcile the ideal of an open, competitive global economy with the reality of meaningless, even perverse, monetary signals across borders? The insights of Volcker—who played such a key role in Nixon's decision to suspend gold convertibility in 1971, and who was subsequently charged with managing an out-of-control money supply as Federal Reserve chairman—are worth noting in this regard. Some twenty years after the United States abandoned the Bretton Woods system of fixed exchange rates, Volcker offered the reflection:

> Increases of 50 percent and declines of 25 percent in the value of the dollar or any important currency over a relatively brief span of time raise fundamental questions about the functioning of the exchange rate system. What can an exchange rate really mean, in terms of everything a textbook teaches about rational economic decision making, when it changes by 30 percent or more in the space of twelve months only to reverse itself? What kind of signals does that send about where a businessman should intelligently invest his capital for long-term profitability? In the grand scheme of economic life first described by Adam Smith, in which nations like individuals should concentrate on the things they do best, how can anyone decide which country produces what most efficiently when the prices change so fast? The answer, to me, must be that such large swings are a symptom of a system in disarray.[78]

A system in disarray. The phrase, so passive in its objectivity, has the effect of masking the seriousness of the problem and glosses over the tremendous losses suffered during the past two decades in both psychological and economic terms. To see U.S. money soar to such heights and sink to such depths, to have the value of the dollar tossed about on a sea of speculative demand, at times seeking to lure fickle global investors with Fed-driven interest rates, at times catering to the protectionist leanings of domestic business interests, is to bear witness to a currency that has lost its credibility. That the dollar was once the anchor currency for the international monetary system makes the fall from grace all the more grievous.

A system in disarray, yes. Recognizing the problem may be the first step toward finding a solution. But it hardly acknowledges the moral lapse of a nation that shirked its responsibility for global monetary stability in the face of economic pressures. And then, too, it is only a first step.

3

The World on Edge

Monetary disorder is rampant throughout the world. At a time when the transition to a postcommunist world holds out the prospect for an international marketplace based on free trade and entrepreneurial initiative, offering new levels of economic prosperity for a growing number of participants, the lack of an orderly global currency system threatens to destroy the vision. The international monetary system currently in existence is no system at all; it is a currency cartel that is operated—badly—by a small group of finance ministers representing the interests of the world's most powerful industrialized countries. As these government officials maneuver to intimidate each other politically and economically, their public remarks are eagerly scrutinized by exchange market speculators who capitalize on every nuanced utterance that might affect future currency movements. Ironically, as the speculators grow more bold and powerful, the direction of influence sometimes moves the other way; when financier George Soros published a letter in *The Times* of London in June 1993 predicting that the deutsche mark would fall against all major currencies, it immediately seemed to cause Germany's currency to do just that.[1]

Global currency arrangements have deteriorated into a high-stakes poker game where exchange rates are determined on the basis of the latest bluff between government officials and speculators. Such shenanigans make a mockery of global free markets, which require accurate price signals to function properly. The real producers and consumers of the world can only be discouraged and disgusted by a game that is biased toward the shrewd practitioners of monetary artifice. Why should private individuals who manufacture useful goods or offer desired services subject their profits to "currency risk" on a scale that swamps whatever comparative advantage they might otherwise seek to provide in the international marketplace?

With the daily net turnover in global money markets now close to $1 trillion, more than one-hundred times the daily total of world trade in merchandise, it is clear that prevailing international exchange rate arrangements offer a playground for currency traders, not an honest countinghouse for producers. As Kenichi Ohmae observes in his book *The Borderless World*, the "tail" of foreign exchange trading has in recent years vastly outgrown the original "dog" of international trade. Based on the relative sums of money involved, "no one can argue that FX [foreign exchange] trading is still a mere adjunct to other kinds of economic activity," Ohmae notes. "It is an end in itself. It obeys rules of its own and displays its own distinctive forms of behavior."[2] It is also clear that as central banks face off against professional fund managers, the behavior of exchange rates is likely to become increasingly erratic and vulnerable to political tensions and market pressures. Estimated currency reserves held by industrialized countries amount to just $550 billion, slightly more than half the daily trading volume in global money markets.[3]

The dilemma is not just over chaos versus order in global monetary relations. It reaches to the deeper question of whether governments believe in free trade among nations or whether they wish to reserve the option of adjusting for the impact of legitimate competition by devaluing their currency. When the monetary rules of engagement among trade partners are subject to the manipulations of government, the message of free trade is compromised: We believe in open markets for our exports, but we don't want any competition from abroad. When a government deliberately devalues its currency against other nations' monies, it clearly shows that it is not above changing the rules when it appears to be losing in the global marketplace. Monetary manipulation is the most insidious form of protectionism.

Certainly the tension of trade disputes and bitter rivalries is hanging heavy in the air as the world's most powerful economic nations and regional blocs accuse one another of cheating in the international arena of economic competition. It starts with a sop from government to a particular domestic industry, such as textiles or steel or livestock, which riles foreign producers who then complain about unfair discrimination and punishing tariffs. Cries of protectionism raise the specter of retaliation and prompt tit-for-tat measures aimed at punishing the offending country and escalating the level of political conflict. Once the process is initiated, it is difficult to stop, as participants seem all too eager to ratchet up the volume of their invective and the menacing tone of their threats.

A decision by the United States in June 1993 to impose steep penalties on steel from nineteen countries accused of selling at prices less than fair market value elicited an angry outcry from European and Asian steelmakers. The European Community steel industry charged that a full-scale trade war had been launched and urged the EC to use all the legal and political means at its disposal to combat it.[4] Community trade ministers had already put the Clinton administration on notice a few months earlier when they denounced the assessment of heavy antidumping duties on EC steel as "unacceptable" and warned Washington that it was "on the wrong track" in its slide towards protectionism.[5] EC trade ministers were likewise upset at threats by Clinton administration officials to bar EC companies from bidding on U.S. government contracts. Niels Helveg Petersen, Danish foreign minister and president of the EC Council of Ministers, noted an ominous trend in the American attitude. "This is not just some minor trade dispute," he declared. "What we are talking about is absolutely the wrong signal for the world economy."[6]

Japan also expressed concern that the United States under the Clinton administration was leaning dangerously toward protectionist solutions imposed by government rather than relying on the free market to resolve trade problems. Hardly a model of free market virtue in terms of opening its domestic markets to foreign competition, Japan nevertheless asserted that the principles of free trade should be upheld and that government-imposed formulas for setting specific target levels for balancing trade relationships are misguided and potentially damaging. In a report issued in May 1993 by the Ministry of International Trade and Industry (MITI), Japan noted that the United States was pursuing policies based on the faulty assumption that the presence of a trade imbalance was de facto evidence of unfair trading. Japan favored an alternative approach requiring that countries simply adhere to international rules without regard to trade imbalances.[7]

Such charges and countercharges of protectionism among major trading partners cast a disturbing pall over the prospects for an open global economy. Where is the leadership in the world to stand up for free markets, not just for their efficiency, but for their fundamental morality? If the world's most powerful nations permit the aims of free trade to be undermined by monetary manipulation and resort to unilateral actions to arbitrarily punish specific competitors, how can lesser nations hope to be treated fairly in the global marketplace? If the United States becomes protectionist, what happens to the dream of democratic capitalism and free markets around the world? Commenting on the MITI report which accused both the United States and the European Community of violating the spirit of nondiscriminatory competition, one of its authors noted: "This report is defending not only Japan. It is to protect the world. We have to say 'no' to managed trade."[8]

Unfortunately, the strength to say no to government intervention in trade relations is weakened when domestic economies are facing recession and concerned producers seek protection from their elected officials. With economic conditions in Europe mired in difficulties, with the highest unemployment rates since World War II,[9] and with citizens in the United States displaying a growing uneasiness about the overall direction of their country, according to a 1993 poll,[10] the search for leadership to connect sound money with free trade seems to be in trouble. Japan's stance is welcomed, but subject to criticism, based on its own shortcomings in providing free access to internal markets. Moreover, Japan also has been struggling with the after-effects of a bubble economy that burst in the late 1980s; a survey of business conditions in June 1993 depicted an economy fraught with hard times and showed Japan's business confidence at its lowest level in almost two decades.[11]

All of these trends bode poorly for the cause of a free market global economy. With much of the industrialized world struggling with recession, developing nations find themselves at the mercy of protectionists who are willing to impose quotas or manipulate currencies to undermine the competition. Just when the world needs to open its doors to exports from formerly communist nations and emerging suppliers in Latin America and Asia, weak leadership in the Group of Seven nations is succumbing to domestic pressures to protect internal markets. The signs are worrisome. Unless the overall advantages to the global economy derived from free trade are strongly championed, they are likely to be lost in the anxiety over depressed economic conditions. Developing nations trying to break out of their state of poverty will find their hopes dashed if negative economic and political factors lead to a breakdown in trade and monetary relations.

EUROPEAN DISUNITY

The United States of Europe. No less a believer in the concept of individual states bound together in a federal union than George Washington, the first president of the United States of America, favored the idea. Washington specifically proposed the formation of a United States of Europe in a letter to Lafayette.[12]

Some two hundred years later, the goal remains far from being fulfilled, although an increasing sense of a common European destiny seems to have begun to permeate the national psyches of the countries involved. Creating a new sense of nationhood is undoubtedly much easier when the population is composed largely of new arrivals who do not have strong attachments to their territory and whose relationships are not framed against a historical background of hostile border disputes and armed conflicts. Jean

Monnet freely admitted that his inspiration for a unified Europe came from the United States. He often lamented during the 1950s and 1960s that only Americans seemed able to comprehend Europe as a group of states.[13]

Europeans who today nurture suspicions that the United States is secretly opposed to European unity might be surprised to learn that another well-known U.S. military leader (who would likewise serve as president of the United States) was also a strong supporter of the cause for a unified Europe. Dwight D. Eisenhower, who served as U.S. commander in Europe during World War II, witnessed up close the horror and devastation that wracked the continent during the 1940s. In 1951 he argued for the establishment of a United States of Europe to bring about a more secure world and materially improve the welfare of humankind. "With unity achieved," Eisenhower stated, "Europe could build adequate security and, at the same time, continue the march of human betterment that has characterized Western civilization."[14]

Eisenhower was sharply aware of the rivalries that divided the continent, which added to the enormity of the task, but he believed the potential benefits of unification would prove a worthy objective. "Once united, the farms and factories of France and Belgium, the foundries of Germany, the rich farmlands of Holland and Denmark, the skilled labor of Italy, will produce miracles for the common good," he predicted.[15] Eisenhower was not simply seeking a more cooperative relationship among the European nations; he believed firmly in the need to specifically create a United States of Europe, complete with its own European constitution and bill of rights. Eisenhower asserted that "so many advantages would flow from such a union that it is a tragedy for the whole human race that it is not done at once."[16]

Certainly, the dream of a united Europe had been pursued for centuries, most eagerly by would-be conquerors who were seeking to dominate the entire continent. But in the decade following the end of World War II, the nations of Europe felt compelled to finally act on the idea of structuring a unified community free of internal nationalistic conflicts and strengthened by integrated economies. In 1957 the European Economic Community, predecessor of the European Community, was born with the signing of

the Treaty of Rome, which aimed to harmonize economic and political development. The original six members were Belgium,
France, Italy, West Germany, the Netherlands, and Luxembourg.
Britain chose not to join, opting instead to establish a separate organization called the European Free Trade Association (EFTA) in
1959. The founding members of that group, besides Britain, were
Norway, Sweden, Denmark, Switzerland, Austria, and Portugal.
Unlike the EEC, which emphasized the importance of setting up
new European economic and political institutions, EFTA was oriented toward facilitating free trade and preventing protectionism.

Britain changed course in 1973, when it abandoned EFTA in
favor of joining the EC. Denmark and Ireland also joined the EC
in 1973, Greece joined in 1981, and Spain and Portugal joined in
1986, bringing the total number of members up to twelve. These
are the twelve member countries represented on the European
flag by twelve yellow stars set against a blue background. The flag
is hoisted at official occasions celebrating the new Europe and
waves continuously over EC institutions located in Brussels, Luxembourg, and Strasbourg.[17]

Lately, however, the flag does not wave so proudly, as the lofty
objectives of unification have been shredded by currency chaos
and trampled by recession and unemployment. The original aims
for a united Europe have gone through several iterations over the
years, with each round contributing a new set of acronyms to the
discussion. But they have remained essentially unchanged: The
goal is still to prevent war in Europe and to integrate human and
material resources to maximize economic returns to the region.
Prior to the debacle over the Maastricht Treaty, two basic tracks
had emerged for pursuing European unity. One was aimed at
defining and achieving political union with the eventual goal of
leading to a Europe with a single foreign policy and a single defense posture. The other was dedicated toward bringing about
economic and monetary union (EMU), completing the transfor-
mation of the European Community into a single market with a
single currency.

But both these objectives were pushed off track by unforeseen
developments in the monetary, economic, and political spheres.
Where European officials were boasting in 1991 that the future

Europe would be the world's largest market and most vibrant economic power—and policy intellectuals such as Jacques Attali were proclaiming the decline of America with barely disguised relish[18]—chronic turmoil among European currencies together with a stunning foreign policy failure to resolve ethnic conflicts have inflicted serious damage on the grand vision of a united Europe.

Uncertain Direction

Europe seems to be adrift, as leaders in individual nations find themselves wholly distracted by pressing domestic problems. Instead of working in concert to build a peaceful and prosperous European community, newly freed from the fear and financial burden of having to defend itself from the Soviet Union, the nations of Europe seem bent on procuring special advantages for themselves at the expense of their neighbors. Bowing to the demands of "Euro-skeptics" who have sheer disdain for the ideals of European unity, leaders in Britain and elsewhere have emphasized national economic priorities and maintained only a vague commitment to political integration across the continent. As Spanish Prime Minister Felipe Gonzalez explained in an early 1993 interview:

> I believe we still have not assimilated the change . . . from the Cold War, from the politics of blocs, when the situation was really an equilibrium of fear and terror but the rules of the game were quite clear. It isn't true that we have a new order. We're in a situation of disorder.[19]

The disorder stems from a lack of leadership and a sense of malaise that have been manifested in social as well as political terms. Instead of moving ahead confidently toward the building of a continental superstate with its own currency and a singular world mission, Europe seems stuck in its old problems of nationalism and protectionism. Individual nations are resorting to beggar-thy-neighbor economic policies. Acts of racism also appear to be on the rise, especially in Germany and France, where vicious assaults on Turkish immigrants have become commonplace.[20] "What is the situation in Europe today?" asked Danish Prime Minister Poul Nyrup Rasmussen in a spring 1993 interview. "Uncertainty, uncertainty, uncertainty. That's a disaster."[21]

What happened to derail the plans for a new Europe? While it is not possible to fully differentiate between cause and effect, the tension that began with Denmark's initial rejection of the Maastricht Treaty in early June 1992 and culminated in the near collapse of Europe's exchange rate mechanism some three months later in mid-September marked a palpable turning point in Europe's movement toward unification. Gone was the confidence in governments and institutions as European currencies were reduced to tiny blips on computer screens that lost their value with alarming speed, despite the frenzied efforts of finance ministers and central banks. When the monetary roiling subsided, government authorities seemed more preoccupied with assigning blame than finding solutions. By May 1993, eight months after Black Wednesday, the exchange rate mechanism that was supposed to evolve into a common European currency was hardly recognizable. Britain and Italy had withdrawn, Spain had devalued three times, Portugal twice, and Ireland once. Only a core group comprised of Germany, France, the Benelux countries, and Denmark was left relatively intact.[22]

The experience was sobering. Government authorities had thought they could impose an agenda for unification on the peoples of Europe by means of a determined blueprint for social, economic, and political convergence. But such hubris came into direct conflict with populist sentiment that resisted the threat of further European bureaucratization under faceless technocrats based in Brussels. Moreover, the power of speculators to move exchange rates undermined the assumption that governments could operate a pegged-rate system based on secret agreements and strategic intervention in currency markets. Most debilitating of all, economic conditions in Europe's major countries took such a downturn as to make a mockery of the convergence criteria specified under the Maastricht Treaty that determine whether a country qualifies for economic and monetary union. As of May 1993, only Luxembourg could meet the stringent 1996 requirements on budget deficits, government debt, and inflation.[23]

In a gloomy economic forecast issued by the European Commission in Spring of 1993, the predicted growth rate for the EC economy was sharply downgraded to zero or even "slightly negative."[24] Shrinking economies mean lower tax revenues and more social spending—a formula for higher budget deficits and increased public borrowing. One of the countries hardest hit was Germany, the reputed economic powerhouse of the European Community. Theo Waigel, Germany's finance minister, announced in May 1993 that his country was suffering "the sharpest economic crisis" since the founding of the German Federal Republic in 1949.[25] Certainly the shock of German unification took its toll on the national budget, but the decline into recession was exacerbated by excessively high labor costs and falling industrial production. In 1993, immigrants comprised 8 percent of the population in Germany (twice the EC average) and furnished ready targets for frustrated Germans as unemployment rose.[26]

The situation was hardly better in the other major European countries. The French economy, according to statements made by Edouard Balladur during the spring 1993 general election campaign, was in its "worst state since the second world war."[27] Unemployment had reached record levels and real interest rates were among the highest in Europe. Balladur took immediate actions as prime minister—including making plans to sell off twenty-one state-controlled companies—to increase revenues to the French budget and help reduce a budget deficit approaching 5 percent of France's gross domestic product.[28]

Britain likewise was faced with a huge budget deficit that amounted to 50 billion pounds ($78 billion) in spring 1993.[29] After three straight years of recession, any attempt to reduce the deficit raised the specter of higher taxes or severe cuts in public spending at a time when British Prime Minister John Major was already under heavy criticism for his economic policies and Britain's humiliating withdrawal from Europe's currency exchange rate mechanism. Major's sagging popularity could also be traced to what some perceived as his pro-European unity stance.[30]

Italy, too, was suffering from what seem to be its four chronic economic diseases: high inflation, unemployment, horrendous budget deficits, and imbalances in its external trade accounts.[31]

Union plans to demand higher wages also threatened to further depress industrial productivity. To make matters still worse, Italy was plagued with Mafia killings of judges and political scandals involving politicians and business leaders at the highest levels. According to *U.S. News & World Report* in June 1993, half of all Italians had lost faith in democracy.[32]

In short, the situation in Europe remains dire. "Any way you look at it," stated an adviser to EC Commission President Jacques Delors in the spring of 1993, "the Community is facing a long period of crisis and doubt."[33] For the 340 million citizens who live in EC member countries, anticipating Europe's gloomy future merely adds to the current misery.

Bundesbank: Culprit or Scapegoat?

Germany is almost universally blamed for Europe's recession. Tight monetary policy may have been the appropriate domestic policy for Germany as it struggled to suppress inflation while incurring the huge costs of absorbing the former East Germany, but the high interest rates that were transmitted through the exchange rate mechanism are seen to have suffocated economic growth for much of the rest of Europe. In the run-up to Black Wednesday, Norman Lamont, Britain's chancellor of the Exchequer at the time, specifically cited the Bundesbank for its intransigence in refusing to lower interest rates and accused Bundesbank president Helmut Schlesinger of further weakening the pound through reckless statements.[34]

Certainly Germany is proud of its money. For a country that has experienced hyperinflation as the precursor to political disarray and war, a solid deutsche mark represents stability and security. A poll by *Stern* magazine in 1992 indicated that 72 percent of Germans were opposed to sacrificing the deutsche mark for a European currency.[35] Little wonder, then, that Bundesbank officials resisted the advice proffered by finance ministers from neighboring countries, which usually hinted of the necessity for easier monetary policy and lower interest rates. In June 1993, when suggestions for improving the European monetary system called for German monetary officials to pay greater attention to conditions in other EC countries, Hans Tietmeyer, serving as vice-president of the Bundesbank, responded with antagonism. Dismissing the suggestions as "deceptive . . . sham proposals," he declared that the Bundesbank would continue to resist laxity and would take all actions necessary "to safeguard the anchor function of the D-Mark." According to Tietmeyer, a monetary system full of loopholes "for all possible contingencies will hardly be able to fulfil its purpose as an instrument of discipline."[36]

Yet the drive toward European economic and monetary unity trudges on, even though most countries seem ill-prepared to make the economic sacrifices necessary to bring their budget deficits and government debts into line. Denmark's approval of the Maastricht Treaty the second time around in May 1993 was widely viewed as a hollow victory given the extent to which the provisions of the treaty were watered down. "The more sophisticated Danes suspect nothing will ever come of this anyway," said a Danish government official. "And they're probably right."[37]

Signing a treaty is not the same as achieving monetary unity, of course, and there's little indication that the proper lessons have been drawn from the September 1992 experience. While there is widespread recognition that the turbulence in Europe's currency system that culminated in Black Wednesday was a disaster—"We must never let this happen again," said Wim Duisenberg, president of the Netherlands central bank—no fundamental changes were made.[38] A report issued by the EC's monetary committee in May 1993 claimed that "current institutional and technical arrangements in the European monetary system remain on the whole appropriate" and asserted that Europe's exchange rate mechanism would retain its ubiquitous "fixed but adjustable exchange rates."[39] Two months later, such complacency resulted in the widening of exchange rate bands beyond any reasonable definition of "fixed."

Britain has continued to distance itself from the system, meanwhile, and has displayed skepticism that exchange rate manipulation through central bank intervention could ever be a replacement for prudent domestic economic and monetary policies. "Attempts to move exchange markets in directions that are not consistent with underlying policies nearly always end in disappointment," observed Robin Leigh-Pemberton, (former) governor of the Bank of England, shortly before his retirement in 1993. Noting that exchange rate stability could not be achieved solely by actions in the exchange markets, Leigh-Pemberton declared that the "primary international responsibility of each country is to set its own house in order."[40]

Leigh-Pemberton's voice of reason clashes discordantly, though, with the bickerings of other monetary officials who still prefer to find scapegoats for their economic woes and who frame monetary policy disputes in terms of national rivalries and personality conflicts. One Bank of Italy official lambasted Germany for its failure to insist on a broad realignment of currencies before the September 1992 debacle and accused it of acting as if it were still "a political dwarf."[41] And an attempt by France to jawbone the Bundesbank into lowering interest rates in June 1993 was met with a sharp rebuff. After French Economics Minister Edmond Alphandery announced in a radio interview that he and his German counterpart, Theo Waigel, would discuss rate cuts in an upcoming meeting, Waigel promptly called the meeting off in what newspapers described as a "snub" by the Bonn government.[42]

Every Nation for Itself

As the *Financial Times* observed in April 1993: "The European Community is in monetary policy limbo."[43] While each nation hunkers down to concentrate on its own economic and financial worries, the cause of European unity takes on the aura of a distant concern. The more individual nations pursue their own agendas without regard to their neighbors' welfare, though, the more difficult it becomes to reconcile divergent policies and amiably resolve economic differences. As EC Economics Commissioner Henning Christophersen warned in June 1993, the temptation to use fiscal stimulus to counter rising unemployment, thus increasing budget deficits, poses the distinct risk of leading to tighter monetary policy, higher interest rates, and a new threat of currency chaos.[44] But nations seem undeterred as high government borrowing continues throughout Europe and soaring unemployment tempts politicians to try to spend their way out of recession while maintaining high levels of social protection.

The more sinister aspect of the new economic nationalism is revealed by governments' resorting to competitive devaluations in their currencies to gain trade advantages over their fellow community members. The exports of Germany, France, Belgium, the Netherlands, Luxembourg, and Denmark suffered big declines in competitiveness as a result of currency devaluations by the other EC countries of 15 percent within eight months after the September 1992 currency crisis.[45] Britain, in particular, seems to have benefitted from the increased price competitiveness of its exported goods and has enjoyed revived economic growth in the wake of its forced withdrawal from the European exchange rate mechanism. Britain's relative prosperity has only bred resentment among its neighbors, particularly France, which threatened to launch a retaliatory devaluation strategy. As Denmark's central bank chief, Erik Hoffmeyer, complained in May 1993, monetary cooperation in Europe had broken down because nations that devalued their currencies had been allowed to win an unjustified advantage.[46]

Competitive devaluations ultimately prove a losing strategy for all concerned, as each round of devaluation-to-match merely reduces the value of the money of every country participating in such tactics. As *The Economist* observed: "Competitive devaluations cancel each other out; they lead only to inflation."[47] Yet desperate governments find the lure of a quick economic fix through increased exports all but irresistible. Despite repeated warnings from Delors that the notion of a single market cannot survive if Europe is hit by further competitive devaluations, the trend toward increased attempts to cheat through currencies is likely to continue so long as Europe remains mired in economic stagnation.

Can anything unify the nations of Europe into taking a single stand on economic policy? Possibly, but the area that garners common support hardly represents a ringing endorsement of free trade. Where EC countries have tended to pull together is on the issue of trade conflicts with the United States. European leaders were put off by what they considered the high-handed manner of the Clinton administration early in its term. Warnings from Washington to "quit subsidizing" Airbus jetliners and threats of retaliation unleashed strong emotions in Europe. French President

François Mitterrand stated in February 1993 that the community should be prepared to assert its power and independence by taking on the United States.[48] Asked by the newspaper *Le Monde* if Europe should launch a trade war, Mitterrand replied: "If we're pushed, I hope so."[49]

When the Cold War was in full swing, disputes over trade between Europe and the United States tended to be resolved amicably in the interests of preserving the all-important Western security alliance against the Soviet Union. But with the military threat from the East vastly diminished, Europe seems less intimidated about expressing its dissatisfaction with U.S. trade policies. Indeed, some observers suggest that collective European antagonism toward protectionist actions undertaken by the Clinton administration may serve as a boon to the campaign for European unity. "Standing up to the United States on trade issues is one subject that gets people to rally round the European flag," an EC ambassador was quoted as saying in the *Washington Post*.[50]

Then again, perhaps not. EC officials angrily accused Germany of breaking ranks with other community members in June 1993 when it was revealed that Bonn and Washington had reached an agreement on their own involving trade in telecommunications equipment. Citing the Treaty of Rome, which gives power to the community to set trade policy, and demanding clarification of Germany's position, the EC's executive commission suggested stiffly that the matter might have to be settled by the European Court of Justice.[51]

AMERICA FIRST

Lack of political leadership is undoubtedly part of the problem in Europe. In the United States, the election of Bill Clinton as president in November 1992 was supposed to bring new vitality and direction to Washington. Clinton promised change. Change, however, does not necessarily connote progress. Clinton promised leadership. But on the issue of free trade, his early policies showed an inclination to lead the United States and the global community in the wrong direction. Clinton has since adopted the rhetoric of a free trade enthusiast in pushing for the North American Free

Trade Agreement (NAFTA) and completion of the Uruguay Round of global trade negotiations. But he has yet to acknowledge the concomitant requirement for stable currency relations among trade partners.

Prior to the election, candidate Bill Clinton emphasized his opposition to unfair competition and protectionist trading blocs. "I am for an open world trading system," he told *Europe* magazine in an October 1992 interview, "but that requires cooperation from every nation and group of nations that has a significant role in the world economy."[52] If the muted disclaimer about requiring cooperation from other key nations imparted a troubling conditionality to Clinton's stance, voters apparently were not alarmed. In February 1993, in his first major speech on the U.S. leadership role in global commerce after being inaugurated, President Clinton proclaimed his commitment to free trade in stirring terms:

> The truth of our age is this, and must be this: Open and competitive commerce will enrich us as a nation. It spurs us to innovate. It forces us to compete; it connects us with new customers. It promotes global growth without which no rich country can hope to grow wealthy. It enables our producers, who are themselves consumers of services and raw materials to prosper. And so I say to you in the face of all the pressures to do the reverse, we must compete, not retreat.[53]

At the same time, Clinton made it clear that U.S. dedication to open world markets would indeed be conditional on the "cooperation" of its trading partners. "We will continue to welcome foreign products and services into our markets," Clinton stated, "but insist that our products and services be able to enter theirs on equal terms." The same terms of reciprocity would also apply to foreign capital flows. "We will welcome foreign investment in our businesses," Clinton noted. "But as we welcome that investment, we insist that our investors should be equally welcome in other countries."[54]

Clinton's quid pro quo approach to free trade touches on American concerns about losing competitiveness—and high-wage jobs—in a global economy where low-wage workers are chomping at the bit to improve their chances for prosperity by selling exports to developed countries. The United States' best shot at remaining competitive, according to Clinton and his economic advisers, is to invest in upgrading the skills of its labor force, raise the level of infrastructure, and provide government support for technology development. "Our trade policy is part of a two-pronged approach to build a high-tech economy and create millions of new jobs," explained Commerce Secretary Ron Brown to Japanese journalists in Tokyo. "As we fight to open markets overseas, we will work to make American industry more competitive."[55]

The idea is to mesh international and domestic economic policies so as to enhance U.S. competitiveness abroad while improving economic and financial conditions at home with increased employment, higher levels of production, and hence, more tax revenues. U.S. Trade Representative Mickey Kantor noted at his Senate confirmation hearing that U.S. trade policy must be part of a coordinated and integrated economic strategy.[56]

But the political rhetoric is hard put to disguise underlying protectionist actions. As syndicated columnist Jim Hoagland observed in May 1993: "Administration trade policy has resembled a series of drive-by shootings more than a considered extension of the philosophy Clinton expounded in the campaign."[57]

Global Neighborhood Bully

Both Europe and Japan are reeling from the new aggressiveness in U.S. trade policy, which seems geared to cracking open markets through intimidation and threats rather than sparkling competitive performance. Kantor said he wanted to use a "sledgehammer" to break down trade barriers; negotiators in Europe and Japan no doubt felt that is what hit them.[58] The European Community was given stiff warnings of punitive trade sanctions for its Buy-Europe policies affecting government contracts for telecommunications, electric power generation, mass transit, and municipal water supplies. Europe received harsh criticism from Clinton for subsidizing its aircraft manufacturing, even as the president was promising larger government subsidies for high technology in the United States.[59] The high duties imposed by Washington in June 1993 against steel imports from a score of countries, seven of them members of the European Community, constituted more than a shot across the bow—it was a shot into the bow.

But such tactics are likely to cause resentment rather than foster cooperation. "Washington's self-righteous indignation over the sins, actual and alleged, of its trading partners is both irritating and depressing," observed the *Financial Times* in spring 1993.[60] Clinton's trade advisers may insist that they are merely seeking fairness and a level playing field for global economic competition. But, as the *Financial Times* counters, if fairness means anything, "what can be 'fair' about reliance on clout available only to a superpower?"[61]

Japan clearly has been the primary focus of Washington's trade policy ire. In an unusually sharp dig in late June 1993, only a week before the scheduled Group of Seven (G-7) economic summit in Tokyo, Clinton accused the Japanese government of deliberately shutting out foreign competition from its domestic market in order to maintain high employment.[62] The White House faulted Japan for running a huge trade surplus with the rest of the world ($132 billion in 1992) and blamed the Japanese government and big business for maintaining tight control over the economy.[63] "The country with the lowest unemployment rate of all the wealthy countries of the world is Japan," Clinton stated. "It would be hard to make a serious case that they have a low unemployment rate because their government is not involved in their economy."[64]

If government economic intervention is the problem, though, can managed trade be the solution? Yet the United States sought to introduce specific economic targets for the G-7 industrial nations at the July 1993 summit that included annual growth rates of 3 percent and restricted trade surpluses. Japan, in particular, was pressed to reduce its trade surplus by one-third to one-half over four years and to increase its purchases of U.S. and other foreign manufactured goods by 33 percent.[65] European reaction to the U.S. attempt to impose common growth targets and trade level ceilings was marked by incredulity. "How can someone promise 3 percent growth?" asked a senior German official. "It's not engineering that we're doing. It's economics."[66]

Indeed, the bizarre request from the United States permitted Japan to take the moral high ground in defending the virtues of free trade and an open global economy. Condemning Washington's emphasis on targets, Japanese Minister for Economic Planning Hajime Funada explained that the demand for specific results is "impossible" and a denial of "the very system of the market economy itself."[67] Coming to Japan's defense, German Chancellor Helmut Kohl argued that Japan, like Germany, garners special criticism when it tries to retake a leading role on the global economic stage because it was one of the losers in World War II. Kohl cautioned that trading partners should not level accusations against one another. "Protectionism is the enemy," he said.[68]

Despite Japanese protests, however, that government-decreed numerical targets are anathema to the functioning of free markets, the Clinton administration seems determined to enforce them to track Japan's "improvement" on reducing its trade surplus and raising the level of foreign imports. In a statement worthy of a communist-era central planning authority, a U.S. official commented: "There is no way to measure progress without measurements."[69]

Such tough talk, however, implies the willingness to take tough actions to back it up. Clinton administration officials let it be known that they would not balk at imposing sanctions if Japan did not conform with Washington's demands. But not all U.S. legislators were comfortable with the prospect of punishing the world's second-richest country and biggest foreign customer for U.S. agriculture and high-tech products. Senate Finance Committee Chairman Daniel Patrick Moynihan (D.-N.Y.) was exasperated when Deputy U.S. Trade Representative Charlene Barshefsky made the assertion that Japan simply must reduce its trade surplus. "Must?" asked Moynihan. "What will you do it if doesn't—bomb Tokyo?"[70]

Lest it seem that the United States' new resolve to stand up for fair trade has been directed solely at Europe and Japan, it should be pointed out that the White House took early steps to impose tariffs and dictate numerical limits on the exports of less developed countries as well. Trade policy expert James Bovard chronicles actions taken in the first five months of the Clinton administration that include: prohibiting Macedonia from exporting more than 80,000 wool suits a year to the United States (a de facto 71 percent cut from earlier levels); imposing import quotas on trousers, breeches, and shorts from Myanmar (Burma); announcing import quotas on women's and girls' suits from China;

imposing an import quota on twills and sateens from Thailand; imposing import quotas on women's wool coats from Bulgaria; imposing import quotas on cotton coats from Pakistan; imposing restrictions on pajamas from Guatemala.[71]

While the Clinton administration may have won points for protecting U.S. industry from low-cost foreign competition, it's hardly clear that American consumers are better off. The whole point of international trade, after all, is to import goods that can be produced more cheaply abroad than at home. It's the theory of comparative advantage. Or as a *Financial Times* editorial put it: "It's the imports, stupid."[72]

Devaluation by Innuendo

Tariffs, quotas, and duties are obvious forms of protectionism. Currency devaluation is much more subtle, but can be equally devastating in its impact on competitors. Initially, at least. Eventually, competing nations retaliate by devaluing their own monies and neutralizing each others' acts of currency aggression in a self-immolating bout of inflation, or they absorb the temporary price disadvantage and strive to make a virtue out of weakness by becoming more efficient and price competitive.

When U.S. Treasury Secretary Bentsen made it known in February 1993 that he would "like to see a higher yen," the impact on the yen–dollar exchange rate was immediate and sustained. The day before Bentsen's remark, the yen was trading at the rate of 119.15 yen to the U.S. dollar. Four months later, in June, the rate hit a postwar record of 104.8 yen for the dollar. At that level, the dollar had depreciated over 12 percent against the yen since Clinton administration officials began talking down their nation's currency.[73] Japanese companies began boosting U.S. prices on a broad array of products as they scrambled to adjust to an exchange rate considerably different than expected. "All the planning for this year had predicated an exchange rate of 115 to 117 (yen) on the dollar," according to a currency specialist.[74] U.S. companies with manufacturing facilities in Japan, such as construction equipment firms, also came under pressure to raise prices on their exports to the United States to compensate for the dollar's weakness against the yen.

For such a high government official to make such incendiary comments about the desired direction of exchange rate movements was so at odds with normal protocol that the first reaction of business journalists was to characterize Bentsen's statement as an unintended revelation. But as weeks went by, it increasingly began to look as if Bentsen's comment was no off-the-cuff quip but part of a purposeful strategy. As reported in the *Financial Times* in April 1993:

> Indeed, in a briefing with reporters this Wednesday an unrepentant Mr. Bentsen came close to admitting that he had deliberately talked the yen up. Referring to his February remarks at the National Press Club, he smiled and said: "It looks like those remarks turned out to be very timely."[75]

If the exchange markets needed confirmation that the Clinton administration wanted a weak dollar to reduce the U.S. trade deficit with Japan, they received it when President Clinton voiced his own satisfaction that the sliding dollar–yen rate was turning out to be an effective tool of U.S. trade policy, one of the things that was "working."[76] Clinton was chastised by the Bank of Japan for making what it considered highly inappropriate and improper comments. "There are some dangerous signs that there is too much toying around with exchange rates," a senior bank official asserted.[77] Yoshiro Mori, Japan's trade minister, said he felt "extremely angry" at the way the Clinton administration had talked up the yen.[78]

But the damage was done. Taking the Clinton clues as a market directive, currency traders persisted in selling dollars for yen and refused to change course even when the Federal Reserve stepped in to buy dollars and sell yen to halt the dollar slide. U.S. Treasury Under-Secretary Larry Summers, who had been a proponent of the strong yen strategy, was forced to concede in May 1993, "The market has moved too far, too fast."[79] Bentsen publicly insisted that the United States didn't want the dollar to fall any further.[80]

Americans have traditionally had a blasé attitude about the value of the dollar relative to other currencies. Until fairly recently, exports were not a particularly important factor in terms of the overall economy, so it was hardly necessary to be concerned about price competitiveness in foreign markets. In 1960, according to the Commerce Department, exports accounted for just 4.9 percent of the U.S. gross domestic product. During the last three decades, however, exports have grown considerably as a percentage of the U.S. gross domestic product; in 1992 they accounted for about 12 percent of all goods and services produced within U.S. borders.[81] Some 14 million workers in the United States now owe their jobs to exports.[82] Moreover, according to economist Jeffrey Garten, author of *A Cold Peace: America, Japan, Germany, and the Struggle for Supremacy*, almost all the growth of high-wage manufacturing jobs in recent years has been attributable to sales abroad.[83]

The United States is thus becoming more integrated with the global economy, and that trend can be expected to translate into increased interest in the dollar's performance in foreign exchange markets. In the past, a cheap dollar has held out appeal for Washington politicians attempting to find a quick fix for certain members of the U.S. business community; as Floyd Norris observed in *The New York Times*, "the Government of this country has tended to see a sinking buck as a painless way out of economic binds."[84] But while devaluing the dollar against the yen or other major currencies may boost U.S. exports for a while—and dampen domestic consumer demand for imported goods—it also poses some offsetting economic consequences that can end up doing more serious damage in the long run.

For one thing, many American consumers continue to purchase imported goods, even in the face of higher prices, because of their perceived higher quality or exotic appeal. Japanese automobiles, in particular, have earned tremendous loyalty among U.S. customers. So as Japanese suppliers raise the price of autos sold in the United States to offset the dollar's decline against the yen, determined U.S. customers swallow the increase and buy them anyway. The resultant impact on the U.S. economy is inflationary, especially because U.S. auto producers generally have tended to mirror price rises in Japanese cars rather than use the opportunity to increase market share.[85]

Then, too, to the extent that foreign producers are hurt by falling export sales to the United States, their own countries' economies suffer from reduced revenues. Mazda Motor Corporation, for example, estimates that it loses about $25 million for each one-yen rise against the dollar over the course of a year.[86] The quick rise of the yen under the Clinton administration has put severe pressure on the sales and profits of Japanese companies that export to America. "Manufacturers are already at the point where they are losing money," commented the research director of DRI McGraw-Hill.[87]

Japan has managed to export its way out of prior recessions by stepping up sales abroad to offset lower sales at home. But Shoichiro Toyoda, chairman of Toyota Motor Co., notes that the yen's strength during the current recession "will prevent an early business recovery."[88] For the first time in twenty-seven years, department stores in Japan registered a decline in annual sales in 1992.[89] Business failures were up 22.7 percent in 1993 from the prior year.[90] In short, Japan's lingering recession is cause for concern in the United States because as the economic slump continues, domestic demand for goods will continue to weaken. And reduced growth in Japan translates into reduced demand for U.S. exports.

The situation is hardly better in Europe, where a severe economic downturn embraces much of the region. While the United States concentrates on its competitiveness and strives to utilize every option—including talking down the dollar—to maximize export sales, recession and high unemployment are snuffing out overall foreign demand for goods and services. Countries need high growth to foster vibrant consumer demand, for domestic as well as overseas products. So when growth is curtailed, in part because companies find that their own sales abroad have been hit hard by tariffs or declining price competitiveness due to currency movements, there is a boomerang effect. The less Europe is able to export to the United States, the more likely it will remain in recession. The longer it stays in recession, the fewer U.S. products it will be able to afford to buy. For U.S. companies that rely on selling products and services to Europeans, trade and currency policies devised in the White House that hurt European competitiveness are self-defeating.

Moral Vacuum

Devaluing the dollar is not only inflationary, then, it is also a misguided protectionist tactic that ends up undermining the objective of selling more U.S. exports around the world. American prosperity cannot be achieved through the impoverishment of its trade partners. But even more important than the economic reasons for avoiding a dollar devaluation strategy are the moral implications. As the *Wall Street Journal* observes, policy-generated attempts to deliberately move exchange rates are disturbing because "they reflect a manipulative policy toward something that should be a standard of value."[91]

When the dollar dropped to record lows against major European currencies in late August 1992, three weeks before Black Wednesday convulsed foreign exchange markets, the financial and economic fallout went beyond currency losses. European stock markets also fell as investors grew concerned at the prospect of a substantial depreciation in the assets of the world's leading economic power.[92] Because the dollar remains the primary store of value for calculating the worth of commodities and equities, a severe drop in its value is destabilizing to the global financial community. "It is, after all, the world's reserve currency," noted Angus Armstrong, an international economist for Morgan Grenfell.[93]

But how meaningful is the dollar as a store of value when it is subject to jawboning by top-level U.S. officials bent on driving its value down against other countries' currencies and when Americans are losing confidence in the economic prospects for their own country? A *Wall Street Journal*/NBC News poll in June 1993 showed that fewer than a quarter of Americans expected the economy to get better over the following year. The biggest worry for most was unemployment, but an increasing percentage also cited federal taxes as the most important economic issue. According to the same poll, more than half of Americans thought their health bills would rise under the Clinton administration.[94] Expressing signs of growing concern in the face of uncertainty over taxes and future financial burdens, Americans convey a somber message to the rest of the world about relying on the dollar.

And if the dollar does completely disavow its role as the leading global currency, if the Clinton administration persists in using the value of the dollar as yet another arrow in its trade policy quiver for fending off foreign competition, how is it possible to continue making presidential declarations in favor of free trade—let alone pursue the ideal of an open global market? U.S. leadership means more than just threatening retaliation and upping the ante for perceived acts of protectionism against U.S.-made goods. Michael Prowse offers the poignant observation in the *Financial Times*:

> In the past the global economy has performed best when an "anchor" country has served both as a guarantor of monetary stability and a champion of the liberal values on which a market system depends. Britain performed this role with distinction during the 19th century; the US performed well after the second world war as the hub of the Bretton Woods exchange rate system.
>
> But towards the end of the 1960s US leadership faltered, mainly because it failed to keep its own inflation rate under control but also because it lost sight of its wider global responsibilities. For the past two decades, for example, the US has perceived the dollar less as a global store of value than as an instrument to be manipulated for the short-term benefit of American exporters.[95]

Certainly, other nations have become increasingly sensitive to the United States' flagrant use of a declining dollar to achieve trade advantages. "The fall in the dollar has been a formidable stimulus to American exports," asserted Elizabeth Guigou, French Minister for Europe, as EC officials struggled to formulate a common position on trade talks with the United States in October 1992. "We cannot negotiate trade in abstraction from exchange rates," Guigou added.[96] For European companies that must cope with fluctuations in currency values, the ramifications of doing business across the Atlantic is most frustrating. Describing the dollar rate as "preposterous" in August 1992, the director of public affairs for Jaguar, a British company that in 1991 had 44 percent of its sales in the United States, noted: "For Jaguar as an operating unit the exchange rate is a disaster. Our cars have little U.S. content. It is still the problem of making cars in pounds and selling them in dollars."[97]

Then there is the problem, too, of buying stocks in one currency and having to translate returns into another. U.S. investors who had been flocking to European mutual funds during the first half of 1992 were whacked with sharp losses when European currencies dropped sharply against the dollar during the September crisis. The irony was that some of the stock markets showed gains during the period. Stocks in Madrid, for example, went up 2 percent the week of Black Wednesday when valued in pesetas, and the London stock market was also up. But currency losses overwhelmed the benefits of higher stock prices; European funds investing exclusively in the United Kingdom and Spain suffered losses for the week of 5 to 15 percent for their U.S. investors.[98]

All of these problems raise the question of whether it is really in the interests of the world's leading economic powers to foster policies that elevate the impact of currency fluctuations over the rewards of efficient production or prudent investment. When the syndrome of competitive devaluation takes hold, everyone loses. "We *are* now in a world of competitive devaluation," observes Anatole Kaletsky, business columnist for *The Times* of London. With morbid humor, he continues:

> Some politicians claim that competitive devaluation is a beggar-thy-neighbour policy like protectionism. But this is quite simply false. To keep their currencies weak, governments around the world will have to keep lowering their interest rates. Of course, it is logically impossible for every country to achieve its ambition of having the world's weakest currency. But the process of trying will, at a global level, promote economic growth. In a world of global depression, competitive devaluation will not cause protectionism, but avert it. So let's do it. Let's fall in love—with the falling pound, dollar, yen, lira, franc and mark.[99]

But there is nothing humorous about global depression. In the past, it has spawned political conflicts with deadly consequences. The world is currently on edge as the most powerful nations wrestle with debilitating economic problems, and the developing world, including the vast region of the former Soviet Union, struggles to assert its presence in the global economy. "Protectionism feeds on world recession, sluggish growth and unemployment," observes Leonard Silk, former economics columnist of *The New*

York Times. So conditions today are ripe. Unless Clinton perseveres in championing the cause of open global markets and presses for a sound global monetary order, even the United States will be unable to prevent nations from falling into the dangerous me-first trade patterns of the 1930s. "Flirting with protectionism," Silk adds, "is flirting with a world catastrophe."[100] The antidote is leadership in the direction of free trade and stable currency relations.

JAPAN SAYS NO

Devastated and humiliated by defeat in World War II, Japan has risen to become one of the world's great economic success stories. Japan's example demonstrates that economic power does not have to be accompanied by military power in order for a nation to exert global influence, although Japan is still groping to find its appropriate leadership role among the industrial nations. Sometimes, to its horror, Japan is accused of shirking global responsibilities; the Japanese harbor a fear of being labeled chintzy when it comes to contributing financial resources to serve the needs of the world community. On the other hand, when Japan suggests that it might play a more prominent role in world affairs or hints at its willingness to help guarantee regional security, its Asian neighbors, as well as the Europeans and the Americans, grow concerned. Old fears are revived about Japanese aspirations to rebuild an empire.

The United States can take pride in the fact that, some fifty years ago, it turned an enemy into an ally by providing economic assistance to rebuild Japan's productive capacity. At the same time, American influence helped transform Japan into a democratic nation that espouses free market principles. But there is an unspoken fear among some Americans that they may have created a monster in the form of an economic threat. "The United States was the model of success that Japan had to learn from," acknowledges Tadao Chino, Japan's former vice-minister of finance for international affairs.[101] Japan, however, is now in a position to teach lessons to other countries—including the United States—about how to be competitive in today's global economy. And Japan is prepared to make certain demands to ensure that its much sought-after capital serves the nation's financial objectives throughout the world.

Japan's approach to free markets was never purist, but instead reflected a combination of tradition and pragmatism that developed into a natural partnership between big business and government. Before World War II, Japan's industrial modernization had been carried out by a handful of family-owned conglomerates that dominated manufacturing, banking, and foreign trade. These huge conglomerates, called *zaibatsu*, were partially dismantled in the postwar free market fervor to break up the monopolistic system that had served the previous totalitarian government. But as Japan began to recover from the war and started gaining confidence in its ability to produce successfully, the old ties between industry and government began to assert themselves once again. It was a partnership with which the Japanese were comfortable, socially and culturally, and one that offered very pragmatic results. Cooperation between the private sector and the public sector worked well to advance the cause of Japan by coordinating economic and financial efforts to maximize production.

The Japanese term for these new groupings of industrial companies with strong links to banking and government is *keiretsu*. Foreigners have a different name for it: "Japan, Inc." While the Japanese have found the *keiretsu* groupings most useful, other nations struggling to gain a foothold in Japanese markets contend that the inside arrangements constitute unfair trade practices. Japanese finance officials make loans available to companies at below-market rates and for extended maturities in order to develop new products. They assist Japanese companies to gain marketing footholds around the world by supplying low-cost capital, thus enabling them to offer the most competitive bids on large-scale projects.

Justification for the cozy relationship between big business and government stems from the fact that the Japanese government looks upon trade as a strategic resource, the source of Japan's survival in the world. To nurture corporations and safeguard Japan's capacity to aggressively export manufactured goods, the government maintains careful control over the economy, largely through actions taken by the Finance Ministry. The Finance Ministry has extraordinary powers to determine interest rates and allocate credit; it even exerts influence over the prices of stocks, real estate, and other investments. Akio Mikuni, president of Japan's only independent credit-rating agency, asserts that for all practical purposes the Finance Ministry "has been running a wartime economy from almost the moment U.S. occupation forces departed."[102]

In a sense, for Japan, economic competition is war, because the nation relies on its ability to trade intelligently, to impart value to goods through manufacturing and then sell the finished products in overseas markets, in order to safeguard its population. Ohmae notes that every Japanese schoolchild is taught this fundamental truth:

> In Japan the "textbook" children learn from starts with the clear and explicit notion that the country is poor. It has no natural resources. It has to import much of what it needs to survive and to export enough to pay for all that. Adding value provides the margin that enables the Japanese to buy the food that is needed. Otherwise they starve.[103]

So when other large industrial nations, Japan's trade partners and trade rivals, attempt to limit that nation's ability to export or force it to accept finished goods from foreign producers, they are treading on cultural imperatives that go beyond the latest trade statistics. Increasingly, Japan will be saying no to such tactics and resisting political pressures to change the way it does business. For one reason, Japan is experiencing severe economic problems and the instinct will be to stick to basics and not deviate from the formula that has brought economic success in the past. Japan will say no because it cannot afford to cave in to Western trade demands at a time when its own economic well-being is threatened.

The other reason Japan is less likely to back down in the future is because Japan has earned its way into the elite circle of nations that wield political power in the world and can act to assert their own will. Japan is aware it has come into its own and is increasingly resentful that other nations—the United States and the countries of Europe—are slow to acknowledge that the world's second-largest economic power should rightly exercise more authority on matters of global importance. Japan exhibits signs of schizophrenia on this point, sometimes backing away from a leadership role, sometimes clamoring to assert a strong position. But increasingly, Japan will want to match its voice in world affairs to its presence in the global economy.

Fool Me Once

Japan is understandably skeptical when the United States attempts to dictate the appropriate fiscal policies that Tokyo should carry out to stimulate its economy. Japan has heard the Keynesian message from Washington before; in the mid-1980s, Japan was pressured to spur its economy to grow very quickly by cutting interest rates and expanding the money supply. The theory at the time was that the resulting high rate of domestic growth would translate into high levels of domestic demand, which in turn would mean higher Japanese consumption of foreign imports.

When members of the Clinton administration today urge Japan to engage in massive government spending to drive domestic growth, they are once again buying into the notion that a heavy dose of internal fiscal stimulus will reduce Japan's trade surplus with the rest of the world. Fred Bergsten, director of the Institute for International Economics, even puts numbers on the supposed efficacy of the theory. His institute calculates that a 1 percent increase in Japan's growth rate would reduce its trade surplus by about $5 billion, of which about $1 billion would represent increased sales of U.S. products in Japan.[104] In combination with a concerted effort by administration officials to jawbone down the value of the dollar against the yen to hurt the price competitiveness of Japanese products in U.S. markets, Washington thus administers a one-two punch aimed at slashing Japan's $50 billion trade surplus with the United States.

The problem with this tidy approach, however, it that Japan is still paying the price for having caved in to such outside pressures the last time around. Japanese finance officials view the earlier decision to succumb to Western demands by loosening the monetary spigot as a mistake; the Japanese economy overheated during the late 1980s and led to speculative bubble prices for real estate and corporate stocks. True, as Japan's growth rate hit over 4 percent a year between 1987 and 1991, Japanese consumption of imports from the United States and Europe likewise increased at gratifying rates. But the economic boom, artificially induced through easy money, could not be sustained indefinitely. When Japan's economy slumped in 1992, demand for imports quickly fell off also.

The financial consequences of the burst bubble left Japanese officials with more serious concerns than just the renewed complaints of trading partners anxious to proffer their exports. By early 1993 it was clear that Japan was sinking into an economic crisis of alarming magnitude and complexity. A sharp fall in land and stock prices was accompanied by a sudden steep drop in consumer and business demand. Manufacturers, who earlier had been induced by the low cost of capital to expand production facilities, now found themselves saddled with excess capacity and huge unsold inventories. As profits dropped, so did share prices and the volume of trade on Tokyo's stock exchange. Bad debts began to mount. In February 1993, the Bank of Japan urged Japanese banks to write off nonperforming loans, while acknowledging that following its advice might result in some banks being forced into net losses for the year. Given that no Japanese bank had suffered a loss in the postwar era, the warning was taken as confirmation that financial authorities believed the Japanese financial system was under more strain than at any time since the 1920s and 1930s.[105]

Small wonder, then, that Japanese Foreign Minister Kabun Muto was somewhat stunned when U.S. Secretary of State Warren Christopher suggested to him in April 1993 that Japan should return to the economic policies of the late 1980s.[106] Official interest rates in Japan were already at an all-time low of 2.5 percent and the government was about to launch a 13.2 trillion yen ($122.93 billion) spending program to rescue the economy from recession. Wasn't this approach satisfactory to the United States? Apparently not. Bentsen offered the stingy assessment that the measures constituted only a "useful first step."[107] Add to Japan's vulnerable economic condition the impact of the soaring yen on export sales and it is easy to understand why Japanese officials have begun to stiffen in response to Washington's recommendations. Noting that his country was not willing to compromise its public finances to the extent necessary to satisfy U.S. demands for greater fiscal stimulus, a senior official from the Bank of Japan asserted: "We will set our policy according to our long-term domestic needs, not international calls for higher growth."[108]

Indeed, the yen's rapid appreciation during the first half of 1993 prompted the Japanese government to appeal to its G-7 compatriots to participate in a coordinated intervention effort to help stop the rise, which was jeopardizing the nation's economic recovery and undermining the hoped-for impact of the public spending package. In May, many of Japan's top companies had filed horrendous earnings reports covering the fiscal year ended March 31. For the corporate sector overall, profits were lower for the third consecutive year—an unprecedented trend. Corporate capital spending was also reported down for two years running; the first two-year drop since the oil shock of the mid-1970s.[109] In late May 1993, news that a small tableware maker, K. K. Watanabe Seisakusho, had gone bankrupt drew nationally televised coverage because it was the first business casualty directly attributable to the yen's appreciation. The seventy-year-old company depended on overseas sales for 70 percent of its revenues. Unable to continue exporting forks, knives, and spoons to customers in the United States and Europe, who were unwilling to pay higher prices, the firm went out of business and left about 438 million yen ($4 million) in unpaid debts.[110]

In the face of gloomy economic prospects and low demand, Japanese firms have been forced to cut output and reduce labor costs. Koichi Yoshimoto, an official in the research department of the Ministry of International Trade and Industry, reported in mid-1993 that Japanese industrial output had fallen for twenty consecutive months, the longest period of decline since Japan's recession in 1974 and 1975.[111] Unemployment statistics were also grim. Japan's Labor Ministry revealed that in spring of 1993, its ratio of job openings to job seekers fell to 0.81—meaning there were 81 jobs available for every 100 applicants. Some two years earlier in March 1991 the situation had been quite the opposite, with 146 job openings for every 100 applicants.[112]

In short, Japan cannot afford to take chances with its economic recovery in order to appease the United States and Europe. As

Kozo Koide, an economist for the Industrial Bank of Japan Ltd., noted in July 1993, conditions in Japan's economy are extremely severe. "We're stuck crawling along the bottom," he lamented.[113] There is no room for error, no slack to accommodate bad advice imposed on Japan by its trading partners that may ultimately prove to be detrimental. Japan does have an island economy, after all. The Japanese people cannot rely on natural resources for their survival. They must import what they need from the outside world and export enough to pay for it. And in doing so, they must utilize their wits.

On the Defensive

If the old Japan used to show a willingness to submit to the demands of more powerful nations, the new Japan is now exhibiting a certain rebelliousness, as evidenced by a more spirited defense of its own policies and a more commanding request for world respect. The arguments put before Japan by its G-7 partners insisting on a lowered trade surplus are being met with counterarguments by Japanese opinion leaders, who do not necessarily accept the notion that Japan exports too much and imports too little. Attempts by the United States to push up the value of the yen against the dollar are viewed with derision. After all, the yen was at 358 to the dollar in 1970, 265 yen to the dollar in 1973, 184 in 1978, 129 in 1988, and 105 in 1993. "During the intervening period," Kenichi Ohmae observes, "Japan's trade performance did not exactly go limp."[114]

If Japanese products sell well in North America and Europe, it is because they offer the consumer high quality and value, argue Japan's increasingly vocal defenders. And regarding the accusation that Japan shuns imports and refuses to open its markets to foreign competition, Japan's ambassador to the European Community begs to differ. Tomohiko Kobayashi asserted in the *International Herald Tribune* in June 1993 that on a per-capita basis Japanese consumers purchase $1,910 worth of imported goods a year, while the comparable figure for Europeans is just $1,788. He noted, too, that Japan is the world's largest net importer of farm products.[115]

If Japan's success in exporting is due to its competitive products, and if Japanese consumers purchase a reasonable amount of goods from abroad, as Japan's supporters insist, what is the point in trying to subvert the rules of free market competition by manipulating the yen–dollar exchange rate? In theory, a higher yen reduces Japan's trade surplus by lowering the amount of exports sold and increasing the amount of imports purchased. But critics of the approach argue that a stronger yen only serves to make Japanese companies even more efficient; squeezed by reduced profit margins on exported goods, Japanese managers restructure their firms to become yet leaner and meaner. A strong yen also encourages Japanese producers to set up facilities in the United States and elsewhere because it is cheaper to invest overseas. Meantime, the high yen makes it virtually impossible for U.S. business to become established in Japan, where real estate prices attain stratospheric levels in dollar terms. "Using the yen–dollar rate to cure the trade deficit makes things worse," concludes R. Taggart Murphy, an expert on the financial relationship between the United States and Japan. "In the past," he notes, "each time the yen got stronger, the trade surpluses retreated a bit and then came back stubbornly higher and more intractable."[116]

Irrational though the policy of exchange rate manipulation may be, Washington still seems enamored of what it perceives as a relatively benign way to dampen the allure of Japanese exports for American consumers. For the Japanese, however, who are sensitive to factors that affect their ability to sell goods abroad, altering the yen–dollar relationship is seen as an act of aggression. While the average American may not track the exchange rate between the dollar and the yen, the situation is quite different in Japan. Reporting from Tokyo for the *Washington Post*, Paul Blustein notes that in Japan everyone ("except maybe the comatose") is aware of currency rate movements:

> On bullet trains, electronic news summaries displayed at the head of each car flash the latest dollar–yen rate. Outside the headquarters of the Bank of Tokyo, an electronic sign displays neither the time nor the temperature—but the current value of the yen. On almost every TV news show, even on a dull trading day, the announcer informs viewers of the yen's latest moves along with the current level of the Nikkei stock index.[117]

For the new, more defiant Japan, an attack on the yen is not only a blow to the nation's sense of economic security, it is also an assault on Japan's role in the global financial system. The yen has attained the status of an international currency as foreigners invest in Japan's financial markets and cross-border trade is increasingly denominated in yen instead of dollars. While the dollar is still the world's most popular reserve currency, it has lost ground to the yen in recent years; according to the *Wall Street Journal*, the world's central banks are holding more yen in their foreign currency reserves than ever before.[118] Driving up the yen's value may stimulate greater foreign interest in Japanese financial assets, such as stocks, as outsiders seek gains from currency appreciation. But it also makes Japan much more vulnerable to sudden market swings that could destabilize the nation's financial system and threaten the global role of the yen.

Japanese people have come to enjoy the prestige their currency is afforded around the world and do not want to see its hard-earned status jeopardized by Washington's jawboning. Takashi Yoneda, a financial consultant in Tokyo, explains that the Japanese "feel the way the Americans used to feel. It makes you feel comfortable, traveling all over the world and using the yen. Now, we'd be shocked if the yen was rejected."[119] Besides making it more convenient for Japanese travelers to pay for purchases abroad, the increasing acceptance of the yen as an international currency testifies to the enhanced role of Japan in terms of the international balance of power. As George Yeo, Singapore's Minister for Information, notes: "The rise of the yen follows the growing economic and political influence of Japan in the world."[120]

Japan knows better than any other nation that its economic and political influence has grown in the world. Japan also knows that this new power is not always explicitly recognized by those lesser nations that traditionally have belonged to the exclusive club that exercises muscle in resolving geopolitical issues. Japan's formal bid for a permanent seat on an enlarged United Nations Security Council, for example, was not immediately embraced by the United Kingdom. In July 1993, Prime Minister Major's response to Japan's request for a seat was that the question needed to be taken "very gently."[121] For its part, Japan suggests that it is ready to discharge all the obligations that would be entailed by the move and notes that in choosing permanent members the UN should give due consideration to a country's political and economic weight.[122]

To the extent that the rest of the world seems reticent to accede power to Japan, whether on trade negotiations or membership in global institutions, the Japanese people can only wonder how much longer they should suffer political indignities not in keeping with their deserved status. Ohmae, pondering why Washington attempts to intimidate Japan with demands for numerical targets and other forms of managed trade, wonders if perhaps the real issue for U.S. politicians isn't just "to show how tough they are?"[123] He points out that retaliation by Japan's government could take the form of a massive withdrawal of funds by Japanese financial institutions from the U.S. bond market; the withdrawal of only $10 billion of Japan's trillion-dollar investment, Ohmae contends, would be enough to trigger a crash.[124]

Retaliation? Is Japan capable of standing up to the nation that restored its economic infrastructure after World War II and helped it to become the economic powerhouse it is today? Signs indicate yes. A report released by the Carnegie Endowment for International Peace in 1993 entitled *Rethinking Japan Policy* points out that Japanese resistance to American pressure is growing and "willingness to overtly challenge the U.S. is becoming an asset for Japanese politicians."[125]

Moreover, the trend toward resisting American and European demands is fueled by emotional factors that raise disturbing questions about the prospects for soothing trade frictions. In the provocative book by Sony chairman Akio Morita and politician Shintaro Ishihara called *A Japan That Can Say No*, Ishihara offers the pointed observation:

> The fact of the matter is that Americans do not trust Japan. . . . American racial prejudice toward Japan is very fundamental and we should always keep it in mind when dealing with the Americans. . . . It is important Americans understand the reality that power in the world, including economic power, is shifting gradually from West to East. We cannot become overbearing, but an inferiority complex is equally harmful.[126]

Sadly, Japanese perceptions of foreign hostility and prejudice may not be wholly unfounded. A poll conducted in Europe by Japan's Foreign Ministry belies the notion that Japan's sense of being discriminated against can be attributed to mere national paranoia. A total of 3,690 politicians, government officials, labor union leaders, scholars, and journalists in Britain, Germany, France, Italy, Belgium, the Netherlands, and Spain were asked the question: "Do you think Japan can be trusted?" The results of the poll, published in July 1993, revealed that the number of people who did not think Japan could be trusted had increased in every country as compared with a previous survey carried out in 1990. In Britain and France, the rise was particularly marked; about 40 percent said they could not or were not inclined to trust Japan, almost double the percentage in the earlier poll.[127]

All of these potential areas of conflict underscore the vital importance of not allowing trade disputes to turn into political—or, much worse, military—confrontations. When not trusting can be defined by citizens of the most powerful countries in ethnic or national terms, the world begins to teeter on the edge of dangerous rivalries. Tactics that involve the United States and the European Community teaming up to seek major trade concessions from Japan are likely to exacerbate existing tensions and provoke the kind of harsh retaliation that is born of resentment and cultural defensiveness.

THE NEW RUSSIA

Russia's break from communism under Boris Yeltsin stands as perhaps the greatest ideological and political turnaround of the twentieth century. Certainly, it constitutes one of the most compelling events in terms of human drama. Yeltsin's willingness to confront a totalitarian government that had lost touch with economic reality and its own sense of purpose—it had long since lost faith with its citizens—must be seen as the embodiment of the human spirit fighting to resist the faceless tyranny of entrenched bureaucracy and to assert the power of the individual. It was a David-versus-Goliath story given the military capabilities of the Soviet government. But with the courageous efforts of a handful of supporters standing by his side, along with a swelling crowd of Moscovites who risked their lives and livelihoods to form a human barricade around Yeltsin's headquarters, and with the spiritual backing of millions of television viewers around the world who held their breath as tanks rolled into place and lifted their guns, Yeltsin prevailed. And with his triumph came a celebration of the idea of democracy and human dignity, against which the old Union of Soviet Socialist Republics soon collapsed.

If a nation could survive on inspiration alone, Russia today would be flourishing. Unfortunately, the transition from authoritarian communism to democratic capitalism has been exceedingly difficult and plagued with missteps. The unworkable economics of central planning do not adapt easily to the supply-and-demand mechanism that drives a free market system. Misguided financial assistance from the world's most powerful industrial nations, former enemies of the Soviet Union, has hampered the process by providing government-to-government transfers rather than fostering private ownership and small business development. By failing to resist dirigiste policies administered through the International Monetary Fund that elevate the bureaucrat over the business leader, the United States has undermined its own vaunted belief in entrepreneurial capitalism.

Russia alone must take responsibility for its economic salvation. But there will be no greater tragedy than to lose what should be recognized as a God-given opportunity to help the Russian people embrace the morality of free markets for themselves. As a first step, Russia needs to wrench itself out of its hyperinflationary spiral and establish a stable monetary environment that will enable citizens and foreign investors to evaluate decisions to buy or sell, save or invest, on the basis of accurate price signals. Russia needs a sound, convertible currency if it is to proceed toward capitalism and become successfully integrated with the global economy.

Warped Money

No greater example of the financial distortions wreaked through central planning and bureaucratic corruption can be found than in the discredited currency of the former Soviet regime. A monetary receptacle for absorbing the massive budget deficits engendered in a hopelessly unproductive economy, the ruble had come to be regarded as "paper trash" long before the events of August 1991. But the decline of the value of the ruble since Yeltsin's ascension to power has been breathtaking in its steepness and rapidity. And heartbreaking in its impact on the lives of ordinary Russians.

Facing nearly incomprehensible levels of inflation—consumer prices increased twenty-six-fold during 1992—the majority of Russian citizens have seen their salaries and savings disintegrate with the dwindling ruble, along with their dreams of improved economic conditions.[128] The only ones who seem to be thriving in the current chaos are the criminals who have abandoned the ruble in favor of foreign currencies and the "speculators" who recycle imported goods at ever-increasing prices. Few people bother to manufacture products; how is it possible to estimate costs and future revenues when the domestic money is increasingly meaningless? For the average Russian, it is difficult not to be cynical.

Russia's money problem has its roots in the misapplications of the past, when Soviet apparatchiks treated the value of the ruble as an accounting plug for reconciling the domestic budget. Stalin deigned to use the ruble's ostensible value as a tool for propaganda purposes; in March 1950 the Soviet government declared the ruble "the world's most stable currency" despite its inconvertibility into Western currencies.[129] Abel Aganbegyan, former economic adviser to Mikhail Gorbachev, provides an amusing behind-the-scenes account of the justification for Stalin's claim:

> Stalin's approach to the whole question of exchange rates is best demonstrated by the following story. March 1950 saw the return to pre-war levels of production in our country, and the question of increasing the purchasing power of the ruble and strengthening its role was raised. Stalin ordered that the exchange rate be calculated. This was carried out in the Central Statistical Agency under Valierian Sobol, the head of the balance section of the Soviet economy. He carried out comparisons between the purchasing power of the rouble and the dollar when applied to consumer goods. Stalin wanted the rouble to be valued high, and those making the calculations knew this. They therefore used types of con-

sumer goods and standards of comparison which were particularly favourable for us in their attempt to overvalue the rouble. . . .
They would compare, for instance, the length of time American
shoes and our hobnailed boots lasted and would then add a correcting factor because our boots lasted longer than American
shoes. Stalin had given them one week for the whole of this task.
Toward the end of that week, everyone who had any part in the
exercise was working literally night and day.

The head of the Central Statistical Agency, Vladimir
Starkovsky, . . . was a talented man and had even been elected a
corresponding member of the Academy of Sciences, a position he
very largely used for the falsification of material to please Stalin.
He was in charge of our statistics for almost thirty-five years from
1939 onwards, and in this time he managed to destroy most of the
data and falsify the rest. For instance, Khrushchev in his published speeches says of the good harvest results for 1970 given by
Starkovsky in the regular digest from the Central Statistical
Agency: "I think only Starkovsky could say this: he is a man who
can apparently make bullets out of shit". . . . At last the calculations were finished in the middle of the night and sent immediately to the Kremlin. Sobol and the others were greatly surprised
when a little while later they read in the newspapers that the new
exchange rate was 1 rouble for 4 dollars. . . . When they asked
Starkovsky what it meant, he rather unwillingly told them that
Stalin had looked at their calculations, frowned, picked up a blue
pencil (apparently he very rarely used a pen, preferring pencils of
different colours) and crossed out their figure, substituting "4."[130]

As Aganbegyan rightly concludes: "This brief story demonstrates that under an administrative system the exchange rate can
only be a formality, not a true rate."[131] The old Soviet Union was
the epitome of an administrative system, and Aganbegyan's story
reveals the folly of having government officials designate the value
of money and set exchange rates by decree: Modern-day supporters of pegged rate systems should take note. But this story also
suggests the heavy burden Russia is carrying today in trying to
turn the rouble into a credible medium of exchange.

Rubles have no intrinsic value—they are not backed by gold or
foreign reserves—and there exists no convincing mechanism for restricting their issuance. Indeed, when Russia's Central Bank made
a ham-handed effort to reduce the supply of rubles in early 1992, in

conjunction with IMF demands, the move led to a sudden shortage of rubles and left huge state-owned enterprises without sufficient funds to pay workers. By June 1992, Yeltsin was forced to bring along 500 million rubles in overdue workers' salaries on an airplane that accompanied his jet when he flew to visit the Siberian region of Altai. Billions more rubles had to be shipped to the Tyumen oil region, the plutonium production facilities at Krasnoyarsk, and the Kuzbass coal mines to prevent threatened strikes.[132] To calm the fears of ordinary Russians anxious to receive back wages and unpaid pensions, Yegor Gaidar, economic reform minister at the time, announced on television that 142 billion rubles would be printed in July—more than all the money issued in 1991.[133]

Printing more rubles, of course, only heightened the monetary tension as inflation came roaring back with a vengeance in the latter half of 1992. "I cannot get used to this; prices change every time I go shopping," noted an exasperated thirty-six-year-old Russian engineer, Ludmila Ulyanova, in a *Washington Post* interview.[134] In July 1992, the ruble was trading at about 130 rubles to the dollar; over the next year, the exchange rate had plunged to about 1,100 rubles to the dollar. Such a dizzying fall in the value of a nation's currency is disorienting and depressing for the people who must use it to carry out their daily transactions. "I can hardly believe in anything any longer," said Ulyanova. "We are just dragging on."[135]

This gloomy attitude is a far cry from the heady days when Yeltsin formally took office in July 1991 as the first popularly elected president in Russia's 1,000-year history and proclaimed: "Great Russia is rising from its knees!"[136] Vowing to turn Russia into a prosperous, democratic, peaceful, law-abiding state, Yeltsin early on put his faith in the creativity of the individual as the key to the nation's economic rebirth. "The initiative and entrepreneurship of the citizens will provide for the welfare of the families of Russia and will become the source of the country's revival," he said in his inaugural address.[137]

Belligerent Beggars?

The danger today is that Russia's frustration over the slow pace of reform and disillusionment with the seeming rewards of capitalism—criminal behavior and social anarchy—could translate into resentment toward the rich industrial nations. Russia's desperate need for hard currency has prompted sales of sensitive military equipment and technology around the world. When Washington protested Russia's agreement to sell India $350 million of liquid fuel rocket technology in June 1993, Premier Viktor Chernomyrdin called off his planned visit to the United States.[138] Russian Vice-Premier Alexander Shokhin accused the wealthy industrial nations of discriminating against their former Cold War enemy and erecting trade barriers to limit Russia's participation in the global economy. "We can't help but conclude that the West is afraid of Russia's economic potential and afraid of Russia as a rival," Shokhin said.[139]

Certainly Russia's neighbor, Ukraine, has adopted the attitude that the only way to capture the attention of the Group of Seven industrial nations is to rattle its saber—that is, to point out it still has hundreds of nuclear warheads within its territorial possession. On the eve of the Tokyo economic summit in July 1993, Ukraine President Leonid Kravchuk sent a message to the G-7 nations asking them not to forget economic assistance to the second most powerful republic after Russia and issued new threats not to relinquish Ukraine's nuclear weapons.[140] Dmytro Pavlychko, chairman of the Ukrainian parliament's Commission on Foreign Affairs, is bitter at what he perceives as blatant Western disregard for Ukraine's future. "Right now all they are doing is looking at the largest beast [Russia] and throwing scraps at him."[141]

Ukraine's struggle with economic chaos and hyperinflation is cause for world alarm. Production has been dropping steadily in this country of 52 million, roughly the same population as France, while the money supply increased fortyfold in 1992 alone.[142] Ukraine's initial attempt to extricate its monetary destiny from the grasp of the undisciplined Russian Central Bank at first seemed promising. But Ukraine's "coupon" approach has been managed with such astonishing recklessness that the value of the interim national currency has plummeted against the dollar even more steeply than the ruble, going from 1,232 karbovantsy to the dollar in March 1993 to more than 3,000 by the end of May. During the first three months of 1993, prices in Ukraine rose fourfold, more than three times the rate of Russian inflation.[143] "It would not be an exaggeration to call the situation catastrophic," notes economist Volodymyr Cherniak. "Those who call it a crisis are dangerous optimists."[144]

Hopeful Signs

Other former Soviet republics are experiencing somewhat more success in their efforts to launch currencies separate from the ruble. Struggling to chart a promarket course apart from the travails of Moscow, Kyrgyzstan, the poorest of the newly sovereign states, introduced a new currency in May 1993. Designated the som, the new money was offered at the official price of four som to the dollar; the stability of the som depends on $400 million worth of aid and support from the IMF, the World Bank, and the Japanese government.[145] While Kyrgyzstan has few resources beyond its natural beauty, it does have a relatively well-educated population. More important, it has a president, Asker Akayev, who is a determined market reformer eager to privatize state property, free prices, and cut state spending.[146] To many Russians, Kyrgyzstan's initiative to dump the ruble is dismissed with anger. "To us this isn't even a serious word, 'som,'" one Russian businessman told a *Wall Street Journal* reporter. "In Russian it means a kind of fish."[147] But the central bank deputy chairman of the National Bank of Kyrgyzstan counters that in Turkic, som means a firm unit of currency.[148] For the citizens of Kyrgyzstan, it's clear that the som symbolizes monetary independence from Russia and a new belief in the future prosperity of the nation. As the premier of Kyrgyzstan, Tursumbek Chyngyshev, explains: "We believe we had no choice but to introduce the som. It allows us to escape from the inflation of the rouble and to create our own economy."[149]

An even more hopeful story surrounds Estonia's introduction of its own currency, the kroon, following a poignant request for the return of the gold it deposited for safekeeping abroad during the late 1930s. Much of the gold held in Britain, France, Sweden, and the United States on behalf of Estonia and its Baltic neighbors, Latvia and Lithuania, had been turned over to the Soviet Union long before or used to settle claims for property seized by the Soviets. But eventually Estonia managed to retrieve 11.3 tons of gold from its prewar deposits in foreign central banks, and together with substantial reserves of foreign currency, began issuing the kroon on June 20, 1992.[150]

As Gail Buyske, a banking consultant who has worked with the Estonian government, explained in an article published in the *Wall Street Journal*, the success of the nation's economic reform stems in large part from Estonia's special currency board system. Under this system, monetary policy cannot be used by government as a tool of economic management and the central bank is not permitted to print money to finance deficits; every kroon in circulation must be backed by foreign currency and gold.[151] Estonia's currency board maintains a conversion rate for the kroon of eight for one deutsche mark. The discipline associated with this approach has helped to bring down inflation in Estonia from almost 1,000 percent at the beginning of 1992 (under the ruble system) to an estimated annual inflation rate of 40 percent in mid-1993. The automaticity of the kroon's exchange rate with the deutsche mark has in addition spurred foreign trade and investment.[152]

While other former Soviet republics, including Russia, teeter near the edge of economic and political disaster, Estonia stands out as a model of stability and promise. There can be no denying that Estonia's early decision to abandon the ruble—it was the first former Soviet republic to create a separate currency—was a necessary condition for achieving economic success. And by imparting intrinsic value to the currency through solid reserve backing rather than merely by designating new paper coupons as legal tender, Estonia has established a sound monetary foundation for building a thriving free market system.

OSTRACIZED EASTERN EUROPE

Long before the nations of Eastern and Central Europe achieved political independence from the Soviet Union, they were already growing bold in their condemnation of the communist trade bloc that chained them to the moribund Soviet economy. Poland and Hungary, in particular, complained that their forced membership in the Council for Mutual Economic Assistance (CMEA) allowed them to be exploited economically by Moscow; if only they could expand their trade relations with the West, they lamented, they could earn hard currency and become prosperous. But when East European nations were set adrift from the CMEA (it had become mockingly known as the "council for the mutual exchange of inefficiency") in January 1991, they were forced to confront the fact that there wasn't much demand in the West for their relatively low-quality goods. When the Soviet Union collapsed later in the year, the nations that had been its satellites suddenly found themselves bereft of the huge trade partner that had always stood ready to absorb their exports, including shoddy consumer goods, in exchange for oil and natural gas at subsidized prices.

The truth hurt—financially and economically. The switch from trade based on political patronage to strictly hard currency accounting has caused economic pain. As noted by *The Economist* in July 1993, the gross domestic product of East European nations has shrunk by about a fifth over the past two years.[153] Even more painful, though, has been the less-than-embracing reaction of the European Community toward its long lost brethren. The gap between the rhetoric lauding free trade and the reality of closed markets has left East European officials feeling betrayed and EC leaders embarrassed. Having arrived at the economic doorstep of their wealthier relatives, the citizens of Eastern and Central Europe might have expected at least an invitation to join the European Community and a hearty welcome to participate in Western markets.

What they largely have received instead have been vague references about the need to meet certain political and economic conditions, such as providing evidence of a stable democracy and a functioning market economy, before being allowed to join the European Community. While the European Commission in May 1993 expressed its "clear commitment to eventual membership" for Poland, the Czech Republic, Slovakia, Hungary, Bulgaria, and Romania, it failed to set any kind of target date for their entry.[154] And the efforts of Eastern Europeans to gain free access to European markets have meanwhile been stymied by protectionist measures to prevent low-cost competition. The citizens of these formerly communist nations express disappointment and frustration; they sense they have been relegated to an economic no-man's-land. "On the eastern front we have the former Soviet republics, once our best customers until their money dried up," complains a farmer in Moravia. "And on the western front we have the rest of Europe, separated from us by a wall of tariffs."[155]

Members Only

The problem for Western Europeans is that their more generous impulses have been overwhelmed by concern for their own economic welfare. Recession has brought more basic instincts for survival to the forefront as EC industries and labor organizations seek to preserve markets and compensation levels. A sudden influx of cheap goods produced in Eastern Europe poses a distinct threat; after all, monthly wages in much of Eastern Europe are comparable to what Western workers earn in just one or two days.[156] To make matters worse, the areas where Eastern Europe is most anxious and most qualified to compete are industries that have traditionally sought government protection from imports: steel, textiles, and agriculture.

As a result, the European Community has imposed an array of tariffs, quotas, and outright bans against goods produced in Eastern Europe. Antidumping duties have been assessed on steel tubes and pipes from the Czech and Slovak republics. Hungary faces tight limits on the number of light bulbs it can export duty free—a blow to joint ventures with U.S. companies such as GE-Tungsram.[157] Poland estimates that it lost millions in export revenues as the result of the temporary EC prohibition on livestock from Eastern Europe enacted in April 1993.

The livestock ban, ostensibly aimed at preventing contamination from hoof-and-mouth disease, was particularly damaging to the cause of European market integration. "This embargo is protectionism and does not reflect the political promises of the West," declared Vladimir Dlouhy, the Czech Trade and Industry Minister.[158] Protesting that they were unaffected by the disease, Hungary and Poland quickly imposed tit-for-tat measures against meat and livestock imports from the European Community. Reporting for the *Financial Times*, Nicholas Denton observed: "The

East European reaction was unprecedented in speed, confidence and anger, with one Western diplomat expressing surprise at Hungary's demonstration of 'backbone.' "[159]

Demonstrations of backbone may be precursors to more aggressive displays of resentment and frustration as Eastern Europe faces the reality that the West is not entirely pleased with its new converts to capitalism. Instead of gathering the nations of Eastern Europe to its bosom, the European Community "is building a new economic Iron Curtain to silently choke off the former socialist countries," accused Hungarian Finance Minister Ivan Szabo at a 1993 news conference.[160] For these fragile democracies attempting to make the transition to free markets, rejection by the West constitutes a severe ideological blow. In the wake of the livestock ban, the former leader of the Communist Party in Czechoslovakia suggested to Prime Minister Vaclav Klaus that the Czech Republic's best friends were not in the West but in the former Soviet Union.[161]

Indeed, it is difficult to redress Eastern Europe's grievance that it is being exploited, rather than assisted, by the European Community. Since 1990, the European Community has gone from running a trade deficit with the core nations of Eastern Europe—Poland, Hungary, the Czech and Slovak republics, Romania, and Bulgaria—to reaping a trade surplus of 2.5 billion ecus ($3.2 billion) in 1992.[162] Given that the far wealthier European Community conducts a mere 3 percent of its foreign trade with its neighbors to the East, while Eastern Europe relies on the community for more than half its total trade,[163] it seems particularly uncharitable to impose stiff import restrictions on East European nations struggling to emerge from the damaging effects of central economic planning.

In recognition of its unseemly behavior, the European Commission moved in June 1993 to liberalize trade relations with Eastern Europe. Specifically, it agreed to speed up the timetable for phasing out import tariffs and quotas against East European goods. The transition period for eliminating duties on most steel products, for example, was reduced from five years to four years under the new agreements. The schedule for lifting quotas on agricultural products by 10 percent annually over the next five years was accelerated by six months. Moreover, starting in 1994, Eastern

Europeans won't be charged an average 10 percent duty for the reimportation of textiles or clothing that they produced for EC companies with materials originating in the community.[164]

Polish Prime Minister Hanna Suchocka in June 1993 expressed her disappointment with the European Community's revised set of trade concessions toward its poorer neighbors, saying it was "less than what we need."[165] But if East Europeans leaders fault the European Commission for what they perceive as a niggardly approach, they underestimate the rising mood of protectionism in France and other EC nations. A poll conducted in 1993 showed that two-thirds of the French, concerned about losing jobs and markets to cheap-labor countries, are in favor of limiting foreign imports into Europe.[166] Against such a prevailing attitude, it is difficult not to question the motivation behind French President François Mitterrand's warning in June 1993 that EC membership could pose "great risks" for the countries of Eastern Europe because their markets might be "invaded" by Western products.[167]

So while Poland, Hungary, the Czech Republic, the Slovak Republic, Romania, and Bulgaria—all former wards of the once-powerful Soviet Union that terrorized the West—console themselves with incremental reductions in the trade barriers erected against them by their fellow Europeans, the world should be contemplating whether it can truly afford to squander this most precious opportunity to spread the gospel of democratic capitalism and free markets. As John Major noted in September 1992, the danger of the European Community's preoccupation with its own economic and financial woes was that it would be distracted from improving relations with its Eastern neighbors. Europe would have far more to gain in the long run if it devoted its efforts to fortifying democracy and encouraging prosperity in these newly unleashed states. After all, Major observed, the rationale for the European Community goes much deeper than trade relations. By joining the nations of Europe in a common economic framework, war becomes all but impossible.[168]

AMBITIOUS LATIN AMERICA

There is no zealot like a convert, and Latin America's conversion from statist policies to free markets over the last decade is nothing short of miraculous. Mexico, in particular, has executed a brilliant about-face by discarding socialism and protectionist trade policies and instead embracing economic liberalism on all fronts. An April 1993 report published by the General Agreement on Tariffs and Trade notes that the structural changes implemented in Mexico since 1983 have transformed that country from an inward-looking state-dominated economy to "a largely open economy driven by private sector initiative."[169]

As investors pour money into Latin America and hail it as one of the hottest new emerging markets, it's useful to remember just how bad the situation was only ten or twelve years ago. The words "Latin American" generally preceded the words "Debt Crisis" in newspaper headlines; Mexico announced in August 1982 that it could not pay its debts. The entire region went into an economic and political stupor of debt and dictatorships that lasted throughout the 1980s: the "lost decade." Wealthy families moved their money to Miami and other offshore destinations. Economic growth stalled and real wages fell, while inflation soared to cover higher public sector spending. Per-capita income in the region dropped by close to a fifth and the area's infrastructure—roads, buildings, communications—became increasingly dilapidated.[170] In 1980, one in four Latin Americans lived in absolute poverty; by the end of the decade the already-dismal ratio had worsened to one in three.[171]

For those who believe that the true measure of success takes into account how far one has come, the Latin Americans deserve tremendous credit for casting off economic autarchy and being willing to open up their markets to foreign competition and outside investment. Their intellectual leap of faith to free trade has paid off. The flow of foreign capital into Latin America more than quadrupled from $13.4 billion in 1990 to $57 billion in 1992.[172] It is significant that even some of Russia's biggest banks, including the International Moscow Bank, have eschewed making business loans in Russia, instead opting to put money into dollar certificates of deposit issued by Mexican banks earning 5 to 6 percent.[173] Latin America is seen as being more ripe for stable economic growth, having gone further toward developing the necessary political, financial, and legal framework for supporting democratic capitalism.

Life After Debt

How did Latin America go from being a disaster zone to becoming a hot financial property? Why are foreign investors so eager to invest in Latin America's future? As Stephen Fidler observes in the *Financial Times*:

> Much of this money is responding to changes in government economic and trade policy. Governments have welcomed international capital, opened their economies to outside influence by lowering trade barriers, and slimmed bloated and inefficient public sectors.[174]

Instead of perpetuating the policies of high tariffs, high taxes, nationalized industry, and runaway inflation that reigned under earlier military governments, the new set of civilian politicians and young technocrats who have risen to power in Mexico, Chile, Argentina, and Venezuela have moved deliberately to restructure their economies in accordance with the doctrine of free markets. The proven winning formula for successful national development is a paean to Adam Smith-style economics: (1) open borders, (2) low taxes, (3) privatization, and (4) sound money.

In Mexico, for example, the average tariff on imports has dropped from 45 percent in 1987 (when Mexico joined the GATT) to 9 percent in 1993.[175] In addition to expanding overseas trade, Latin American countries have spurred the benefits of competition within the region by knocking down existing barriers. "Historically, Latin America's intraregional trade has been zilch," according to Peter B. Feld, director of the Enterprise of the Americas program at the North-South Center in Miami. "But in the last two years, intraregional trade has exploded," he noted in a *New York Times* interview.[176] By agreeing in early 1990 to phase out the tariffs that were an anachronism of earlier nationalistic policies, trade between Brazil and Argentina jumped 50 percent in 1991 and 50 percent again in 1992.[177]

Tax reform in Latin America has concentrated on moving away from old class-conscious economic models that sought to impose punitive taxes on those who were distinctly wealthy or who enjoyed large-scale business success. Until 1990, the Mexican tax system granted special status to "small businessmen" and thus discouraged them from growing into big businessmen. Why give up nearly tax-free status to move into the 35-percent bracket and be forced to handle additional paperwork as well? As reported in *Forbes*:

> Small businesses proliferated but remained mired in the informal economy, preferring hassle-free anonymity to government-harassed growth. Small businesses were exempt from breaking out value-added taxes on their invoices but could not sell their products to bigger companies that required receipts showing the VAT. Emerging companies could not issue stock without already showing a substantial balance sheet and offering a minimum issue of about $4 million. Thus much of Mexicans' economic vitality remained bottled up. Small companies lost growth prospects, Mexico lost economic growth, and the government lost tax revenues.[178]

In 1990 the Mexican government cut the top marginal income tax rate to 35 percent (continuing the reduction from 60 percent in 1986), reduced corporate taxes, and abolished special tax status for small business and other sectors of the economy. The results of the tax reform were discussed in an interview with President Carlos Salinas de Gortari conducted by the *Wall Street Journal*:

> *WSJ*: Have you gained revenue by lowering rates and broadening the tax base?

> *President Salinas*: Yes, we have. On the one hand we made tax rates competitive on international levels. I believe in the U.S. the corporate rate is 35%; in Mexico it's 36%.
>   We have also broadened the base: 20% of GNP was tax-exempt in Mexico. Imagine the loopholes. Farming was tax-exempt. So you used to find industrialists who owned a farm and all the profits went to the farm, which was tax exempt, and the industry was in the red. And intellectual rights were tax-exempt. So you could find businessmen who designed a logo and charged a million dollars for the copyright. So we broadened the base and the revenue is growing.[179]

Besides the additional tax revenues that have been derived through growth-oriented policies, Latin American governments have taken great strides toward improving the fiscal health of their nations by selling off state-owned enterprises, including such traditional sacred cows as banking, utilities, and agriculture. The Argentine government has gone so far as to sell off half of its interest in the national oil company it has held since 1922, Yacimientos Petroliferos Fiscales; this move constitutes the largest privatization of a state-owned company in Latin America. "This is the last big step in Argentina's privatization program," said Daniel Marx, Argentina's finance secretary, "and will be a driving force for increasing the efficiency of the economy."[180] The Mexican government sold off the last of its eighteen banks (nationalized in the throes of financial panic a decade earlier) in July 1992.[181]

Breaking the syndrome of inflation has been the key factor in Latin America's most impressive economic success stories. Burdened with a massive government deficit that stood at 16 percent of gross domestic product, Mexico had an inflation rate of 159 percent in 1987; in 1992 the government ran a surplus equal to 1 percent of GDP[182] and achieved its long-awaited goal of single-digit annual inflation in June 1993.[183] Venezuela likewise has reduced inflation significantly and also boasts an independent central bank whose sole focus is to maintain monetary stability; the *Financial Times* credits the bank's autonomy, which became law in December 1992, for "breaking the vicious cycle between political and economic stability" that destabilized Venuezuela in times past and prompted runs on its currency.[184]

The truly shining star of monetary reform, though, has been Argentina. Under the guidance of its economy minister, Domingo Cavallo, the Argentine government in April 1991 adopted a law on convertibility that requires parity between its currency and the U.S. dollar. The central bank can issue money only if it is backed by foreign exchange reserves, including gold. By establishing a fixed exchange rate with the dollar and rigorously applying the discipline of convertibility, Argentina has achieved a monetary miracle: inflation has come down from a raging 5,000 percent in 1989 to 14 percent in early 1993.[185] Side benefits from this striking achievement include a 9 percent annual economic growth rate in both 1991 and 1992, the creation of 670,000 new jobs during the same two-year period, and an influx of foreign capital. Tax revenues have tripled since 1989 and the Argentine government began running a budget surplus in 1993.[186]

No wonder Cavallo dismissed as "madness" suggestions from outside advisers that Argentina should devalue its currency to increase export competitiveness; he countered that such a move would only raise inflationary expectations.[187] Roque Fernandez, president of Argentina's central bank, likewise rejected demands from the International Monetary Fund for the government to impose limits on the heavy inflow of private capital. "We do not think this is a good idea," says Fernandez. "If capital inflows are too great, interest rates will decline sufficiently for [capital] not to come."[188] Argentine finance officials have little faith in the ability of bureaucrats to orchestrate economic and financial developments. "Either we believe in market prices or we do not," insists Fernandez. "It is not consistent to look for restrictions at a time when we are integrating Argentina with the rest of the world."[189]

In contrast to those nations that have brought down inflation and opened up their economies to foreign competition by reducing trade barriers, Brazil stands apart as the country that has largely failed to adopt free market solutions and continues to remain mired in poverty and misery. An estimated 65 million of Brazil's 150 million people live below the poverty line; according to the World Bank, the gap between rich and poor is the second largest in Latin America, after Panama's. Inflation is running at more than 1,200 percent a year. Brazil's budget deficit is almost 30 percent of its gross domestic product.[190]

Instead of trusting entrepreneurial initiative, the Brazilian government tried to manage the nation's vast economy by restricting imports—of computer hardware and software, for example, in 1984—and by imposing a freeze on wages, prices, and the exchange rate in 1986 in a misguided effort to stop inflation. Not surprisingly, inflation came roaring back within months. In 1990, the government tried again to suppress inflation, this time by freezing all personal and corporate bank assets.[191] For investors, that was the final straw. Where there are no rules, there can be no stability.

Brazil is rich in natural resources and has the potential to join the ranks of Latin America's most successful economies. But the impact of inflation is devastating. As an economist from São Paulo University, Eduardo Giannetti da Fonseca, explains: "Inflation breaks the connection between what you sow and what you reap. It's a school of opportunism where what matters is financial wizardry rather than supply and demand."[192] The financial director of Autolatina, William Cosgrove, notes the negative effect on productivity. "Everyone's working on the constant battle to recover last month's inflation rather than concentrating on competing with Korea."[193]

Brazil's president, Itamar Franco, is keenly aware of the destructive aspects of inflation. In a televised speech in April 1993, he stated that the value of Brazil's currency had become distorted; that in turn had distorted all values in society. "In an effort to preserve their assets and their family, many people have lost all references to the indispensable values of a civilized society," Franco said.[194]

But it's not clear that Franco will be able to muster the political will to carry out meaningful economic reform toward free markets. No progress seems possible in the absence of a sound currency. As a Western diplomat commented in the *Financial Times*: "Brazil's high inflation is damaging its credibility as a place to invest or do business. It's the world's ninth-largest economy and fifth-biggest country but people just don't take it seriously."[195]

Fair Weather Amigos?

The focus of aspirations in Latin America, particularly in Mexico, is to tap into the economic strength of the United States and expand the benefits of free markets and democracy into a common prosperity throughout the Americas. Mexico's President Salinas has remained true to the course of genuine economic reform, even in the face of tremendous pressures to revert back to government control of economic and financial variables. Salinas is determined to maintain Mexico's attractiveness to foreign investors despite the punishing effect of high interest rates on the domestic economy. Economic growth rates are declining and unemployment is rising as foreign competition takes its toll on inefficient domestic operations. Some economists, such as Mexico City-based consultant Rogelio Ramirez de la O, are concerned that Mexico is becoming too dependent on unstable foreign capital; they have recommended that Mexico devalue its currency by 10 to 20 percent to cool the domestic demand for imports and make Mexican exports more competitive. But Mexico's finance minister, Pedro Aspe, has resisted calls to manipulate the peso's exchange rate and has declared that a devaluation would ultimately lead to higher inflation rather than increased competitiveness. "It would be like committing suicide because you're afraid of death," declared one senior Mexican official.[196]

For Mexico, much depends on how the United States proceeds in implementing the terms of the NAFTA accord, which is intended to dismantle most remaining trade barriers and help cement the economic gains achieved in recent years under Salinas. Confronting the vast populist undercurrent of antigringo sentiment, Salinas has put his faith in the free market virtues espoused by Mexico's wealthy and powerful neighbor to the north. Washington's willingness to embrace NAFTA (which was first floated as an idea by Ronald Reagan in 1980 and has been vigorously pursued by Salinas since 1990) thus has political and psychological implications that go well beyond the economic and financial benefits expected to accrue as the result of its ratification. U.S. approval of NAFTA carries a strong symbolic message concerning the future of democratic capitalism, not only in Mexico, but throughout Latin America.

Contradicting that message, however, have been cries of concern in the United States over the prospect of losing jobs to Mexican workers, who are willing to work for lower wages. References by presidential aspirant Ross Perot to a "giant sucking sound" as U.S. jobs are drawn south play on the fears of American workers already hit hard by recession and gloomy economic forecasts. In tragic irony, just as Mexico seems ready to shed its resentment toward the long-hated Yanquis and begin working together to achieve mutually beneficial economic rewards, the United States is leaning toward protectionism and displaying signs of short-sighted nationalism.

Countering American workers' concerns over lost jobs are the statistics that explain how much is to be gained: Mexico is the fastest-growing market for U.S. goods. According to the *Financial Times* in June 1993:

U.S. exports to Mexico expanded to $44 billion last year. If, as is commonly supposed, each $1 billion of U.S. exports is worth 20,000 U.S. jobs, the Mexican market—growing in part because of the prospect of a free trade agreement—has been responsible for the creation of nearly 500,000 U.S. jobs in the past few years.[197]

Mexico is the United States' third-largest trading partner after Japan and Canada. Unlike Japan, however, Mexico has run a considerable trade deficit with the United States; in 1992, Mexicans purchased $11 billion more of U.S. merchandise than they sold to Americans.[198] Mexico's economy is crucially dependent on the United States' because about 70 percent of Mexico's total trade is with its dominant neighbor.[199]

The intensity of the struggle for acceptance of the North American Free Trade Agreement by the U.S. Congress sent mixed signals to Mexico and its fellow reform-minded nations in Latin America. While the treaty was ultimately approved in November 1993, the hesitation displayed by U.S. legislators to commit to a free trade relationship suggests there exists a latent hostility toward sharing the benefits of democratic capitalism across borders. When the rhetoric goes beyond arguments about the economic impact of removing tariffs and crosses the line into thinly veiled insults about the aspirations of whole populations, national sensibilities are deeply offended and real political damage is done.

Reluctance to fully embrace Mexico as a free trade partner also carries negative financial implications that can have devastating effects if foreign investors are frightened off by the seeming strength of protectionist sentiment in the United States. A sudden drop-off in outside capital flows would put pressure on Mexican officials to resort to the humiliating tactic they have so steadfastly opposed as a matter of principle: devaluing the national currency. While Aspe has acknowledged the "risk of social instability" if the economic and financial benefits expected under NAFTA are not forthcoming, he is clearly loathe to sacrifice the hard-gained credibility of the peso.[200] "Politically, it would be a disaster," notes Jonathan Heath, who heads Macroeconomia Asesoria, a private economic consulting firm in Mexico City. "Nearly every Mexican devaluation has been accompanied by the resignation of the finance minister and central bank governor."[201]

By emphasizing the opt-out clause in the NAFTA agreement, U.S. officials indicate a lack of confidence in the very ideals of free trade and global competition. Such wavering undermines the tenets of the accord and threatens to diminish its potential impact throughout the Western Hemisphere. When Mexico's willingness to abide by the rules of free markets stirs up protectionist resistance, the fundamental values of the United States are called into question. Faced with economic problems of its own, is the United States nevertheless dedicated to supporting democratic capitalism around the world and helping developing countries find their place in the global economy? If not, the efforts of Salinas and Aspe, Cavallo, and so many other courageous reformers in Latin America are seriously demeaned by the nation whose values once inspired them. The United States cannot deviate from its commitment to global free trade without risking the loss of political and economic good will embodied in NAFTA. A turn toward protectionism would subject the ambitious nations of Latin America to a profound sense of social rejection and ideological disillusionment.

CHINA: RED HOT

For sheer volume, the statistics on China are impressive. A nation of 1.2 billion people, China can boast—or complain—that it has 22 percent of the world's population living within its borders.[202] Indeed, whether it views its population as a burden to be controlled by the state or as a vast pool of human talent capable of creative, productive work says much about the ideology of the nation and its leaders. In the past, China has practiced communism with a vengeance; people who dared to show personal initiative or any other display of individualism were sent to the countryside for "re-training." The objective was to have each human function as a perfect cog in a vast communist machine controlled by the state. People who didn't conform to that plan, or who desired to achieve their own goals in life, were branded enemies.

But something has changed in China. Entrepreneurship, the very essence of individual initiative, has not only turned around China's economy, it has electrified the Chinese people. Barely tolerated at first, like a small boy permitted to steal food to feed the family, China's growing class of entrepreneurs is fast becoming an important political force with the power to influence the leadership of the nation. China is sensing its new role in the global economy as a massive producer and a huge market, even as it is wrestling with the fear of sudden, almost unimaginable economic growth and success.

Since the early 1980s, China's economy has been growing at an average of 8.6 percent a year, driven by the booming "special economic zones" along the coast, particularly the thriving Guangdong province.[203] The economic growth rate in China was 12.8 percent in 1992; in the first six months of 1993, China's gross domestic product grew by 13.9 percent and industrial output jumped 25.1 percent.[204] Those growth rates translate into markedly improved statistics for the per-capita wealth of the citizens of China. Although the official per-capita income in China is just $370 a year, calculations by the World Bank based on purchasing power parity measures suggest a more relevant figure of $1,950 per year.[205] Using the revised calculations, China has the third-largest economy in the world, coming in behind the United States and Japan, but leading Germany, Canada, and Britain.[206]

China's sudden rise to economic prominence has taken much of the industrialized world by surprise. It is one thing to smilingly acknowledge the improved living standards of a population largely isolated from the rest of the world; it is another to realize that China intends to interact with the other leading economic powers and to assert its presence in the global economy. China's foreign trade grew by 22 percent in 1992; with exports and imports totaling $165 billion, China ranked as the world's eleventh largest trader.[207] "Given economic growth and open markets," *The Economist* projects, "that figure could easily double in the next five years, and again in the next five, putting China into the top rank of the world's traders and helping maintain the growth rates of its Asian neighbors."[208]

China is here. Is the world prepared to welcome this nation of former Mao-adoring communists whose rush to capitalism threatens to become a stampede? Even as China's aging leadership vacillates between embracing capitalism for the prosperity it brings and disavowing it for the "money worship" it fosters, the leading nations of the world must also come to terms with China's new hunger for material wealth and economic opportunity. The nation whose leader in 1793, Emperor Qian-Long, refused to permit trade with the West, declaring, "Our Celestial Empire possesses all things in prolific abundance," has now decided that it wants very much to buy whirlpool tubs made by American Standard, Avon cosmetics, and shampoo from Procter & Gamble.[209]

Money Is Power

For China's new generation of small-scale entrepreneurs, *quiyejia*, the lure of accumulating personal wealth has become an all-consuming passion. "Everybody wants to do this," Xia Deming, a thirty-nine-year-old former cement worker told *Insight* magazine. Deming had quit his job a year earlier to open a tiny noodle shop near Shanghai. He exults: "I'm making money!"[210] Other former cogs in the state apparatus have made more spectacular progress under the new rules that permit individuals to take financial risks—and earn rewards. Bai Mei was a lowly worker in a state-owned metals factory earning less than $40 a month, according to a *Washington Post* account; in 1988 she quit her job to start her own business and is now a real estate developer on China's southern coast, with a net worth of nearly $2 million.[211]

While the communist *People's Daily* newspaper continues to rail against the "shockingly uncivilized" behavior of China's nouveaux riches and calls for the broad masses to be educated in "patriotism, collectivism, socialist thought and the spirit of working arduously for the great cause,"[212] China's new capitalists have redefined the great cause for themselves in terms of getting rich and acquiring fax machines and cellular telephones. And for those who have long argued over whether or not economic reform and political reform are inextricably linked, China's savvy young entrepreneurs go straight to the bottom line. "We don't have power, but we have money," observes Chen Mei, a twenty-six-year-old businesswoman who owns a Beijing-based computer company with her twin brother. Then she adds, knowingly: "With money, you can get power."[213]

Even though it might appear that China's new rising class of entrepreneurs has abandoned political aims in pursuit of economic gains, in fact the two cannot be separated, because China's burgeoning prosperity is creating a powerful middle class to which government authority increasingly will have to answer. Gone are the days when communist leaders could impose their decrees on a faceless army of peasants dressed in drab uniforms. In today's China, professors of Marxist philosophy at Beijing University must contend with the constant interruption of beepers as they attempt to deliver their staid lectures to students who are busy ministering to their entrepreneurial activities on the side.[214] As David Shambaugh, a professor of Chinese politics at the University of London, notes:

> These people are creating a middle class, they are creating wealth, and, as elsewhere in East Asia, somewhere down the road they will be creating a demand for an improved quality of life and meaningful political participation.[215]

Not that China is completely safe from the ideological tyranny that branded profit-motivated individuals in the past as "economic saboteurs" and squelched the development of private enterprise. In June 1993, Beijing officials reportedly ordered the execution by firing squad of several individuals accused of financial fraud, including a bank president.[216] When a group of Chinese migrants attempting to gain entry into the United States was repatriated back to southern China in July 1993, the response of Chinese authorities was to upbraid those who sought to flee—"they are selfish and want to get rich"—and to subject them to "some ideological work" to help them draw the appropriate lessons from their ordeal before being allowed to return home.[217]

Still, the cultural pendulum is swinging away from trumpeting selfless servitude to promoting individual initiative of the sort that leads to the accumulation of vast personal wealth and that often enriches extended families and whole communities in the process. Deng Xiaoping, China's supreme leader, gave a great boost to economic decentralization when he paid a visit to southern China's go-go coastal region in early 1992, took in the scene of frenzied growth and investment activity, and urged even swifter reform with the simple pronouncement: "Do it faster."[218] Approval from this huge nation's modern-day emperor unleashed a torrent of suppressed entrepreneurial instincts and stepped up the momentum behind China's lurch toward capitalism. Self-made millionaires are assiduously cultivating their connections with influential politicians and seeking to influence the pace and direction of China's economic and financial restructuring to favor increased latitude for business activity. "But the most potent force for opening China's political system is the rising middle class emerging from rapid modernization," reaffirms Robert B. Oxnam, former president of the Asia Society and a member of the national committee on U.S.–China relations. "They are office workers, industrial managers, private entrepreneurs, technocrats in government and private service, and substantial numbers of rich peasants."[219]

Newly empowered with a gratifying degree of economic autonomy, these individuals now become potential catalysts for democracy in China. Surely it is in the interest of the United States, Europe, and Japan to foster this development and encourage China's integration into the community of nations, both economically and politically. To do so, it is important to guard against protectionist barriers that discriminate against Chinese products. To deny consumers in highly developed countries access to low-cost goods from China that serve their needs is to lose the benefits of "comparative advantage" in international commerce. At the same time, Western governments should be quick to condemn authoritarian actions on the part of Beijing that seek to suppress entrepreneurial activity in the name of achieving "stability." China's Communist Party needs to be reminded that it cannot have it both ways. It cannot enjoy the fruits of private enterprise without granting the personal liberties that attend economic self-determination at the level of the individual.

The communist mindset persists in viewing the national population as an amorphous economic input to be channeled into productive labor in accordance with a central plan administered by bureaucrats. According to this world view, economic and financial development must be carefully controlled and directed; the rationale is thus provided for intervening in private commerce as deemed necessary by government overseers. The capitalist approach, in contrast, envisions possibilities for success in every individual, subject only to their personal level of ambition, creativity, and determination. It sees growth—even disorganized growth—not as a threat but an opportunity. Officials in China's thriving provinces are increasingly coming to understand and appreciate the difference. They see that economic liberalization and the rapid inflow of foreign investment have brought better jobs to the Chinese people and raised their living standards. For Ye Disheng, the vice-mayor of Tianjin, an industrial city in northeast China, the concerns expressed by officials in Beijing about an overheated economy are misplaced. "It's not nearly hot enough in Tianjin," he told the *Financial Times* in June 1993. "We want more heat."[220]

FALLEN COMRADES

If the formula for economic success in developing countries is to foster private enterprise and free trade, the recipe for disaster is just the opposite. And, indeed, the world's basket cases today are those countries whose governments have refused to trust in the aggregate economic decisions of individuals participating in free markets and, instead, have assumed an exalted role in managing the economy. A case in point is Ghana. In 1957, as *The Economist* explains, Ghana was the richest country in sub-Saharan Africa and had the best-educated population. It was the world's leading exporter of cocoa and mahogany, and it was a major supplier of gold, diamonds, bauxite, and manganese. Ghana's per-capita annual income was $490 (in 1980 dollars), virtually the same as South Korea's at $491. But an oppressive government, anxious to assert an ambitious model program for the new independent Africa, began nationalizing industries at will. It spent vast sums on huge, largely useless capital projects. It granted monopoly powers to government-appointed boards to buy up farmers' crops at controlled prices and took over international trade. The economic and financial impact was devastating: capital flew abroad, investment slumped, wages fell. Exports dropped from more than 30 percent of gross domestic product in the 1950s to just three percent by 1982. Ghana's annual $400 per-head income in the early 1980s was lower than it had been twenty-five years before. In the meantime, South Korea's per-capita income had climbed to $2,000. "Here was a potentially prosperous economy," concludes *The Economist*, "razed by bad government in the space of two decades."[221]

The message is clear. When it comes to government, less is more—certainly in terms of allowing economies to develop in accordance with free market signals. But in the areas where government should exercise authority, guaranteeing property rights and preserving law and order, it often comes up short. For those poor countries most desperately in need of outside investment, the inability of government to provide a reliable legal framework and a stable monetary environment effectively deals a fatal blow to economic prospects. Investors, by definition, are willing to incur financial risk. But in the absence of a dependable rule of law—where profits are easily confiscated through corruption or fraud, the imposition of rash government decrees, or blatant monetary manipulation—it is almost impossible to provide investment returns sufficiently high to compensate even the most free-wheeling of venture capitalists. There are too many reasonable business opportunities around the world to waste time with crooked politicians and social conditions that border on anarchy.

To speed development, governments should capitalize on the lessons from the past. Following the example of Mexico, Argentina, and Chile, they should undo the damage wrought by nationalization by privatizing state-owned companies. They should resist the temptation to interfere in foreign trade; for example, India's long preoccupation with bureaucratic "input-output analysis" to determine what goods it would allow to be imported from abroad acted as a straitjacket on economic growth. Governments need to reduce taxes to spur greater entrepreneurial activity and higher capital flows (and to compensate investors for the heightened risk factor in less-developed countries). Citing the excessively high marginal tax rates in Nicaragua of 70 percent, Haroldo J. Montealegre, an economic adviser appointed by President Violeta Chamorro, noted in June 1990 in the *Wall Street Journal*: "Moderate tax rates can attract back the many professionals, entrepreneurs and technicians who have left the country, as well as attract foreign investment."[222]

Finally, government officials in developing countries should concentrate on providing sound, convertible money. Argentina's 1991 monetary reform provides an excellent prototype for other nations to emulate; by backing the peso with hard currency and gold, Argentina has succeeded in imparting intrinsic value to its money rather than subjecting it to the vagaries of political wrangling and budget deficits. Russia's move in the opposite direction—its decision in July 1993 to invalidate currency issued between 1961 and 1992 marked the essence of arbitrary rule by men, not by law—undermines progress toward free markets and democracy. A system based on supply and demand cannot function properly if prices do not impart accurate signals to market participants. A solid monetary foundation is a necessary prerequisite for eliminating price distortions that compromise the returns from capitalism.

It is worth noting that Bolivia's determined, if rudimentary, effort to instill discipline over the issuance of money has produced gratifying results. In August 1985, the Bolivian government publicly adopted a simple rule: the government would not spend more than it received, period. The rule was effective on a daily basis; the finance minister could only dispense checks up to the value of the revenues in the hands of the Treasury that day. Spending for projects approved by Congress was subject to the availability of cash, and hence, many outlays were curtailed.[223] "By insisting that money would not be spent until the Treasury had received it," *The Economist* observed, "the government left no room for argument, and confronted the people with a gimmick-free rule they could understand."[224] Inflation in Bolivia, which had reached 25,000 percent in 1985, stood at 10.5 percent in 1992.[225]

By refuting the tenets of central planning and strictly limiting government intervention in the economy, then, developing nations have every chance to improve the living standards of their populations and find their niches in the global economy. More advanced industrial countries should not undermine their progress by inflicting tariffs against their exports or otherwise foiling their efforts toward achieving economic and financial integration. Sadly, even as rich countries provide aid to poorer countries and urge them to move toward free markets, they often impose tariffs and quotas at the same time that severely restrict the ability of low-cost nations to export their products. In September 1992, the finance ministers of twenty-four developing countries called on rich nations to buy more goods from the third world.[226] Pakistan's finance minister, Sartaj Aziz, voiced the complaint that the developing world had followed rich countries' prescriptions for pursuing economic growth by eliminating their import barriers, only to find that barriers against their own countries' exports remained as world trade talks bogged down.[227]

Federal Reserve Board Chairman Alan Greenspan underscored the same message in May 1993 with respect to Western trade relations with former Soviet republics and the nations of Eastern Europe. Noting that "there is no reason why these countries cannot substantially expand their exports in the years ahead," Greenspan added:

> However, in order to integrate the former Soviet Union and East European countries meaningfully into the global economy, the West must be ready to allow the goods for which these countries have a comparative advantage into their markets. Protectionist measures directed against these countries give these countries the wrong message—namely, that we ourselves are not prepared to accept the verdict of competitive market forces at a time we are endorsing the virtues and benefits of competition for these countries. The avoidance of trade protection and the reduction of existing trade barriers for manufactured goods, agricultural goods, and services, therefore, should be high on the international agenda.[228]

The most desperately poor countries, mostly in Africa and South Asia, still look to the rich industrialized countries largely for charitable aid rather than private investment. But as Europe, the United States, and Japan wrestle with their own domestic economic concerns, they are less willing to offer generous financial assistance to less fortunate countries. Indeed, when currency markets in Europe collapsed in September 1992, the problems of the developing world were largely shunted aside at the annual meeting of the World Bank and International Monetary Fund. "Donors are turning inward," explained Ernest Stern, World Bank managing director, to the *Washington Post*. As a result of "not dealing with their own structural [economic] problems . . . they are always in a fiscal [budgetary] bind," he noted.[229]

Not that official aid represents purely altruistic aims on behalf of the world's richest nations. As *The Economist* noted in July 1993: "Countries that spend most on guns and soldiers, rather than health and education, get the most aid per head. And about half of all aid is still tied to the purchase of goods and services from the donor country."[230] Criticizing the G-7 economic summit in Tokyo in July 1993 as a "huge missed opportunity" for alleviating the suffering of millions of poor people, David Dryer, director of the charity Oxfam, pointed out that the African continent was paying four times more on debt repayment than health care.[231]

Such dire situations bring to the forefront the need to emphasize the importance of free market solutions for humanitarian as well as economic reasons. Cursing the vicious circle of poverty and political instability, an economist for the African National Congress (ANC), Tito Mboweni, told the *Wall Street Journal*: "A good economy is vital for sustaining democracy, and democracy is vital for sustaining a good economy."[232] While the ANC used to speak of nationalizing industries and redistributing wealth through government intervention, its spokespeople now stress the need to make South African products more competitive. Anne Moore, general manager of the South African Foreign Trade Organization, a private enterprise that promotes trade, told *U.S. News & World Report*: "It needs input from outside. And that depends on the new government providing the right framework for investment. Then we can see sustained growth." Mboweni hopes to tranform South Africa into an exporter of manufactured goods, such as steel.[233]

But will the rich industrialized nations stand ready to buy the exports of these aspiring developing nations and permit them to find their economic place in the sun? By one estimate, according to *The Economist*, if rich countries abolished all their barriers to goods from the third world, the increase in developing nations' exports would be worth twice what they receive in aid.[234] Presumably, the wealthy importing countries would benefit as well. Once again, comparative advantage. The 1993 economic survey issued by the United Nations indicates an intellectual shift back to this classic thinking on economic development. Explaining the reversal of the UN's former position, which stressed government economic management and international aid as the keys to growth for developing countries, Jean-Claude Milleron, Under-Secretary General for Economic and Social Information, told the *International Herald Tribune* in June 1993 that new research indicates that "growth is led by the vitality of individual firms. And opening up a country to imports means less inflation, less protection, and more competitiveness by local firms, which also leads to growth."[235] That message should be taken to heart by the governments of rich industrialized nations as well as by their less developed neighbors.

4

Theory Versus Reality

For in every country of the world, I believe, the avarice and injustice of princes and foreign states, abusing the confidence of their subjects, have by degrees diminished the real quantity of metal which had been originally contained in their coins. . . . By means of those operations the princes and sovereign states which performed them were enabled, in appearance, to pay their debts and to fulfil their engagements with a smaller quantity of silver than would otherwise have been requisite. It was indeed in appearance only; for their creditors were really defrauded of a part of what was due to them.

—Adam Smith, *The Wealth of Nations* (1776)[1]

Money makes the world go around. At least, it makes goods and services go around the world. If we are to have a global economy that permits producers and consumers to recognize each other and respond appropriately to price signals, we must have a monetary system in place that permits individuals to measure the value of competing goods fairly and properly. If the money isn't right, the prices aren't meaningful; if prices aren't meaningful, markets cannot function.

It's one thing to rail against the currency chaos that exists today and to warn that monetary disorder threatens to undermine hard-earned progress toward democratic capitalism in many parts of the world. It's another to put forward an alternative monetary regime that can be expected to deliver all the tasks required of money—that it serve as a reliable unit of account, a meaningful standard of

171

value, an acceptable medium of exchange—and not be subject to intrinsic erosion or political compromise over time. The problem, though, is that theories regarding the issuance of money, such as the theory of floating rates, do not necessarily work out in practice. And some practices regarding international monetary relations (for example, Europe's pegged rate approach) have no theoretical validity but instead rely on government pronouncements that are gleefully challenged by private currency speculators.

The search for a stable international monetary order is complicated by the unique nature of money and human behavior concerning it. The story of money, as Adam Smith notes above, has largely been a story of deceit and fraud on the part of the money issuer. Like power in general, the power to print money tends to corrupt. Any anecdotal history of money includes some reference to the jewelsmith of old who safeguarded gold and other valuables on behalf of his clients and issued a receipt to acknowledge their personal claim to materials kept in his safe. These receipts, representing entitlement to stored wealth, eventually started to take on value of their own as they were circulated among individuals to make purchases or pay off debts. It was much more convenient to trade pieces of paper, naturally, than to visit the jewelsmith, open the safe, and physically transfer possession of gold or other valuables. Much safer, too.

But as the paper claims to wealth became as acceptable as the wealth itself—as good as gold, so to speak—the temptation arose to take advantage of the public trust by indulging in the excess issuance of paper claims. The storied jewelsmith soon discovered that by writing out additional paper claims, he could create purchasing power even when the value of the goods held in his safe was not sufficient to cover the titular claims to the physical wealth. So long as all the paper claims were not presented at the same time, the jewelsmith could manage to honor the occasional demand for redemption of a note in gold. The trick was to guess how much gold was sufficient to keep on hand to convince patrons that all their claims to wealth were perfectly legitimate and could be redeemed at will. At the same time, the more paper claims the jewelsmith dared to issue, the more purchasing power he could create and thus set himself up to earn profits by lending it to others for a price.

What sounds like an unsavory abuse of stewardship eventually developed into the button-down business of banking. Banks do create money on the basis of fractional reserves that do not come close to covering the amount of purchasing power generated by the issuance of loans. Their actions significantly complicate the task of controlling the money supply, because the paper claims created by banks are sold and resold after they are issued, each time functioning as purchasing power for the individual who utilizes them. Governments may have some ability to influence the amount of claims that can be issued by banks by redefining the fraction of reserves that must be maintained, by influencing the cost of attaining additional reserves, or by buying or selling some of the bank claims on their own account. But whether the presence of a governmental role within the banking industry serves to protect citizens against monetary abuse or instead constitutes an unholy alliance among "princes and sovereign states" is open to debate.

One thing is clear: Money is a product that people find useful, particularly as a medium of exchange. Money is also something that lends itself to exploitation because it easily can be reproduced in amounts that quickly violate the requirement that printed claims be convertible into assets. To validate the authenticity of paper money, people have often turned to governments and granted them sole authority over the issuance of money in order to provide a public guarantee of its value. But like the jewelsmith, or any producer with an effective monopoly, governments are prone to the temptation to abuse the privilege and reap profits for themselves by steadily shaving away at the ratio between issued money and the assets that constitute its underlying value.

What have we learned as the result of all our experiences with money, whether issued by private producers or governments? Can some lesson be applied on a global basis, some basic design that represents the best system yet devised for providing money to individuals so they can carry out transactions in an efficient, accurate manner without having to make allowances for the behavior of an exploitative monetary authority? In relatively modern times, the world community has relied on both a gold standard and a gold-exchange standard to serve as the basis for aligning national currencies into a unified monetary system. It has also tried a floating rate approach that permits individual governments to set their own monetary policies and then invites foreign exchange markets to sort it all out.

Should we be evolving toward something new in terms of providing good, solid money for national and international use? Or should we be thinking in terms of resurrecting the kind of system that worked well in the past and might serve the needs of the future global economy? Can we incorporate what we have learned from the Bretton Woods experience, or do we need to start from scratch?

There are plenty of theories around purporting to explain the role of money in society, chock-full of scholarly advice on how to construct the best monetary system. Discussed here are four major approaches, ranging from (1) floating rates to (2) government pegged rates to (3) commodity-backed money to (4) competitive private currencies. The problem throughout the history of money has not been the lack of academic rationale for various approaches; the problem has been the difference between monetary theory and practice. In theory, it seems possible to draw up a reasonable plan to ensure that a stable value for money would be preserved through time and across borders, either by controlling the number of paper claims issued or by guaranteeing its value through the full faith and credit of a powerful government, or by stipulating its conversion into physical assets, or by subjecting its production to competition in private markets. However, the goal has proved quite elusive in recent decades and quite vulnerable to the "avarice and injustice" of governmental authorities.

Human behavior is an important component when it comes to money. When humans authorize other humans to regulate the value of the standard by which their individual productivity and wealth is measured, they invite trouble. When the value of money can be manipulated to reward some at the expense of others, it leads to tension and turmoil. Whether it is governments squaring off against speculators, or citizens confronting their governments, or governments confronting other governments, the more the value of money is subject to the influence of individuals, rather than being fixed by law, the greater the potential for hostility and conflict.

DIRTY FLOAT

In theory, floating rates offer an appealing solution to the problem of aligning national currencies for purposes of carrying out international transactions. Governments ostensibly are precluded from manipulating exchange rates for their own economic gain because, just as in the stock market, the price of their nation's currency is determined by market forces. Demand for the dollar, say, is met by some level of supply; buyers and sellers of dollars make private assessments concerning the value of the currency and establish its market price at any given moment. The market for dollars, or any other currency, is deemed capable of incorporating all the relevant information pertinent to the value of the asset. Hence, the price for dollars in relation to other currencies is the right price by definition.

Even as the relative values of national currencies are being equilibrated through the magic of the marketplace, floating rates theoretically permit individual countries to concentrate on resolving domestic economic and financial problems without being distracted by the need to preserve fixed exchange rates for the sake of international monetary stability. Floating rates thus offer an intellectual out for those who resent the idea of having to constrain U.S. monetary policy so as to garner world approval. Instead of defining the value of the dollar in terms of some arbitrary metal and subjecting the financial health of the United States to the recriminating demands of foreign governments, why not let each nation mind its own currency and its own business?

By letting the market decide what different national monies are worth, government can shrug off the "standard of value" and "unit of account" aspects of money. Within the capitalist paradigm, there is no more respectable arbiter of value than the free market. So rather than establishing fixed exchange rates among currencies through governmental dictate and then insisting they remain forever in lockstep despite the changing economic fortunes of the countries involved, why not let those values float with the forces of demand and supply? Instead of being concerned with the inherent quality of a nation's money, based on its link to physical wealth, the floating rate approach focuses on its quantity.

Just Another Good

One of the primary assertions made by Milton Friedman, Nobel laureate and intellectual father of floating rates, concerning the nature of money is that it is not so much a standard or measurement tool with which to value assets, but that money is an asset itself. That is, people choose to hold money on the same basis they might choose to own a washing machine or other asset. "The most fruitful approach is to regard money as one of a sequence of assets, on a par with bonds, equities, houses, consumer durables," Friedman has written.[2]

We can readily understand why people choose to own washing machines or houses; they provide a useful service. But why would people choose to own paper money, which seemingly has no innate value? The answer is that it provides a useful service as well. When one has money, one can use it to exchange for other goods. The service provided by money, then, is its usefulness in carrying out transactions to procure other assets. The collective demand for money thus reflects the relative value people place on holding an asset that permits them to efficiently change or augment their portfolio of assets.

So money is just another commodity, just another good that people can choose to hold in the same way they might own cars or computers. It performs a service. Contrary to John Maynard Keynes's earlier assertion that the desire to hold money balances is dependent on interest rates—the higher the rate, the less money people keep as idle balances—Friedman held that interest rates exert very little impact on the demand for money. Much more important to people, in terms of deciding how much money to hold, was the "transactions demand."

Because people look upon money as just another useful asset, according to Friedman, one that enables them to carry out personal transactions, the demand for money tends to be stable. From this assumption it follows that any major increase in the money supply ultimately will show up in the form of higher prices. In other words, money matters: If you increase the quantity of money in the system, the price level will likewise increase. "There is perhaps no empirical regularity among economic phenomena that is based on so much evidence for so wide a range of circumstances," Friedman observes, "as the connection between substantial changes in the quantity of money and in the level of prices."[3]

If changes in the money supply are reflected as changes in the price level, then the occurrence of inflation or deflation can be traced to increases or decreases in the supply of money that are not matched by an increase or decrease in the level of available goods and services. Whether the amount of money in any system is dictated by its gold supply, controlled by a central bank, or issued by private suppliers, when the money supply is out-of-kilter with economic output, inflation or deflation will result. As Friedman summarizes: "It follows . . . that *inflation is always and everywhere a monetary phenomenon* in the sense that it is and can be produced only by a more rapid increase in the quantity of money than in output."[4]

Friedman's characterization of money carries important but seemingly contrasting implications for domestic economic policy and international currency relations. Domestically, it suggests that the Federal Reserve system, with its power to control the U.S. money supply, has an awesome responsibility to do the right thing. Mishandling of the money can bring about disastrous internal economic consequences. Internationally, though, the supplier of dollars cannot be held culpable because market forces will take responsibility for its value relative to other currencies.

Intuitively, it's not clear why the prescriptions should be at odds domestically and internationally. Friedman's monetary theory at home attributes so much power to the Federal Reserve, for example, that the mere mortals who run the system (particularly the chairman) might scarcely be deemed capable of carrying out their responsibilities. Because money is treated by citizens as a commodity like any other, it's vital that the government authorities who control the money do not put too much of it into the system or else people will endeavor to get rid of their personal excess balances by trading them for other assets. That trend, in turn, will cause the prices of all other assets to go up and, voila: inflation.

Domestically, viewing money as just another good means that monetary authorities must take their duties extremely seriously. Friedman does prefer to limit their ability to exercise discretionary control over the rate of monetary growth. He would rather establish in advance a stable growth rate in the money supply—one that would not vary from one month to another or even from one year to the next—and then charge the governors of the Federal Reserve Board with the duty to meet the target growth rate. As Friedman puts it, "The conduct of monetary policy is of major importance: monetary instability breeds economic instability."[5]

Yet sovereign monetary authorities seem to be off the hook when it comes to the international currency system. Friedman's approach of looking at money as just another commodity that can be subjected to the market forces of supply and demand takes away the idea that governments are somehow responsible for maintaining the value of their currency. That money should have any intrinsic value is no longer important; what matters is the quantity of money. And even the issue of quantity is relative since the value of the currency is determined by the aggregate international demand for a particular nation's money, and no government can anticipate such an indeterminable market variable. All the government (i.e., the central bank) can do is put out the supply it deems appropriate for domestic economic needs and let the outside world bid whatever it wants for the nation's currency.

Friedman contends that the market is the best judge of an asset's value and that the value of money should submit to the market's judgment as well. The "price" of money is not the interest rate; the interest rate is the price of credit, Friedman explains. The price of money is the quantity of goods and services—"analogous to the price of land or of copper or of haircuts"—that must be given up to acquire a unit of money.[6] Because the prices of other nations' currencies are likewise established in terms of other assets, the price of the dollar can appropriately be established in terms of those other currencies. The market for currencies thus should accurately reflect, at any given moment, the aggregate choices of consumers for different brands of money to complement their asset portfolio holdings.

Automatic Pilot

To make this theory work, the money supply must be expanded at an appropriate rate that is both stable and predictable. But Friedman is convinced that the erractic actions of monetary authorities not only fail to stabilize money and the economy but instead exacerbate the damaging gyrations. Rather than allowing them to attempt to offset cyclical variations in the domestic economy by tightening to curtail a boom or by easing to pull out of recession, Friedman would render them impotent with a long-run monetary growth rule that effectively puts control of the money supply on automatic pilot. In his presidential address to the American Economic Association in 1967, Friedman stated:

> My own prescription is still that the monetary authority go all the way in avoiding such swings by adopting publicly the policy of achieving a steady rate of growth in a specified monetary total. The precise rate of growth, like the precise monetary total, is less important than the adoption of some stated and known rate. I myself have argued for . . . something like a 3 to 5 per cent per year rate of growth in currency plus all commercial bank deposits.[7]

But Friedman is the first to recognize that central banking authorities are likely to resist any outside rules that diminish their importance or scope of authority. "As with any bureaucratic organization, it is not in the self-interest of the Fed to adopt policies that would render it accountable," he notes. "The Fed has persistently avoided doing so over a long period."[8] Friedman essentially accuses Fed members of exposing the nation to all the evils of monetary instability to preserve their personal power and prestige. In Friedman's view, U.S. central bank authorities invent all sorts of elaborate excuses to explain away their inability to deliver a steady growth rate in the money supply rather than admitting that the failures result from their own bungling:

> One chairman after another, in testimony to Congress, has emphasized the mystery and difficulty of the Fed's task and the need for discretion, judgment, and the balancing of many considerations. Each has stressed how well the Fed has done and proclaimed its dedication to pursuing a noninflationary policy and has attributed any undesirable outcome to forces outside the Fed's control or to deficiencies in other components of government policy—particularly fiscal policy. The Fed's pervasive concern has been and continues to be the avoidance of accountability—a concern with which it is easy to sympathize in view of the purely coincidental relation between the announced intentions of Fed officials and actual outcomes.[9]

Friedman may be attributing bad motives to a group of well-meaning individuals when the real culprit is the difficulty of controlling the money supply. Attaining preset monetary targets is not that simple. It is one thing to state in advance that the money supply should grow at a specific rate; it is another to make it do so. Friedman is the first to point out that central bank authorities are often ham-handed about achieving monetary targets. He notes that the lag between the time when action is taken and when the results of that action are manifested in the economy is unpredictable. He recognizes that the definition of monetary targets can be blurred by innovations in the financial industry. The development of "money market" accounts, for example, which enabled people to write checks on deposited money, changed the definition of money.

Yet Friedman nevertheless asserts that if the Federal Reserve were confined to behavior within a narrow band of restricted actions governing the money supply, economic growth could be much more steady and predictable. To bring that about, Friedman proposes to pass a constitutional amendment to impose a monetary rule on the Federal Reserve. In his book *Free to Choose*, written with his wife and fellow economist, Rose Friedman, he suggests the wording:

> Congress shall have the power to authorize non-interest-bearing obligations of the government in the form of currency or book entries, provided that the total dollar amount outstanding increases by no more than 5 percent per year and no less than 3 percent.[10]

But what might seem like a straightforward monetary rule to economists might be less comprehensible to nonexperts. While specialists argue over precise definitions of money and attempt to structure an array of monetary aggregates, the general citizenry is left wondering what the experts have concluded about money supply growth and whether interest rates in the future will be higher or lower. Realizing that ambiguity provides the shield behind which monetary authorities mask their failings, Friedman even ventures to propose the admittedly radical suggestion: Why not simply freeze the quantity of high-powered money—non-interest-bearing obligations of the U.S. government—at a fixed amount? Basically he is referring to the currency and bank deposits at the Federal Reserve. Freezing the level of this component of the money supply would effectively mean a zero rate of monetary growth. In conjunction with a plan to eliminate bank reserve requirements and deregulate financial institutions, Friedman proposes such a strategy as a way to end the arbitrary power of the Fed to determine the quantity of money. While zero growth in high-powered money might strike some as unnecessarily restrictive, Friedman explains:

> Zero has a special appeal on political grounds that is not shared by any other number. If 3 percent, why not 4 percent? It is hard, as it were, to go to the political barricades to defend 3 rather than 4, or 4 rather than 5. But zero is—as a psychological matter—qualitatively different. . . . Moreover, by removing any power to create money it eliminates institutional arrangements lending themselves to discretionary changes in monetary growth.[11]

Slippery Measures

Even as Friedman and other devoted monetarists continued to seek radical solutions to achieve the objectives promised by the monetarist paradigm, others were beginning to question whether the monetarist experiment hadn't already had a reasonable opportunity to prove its worth and failed. In the translation from theory to practical reality, problems arose of both a political and technical nature. The political problems reflected very human concerns over personal power, economic cycles, and future elections. As Friedman anticipated, government officials do not like to be restrained by strict monetary targets if it means losing the ability to influence economic developments. The voting public might not get emotional over whether or not a particular monetary target was achieved, but people definitely complain about recessions and unemployment. And because Friedman opposes having independent central banks—he believes it is undemocratic to concentrate so much power in a body free from political control—it is difficult to eliminate the possibility (or the perception) that Federal Reserve officials might succumb to pressure to accommodate the political agenda of the White House or Congress.[12]

The technical problems revolve around the basic assumption in monetary theory that velocity is fairly stable. As it turns out, the demand for money seems to be neither stable nor predictable. In 1983, British econometrician David Hendry, in collaboration with Neil Ericsson, tested the equations generated by the data for Milton Friedman's and Anna Schwartz's 1982 work *Monetary Trends in the United States and the United Kingdom* and concluded that the statistical evidence did not support the notion of a stable demand for money.[13] Moreover, as the definitions of money have changed with new innovations in the banking and financial industry, it has become increasingly difficult to measure monetary aggregates and even more difficult to meaningfully compare their behavior over time. Testifying before Congress in July 1993, Federal Reserve Chairman Alan Greenspan suggested that the M-2 money supply growth target, which had formerly functioned as a key policy guide, was no longer reliable and should not be viewed as an indicator of future Fed actions.[14]

Measuring the money supply is a crucial part of carrying out monetarist theory. The whole idea is to facilitate stable growth by providing the appropriate increase in the money supply to accommodate productive economic activity. But how can you designate a target growth rate and hope to achieve it if the target is constantly and unpredictably changing form? Redefining the monetary aggregates becomes an intellectual cottage industry as specialists attempt to reconcile policy decisions, economic data, and changes in selected monetary measures that take turns functioning as surrogates for the money supply.

Another complicating factor in measuring the money supply—certainly the U.S. money supply—is the fact that vast amounts of dollars have gone abroad and taken up residence in other countries as the local currency. The Fed estimated in July 1993 that nearly two-thirds of the $300 billion of U.S. currency in circulation had gone abroad; that figure represented a 14 percent jump within two years.[15] Cash comprises about 9 percent of the U.S. money supply. So while the inability to account for some $200 billion in printed dollars that may or may not ever slip back across U.S. borders does not completely invalidate the usefulness of domestic money measures, it is one more reason to feel less than confident about relying on estimates of growth in basic monetary aggregates as a strict guide to policy.

Finally, even assuming that the amount of money in circulation could be measured accurately at any point, the tools at the disposal of Fed officials have proved insufficient to alter the domestic money supply to bring it into conformance with the desired target growth rate. One of the most potent instruments, presumably, is the ability to influence money creation through commercial bank lending. Because central bank authorities effectively can determine the interest rate, the assumption has been that they can control the amount of loans issued by banks. But experience has proved otherwise; when interest rates are high, banks find themselves making more loans to enable troubled companies to keep paying on their old debts. And when interest rates are low, many private borrowers find they still cannot get financing from cautious banks. Regulatory overkill no doubt has had an inhibiting effect on banks' decisions to make loans to individuals and businesses. Even when banks are willing to lend, borrowers are likely to use the cheaper funds to pay back debt rather than to create new purchasing power. Federal officials have thus learned that their efforts to control the money supply by manipulating interest rates often amount to "pushing on a string."

Rigged Market

Where the monetarist approach seemingly has failed the test most severely is in the area of international monetary stability. In theory, by allowing exchange rates to float freely, differences in the monetary and fiscal practices of various countries should be smoothed out by the forces of demand and supply in currency markets. Because the underlying conditions that define a country's productivity or trade position relative to its partners tend to be fairly constant, with changes occurring only over a lengthy period, one could logically expect freely floating exchange rates to stabilize against one another. Indeed, the appeal of floating rates was that governments would no longer be able to execute jarring changes in the exchange rates to secure unfair economic advantage or to make sudden corrections to accommodate built-up pressures.

Free market money seemed the perfect complement to free markets and free trade in general. Market participants were expected to do a better job of coordinating currencies than government officials (who had an inherent conflict of interest). Even if floating rates fostered some confusion and caused exchange rates to move erratically at first, the market would eventually calm down and rates would stabilize as economic and financial trends became clear and observers could reasonably compare the impact of domestic policies among various nations.

Rather than smoothing out the economic differences among trade partners, however, floating rates seemed to exacerbate them. "Instead of exchange markets moving along a learning curve toward greater stability as time has passed," noted former Federal Reserve Chairman Paul Volcker some fifteen years after floating rates had come into play, "various measures of exchange-rate volatility—daily, monthly and cyclically—have plainly increased."[16] If the goal was to promote international monetary stability, the evidence showed that floating rates had failed to deliver.

Disillusionment with floating rates, though, did not mean finance officials of major countries were prepared to officially adopt an alternative system. For James A. Baker III, serving as Treasury Secretary in 1985, the answer was not to go back to a fixed rate system of the Bretton-Woods type, where official exchange rates were publicly declared and honored through the gold redemption privilege extended to foreign central banks. Instead, Baker sought to secretly engage foreign finance ministers in a plot to coordinate exchange rates in accordance with an overall strategy to drive down the value of the dollar. Participating governments would intervene in currency markets as necessary to move exchange rates among their currencies in the direction of preagreed target zones. The market, ostensibly, would still be the basic mechanism for determining exchange rates. But governments would become extremely heavy players in the market.

Clearly, such a blatant attempt to influence currency markets was anathema to the idea of letting floating rates determine the free market value of money. When Secretary Baker, assisted by his deputy, Richard G. Darman, began working to bring about a coordinated effort by the United States, Germany, France, the United Kingdom, and Japan to engage in intervention to deliberately lower the value of the dollar, they were wary of alerting the floating rate ideologues in the White House. According to Yoichi Funabashi, author of *Managing the Dollar*:

> Baker and Darman applied a gradualistic approach knowing that the Reagan administration suffered from an overdose of ideology and that some Republican heavyweights, Representative Jack Kemp (R-NY) for one, were keeping a vigilant eye on the course of economic policy making. After all, as late as the summer of 1984, the Republican presidential platform included a gold standard, while other conservatives clung zealously to floating exchange rates and nonintervention. Moreover, the President himself had put his political prestige on the "strong dollar means a strong America" bandwagon. One senior administration official said, "We did not say that it was a radical departure, in fact, within the administration, we took pains to say that it was really just a modest change, that it was not all that significant a change."[17]

But the new approach constituted a considerable deviation from the reigning practice of nonintervention. When Darman explained his ideas for achieving a new international economic regime by means of policy coordination and intervention in currency markets, Volcker reportedly responded: "My gosh, it is a big change."[18] But Baker and Darman proceeded to work out what came to be known as the "Plaza Agreement," an accord by the finance ministers and central bankers of the G-5 leading industrial nations to influence the price of the dollar against other major currencies through concerted intervention in the exchange markets.

Although officials from the participating nations were hesitant to acknowledge that the Plaza Agreement (enacted at the Plaza Hotel in New York in September 1985) meant they had agreed to distort the normal demand-and-supply mechanism of currency markets around the world, it was obvious that the agreement engendered a mutual obligation to steer the value of the dollar toward some preordained level. The word intervention was politically sensitive. So, too, was the notion that the dollar was going to be deliberately depreciated. To avoid accusations that they were rigging the market or violating the doctrine of free markets, participants shrouded their intentions by merely expressing their readiness "to cooperate more closely" and by indicating their general desire to see an appreciation of the yen and the deutsche mark. Baker and Darman scrupulously avoided any mention of a specific target value for the dollar lest they anger administration officials who were philosophically opposed to manipulating exchange rates; instead, they talked only in terms of the intention of the Plaza participants to "aim at" lowering the dollar by about 10–12 percent over a six-week period.[19]

Currency Collusion

Employing suitable rhetoric could not hide the fact that the finance ministers and central bankers of the five leading Western nations had agreed to engage in a cartel to fix the price of the dollar. Why did Japan go along with it? U.S. policy makers were accusing Japan of unfair trade practices; rather than risk large surcharges being imposed against the imports of countries that had large trade surpluses with the United States, Japan was willing to accept the less overt form of protectionism inherent in realigning the dollar–yen exchange rate through central bank intervention. Germany, France, and Britain grudgingly took part because they saw they also could be potential victims of U.S. protectionist measures. Then, too, the European powers had long argued that the U.S. position of benign neglect on exchange rates was naive. In their view, the dollar was plainly overvalued and they were concerned about the disruptive effects of a hard landing should the dollar suddenly start tumbling against their own currencies. If the market couldn't remedy the situation in an orderly fashion, governments were obligated to step in.

Baker and Darman did not claim to have deep knowledge of the field of international monetary relations, but they were consummate political players. Anxious to address the growing economic problems that were increasingly being blamed on the strong dollar—domestically and internationally—they were willing to exploit disagreement among leading conservatives over the proper framework for structuring international monetary relations. President Reagan was torn by the debate over whether floating rates or a gold standard provided the best monetary foundation for global free trade. As Martin Feldstein noted in a personal interview with Funabashi:

> [Reagan] has ambiguous views about exchange rates. On one hand he liked the idea of fixed exchange rates. He knew them as a young man. That was one of the solid things. But, at the same time, he realized that the exchange rate is a relevant price and that's part of believing in the market in general: to believe the exchange rate should be set by the market rather than government intervention.[20]

Baker and Darman appealed to Reagan and other stable money advocates with the argument that managed floating rates would be an important step toward establishing a new international monetary regime of fixed rates. At the same time, they emphasized to influential Democrats, such as Senator Bill Bradley of New Jersey, that a coordinated intervention approach would serve the interests of farmers and other exporters who were suffering from the overvalued dollar. Bradley had been the sponsor of a bill that would mandate government intervention in currency markets to lower the dollar against the currencies of the United States' trade partners. Senators Max Baucus (D.-Mont.) and Daniel Patrick Moynihan (D.-N.Y.) also had introduced a bill to steadily bring down the value of the dollar through concerted market intervention.

By appealing to the concerns of both Republicans and Democrats, Baker and Darman managed to portray their initiative to reduce the exchange market price of the dollar through internationally coordinated intervention as a positive development in monetary relations. Only a few astute economic observers caught the irony behind the strategy. As Robert Kuttner declared:

> If, say, Walter Mondale had proposed this scheme, it would have been dismissed as a naive call for global planning. . . . Like Eisenhower's pull-out from Korea, de Gaulle's accord with Algeria, or Nixon's embrace of China, it could have been done only by a conservative administration.[21]

It's easy to appreciate the cynicism inherent in such an observation. If floating rates represent the epitome of free market principles applied to international monetary relations, what happens when governments deliberately attempt to influence the price of their currencies by intervening in the market? Can they be considered legitimate players? Or are they market manipulators operating on the basis of the ultimate insider information?

What does it mean when the financial officials from the world's most powerful countries meet in private and form a pact to buy and sell currencies to move the relative market prices of the different monies to predetermined levels? While the professional currency hedgers scavenge for tips and inside information like so many feverish handicappers, the hapless entrepreneurs attempting to legitimately compete in the international marketplace are left to take their chances at the currency racetrack without being privy to secret negotiations that already have fixed the outcome.

The presence of a few privileged and powerful players with considerable financial resources fundamentally alters the nature of presumably free foreign exchange markets. On the pretext of "correcting trade imbalances" or "restoring competitiveness," government officials find it all too tempting to take market positions to achieve their own domestic economic objectives. Why address longer-term issues of domestic productivity or comparative advantage when an orchestrated jolt to the currency markets can seemingly correct the most pressing trade problems? As Kenichi Ohmae writes in *The Borderless World*:

> In the past currency fluctuated to reflect the relative purchasing power of nations. Financial fundamentals prevailed. Differences among nations in the rates of interest and inflation were adjusted so as to make the return on investment nearly equal in interlinked economies.
>
> Politicians and macroeconomists, not fully understanding this, started to intervene in the natural flow of money. Today "political paradigms," not fundamentals, have become the major force influencing exchange rates. When Reaganomics called for a "strong America through a strong dollar," the dollar got strong. When James Baker argued that the strong dollar was the cause of the nation's lost competitiveness and hence of its trade deficit, the dollar declined against the yen almost to one-half (from 240 to 120 yen to the dollar) in the year after the Plaza agreement.[22]

In retrospect, it almost seems laughable that one of the main arguments at the time for accepting floating rates was that governments would be relieved of the duty to support official exchange rates. Instead of having to maintain the price of their currency at a specified level, governments could concentrate on domestic monetary targets and defer to the market as the final arbiter of the relative value of their nation's money as measured against other currencies. Certainly no one expected that the amount of government intervention in exchange markets would be higher under floating rates than it had been during the Bretton Woods years when fixed rates still prevailed.

According to an IMF study published in the mid-1980s, however, official intervention had been "very substantial" under floating rates. Citing separate studies by John Williamson and Esther C. Suss, the IMF report conceded that official intervention after the dissolution of the Bretton Woods system was "perhaps even greater than under fixed rates."[23] This finding was despite the fact that the IMF, after amending its original articles to conform to the new era of floating rates, explicitly warned member countries to avoid manipulating exchange rates either "to prevent effective balance of payments adjustment" or "to gain an unfair competitive advantage over other members."[24] The IMF report acknowledges, somewhat defensively, that it is not enough merely to establish a set of principles for proper government conduct toward intervention in currency markets:

> The actual achievement of a stable system of exchange rates rests, of course, not only on the existence of clearly specified and well understood codes of conduct but also on their *implementation*. If a stable system of exchange rates has not been forthcoming during the period of floating rates, it is not because of the lack of codes of conduct.[25]

In other words, after tailoring its charter to accommodate floating rates, even the IMF was forced to admit that governments cannot be expected to abide by prescribed codes of conduct in the absence of any kind of enforcement mechanism. As long as they can get away with it (and official intervention in exchange markets is very difficult to measure because of the secrecy surrounding such actions), governments will find it overwhelmingly tempting to seek short-term domestic economic benefits by deliberately influencing currency exchange rates with their trade partners. If it weren't for the sovereign status of money, governments seemingly could be found guilty of violating antitrust legislation. "Adam Smith once remarked on the fact that any meeting of businessmen results in a conspiracy to raise prices," noted Sir Alan Walters in a 1990 essay in *National Review*. "I would add that any meeting of governments for the 'coordination' of exchange rates results in higher inflation."[26]

Governments, not surprisingly, don't see it that way. They defend their collective actions to counteract the currency market as being prompted by the desire to correct "exchange rate misalignment." Commenting on a U.S. Treasury Department press release issued in September 1985 to justify the need to intervene, I. M. Destler and C. Randall Henning observe in their book *Dollar Politics*:

> With understatement typical of official exchange rate pronounce-ments, they declared that "fundamental" economic conditions and policy commitments among their countries had "not been reflected fully in exchange markets" and that "exchange rates should play a role in adjusting external imbalances." For this reason, they con-cluded, "[S]ome further orderly appreciation of the main non-dol-lar currencies against the dollar is desirable."[27]

Interpretation: The U.S. government was getting ready to sell huge amounts of dollars and buy huge amounts of yen and deutsche marks. Moreover, U.S. trading partners could be count-ed on to "coordinate" their own currency buying and selling activi-ties to reinforce the effort by the U.S. government to compensate for what it saw as the shortcomings of the market in evaluating the proper rates of exchange among the world's leading currencies.

But what if the market had it right? As Henry Nau, a former Reagan strategist, asks: What recent shifts in fundamental eco-nomic policies had occurred? What major economic conditions or fiscal policies had dramatically changed that currency market par-ticipants had somehow failed to notice? The United States was moving in the direction of higher budget deficits and easier money. Was the effort to devalue the dollar orchestrated to alert currency markets to some unforeseen economic development? Or was its purpose to drive exchange rates to levels that would permit the U.S. government to perpetuate existing domestic policies and to pressure other countries to go along? Nau concludes:

> (T)he campaign to lower the dollar was never, as officials asserted at Plaza, an attempt to adjust exchange rates to reformed economic fundamentals. It was instead an attempt to override unreformed fundamentals (namely, fiscal deficits in the United States and structural rigidities in Europe and Japan) with loose monetary policy, not only in the United States but also in other industrial countries.[28]

Futile Exercise

Manipulation of exchange rates by government authorities does not solve domestic economic problems; it merely staves them off temporarily. But that reality doesn't prevent officials from proclaiming that an agreement to coordinate their activities in currency markets somehow demonstrates the renewed resolve of participating countries to address their domestic economic failings. In seeking cooperation from its leading trade partners to target exchange rates, the United States consistently stressed that each nation would improve its own financial and economic "fundamentals" to justify the exchange rates being pursued through intervention.

Recognizing the potential for high-profile exercises in international economic diplomacy to become substitutes for genuine domestic policy reform, Secretary of State George Shultz emphasized underlying economic imperatives in a speech at Princeton University in April 1985. As Nau recounts:

> [Shultz] warned that "intervention in exchange markets addresses only the symptoms of the dollar's strength—and not at all successfully." Growth, he added, was a "result of the interaction of sound national policies." Thus, the United States must cut budget expenditures "*now*," Europe "should reduce . . . obstacles to change and innovation," Japan should "liberalize the Japanese capital markets . . . to channel Japanese savings more efficiently to both foreign and domestic uses," developing countries should concentrate on structural adjustments, and "all nations should support freer international trade."[29]

Despite solemn vows to make the necessary improvements at home, however, most government officials tend to view international coordination efforts as a way to force offending trade partners, rather than themselves, to make adjustments in domestic policies. According to Destler and Henning, "each finance minister denied on returning home that the Plaza Agreement implied any substantial changes in his own country's fiscal and monetary policies; the major policy adjustments would be required of the others!"[30]

In short, the solutions seemingly achieved by manipulating exchange rates were not meant to provide breathing room so that each government could put its domestic economic house in order; instead, officials attempted to move exchange rates to accommodate chronic fiscal imbalances and indulgent monetary policies. The implicit message of the Plaza accord was that the United States would continue to run a huge budget deficit and the rest of the world would have to deal with the consequences. If trade partners such as Japan protested the United States' lack of budgetary restraint, the United States could blame its domestic economic problems on its trade deficit with Japan. By raising the specter of protectionist legislation, Washington was in a position to coerce Japan into cooperating to realign the dollar–yen rate.

What was the final outcome of the deliberate government effort engineered by Baker and Darman to lower the value of the dollar against the yen? It's true that, in the year following the Plaza Agreement, Japanese products became more expensive for American consumers. But instead of taking advantage of rising prices caused by the higher yen, U.S. producers of competing goods opted to hike their own prices rather than carve out broader market shares. Although the dollar lost about half its value against the yen from 1985 to 1988, notes Kuttner, the price of American cars sold in the United States rose slightly faster than the price of Japanese cars during that period.[31] Detroit automakers were anxious to recoup some of their losses from the early 1980s; rather than sell more cars, they chose to reap windfall profits from the currency gains. "Meanwhile," Kuttner observes, "the Japanese held their price increases to about half of what was indicated by the currency fluctuations—by shifting some production to the United States and other cheap-currency countries and by redoubling productivity improvements."[32]

Another aspect of having become a "cheap-currency country" was that U.S. assets increasingly began to look like bargains to Japanese investors. Japanese capital started flowing heavily into U.S. real estate, banks, and corporations, as well as Treasury bills and bonds. While the surge was no doubt welcome in some circles, it was the result of distorted financial signals, not legitimate investment opportunities. The financial capital was flowing overwhelmingly in one direction—from Japan to the United States. U.S. investors had little incentive to buy real estate in Tokyo at any exchange rate lower than 300 yen to the dollar.[33] Indeed, U.S. complaints in later years about the difficulty of penetrating Japanese markets would reflect the impact of Washington's efforts to manipulate the yen–dollar currency relationship. As R. Taggart Murphy, writing in *The New York Times* in May 1993, observed: "A combination of inflated Japanese real estate prices and a quarter century of dollar-bashing by successive U.S. administrations has made it impossibly expensive for U.S. business to establish more than a toehold in Japan."[34]

So asset prices in the United States became inordinately cheap for Japanese investors and spurred purchases not otherwise warranted by economic factors. Asset prices in Japan, meanwhile, soared beyond the price limits of prudent U.S. businesses. Responding to the exchange rate pressures, Japanese manufacturers strived to become even more efficient at producing goods for U.S. consumption, even though these goods sold for dollars that yielded substantially lower profits after being converted back into yen. U.S. producers merely soaked up unearned profits as their Japanese competitors wrestled with the blow dealt by U.S. finance officials.

The lesson from evaluating the experience of floating rates is that governments cannot resist the temptation to intervene and that government intervention causes perverse financial effects. Who ends up paying the price? Consumers, of course, who are deprived of the benefits of genuine comparative advantage. But also producers— the individuals who would prefer to avoid the risk of currency gyrations altogether and concentrate instead on delivering products that are competitive on their own merit. As Ohmae explains:

Plants and factories are not the kinds of things you put on a trailer or steamer and move about. They tend to be fairly well bolted to the ground on which they stand. You can close them down, of course, but you cannot set them running about the world like a pack of bloodhounds hot on the trail of sweet-scented exchange rates. Nor do these facilities exist in a vacuum. They have critical linkages with all sorts of industrial infrastructure—suppliers, distributors, logistics networks, academic researchers, labor pools, and the like.

Money slips across borders in the blink of an electronic eye. Infrastructure cannot. The weight of historical evidence shows that most producers will try to sit out unfavorable FX [foreign exchange] movements where they are rather than starting from scratch in a new location to build up whole new infrastructural networks. Even if they were tempted to do otherwise, the time scale is off. By the time they get their new networks in place, the FX rates may have shifted again.[35]

Governments do their citizens no favor by colluding in secret to alter the basic terms of international competition in ways that have nothing to do with the inherent value of goods and services. Manipulating exchange rates may seem an effective way to temporarily defuse protectionist pressures. Protectionism, though, is hardly the answer in the long run for nations whose competitiveness is declining in global markets. Improved productivity, greater efficiency, and higher quality should be the goals for those who aspire to successfully compete internationally.

As far as reconciling theory and practice, the dirty float system that exists today provides a corrupt basis for international monetary relations. The purported advantage of a freely floating currency regime is its ability to transcend governmental interference in favor of market-determined forces; that objective has been irrevocably compromised by actual practice. Governments have proven to be the worst abusers of the free market approach to exchange rates by shamelessly engaging in currency price-fixing as they seek to reap unfair advantages at the expense of less powerful market participants.

PEGGED RATES

What if the colluders decided to go public? That is, what if governments stated up front what set of exchange rates they were attempting to achieve among their currencies and then intervened in the markets as necessary to maintain that preannounced matrix of rates? Rates would be managed as before in the sense that governments would manipulate the market value of their currencies by buying or selling them in sufficient quantities to neutralize market pressures up or down, but at least the arrangements would all be very public. Once governments agreed to a certain set of exchange rates among their currencies, the world at large would be informed. Private citizens involved in foreign trade could count on a certain amount of currency stability across borders, at least to the extent that governments fulfilled their responsibility to intervene automatically and to whatever degree necessary whenever market forces pushed the price of one nation's money out of kilter against other nations' monies.

To take on such a responsibility, though, is to accept certain constraints on domestic financial behavior. No government can forever resist overwhelming market pressures that drive the value of its currency up or down in response to fundamental economic factors. At some point, each government must reconcile its own budgetary and monetary policies with the value of its currency in the global economy; otherwise, it will find itself unable to make a market in its own money and agreed-upon exchange rates with other currencies will become unsustainable.

If nations thus resolve to keep exchange rates among themselves stable over time, they are likewise bound to pledge that they will abide by certain restrictions limiting the scope of their internal spending and financing decisions. In essence, they have to agree in advance to sacrifice a certain amount of national economic sovereignty in order to reassure other nations participating within the fixed rate system that they will be able to uphold their end of the bargain. They must convince their trading partners that they will have the capacity to support a prespecified exchange rate and that they will refrain from policies that would put the value of their currency out of sync with market assessments.

But the matter of constraints forces the issue: Are nations ready to work together to achieve international monetary stability if it means placing a higher priority on global currency relations than on domestic financial and economic problems? Where should a government's loyalties lie—in promoting the narrow economic interests of its citizens or in preserving monetary stability for the sake of the global economy? As distinguished economist and former Federal Reserve Governor Henry Wallich expressed it, there are four ways in which nations recognize that they are not alone in the world: through coordination, harmonization, cooperation, and consultation. These terms suggest, in descending order, the degree of constraint exercised over their individual actions. " 'Cooperation' falls well short of 'coordination,' a concept which implies a significant modification of national policies. . . . It falls short also of 'harmonization,' a polite term indicating a somewhat greater reluctance to limit one's freedom of action. But 'cooperation' is more than 'consultation.' "[36]

Europe's Experiment

In the aftermath of the collapse of the Bretton Woods system, the countries of Europe sought to cling to one another to preserve some semblance of monetary order. If the United States would no longer serve as the anchor for international monetary relations, at least they could find some comfort in relying on each other to cooperate within European borders. Setting up a sort of mini-Bretton Woods system, minus the provision for gold convertibility, the Europeans decided to establish a mechanism for pegging their currencies to each other while maintaining a joint float against the dollar. Chancellor Helmut Schmidt of Germany and President Valéry Giscard d'Estaing of France announced in 1978 their intention to create a "zone of monetary stability" that would link the currencies of Europe together and stimulate increasing economic and financial integration among European nations. This initiative brought forth the birth of the European Monetary System (EMS) on March 13, 1979.

Besides ensuring monetary stability, characterized by both low inflation and stable exchange rates among participating European nations, it was hoped that the EMS would improve policy coordination and spur the economic convergence of the countries involved. But during the first few years, from 1979 to 1983, individual member countries continued to function independently, with diverse levels of inflation, budget deficits, and monetary policies. While the goal was to preserve a set of fixed exchange rates, realignments among the EMS currencies took place frequently. Afraid of being too rigid, the participating countries overemphasized the need for flexibility and ended up with a slow-motion floating rate system.

By striving for more stable rates among their currencies, though, and by lauding the benefits of economic convergence, the Europeans were giving expression to the long-held dream of a Europe without frontiers. Separate nations would intertwine their fates by giving up a certain amount of individual sovereignty for the sake of achieving a common economic objective. If not actually becoming a single entity, at least they would create a level playing field to carry out trade and financial relations among themselves.

At the same time that Europe's new monetary system was implemented in 1979, a new monetary unit was invented. The new unit was a concept more than an actual currency. Its very invention, though, even in the abstract, meant that the nations of Europe were serious about the longer-term goal of melding together in the future to stand as a unified economic entity, perhaps one unified politically and even militarily as well. The new money was designated the "ecu," or European currency unit. According to the 1979 agreement, the ecu was to be "at the centre of the European Monetary System" and would be defined on the basis of the value and composition of the European unit of account, which in turn was defined as the weighted average value of the European member currencies.[37] A set of pseudo-fixed exchange rates among the European currencies was established, with each nation's currency being specified in terms of the ecu. As laid out in the 1979 agreement:

> —each currency will have an ecu-related central rate and the central rates will be used to establish a grid of bilateral parities or central rates,
> —fluctuation margins of 2.25% will be fixed around these bilateral central rates, although Member States not at present participating in the narrower margins mechanism may in the initial stage of the European Monetary System opt for wider margins of up

to 6%, which must be progressively reduced as soon as economic
conditions permit.[38]

So the original members of the EMS were expected to keep
their currencies linked to one another at fixed rates that permitted some fudging of plus or minus 2.25 percent. If a nation's currency went above or below the established central rate of
exchange with another currency by more than the stipulated percentage, that member would be guilty of having allowed its currency to drift out of the target range defined by the plus or minus
2.25 percent band around the central rate. Participating governments were expected to intervene in the market if currencies
started to approach the top or bottom of their allowable range by
buying and selling as necessary to push the exchange rate closer
to the central parity rate.

Ostensibly, the EMS system did not have a key currency or outside commodity anchor. The grid of desired exchange rates was
spelled out in terms of the ecu value of member currencies, and
target zones were set up for official government reference. Peer
pressure among the member nations was deemed sufficient to
provide the necessary incentive to force them to keep their currencies within the acceptable range so that the whole system
would hold together.

Starting in 1984, EMS member countries started in earnest to stay
within the allowable ranges and to coordinate their monetary policies so as to achieve currency stability within Europe. Not only did
governments cooperate on intervention tactics, they also seemed to
embrace the notion of their economic interdependence and to work
more seriously toward convergence on key economic variables such
as interest rates and inflation. They agreed on the need to remove all
restrictions on capital movements as an important step toward
achieving a single European market. As governments took actions
that gave momentum to the single Europe movement, financial securities began to be denominated in terms of ecus. Corporate trea-
surers, along with public debt issuers, indicated their increasing
acceptance of the new currency unit as a legitimate entity. The ecu, a
basket of various European currencies, was on its way to becoming a
prototype for a full-fledged single European currency.

Trouble Beneath the Surface

The closer the concept of European economic and monetary union moved toward reality, the more friction developed between those who were eager to fulfil the vision of a unified Europe and those who felt increasingly threatened by the potential loss of political identity and economic self-determination. The acronym for European monetary union, EMU, figured prominently in the highest levels of debate over Europe's destiny. Attempting to convey the meaning of EMU to a largely American reading audience, Anne Bagamery wrote in *Investment Vision* magazine:

> Depending on which authority you consult, this controversial entity is either "critical to the completion of the single European market" (European Commission President Jacques Delors), "socialism by the back door" (former U.K. Prime Minister Margaret Thatcher), or "a flightless bird of Australia, weighing over 100 pounds" (*Encyclopaedia Brittanica*)[39]

Was Europe finally ready to bury old hostilities and redefine itself in continental terms? Could the independent nations of Europe merge into a single financial system with a single currency—run by a single central bank and subject to a single set of financial regulations—without submerging their individual identities as well? Who would control this vast empire? Countries with glorious histories of their own were suddenly wary about the possibility of having their distinctive cultures swallowed up by the concept of a behemoth single Europe.

In response to such concerns, proposals surfaced for separating out the monetary issue from broader plans for unification. All the European nations could see the advantages of using a single currency to carry out intra-European business; transactions costs could be eliminated and exchange rate risk would no longer exist. If it were simply a matter of unifying the currencies without having to delve too deeply into questions concerning political control over the monetary authority, EMU would not be such a contentious issue.

But the power to issue money is intensely political, and no government gives up that power lightly or without recourse. The rules must be clearly defined before any nation will accept an agenda that would ultimately result in the loss of its monetary sovereignty. To whom will the power to regulate the supply of money on behalf of all nations be granted? Will it be an independent central bank whose members are beyond the political influence of any one country? Given that human beings are necessarily citizens of some country or another, is it even possible to create such an institution? Could the chairman of a so-called supranational central bank proceed with monetary policies that were seen as benefiting his homeland at the expense of other countries without being accused of subtle favoritism, if not blatant nationalism?

In their quest to unite currencies, pro-European officials were diligent to step lightly around such sensitive questions. From the beginning, they avoided making overt reference to any hierarchical standing among national currencies or monetary authorities. Instead, rhetorical prominence was granted to the ecu, which, while still an artificial currency construct, served as the symbol of European monetary cooperation. The ecu was designated Europe's currency because it represented the politically neutral weighted inputs of member countries' monies. Instead of explicitly identifying an anchor currency on which the value of all the other currencies would be determined, the Europeans evaded the issue by focusing attention on the ecu.

But such a strategy of denial could not go on indefinitely. The ecu could never define the value of Europe's currencies; it could only reflect them. To portray the ecu as some kind of foundation for a monetary system was to suggest a system of currencies tethered to each other like a cluster of floating balloons, but with no guide line connecting them to the ground. If Europe wanted exchange rate stability and low inflation, it would have to link its system to something more solid than a monetary accounting construct.

Of course, there had been an anchor currency all along and there was a national monetary authority at the top of the European hierarchy: Germany. Whether or not they cared to acknowledge it explicitly, the governments of Europe had effectively acceded the power to dictate monetary policy to Germany's central bank, the Bundesbank. Each nation quietly endeavored to keep the value of its currency aligned with the deutsche mark.

Europe's choice was hardly a novel approach to achieving international monetary stability; Germany's role in the European monetary system could be seen as paralleling the former U.S. role in the Bretton Woods system. As the anchor country, Germany was expected to prudently manage its money supply so that other participants only had to make sure that their currencies stayed firmly pegged to the anchor currency. To the extent that people in other European nations believed Germany would exercise restraint and deliver sound money, they thought the soundness of their own nation's money was likewise ensured. According to U.S. economist Paul Krugman:

> In order to control inflation, a central bank needs both a strong backbone and credibility with the public.
>
> What the nations of Western Europe discovered during the 1980s was that they could stiffen their own backbones and gain credibility with the marketplace, by tying their currencies to the Deutsche mark. West Germany has a famed commitment to price stability, rooted in bitter memories of the great inflation of the 1920s, reinforced by a generous welfare state that makes it easier to accept the pain of recession. In the 1980s, European nations found that by accepting German leadership, they could hitch a ride on that German resolve.[40]

Germany earned the top spot not just because it had credibility in fighting inflation but also because it was a bastion of economic power in Europe that accounted for almost one-third of Europe's total GNP. Krugman notes that the United States produces nearly 40 percent of the industrial world's output—"yet the days when the U.S. could dictate global monetary policy are long gone," he asserts.[41] The combination of the two factors, considerable economic strength and a demonstrated commitment to price stability, cast Germany into the role of disciplinarian for Europe's monetary system.

For all the egalitarianism implied by the ecu, then, the currency order among European countries was actually controlled by Germany, that is to say (and the distinction would figure crucially in the turmoil to follow), by the Bundesbank. At the time, this arrangement seemed good. One reason Germany's monetary policy was perceived to be so resolutely anti-inflationary was precisely because Germany's central bank was reputed to enjoy considerable independence from political institutions. Monetary decision making was thus thought to be insulated from political pressures to accommodate indulgent fiscal policies with easy money. Certainly, the Bundesbank turned in an admirable performance during the 1980s; Germany's annual inflation rate averaged a mere 3 percent.

Deutschland uber Alles?

Even as the nations of Europe linked their monetary policies to the reliable German anchor, it was never clear that Germany particularly relished the role or sought the responsibility. As more countries began to cling to the Bundesbank's monetary policy to help stabilize their economies, Germany began to fear that the additional burden might pull it adrift from its own rock solid commitment to low inflation. Moreover, it was becoming clear that the European monetary system, which now relied on the deutsche mark for its credibility, was viewed as merely an interim step on the way to achieving full European economic and monetary union. If so, German central bank authorities would want some guarantees that the future system would be at least as good as the one they already had. According to an account published in March 1989 in *Europe* magazine about the "Delors Committee" meetings:

> West Germany's independent Bundesbank made clear that it would agree to the creation of a European central bank only if it were as independent of E.C. Governments as the Bundesbank is of Bonn and had price stability as its prime goal. A common currency in the Bundesbank's eyes would have to be every bit as solid as the German mark.[42]

Germany had earned the right to make such demands. As long as Germany continued to maintain its reputation for putting monetary stability ahead of politics, it was altogether appropriate for the Bundesbank to raise concerns about the structural independence of any future European central bank. It also was understandable that Germany sought price stability as the chief objective for any supranational monetary authority, even if it meant undertaking politically unpopular measures such as raising interest rates. To remain unperturbed in the face of a domestic economic crisis and to rise above the fray of political demands were considered the duties of any central bank worth its salt. But then the Berlin Wall came down. In November 1989, to the deep satisfaction of observers around the world, jubilant protesters began to physically dismantle the Berlin Wall after months of mass demonstrations and the furtive exodus of thousands of East Germans via Hungary. The long-suppressed hope that Germany's two halves might one day be rejoined suddenly loomed as a distinct possibility. Over the next eight months, German and U.S. officials carried out high-level negotiations with their counterparts in the Kremlin to ensure not only that German unity would not be opposed by Moscow but that the new Germany would be allowed to retain its membership in the North Atlantic Treaty Organization (NATO). The Soviets were willing, but there would be a price: The Germans had to promise that they would (1) redefine the mission of the NATO alliance and (2) lobby the other major economic powers for a $15 billion aid package for the Soviet Union. In exchange, the Soviets would acquiesce on unification and recognize Germany as a fully sovereign nation, free to join whatever bloc or alliance it wished. Following a private meeting between German Chancellor Helmut Kohl and Soviet President Mikhail Gorbachev, the deal was settled and an accord was announced on July 16, 1990. "From that moment on," reported correspondents for the *Washington Post*, "the chancellor could not stop smiling. He wore the huge grin of a little boy, even in public. He was the chancellor of German unity."[43]

Kohl's grin later became strained, however. The euphoria over unification was dampened by more mundane questions concerning how to pay for it. Attempting to reconcile East Germany's feeble ostmark with West Germany's vibrant deutsche mark was causing great financial consternation. Against the advice of Karl Otto Pöhl, president of the Bundesbank at the time, Kohl insisted that monetary union with East Germany should proceed quickly and that ostmarks should be converted into deutsche marks at a rate extremely favorable for the East Germans. Pöhl's first reaction was to call the idea a "fantastical illusion."[44] But as reported in *The Economist*, Pöhl soon realized he had little choice in the matter. Despite the Bundebank's much-vaunted independence, it did not have the power to decree where the deutsch mark could be used. And its control over the money supply was protected only by a simple law that could be amended by the government should a sufficent political imperative present itself.[45]

East Germans ended up being allowed to exchange up to 4,000 ostmarks per person into deutsche marks on a one-for-one basis. Before unification, the official rate of exchange had been three ostmarks for one deutsche mark, with a considerably higher black market rate that had ranged between five and ten ostmarks for one deutsche mark. The one-for-one conversion rate was expected to increase the growth of the money supply by some 13 percent—much more than East Germany's contribution to gross national product.[46] In addition, government spending to help alleviate the social costs of rebuilding eastern Germany's crumbling economy was expected to push the nation's budget deficit as high as 125 billion deutsche marks ($65 billion) in 1991—more than five times greater than its budget deficit for 1990.[47]

Suddenly Germany seemed less interested in preserving its reputation for fiscal prudence and more preoccupied with making Germany whole at any price. The other nations of Europe began to wonder if they hadn't perhaps counted too much on the notion that Germany would continue to place the highest priority on monetary stability even in the face of pressing domestic economic and social problems. In an attempt to keep a lid on inflation while accommodating the costs of unification, the Bundesbank began to raise interest rates steeply. The prescription may have made sense for Germany, given its unique circumstances and its deep-rooted aversion to a runaway money supply, but it was hardly the formula the rest of Europe wanted to embrace. The other European nations had little to gain economically from the increased consumer demand of East Germans for West German goods, yet they found themselves paying the price of unification. They were locked into a monetary policy that was aimed at staving off inflation in Germany rather than fueling economic growth throughout the rest of Europe.

The example of Germany brings to the forefront the issue of whether it makes sense to rely on any single country or any single central bank, even one ostensibly immune to political loyalties, to serve as the anchor for an international monetary system. Concern over German actions quickly took on ugly overtones in the European debate over economic and monetary union. Shortly after German monetary union was enacted on July 1, 1990, the late Nicholas Ridley, a senior British Cabinet minister, was quoted in the magazine *The Spectator* as suggesting that Germany had ulterior motives in promoting European monetary union. "This is all a German racket designed to take over the whole of Europe," Ridley said. "It has to be thwarted. This rushed takeover by the Germans on the worst possible basis, with the French behaving like poodles to the Germans, is absolutely intolerable."[48]

Ridley had little better to say about the prospect of yielding national economic sovereignty to centralized European institutions, which he likened to the very symbol of German tyranny:

> Seventeen unelected rejected politicians with no accountability to anybody, who are not responsible for raising taxes, just spending money, who are pandered to by a supine parliament which also is not responsible for raising taxes, already behaving with an arrogance I find breathtaking—the idea that one says, 'O.K., we'll give this lot our sovereignty,' is unacceptable to me. I'm not against giving up sovereignty in principle, but not to this lot. You might just as well give it to Adolf Hitler, frankly.[49]

A System Undone

Over the next three years, the European monetary system was subjected to mounting political tensions and increasing financial strains. The exchange rate mechanism through which European currencies were aligned with the deutsche mark by means of central bank intervention was pummeled by speculative pressures as currency traders saw signs of weakness and lack of resolve among European governments to move forward on monetary union. The currency chaos that took place in September 1992 gravely injured the cause of a single currency and left deep psychological scars;

the leading nations of Europe no longer seemed to share the same aspirations, let alone the same economic circumstances.

Even so, the system still limped along for almost another year—held together by an unspoken determination between France and Germany to prove that European solidarity would not succumb to currency pressures—until August 1, 1993, when an emergency meeting of Europe's finance ministers resulted in a decision to widen the bands around central exchange rates from the earlier 2.25 percent margins to much more relaxed margins of 15 percent. The meeting had been prompted by a tumultuous war of nerves the prior week between central banks and currency speculators and by an increasing sense among government officials that the speculators were bound to win.

Under the new rules (which were widely viewed as a disingenuous attempt by the governments involved to insist that the European rate mechanism system, and all it symbolized, remained intact when it had collapsed), currency values would be permitted to fluctuate 30 percent against each other before prompting official intervention. Effectively, exchange rates were no longer fixed in even the contrived sense of Europe's pegged system; they were left to float. Europe's experiment in maintaining a set of parity rates among its currencies to provide a stable monetary environment for trade and financial transactions among EC members had seemingly ended in failure.

French and German leaders quickly endeavored to put a positive slant on the decision to make Europe's monetary system more "flexible." French Prime Minister Edouard Balladur declared the next day following the decision to relax margins: "The European Monetary System remains in working order with a considerable loosening, but its founding principles remain in effect."[50] German Chancellor Helmut Kohl observed that the timetable for creating a single European currency might have been delayed a year or two, but he stressed that Germany's commitment to the goal of European union remained unchanged.[51]

Behind the public facade of camaraderie, though, the national resentments were bitter. France had tried to perpetuate the notion that it enjoyed equal monetary and financial status with Germany within Europe's monetary system; if any country should temporarily excuse itself from the exchange rate mechanism to get its own currency in order, French officials suggested, it should be Germany. Gallic pride was riding on the outcome of the tense negotiations that took place during the last days of July 1993. Balladur had long championed the cause of stable monetary relations and supported a *franc fort* policy for solid money. Indeed, he had vowed to resign rather than allow the French franc to float.

But Germany was not about to let France's arrogance displace the deutsche mark from its central role among Europe's currencies. Kohl all but ridiculed the suggestion that any nation other than France considered the franc the key to European monetary stability. "We did not isolate the French," Kohl insisted, defending Germany's decision not to withdraw the mark from the exchange rate mechanism. He did inform the French, however, that the other EC countries would likely reject the idea of keeping the franc at the expense of the deutsche mark. "And that is what happened," Kohl affirmed.[52]

So the dream of European unity that had rested so prominently on currency coordination among members of presumed equal political standing was dashed, although with a minimum of official recognition and nary a ministerial resignation. French aspirations for political solidarity with Germany had come up against German pragmatism and concern over inflation. And Germany had good reason to be concerned; in an ironic twist of fate, the nation that was deemed most capable of anchoring the stability of European currencies was turning in the worst monetary performance. As the *Sunday Times* of London reported in June 1993: "The Bundesbank, guardian of price stability in Germany for nearly 40 years, is presiding over the highest inflation rate among the Group of Seven industrial economies and appears confused and indecisive."[53]

What had gone wrong? Had Buba—the Bundesbank—really become "confused and indecisive," or was something fundamentally wrong with a pegged rate approach to international monetary relations that relied on central bank intervention to counteract the forces of supply and demand in currency markets? By stating in advance the target exchange rates, along with the margins that would trigger central bank activity, governments tipped their hands to speculators. It was then easy to target the most vulnerable currencies and anticipate the next likely moves of central banks. A favorite strategy was to sell currencies "short" (selling them in advance of owning them) and drive down their value to the bottom of the allowable range, thus forcing central banks to start buying; it was a sure bet that central banks eventually would balk at spending additional billions to support the currency and would succumb instead to devaluation. At that point, the short-sellers could cover their open positions by purchasing back the targeted currency at its new lower price and pocketing the difference as trading profits.

To combat such tactics, the general manager of the Bank for International Settlements, Alexandre Lamfalussy, warned in June 1993 that the world's central banks would have to coordinate their efforts to manage exchange rates more closely and avoid "piecemeal" approaches that permitted individual currencies to be picked off one by one.[54] At the same time, Lamfalussy pointed out that financial markets had attained increased powers to determine the relative value of currencies and that exchange rate targets could only be met where government policies were in conformance with market expectations. "If [authorities] want to meet exchange rate targets they will have to influence these expectations, or at least avoid giving rise to adverse ones."[55]

Though Lamfalussy exhibited a very civil tone with regard to the evaluations of financial markets, others harbored much less charitable feelings toward the currency speculators who dared to question the wisdom of finance ministers and central banking authorities in determining the appropriate exchange rates among Europe's currencies. At the height of the turmoil during the final week of July 1993, currency traders were denounced as "parasites" and "terrorists" willing to destroy Europe's monetary order to enrich themselves.[56] Newspapers vied to attribute the most sinister motives to the arbitrageurs; French newspapers particularly disparaged the "Anglo-Saxon speculators" who launched their attack on the European exchange rate mechanism because they were hostile to the idea of a fixed currency system.[57] *Le Monde* offered the editorial opinion: "The war between the international speculators and the central banks is a shock between two cultures."[58]

One cultural trait they apparently had in common was an appreciation for money. Central banks spent vast sums attempting to reverse market pressures; according to *U.S. News & World Report*, the Bundesbank and the Banque de France spent an estimated $100 billion between them to buy up francs in a bravado attempt to dam the speculation.[59] Figures released by France's central bank showed that French foreign currency reserves fell by more than 100 billion francs ($17 billion) during the week prior to the decision to widen the currency fluctuation bands—to little avail, because the franc fell back to its old floor in the exchange rate mechanism on the Friday before the emergency Sunday meeting of finance ministers.[60]

If central banks were feeling the pain of having billions slip off their books and disappear into the currency trading pits, speculators were joyfully accumulating the rewards of their investment activities. Currency dealers thrive on market volatility and exchange rate bedlam. In the aftermath of Black Wednesday in September 1992, they enjoyed a banner year and were chomping at the bit to test the mettle of French and German central bankers in the final weeks before the exchange rate mechanism finally succumbed to their onslaught. "The speculators have one thing on their side—they made a fortune this year already. They can take a much bigger fling," noted Rudiger Dornbusch, a professor of economics at the Massachusetts Institute of Technology.[61] The "fling" brought huge profits to currency traders who took short-term positions—sometimes for only a few minutes—that enabled them to capitalize on the market frenzy that reigned in late July 1993. "A lot of people, I think, must have made a lot of money over the last few days," observed Gabriele Otto, a trader at Bank of America in Frankfurt.[62]

Indeed, foreign exchange trading has become an extremely lucrative business as monetary relations change unpredictably and international businesses seek to insulate their transactions from currency risk. Per Kaalby, the foreign exchange manager at Bayerische Vereinsbank AG in Munich, noted in the *Wall Street Journal* that foreign exchange turnover at his bank had increased 200 to 300 percent during the first week of August 1993.[63] He estimated that, in the wake of the Black Sunday decision to widen bands, currencies would fluctuate even more and subject cross-border business transactions to even greater risk. Not a bad situation for currency traders. "Let's just say we're certainly not worried about where to find work anymore," said Kaalby. He added: "Everyone needs to look at Europe country-by-country now, and that requires more resources, more people and more potential for profit."[64] U.S. banks have taken to the foreign exchange business with gusto; according to *The New York Times*, the six top U.S. banks derived 40 percent of their total profits from trading currencies and securities in the second quarter of 1993.[65]

No wonder central bankers are peeved at speculators who seemingly delight in profiteering off the demise of the dream of European monetary union. As business reporter Allen R. Myerson observed: "The central bankers propose, the markets dispose."[66] There appears little sign that foreign exchange dealers are much deterred by the disapproval of central banking authorities or finance ministers, although George Soros did volunteer in a letter to *Le Figaro* on July 26, 1993, that he was not speculating against the franc because he did not want to be accused of destroying Europe's monetary system. Four days later, however, according to *The Economist*, Soros notified various news agencies that he no longer felt bound to refrain from betting against the franc.[67] In general, the savvy traders who earn their money by staying one step ahead of government officials seem to enjoy the game. For profit-motivated young dealers, the phrase "Anglo-Saxon conspiracy" evokes laughter.[68] French politicians often refer to it, but the only conspiracy among the hottest players in currency markets is their universal desire to make big bucks—or sterling or deutsche marks or yen.

Far from being the sleaze operators of the global monetary marketplace, *Newsweek* magazine improbably suggested in August 1993 that the foreign exchange dealers eventually might emerge as economic policy heroes:

> The five-day crisis highlights two emerging realities. One is that control over the world's financial markets has shifted from central banks to private institutions. The other represents a startling role reversal. Currency traders and speculators, despite their bad rep,

have become a force for stable growth. Europe's central banks and monetary "policy planners," supposed bulwarks of economic order, actually impede it.[69]

Truth to tell, there are no heroes in the events leading up to Black Sunday. But if Europe's monetary debacle and the billions in financial resources it wasted cannot be blamed on the speculators, responsibility squarely returns to the shoulders of central banks. That, in turn, means the governments of the nations of Europe are left to smolder in their resentment of each other while they rethink the whole matter of European unity. As *Le Monde* snapped: "German selfishness is the root of the crisis."[70]

HARD MONEY

Resentment based on nationalistic suspicions and political rivalries seemingly could be avoided by turning to an inanimate object to function as the monetary anchor. Instead of inviting the economically dominant country to dictate monetary policy for its neighbors through a mechanism of pegged exchange rates, governments would assume individual responsibility for keeping their own currencies in alignment with an outside standard that transcends the control of any one nation.

Turning to an outside anchor permits trading partners to safely transcend politics in their monetary relations. Unlike a pegged rate system, an outside anchor offers an objective monetary point of reference instead of requiring countries to coordinate policies or subjugate their own economic agenda to the domestic priorities of the dominant regional power. While economic hegemony may be associated with monetary credibility, it provides no guarantee against abuse; indeed, the most powerful country is the one most apt to pursue its own domestic priorities without worrying about the economic fallout transmitted to other nations. Then, too, hegemonic authority has a tendency to shift over time. So if one of the primary goals of the monetary anchor is to provide a standard of value that has meaning across the decades, perhaps even for a century or more, then it is better not to link it too closely with the political fortunes of empires that may rise or fall.

By designating an outside anchor, the potential for monetary manipulation is vastly reduced, not just in terms of international currency relations, but also with respect to the validity of the money issued to citizens by their own governments. By fixing the value of currency to a specific commodity or group of commodities, government officials are deprived of the option of devaluing their own nation's currency against foreign currencies to gain a trade advantage. Equally important (arguably, more important), they are prevented from devaluing the money in the hands of the domestic population through inflationary policies. So long as citizens maintain the right to convert paper or "fiat" money into genuine assets at a fixed rate, the money supply is effectively controlled by the people—not the government.

Built-in Constraint

Certainly, the idea of designating an objective monetary standard beyond the reach of government has long been championed as a way to prevent the value of money from being compromised for political ends. As Hans F. Sennholz observes in his book *Age of Inflation*:

> Throughout the long history of money a clamor for this stability always arose when governments engaged in coin debasements and paper money inflation. Certainly the Romans yearned for monetary stability when their emperors resorted to every conceivable device of monetary depreciation. Medieval man longed for stability when his prince clipped, reduced, or debased the coins and defrauded him through such devices. Throughout the seventeenth and eighteenth centuries the early Americans sought monetary stability when the colonial governments issued legal tender "bills of credit," regulated the exchange ratios between British and Spanish coins, and imposed wage and price controls. Americans were dreaming of monetary stability during the Revolution when the Continental Congress emitted vast quantities of Continental Dollars until they became utterly worthless.[71]

To maintain the integrity of money, then, it is necessary to impose some kind of outside discipline—that is, to make money subject not to the actions of government but to the untainted value of a concrete commodity or set of commodities. Fiat money could be compromised too easily. Roger Sherman, an American statesman in the mid-1770s who resided in Connecticut, captured this concept in a statement he wrote to protest against allowing bills of credit issued by Rhode Island and New Hampshire to serve as legal tender in his home state:

> [I]t is a principle that must be granted that no Government has a Right to impose on its subjects any foreign Currency to be received in Payments as Money which is not of intrinsic Value: unless such Government will assume and undertake to secure and make Good to the Possessor of such Currency the full Value which they oblige him to receive it for. Because in so doing they would oblige Men to part with their Estates for that which is worth nothing in it self and which they don't know will ever procure him any Thing. . . . And since the Value of the *Bills of Credit* depend wholly . . . on the Credit of the Government by whom they are emitted and that being the only Reason and Foundation upon which they obtained their first Currency . . . , and therefore when the Publick Faith and Credit of such Government is violated, then . . . there remains no Reason why they should be any longer current.[72]

Sherman was opposed to government-issued bills of credit being circulated as money not just on legal or political grounds, but for moral reasons:

> [I]f what is us'd as a *Medium of Exchange* is fluctuating in its Value it is no better than unjust Weights and Measures, . . . which are condemn'd by the Laws of God and Man, and wherefore the longest and most universal Custom could make the Use of such a *Medium* either lawful or reasonable.
>
> Now suppose that Gold and Silver Coines that pass current in Payments . . . should have a considerable Part of their Weight filed or clipp'd off will any reasonable Man judge that they ought to pass for the same Value as those of full Weight. But the State of *R———I———d Bills of Credit* is much worse than that of Coins that are clipp'd because what is left of those Coins is of intrinsic Value: But the General Assembly of *R———I———d* having depreciated their *Bills of Credit* have thereby violated their Promise from Time to Time, and there is just Reason to suspect their Credit for the Future.[73]

The rationale, then, for a commodity money versus a government bill of credit or other form of paper money is that it has intrinsic value of its own rather than just relying on the continued authority and viability of the issuing government. Indeed, the word fiat is defined in *Webster's* dictionary as "a command or act of will that creates something without or as if without further effort."[74] So fiat money implies the creation of money through the issuance of a bill of credit with no further effort being made to guarantee or otherwise provide the holder with something of value equal to the amount nominally represented by the paper claim.

The preference for commodity-linked money is largely a reflection of distrust of government. Friedrich A. Hayek, recipient of the 1974 Nobel Memorial Prize in Economics, believed it imperative to impose discipline on government in monetary matters because "government will behave reasonably only if it is forced to do so."[75] Yet Hayek also feared it had become impossible to subject the government to the outside discipline inherent in a commodity standard:

> I am afraid I am convinced that the hope of ever again placing this discipline on government is gone. The public at large has learned to accept, and I am afraid a whole generation of economists has been teaching, that government has the power in the short run to relieve all kinds of economic evils, especially unemployment, by monetary stimulus. Experience has shown, however, that rapid increases in the quantity of money—although they may temporarily reduce unemployment—become in the long run the cause of much greater unemployment. Yet, what politician can possibly care about long-run effects if in the short run he buys support?[76]

For Hayek, the problem with putting government in charge of producing domestic money is that it always tends to abuse the privilege unless it can be properly constrained, and Hayek had grave doubts that any mechanism could prove up to the task. Hayek believed that government officials always will be overly receptive to the views of Keynesian economists who recommend easy money to stave off recession. Hayek yearned for some form of outside discipline that would exert proper control over the actions of government, and while he was attracted to the gold stan-

dard, acknowledging that it had worked fairly well over a long period, he worried that government officials would somehow find a
way to circumvent the requirement of gold convertibility. Hayek
was convinced that even if the gold standard were reintroduced by
means of an international treaty, it still would not provide adequate protection from monetary abuse because "there is not the
slightest hope that governments will play the game according to
the rules."[77]

Not everyone is so pessimistic about the prospects of trusting
governments to exercise sovereignty in money matters; the trick is
to ensure that governments behave within publicly acknowledged
constraints that limit the scope of their actions in creating money.
Long-term monetary stability should never be compromised to
achieve short-term political gains, and this principle applies to domestic economic policies as well as to international currency relations. Balladur, who served as finance minister in Jacques Chirac's
government from 1986 to 1988 before becoming prime minister in
1993, has called repeatedly for some kind of outside standard or
unit of reference on which the values of other currencies would be
based. While he does not disparage the importance of central
banks in controlling currency relations—Balladur played a primary role in getting the finance ministers and central bankers of the
major industrialized countries to coordinate their exchange rates
through concerted intervention tactics—he nevertheless notes:
"The world suffers from the lack of a true international monetary
system, one with built-in . . . constraints independent of the will of
governments."[78]

Choice of Standard

If one accepts the argument that it makes sense to control the
monetary authority of government by imposing some kind of outside discipline to impart intrinsic value to currency and thus ensure that its quantity cannot be manipulated to satisfy political
ends, the next question is: What kind of commodity or group of
commodities would provide the best, most workable standard?
Should the standard be a metal or combination of metals or a sophisticated index of consumer goods?

Before making that decision, it's important to ascertain exactly what one hopes to achieve by linking the money supply to a specific commodity. The main objective, clearly, is to remove from government the ability to distort the nominal value of prices and wages by issuing excess monetary claims. But what constitutes good money? Is it defined by stable prices? Is the goal to produce a form of money that is economically neutral in the sense that it exerts no disproportionate effects on the level of savings, investment, or productivity?

Stable money, if it means stable prices, may not be the desired outcome. The value of goods is most appropriately determined by changes in demand and supply that occur through time and that may be significantly affected by new technologies that enable a particular good to be produced more cheaply. Other changes in circumstances may cause goods or services to become more or less desirable to consumers. The price for a good easily might change over time as consumer tastes change and as the dynamics of supply and demand change in the context of a continuous free market. A stable price, then, is not necessarily the correct price, because the interplay of so many market factors easily can move prices up or down. As Ludwig von Mises explained, the establishment of a stable money would mean that all the relative prices among goods would be frozen, and that the relationship between all goods and money would likewise be frozen.[79]

The concept of "neutral" money likewise may miss the mark in defining a desirable policy objective for administering the money supply. Again, as Mises has pointed out, it is not possible to separate money from the economy, to treat it simply as a numeraire for measuring the value of commodities. Money is a commodity itself, albeit a unique one because it enters into every act of exchange. Every transaction involving money, according to Mises, results in a new configuration of the relative demand of consumers for all goods, including money.[80]

If neither stable prices, then, nor neutral money, are the most desirable objectives of monetary policy, what can one hope to achieve by imposing an outside commodity standard to properly discipline government monetary authorities? Richard Ebeling, a Mises scholar, provides the explanation:

For Mises the answer was "sound" money. Sound money was a commodity money neither stable in value (because money's value, like all other goods' value, was a matter of relative prices) nor neutral in its effects on the economy (because of the pervasive presence of money in the nexus of exchange, which meant it was always a dynamic element for change). What sound money connoted was a monetary system fully integrated into and a part of the very market process which the use of money facilitated in growing, developing, and enhancing. What sound money was to be free of was the intervention of the political authorities, intervention that only succeeded, as Mises saw it, in producing economic disruption, social upheaval, deceptive taxation, and squandered capital—all through the false signals of manipulations of the money supply.[81]

What form of outside discipline would be necessary to bring about sound money? For Irving Fisher, a Yale economist who sought through numerous personal letters to educate President Franklin D. Roosevelt on the subject of money, the answer was to link the dollar to a basket of commodities.[82] In contrast to the views developed by Mises, Fisher believed that the ultimate objective of monetary policy should be to maintain a constant price level. People who held dollars should have some guarantee that the purchasing and debt-paying power of those dollars would not depreciate over time; if they could purchase a basic set of consumer goods with so many dollars today, they should be able to purchase that same basket of consumer goods with the same amount of dollars in the future. Likewise, they should be able to pay back debt in dollars whose value had not been distorted during the time the loan was issued and the date of maturity.

Fisher came to the conclusion that it was not necessary that the dollars be convertible into a specified basket of commodities. It could all be handled financially. People who held dollars should have the right to convert them into a financial asset that would be worth whatever amount was required to pay for the basket of commodities.[83] Fisher thought of this concept as providing a "compensated dollar" in the sense that holders would be entitled to receive sufficient financial resources to maintain their purchasing power through time. Under Fisher's proposal, governments would be obligated to make sure that the value of the currency they issued remained stable in terms of a broad official index of commodities.

Not everyone accepts that it is necessary to identify an elaborate collection of goods, however, to provide a suitable standard for maintaining the purchasing power for money. Long before Fisher offered his scheme for a commodity-linked dollar, others had argued that precious metals could serve effectively as surrogates for an array of commodities. It was only necessary to link the value of currency to silver or gold or some combination of metals in order to simulate the effects of a stable price level across all commodities in general.

Indeed, English common law suggests that metal provides the "most proper" standard for guaranteeing the value of money. As stated in W. Blackstone's *Commentaries*, published in the early 1770s:

> Money is an universal medium, or common standard, by comparison with which the value of all merchandize may be ascertained: . . . a sign, which represents the respective values of all commodities. Metals are well calculated for this sign, because they are durable and are capable of many subdivisions: and a precious metal is still better calculated for this purpose, because it is the most portable. A metal is also the most proper for a common measure, because it can easily be reduced to the same standard in all nations: and every particular nation fixes on it it's own impression, that the weight and standard (wherein consists the intrinsic value) may both be known by inspection only.[84]

For the United States Founding Fathers, precious metals were literally money. It wasn't a matter of having the right to redeem paper for gold or silver on demand, prominent patriots asserted; only actual gold or silver could constitutionally be allowed to function as money. As Daniel Webster explained:

> If we understand, by currency, the legal money of the country, and that which constitutes a lawful tender for debts, and is the statute measure of value, then undoubtedly, nothing is included but gold and silver. Most unquestionably, there is no legal tender, and there can be no legal tender in this country under the authority of this government or any other, but gold and silver, either the coinage of our mints or foreign coins at rates regulated by Congress. This is a constitutional principle, perfectly plain and of the very highest importance. The states are expressly prohibited from making anything

but gold and silver a tender in payment of debts, and although no such expressed prohibition is applied to Congress, yet as Congress has no power granted to it in this respect but to coin money and to regulate the value of foreign coins, it clearly has no power to substitute paper or anything else for coin as a tender in payments of debts in a discharge of contracts.[85]

In Webster's opinion, the question of a suitable monetary standard for the United States was not open to debate:

> The legal tender, therefore, the constitutional standard of value, is established and cannot be overthrown. To overthrow it would shake the whole system.[86]

To accept both silver and gold as monetary standards is to effect a bimetallic system. The Coinage Act passed by Congress in 1792 did establish a bimetallic dollar standard in the United States. A dollar could be defined in terms of 371.25 grains of pure silver or 24.75 grains of pure gold. Thus the value of silver money was equal to gold money at the fixed ratio of fifteen to one, reflecting their relative market values. The U.S. Mint accepted either silver or gold to be coined on demand.

By the early 1800s, though, increased silver production from Mexico caused the market price of silver to decline in relation to gold. Because the U.S. government maintained the original 15:1 ratio, people began bringing in the cheaper silver to exchange for gold and then shipped the more valuable gold abroad. Soon only silver coins were circulating as legal tender in the United States, fulfilling the prediction of Gresham's law, which posits that if two types of metallic money circulate in parallel at a fixed rate of exchange, the bad (less valuable) metal money will drive out the good money as people opt to pass on the former and hoard the latter.

To avoid this situation, why not choose a single precious metal to serve as the monetary standard? Either silver or gold would be likely candidates given their status as the precious metals most often tapped through the ages to serve as money. Gold, the more valuable of the two, is the efficient choice because more value can be represented by a smaller mass—that is, gold is more comfortable. Gold, too, is more widely viewed by individuals, as well as central banks, as the primary alternative to paper currency. Gold has a legacy of serving as sound money.

Even John Maynard Keynes, despite his reference to the gold standard as a "barbarous relic," had to admit that it protected the purchasing power of citizens from the efforts of governments to debase the value of money. "The metal *gold* might not possess all the theoretical advantages of an artificially regulated standard," Keynes wrote in his book *Monetary Reform*, "but it could not be tampered with and had proved reliable in practice."[87]

To Mises, the fact that gold could not be tampered with by governments or special interest groups was reason enough to employ it as the peoples' money. Gold was the proper choice, Mises argued,

> Because, as conditions are today and for the time that can be foreseen today, the gold standard alone makes the determination of money's purchasing power independent of the ambitions and machinations of governments, of dictators, of political parties, and of pressure groups. The gold standard alone is what the nineteenth-century freedom-loving leaders (who championed representative government, civil liberties and prosperity for all) called "sound money."[88]

Contemporary Appeal

It may seem difficult at first to bridge the seeming theoretical gap between modern attempts to maintain the value of money through time and across borders—such as the failed European exchange rate mechanism—and older theories regarding sound monetary practices. But a number of influential economists and political leaders have tackled the issue and come up with contemporary proposals that have clear antecedents in the earlier approaches that sought to guarantee the intrinsic value of money by making it convertible into commodities. An outside commodity anchor is still deemed necessary to provide the discipline required for international monetary stability. From Sir Alan Walters's proposal for a stable commodity-backed money to conservative leader Jack Kemp's call for a U.S. dollar defined in terms of a fixed weight of gold, the objective is still to provide users of money with a reliable standard that cannot be manipulated by governments in the name of political expediency.

Sir Alan Walters served as former British Prime Minister Margaret Thatcher's personal economic adviser in 1989 during the crucial period when Britain was strongly resisting the drive among European nations to achieve full economic and monetary union. Sir Alan was opposed to the idea of transferring significant powers to any future EC central banking authority because he felt the loss of sovereignty was unacceptable. "He's violently anti-European Monetary System," observed an aide to European Community Commission President Jacques Delors in August 1989.[89]

But Sir Alan's quarrel with turning over the authority to control Britain's money supply to a central bank of Europe did not so much stem from fear that it would take away money-creating powers from the British government and the Bank of England but that it would turn over such powers to an institution with discretionary authority, whether it would be the Bundesbank or a yet-to-be-created European central bank. Any organization with discretionary powers to expand the money supply, Sir Alan pointed out, is likely to have an inflationary bias. What Sir Alan posits instead is that states may be willing to give up their sovereignty over money creation to an automatic monetary mechanism that could be counted on to provide a noninflationary money for Europe. "A German Master is an anathema," writes Sir Alan, "but a monetary rule guaranteeing price stability *may* be tolerable."[90]

What kind of monetary rule would be necessary to guarantee price stability? According to Sir Alan, the best rule would be one that required the monetary authority to stand ready to redeem its currency on demand in the form of a financial asset whose value was indexed to a basket of goods. Effectively, the money issued under such strict rules would be a commodity currency. If consumers believed that the value of their currency had dropped, they would have the right to bring it to the monetary authorities and receive in exchange a financial instrument with which they could buy the designated basket of goods. A unit of the currency would thus always be worth a certain amount of purchasing power defined in terms of the goods that could be purchased with it.

Sir Alan, like his predecessor Irving Fisher, seeks to capture all the inflation-fighting advantages of a currency backed by gold without subjecting overall price stability to the vagaries of new gold discoveries and updated technologies that might affect the world supply of gold and, hence, its inherent price. In his 1990 book, *Sterling in Danger*, Sir Alan asserts that the "idiosyncracies" of gold supplies can be avoided by specifying a commodity basket comprised of a broad selection of representative goods and services.[91] The monetary authority would not have to actually hold vast quantities of the commodity basket as reserves to guarantee convertibility; it would, though, have to be prepared to accommodate members of the public who wished to redeem their currency by supplying them with a financial asset which would give the holder sufficient resources to buy the commodities if he so wished. "The point is that the value of the currency will be preserved through its convertibility into a reserve asset which has a value defined as constant in terms of the commodity basket," Sir Alan explains.[92]

How would such a commodity-linked currency come into play in terms of Europe's potential movement toward monetary unity? Sir Alan has proposed to introduce his particular type of money as an alternative parallel currency to the existing national monies in Europe. This new Euro-Commodity money, dubbed by Sir Alan as the ECOM, would be the thirteenth currency operating in the twelve-member European Community. People would be able to choose from among any of the national monies or they could opt to utilize the ECOM to conduct their business and carry out economic and financial transactions. What is essential, according to Sir Alan, is that citizens be allowed to use whatever currency they wish; if people value the stability of an inflation-proof currency, they will increasingly turn to the ECOM as their preferred money.[93] Presumably, national monies would then come under competitive pressure to match the inflation-proof qualities of the ECOM.

Sir Alan's contribution to the debate over European monetary union was consistent with the views being expressed by Thatcher in late 1989; she long had been suspicious of a federalized Europe on both philosophical and political grounds. Thatcher argued that plans to accelerate economic integration and to establish a single

European currency under the authority of a centralized institution would "destroy democracy" by robbing nations of their sovereignty.[94] What could be more democratic than to offer European consumers a choice in currency, including a new hard currency linked to commodities?

John Major, who was serving as chancellor of the Exchequer and who later would succeed Thatcher as prime minister, soon began extolling the virtues of creating a "hard ecu" to serve as the thirteenth currency to be issued in parallel with the other national European monies.[95] Major's proposal envisioned a currency that would be backed by foreign currency reserves and that would be more resistant to inflation than even the deutsche mark; he portrayed the introduction of a hard ecu as an important evolutionary step toward European monetary union. While Delors continued to pursue his design for a centrally run community with a single currency managed by a federalized central bank, British officials insisted that exchange rate stability could be achieved without taking the step of forming a single central bank and subjecting national economic policy decisions to community-wide approval. Instead, they offered an alternative common currency as an option available to all Europeans—and may the best money win. "The difference in approach is quite simple," Major observed. "The Delors approach is centralist and ignores the market; ours is based on the market."[96]

But as *The Economist* observed in September 1990, people do not necessarily exhibit a market mentality when it comes to choosing a currency. They are more apt to stick with the money to which they have become accustomed. So while the British proposal for a hard ecu might be useful to the extent that it would introduce "an extra anti-inflationary check on national governments that wanted to relax their monetary policies," it could never deliver the microeconomic benefits of a single currency.[97] As stated further in *The Economist*:

> Down the decades of this inflationary century, people have shown a remarkable attachment to their national currencies, almost irrespective of how debauched those currencies become, how useless as measuring rods or as stores of value.

>   That history shows that Europeans will not embrace a 13th cur-
> rency, leaving the other dozen to wither away. If the single-curren-
> cy prizes are to be won, the single currency must be legislated into
> life, deliberately and permanently.[98]

Once you begin to get into distinctions between offering a common currency versus a single currency, the concepts can sometimes start to blur. Indeed, when Major used the occasion of the
collapse of the European rate mechanism to revive his proposal
for a hard ecu in August 1993, a Labour Party critic dismissed the
proposition with the statement that it would be "laughed at by
those with a serious knowledge of the topic and not understood by
anyone else."[99] Even other members of the ruling Conservative
Party expressed skepticism about plans to create a parallel common currency that would trade alongside Europe's national
monies; Michael Spicer, a hardline tory who opposed European
unity, labeled it "pie in the sky."[100]

In any case, it is important to note that Major's proposal for a
hard ecu is not the same as Walters's concept of a commodity-
backed European currency. While the envisioned hard ecu would
offer a common unit of account and ostensibly perform as a reliable standard of value, its stability would not derive from any direct link to commodities but, rather, would result from being
properly "managed" by a European monetary fund so as to never
be devalued against any EC currency.[101] Major's hard ecu would be
guaranteed by the governments of participating nations; Walter's
ECOM would be redeemable by its holders for a financial instrument sufficient to enable them to purchase a prespecified basket
of goods.

The Role for Gold

Then there are those who are not afraid to invoke the word gold
in the midst of sophisticated discussions concerning the proper
regulatory mechanism for an international monetary system.
Granting that it would be desirable to impart stable purchasing
power to money by providing for its convertibility into real assets—a basket of goods, for example—should that basket contain
a certain barbarous relic that has occupied a primary place in the

monetary history of the world? Should gold be included in the basket? Should gold *be* the basket?

In September 1987, then–U.S. Treasury Secretary Baker suggested a role for gold in setting world economic policy during his remarks at the annual meeting of the World Bank and International Monetary Fund; his remarks set off rampant speculation that the Reagan administration might be drifting back to a Bretton Woods-type system or even a classical gold standard. World finance officials present at the Washington meeting clearly were caught off guard by Baker's reference to gold and responded cautiously. According to a *Wall Street Journal* account, Japan's vice-minister of Finance, Toyoo Gyohten, was surprised by the proposal and told reporters: "I think we need to study it. We should know exactly what is implied in that." Bundesbank President Pöhl likewise conveyed through a spokesman that he needed to study the Baker statement before commenting on it.[102]

Baker knew full well that the mere mention of gold would arouse the "gold bugs" because he had never before made reference to the use of gold with regard to setting exchange rates among the world's leading currencies.[103] As supply-side advocate Jude Wanniski quipped, Baker was "the first secretary of the treasury to use that four-letter word since George Shultz said it in 1973 in throwing it out."[104]

But even as Baker raised the hopes of those who had long championed the use of gold to restore soundness to the dollar, he was careful to make clear that his suggestion to include gold among a basket of commodities that might figure into the calculations of finance officials was strictly an attempt to utilize all available tools and indicators to assist in the process of managing exchange rates among the major industrial nations. Baker did not wish to suggest in any way that the United States was preparing to go on a commodity standard—only that the price of a basket of commodities, including gold, would be monitored along with other indicators to provide information to finance officials and central bankers concerning potential inflationary trends.

Baker was hardly advocating that the existing system of managed floating rates be abandoned in favor of an automatic standard; he was only suggesting a method for improving the international currency management approach. His statement was that the major industrial nations should base their joint economic policy planning in part on "the relationship among our currencies and a basket of commodities, including gold."[105]

If Baker was prepared to admit the use of gold only as an analytical tool, other top officials have expressed willingness to consider a more exalted role for the yellow metal. In February 1988, in an article published by the *Wall Street Journal*, Balladur outlined three possible approaches for reforming the international monetary system.[106] The approaches differed in terms of the level of constraint they would exercise over the decision-making powers of governments and central banks. Balladur suggested that the least restrictive approach would be to continue to strengthen the level of economic coordination among central banks, especially in the area of interest rates, and to make public the acceptable margins within which exchange rates could fluctuate. A more rigid approach would be to set up an exchange rate mechanism similar to the European monetary system on a world basis. Fixed rate parities would be established among the various national monies, and each country would be required to intervene on exchange markets to ensure that its currency remained within a specified margin around its "central" rate in relation to other currencies. The third and most constraining approach would be organized around a universal standard and would create a monetary unit of reference on which the values of the world's currencies would be based.

The advantage of the third approach, in Balladur's view, is that it would offer an objective international monetary system whose integrity would be protected by automatic mechanisms and sanctions beyond the control of governments. The monetary unit of reference would function as the main world reserve asset. Each national currency would be convertible into the world currency at a fixed exchange rate. Settlements among central banks would be made in the same way as under the classical international gold standard—that is, through transfers of the world currency that would be "the reserve asset held by each national central bank and the central reserve asset of the system."[107]

Balladur speculates that there are two possible ways to create such a world monetary unit: either by (1) designating a commodity standard including gold or (2) establishing a basket of currencies to which gold might be added. In either case, Balladur envisions an important role for gold in any future monetary system. As he noted in an interview in December 1990: "I don't see how a true world system that by necessity must create a new monetary standard could avoid a reference to gold."[108]

A mere reference to gold, though, is not what some advocates have in mind when they talk about creating a new global monetary standard. Lewis Lehrman, for example, a political activist for conservative causes who narrowly lost the gubernatorial race in New York in 1980, has long gone on record as favoring the restoration of a dependable monetary standard in the United States. For Lehrman, that means a genuine gold standard—"the true American monetary standard."[109] As Lehrman asserts:

> Under the American Constitution, a free monetary order consists in a currency of intrinsic worth, a gold dollar, ruled by a moral principle—the unimpeachable integrity of a true money. The substance and integrity of the dollar, until 1934, rested upon the right of every American to bring precious metal to the mint to have it freely coined into standard money. Free coinage gave rise to the right to *convert* all paper and bank deposit claims, such as Federal Reserve notes and checking accounts, into the monetary standard. Thus was the dollar referred to as a *convertible* currency.[110]

Lehrman was one of four "distinguished private citizens" appointed in June 1981 to serve on the Gold Commission, which was charged with making policy recommendations to the U.S. government concerning the role of gold in domestic and international monetary systems. Despite opposition from other members of the group, Lehrman never demurred from his conviction that a gold-backed dollar was necessary to achieve true monetary integrity. In the commission's report to the Congress in March 1982, Lehrman makes the unabashed declaration: "I favor the restoration of a gold standard with a fixed price of gold. It is the means to achieve discipline in the U.S. monetary base which will then increase or decrease with gold purchases and sales by the monetary authorities."[111] With regard to international monetary policy, Lehrman affirms: "I support fixed exchange rates for the U.S. dollar to be introduced at the earliest possible date."[112]

Robert Mundell, a professor at Columbia University who has achieved renown as an international economist and monetary scholar, likewise has argued in favor of abandoning floating rates and reinstating an international monetary system based on fixed exchange rates and linked to gold. As Mundell stated at a monetary conference held in Washington in May 1983:

> It is time to cut our losses with flexible-exchange-rate monetarism and go back to the internationalist approach to dealing with inflation that was successful in the heyday of gold and Bretton Woods. That approach involves readoption of a system of exchange rate parities by convertibility of a major currency or collective reserve asset into gold. If the dollar is stabilized in terms of gold, the other countries should fix their exchange rates to the dollar using the balance of payments as the guide to appropriate monetary policy. For its part the United States should commit its monetary policy to stabilization of the price of gold.[113]

Mundell is sometimes referred to as the godfather of supply-side economics.[114] He has long maintained that a truly integrated global economy would be served best by a single money; prices would then provide meaningful and consistent signals to market participants around the world. One way to capture the benefits of a single world currency would be to have a strictly fixed rate system in which every nation's currency would be defined in terms of the same commodity. That commodity wouldn't have to be gold, Mundell concedes.[115] On the other hand, gold has long played an important role in the history of central banking and could serve quite well in the future. For Mundell, what is important is the need to reconcile domestic monetary policy with the notion of a unified global market; that is the way to avoid the inefficiencies of distorted prices across national boundaries. Robert L. Bartley, editor of the *Wall Street Journal*, recalls Mundell's aphorism: "The only closed economy is the world economy."[116]

One of the most ardent and faithful supporters of sound money has been Jack Kemp, a former congressman from New York who served as Housing and Urban Development Secretary in the Bush administration cabinet. Dubbed "Mr. Gold Standard" in the *Washington Times* in May 1992,[117] Kemp has long championed the cause of making the dollar as good as gold, even in the face of stiff political opposition and haughty derision in certain economic circles. "Gold convertibility may not be fashionable," Kemp noted in remarks before the Federal Reserve Bank of Atlanta and Emory University in March 1982, "but I am convinced that it is imperative, for the simple reason that if we do not choose to remonetize gold, people in the market will progressively choose to demonetize the dollar."[118]

In calling for a reliable monetary standard, Kemp has emphasized the moral dimension of sound money. "People trade with each other in time because they believe they will not be defrauded by a change in the currency," he observes.[119] For Kemp, the restoration of an honest dollar with predictable and constant value over time would not only serve the best economic interests of the American people, it would also assist countries whose "currencies and fates are tied to ours."[120] Most importantly, perhaps, it would help move the whole world toward liberalized trade and strong growth.

How best to achieve the objective of a sound dollar and a stable international monetary system? Kemp has argued strongly for convertibility of Federal Reserve notes and credit into gold on demand and for establishing a system in which official international settlements are made in gold:

> We need gold convertibility because it's not enough to simply have a rule for monetary policy; there must also be a mechanism for putting it into effect. The most stable monetary mechanism we have seen was the classical international gold standard.[121]

PRIVATE CURRENCIES

Some of the most prominent monetary economists have come to the conclusion that even a gold standard can be compromised by government manipulation. No statist by anyone's definition, Friedrich Hayek would not trust government even to maintain an honest gold standard. But if government cannot be relied on to issue the money, who can? Hayek had an answer. In November 1977, he stated, "I am more convinced than ever that if we ever again are going to have sound money, it will not come from government; it will be issued by private enterprise."[122]

Private enterprise? What would it mean to have private enterprise money? It's difficult to think of any commodity more public in nature than money. Defining it as the medium of exchange suggests its acceptability as a measure of value whose validity is acknowledged by the parties concerned in any economic transaction. To compete with government-issued money, or to replace it, private money would have to be at least as acceptable to its users as government-issued money. To attain that level of legitimacy would require going beyond legal definitions or economic comparisons; private money would have to be culturally acceptable. The fact that humans still tend to think of themselves as citizens of specific nation-states, subject to the authority of their governments, suggests there might be a higher psychological comfort level associated with using government-issued money. Money has an official air about it with its exotic symbols, numbers and signatures, and its illustrations of cultural heroes and important historical events. It conveys the very essence of national sovereignty.

Just because the issuance of money has long been one of the sovereign rights claimed by governments, though, does not mean that it cannot be produced and managed more effectively by private enterprise. Indeed, Hayek argues that "governments have invariably and inevitably grossly abused that power throughout the whole of history" and concludes that a system based on competing private currencies offers a much more promising avenue for achieving sound money.[123] But can money truly be "denationalized"? Would private competition to produce money result in a more orderly monetary regime, or would it lead to even greater currency chaos?

Competitive Brands

People who believe in the efficacy of private money derive their faith from a basic belief in free markets as the least arbitrary, most efficient, most fair mechanism for producing and distributing goods and services for society. Under a laissez-faire monetary regime, competition among money producers ultimately would lead to the development of an identifiable brand of money that would fulfil consumer demands for a reliable unit of account, a store of value, and a medium of exchange. To gain more customers, while at the same time retaining old customers, money would have to outperform its competitors. To do that, it would have to become better and better until it would provide the ultimate stability in the form of zero inflation for its users.

This kind of scenario predicting the emergence of superior money under laissez-faire conditions seems to suggest a reversal of Gresham's law: The good money would drive out the bad. But the observation is not apt because Gresham's law is only applicable where the choice of one currency over another comes about because the government maintains a fixed rate of conversion between two metallic currencies—for example, gold and silver—that becomes out of sync with market-determined values. People then arbitrage the difference by circulating the overvalued currency and hoarding the undervalued one or selling it abroad for a profit.

The idea that good money would drive out bad money under conditions of private issuance is just a reaffirmation of what happens when producers strive to excel in a competitive marketplace: They produce better products. To out-perform rivals, a money producer would have to offer the public a better brand of money than the competitors. As Richard Rahn, former vice-president and chief economist at the U.S. Chamber of Commerce, has argued:

> Private issuers of money have stronger incentives than governments to maintain the real purchasing power of a currency because the only way to make a profit by issuing money would be to provide a currency that people consider superior to government money. People making long-term contracts or investments would be eager to rely on a private currency only if they thought it would maintain its value better than the U.S. dollar or Japanese yen or other currencies.
>
> Proponents of competitive currencies and free banking do not suggest that decisionmakers in the private sector are more honest and responsible than those in the public sector, only that competition ultimately would weed out the crooked and incompetent. Superior money will drive out inferior money.[124]

Whether this superior money would derive its value because it was backed by commodities, or was redeemable in gold or silver, or whether it would be merely a fiat money cannot be ascertained in advance. The market would decide what type of money it most preferred. Hayek noted that although gold has been a useful mechanism for forcing governments to control the quantity of money in an appropriate manner, gold may not be a requirement for bringing about a good private currency:

> I think it is entirely possible for private enterprise to issue a token money, which the public will learn to expect to preserve its value, provided both the issuer and the public understand that the demand for this money will depend on the issuer being forced to keep its value constant; because if he did not do so, the people would at once cease to use his money and shift to some other kind.[125]

Thus the key to providing a sound currency through private markets is to offer money that can be relied upon to retain a stable value either because it can be converted into precious metals or commodities at a fixed rate or because the issuer has credibility among consumers, who trust that the quantity of money placed in circulation will be managed in such a way as to maintain consistency in its value over time. Like zealous monetarists, who believe the supply of money and credit can be regulated to achieve stable domestic prices, Hayek concedes that money need not have intrinsic value to fulfill its chief functions. By controlling its quantity relative to demand, Hayek explains, it is possible to keep the value even of a "token" money constant.[126]

What kinds of entrepreneurs would arise to offer their wares in a competitive currency market? How would the market differentiate among their various products? The money issued by individual suppliers would have to be uniquely identifiable so that consumers could distinguish one brand from another and choose accordingly; the best type of money would emerge as the leading product in the field. Arguing the case for competing currencies, Roland Vaubel suggests that barriers to entry should be removed to allow both foreign central banks and private enterprises to offer their money product to consumers. "The existence of these barriers to entry raises three questions," notes Vaubel:

> (1) What welfare-theoretic grounds are there to justify restrictions of currency competition from foreign central banks? (2) If there is

a case for free currency competition from foreign central banks, why doesn't this case extend to private banks as well? (3) If private banks should be free to supply currencies of their own, why should the government (its central bank) supply money, or a monetary unit of account, at all?[127]

Vaubel thus contends that currency users should be free to select their preferred money from an array of choices and not be limited by governmental restrictions that might narrow the consumers' freedom of choice. But how can people know in advance whether the producers of money are reputable? Doesn't there need to be some kind of good housekeeping seal to signify that the money can be trusted? Otherwise, what is there to prevent fraudulent producers from reaping unearned gains by supplying paper money to the public at virtually no cost beyond the price of newsprint and collecting great sums of genuine value for it? Can market competition really lead to the development of sound money?

Free Banking

The type of competitor likely to emerge from a free market environment of alternative currencies is a bank. People are accustomed to obtaining purchasing power from banks in the form of deposits on which they write checks to pay for goods and services. Banks have always been creators of money; whenever paper IOUs issued by banks are circulated by the public and used to settle personal debts, money is created. Unless the IOUs are immediately presented to the bank for payment—and are covered 100 percent by hard cash reserves or commodities—they represent an additional increment to the basic money supply.

The fact that private banks create money in the process of providing credit to the public remains a complicating factor in control of the money supply. Central banks typically have sought to influence the level of private bank-created credit by imposing reserve requirements (subject to change at the discretion of the government) or by intervening in credit markets or by adjusting the interest rate. Yet under a competitive currency regime, private banks would control the level of credit they issued, and thus the amount of money they created, not to comply with government regulation or supervisory authority, but in pursuit of profit. Monetary discipline would be a competitive advantage among producers of alternative currencies.

Free banking means that private banks would be able to issue currency and create deposits without being subject to government regulation or restrictions. The acceptance of this privately created money by the public would be a function entirely of the bank's credibility in promising not to overissue its particular currency. Profit-maximizing managers of money-issuing banks would necessarily become sensitive to market signals that reflected on-the-spot consumer demand for their money. As George A. Selgin writes in his book *The Theory of Free Banking*:

> In the money industry as elsewhere, the free interplay of market forces leads to effective resource administration. The key to the market solution in this case is the guidance provided by the clearing mechanism. That mechanism is the source of debit and credit signals that rapidly (and timing is critical) follow free banks' over- and underissue of inside money. By responding to these signals free bank managers are led to adjust their liabilities to conform with the public's demand for inside money balances as if they had direct knowledge of, and were concerned with satisfying, consumer wants. It is not just the costs connected with the *issue* of inside money which regulate its supply under free banking; rather, it is these costs plus the costs associated with the return of notes and checks to their issuers for redemption in base money, that is, *liquidity* costs.[128]

In short, free banking ostensibly would capture all the benefits of competitive free markets by responding to consumer demand for money balances and, in so doing, would provide the desired aggregate supply of money. Individual bankers who made good decisions in regulating the amount of the currency they produced to conform to consumer demand would be economically rewarded, while bankers who made bad decisions in issuing their currency would be punished by the market. Competition in money would not lead to chaos, argue the proponents of free banking, but would bring about order and efficiency. They point to central bank monopoly issuance of money as lacking the advantage of continuous market signals and rapid managerial response.

If free banking were to become the accepted form of organization for issuing money and creating credit—in essence, for managing the level of purchasing power in accordance with the demands of consumers—would the risk of wide-scale economic or financial failure be increased or decreased? Skeptics argue that a free banking regime would bring forth hoards of wildcat operators anxious to exploit short-term profit opportunities with little concern for longer-term stability. Disreputable producers could create an explosion of excess money and leave consumers with a debilitating "buyer beware" attitude about accepting any but the most familiar forms of currency. The proliferation of fast buck operators might finally lead to a crescendo of total monetary anarchy and a paralyzing crisis of confidence that would bring internal economic transactions to a halt.

Free banking advocates are quick to negate the possibility of such a doomsday scenario, but beyond a certain point economic theory cannot provide all the answers. Social behavior injects itself into the formula. Ask most people (not economists) what events brought on the Great Depression and they are likely to cite the absence of regulatory control over the activities of banks and financial markets. Laissez-faire creation of credit and purchasing power is somehow not acceptable to the public at large. The government is expected to play a prominent role in regulating something as basic and important as money. Indeed, the establishment of the Federal Reserve is generally viewed (again, outside of professional economic circles, where the matter is decidedly more contentious) as having been necessary as a countermeasure to rein in the less-than-responsible activities of private sector banks. Like food inspectors or traffic police, Federal Reserve regulators are seen as being necessary to protect the interests of society at large from the greedy and damaging actions of profit-seeking banks. The Great Depression could never happen again, it is widely believed, because the Federal Reserve now functions as a watchdog to ensure the orderly process of money creation.

The point is this: The most rational theoretical model, though derived through impeccably logical deduction and rigorous analysis, may not be an acceptable model for society. That is, society may reject it. Does that mean monetary historians, researchers,

and theorists should not even attempt to overcome public mis-
conceptions and strive to bring about what they consider to be a
superior form of money for a capitalist system? No. But they
should accept the fact that government-issued money is an entrenched cultural concept that cannot easily be displaced. As
Hayek recognized:

> The great obstacle is that the denationalization of money involves
> such great changes in the whole financial structure that, and I am
> saying this from the experience of many discussions, no senior
> banker who understands only the present banking system can really
> conceive how such a new system would work, and he would not
> dare to risk and experiment with it. Hence, I think we will have to
> count on a few younger and more flexible brains to begin and show
> that competing private currencies are a viable alternative to gov-
> ernment monopoly of issuing money.[129]

Historical Precedents

In theory, it is difficult to argue with Hayek's logic: Money, the
most basic of goods, should be subjected to the ultimate discipline
of free market competition in order to develop the highest quality
product. But how has this idea worked in practice? Can we review
the historical experience with private money to get a feel for
whether this approach might offer a feasible option for today's
global economy?

Adherents of private money and the free banking environment
associated with it point to several instances in the past where competitive currencies have delivered a level of monetary stability far
superior to the results achieved under government-influenced
central banking systems. Selgin, for example, recounts the era of
private note issuance and free banking that took place in Foochow, China, between 1800 and 1935.[130] According to Selgin, the
issuance of currency during this time was exclusively a private undertaking (except for a brief period during the 1850s when the
government unsuccessfully attempted to issue notes) and private
paper currency grew in importance and popularity.

Selgin notes that, unlike government issues, the private offerings of currency typically did not depreciate and were widely pre-

ferred over bulky copper cash. An efficient note-clearing system cropped up, and the notes of larger banks were circulated throughout Foochow at par. Failures among smaller banks occurred often, but during the whole episode of private note issuance and banking only one large local bank failed. By the end of the private money era in Foochow there were approximately forty-five large banks in operation. These banks issued paper notes redeemable in copper cash, in most cases on demand, and functioned completely free of government regulation. Based on Selgin's assessment, they "commanded a high level of public confidence and respect."[131]

During much of the same time period, from about 1830 to the early 1900s, Sweden also experimented with private currencies and free banking. Sweden's Parliament decreed in 1824 that there would be no state support for commercial banks because the government was not willing to take the responsibility of having to protect depositors.[132] On the plus side, though, banks would not have to comply with any government regulatory requirements beyond the filing of quarterly reports. Still, commercial banking was not considered a worthwhile pursuit until the law against private note issuance was lifted in the 1830s. Once private banks had the right to compete with Sweden's state bank, the Riksbank, competitive currencies proliferated and commercial banking became quite profitable. Mary L. King points out that at the end of 1850 the state bank's note issuance stood at about 34 million kroner while private notes amounted to some 15 million. By 1870 the situation had reversed; the state bank's notes amounted to just 26 million kroner while the private banks had some 40 million kroner in notes in circulation.[133]

One reason Sweden developed such a thriving paper currency market perhaps may be explained by that country's unique monetary history. King explains that Sweden was the laughingstock of Europe in the seventeenth century because it had ridiculously heavy coins. That particular development was the result of a decision in 1624 by Sweden's king to put the country on a bimetallic standard based on silver and copper; copper's prominence had much to do with the fact that Sweden had a virtual monopoly on copper and the Swedish government was part owner of the nation's largest mine. Eventually, reflecting the effect of Gresham's law, the silver coins were driven out of circulation by the copper coins. Because the price of copper was barely one-hundredth that of silver, King explains, the ten-dollar coin was a back-breaking forty-three pounds. The most common coin, the two-dollar piece, was almost ten inches across and weighed close to nine pounds.[134]

The instance of successful private free banking cited most often by advocates of competitive currencies is Scotland's experience from 1716 to 1844. Lawrence H. White, who chronicled this 128-year period in his book *Free Banking in Britain*, asserts that a nonregulated banking environment offering consumers a plethora of private banknotes functioned quite smoothly. "During its free banking era, Scotland experienced remarkable economic growth with relatively little macroeconomic instability," White notes. "The banking system enjoyed complete immunity from panics and runs."[135]

The success of the Scottish free banking period, though, has been challenged by other monetary scholars. Larry J. Sechrest contends that White's portrait of free banking in Scotland does not necessarily provide evidence on the workability of monetary freedom in a private market setting, nor does it prove the efficiency or stability of an unregulated monetary system.[136] Sechrest disputes the notion that Scottish banks were less prone to failure than English banks (which operated under a rigid central banking system) and points out that Scottish banks often demurred from redeeming depositors' claims in gold or silver. To the extent that the immediate convertibility of private note issuance constitutes a defining characteristic of competitive currencies, Sechrest concludes that "a significant element of free banking was absent."[137]

In his historical work *Money in Britain*, C. R. Josset also provides information that undercuts the concept that citizens were largely insulated from monetary concerns during Scotland's free banking periods:

> Many of the early private banks of the eighteenth century in Scotland issued notes far in excess of their resources, with the result that they used every measure possible to prevent the notes being presented too soon in order to avoid financial embarrassment. This

caused the two large banks to find a more reliable method of circulating money, especially in times of panic, and to refuse to accept the many notes of other banks which were circulating in Edinburgh. This decision unfortunately meant 'a loss to the people of Edinburgh who when they became possessed of notes of private bankers, in which indeed most of their wages were paid, were obliged to keep them dead sometime on hand or pay 1 1/2*d*. every 20*s*. for changing them' (Scots magazine).[138]

The U.S. Wildcat Era

The United States' experience with private banking and competitive note issuance has received mixed assessments. The term "wildcat" refers to the concept that private bankers who wanted to issue excess notes without having to contend with heavy demands for redemption from their customers tended to locate out in the frontier regions where wildcats roamed. Transportation costs and lack of communications hindered the ability of note recipients as well as professional money brokers to verify the integrity of the numerous forms of private currency. Notes issued by these backwoods operators were accordingly discounted. Catalogs—called banknote detectors—were published to assist in establishing appropriate exchange rates for notes offered by nonlocal banks.[139] Still, as King notes, unscrupulous bankers in obscure regions managed to delude state regulators:

> The coin reserves some wildcatters showed state officials were only kegs of nails with a layer of coins on top, and while the examiner was tromping through the brush to the next bank, the keg would be whisked ahead for display there.[140]

Another problem during the U.S. experiment with free banking from 1836 to 1863 was the prevalence of counterfeiting. Citing the *Nicholas Bank Note Report* of 1858, King points out that some 4,500 notes in circulation were described as fraudulent at a time when only 7,000 legitimate ones existed.[141] It was a period when the consumer had to pay attention; there was no federal regulation of banks and the notes issued by banks in various states were no more than private promises to pay on demand. The Bank of the United States was abolished in the 1830s, so no central bank existed to provide a benchmark for the amount of notes that might be issued against gold or other reserves.

Some defenders of the U.S. free banking era point out that a legacy of government interference in issuing money hampered the development of authentically free banking. Instead, banks enjoyed special privileges that allowed them to rise above the normal contractual obligations incurred by other businesses. If a bank issued a note promising the recipient that the note could be redeemed in specie—that is, silver or gold—on demand and then failed to honor such a demand, that bank should be declared bankrupt and liquidated to pay off claims held against its assets. But the practice had arisen earlier in the United States, starting in August 1814 and lasting until February 1817, to effectively exempt banks from having to honor their convertibility clauses in times of monetary crisis. For two and a half years, in the wake of the inflationary aftereffects from the War of 1812, the federal government had permitted all banks to suspend specie payments while allowing them to continue to operate and expand the level of paper claims. As observed by former congressman Ron Paul and Lewis Lehrman in their minority report of the U.S. Gold Commission:

> From then on, every time there was a banking crisis brought on by inflationary expansion and demands for redemption in specie, state and federal governments looked the other way and permitted general suspension of specie payments while bank operations continued to flourish. It thus became clear to the banks that in a general crisis they would not be required to meet the ordinary obligations of contract law or of respect for property rights, so their inflationary expansion was permanently encouraged by this massive failure of government to fulfill its obligation to enforce contracts and defend the rights of property.[142]

An even more insidious incursion of government interests into the banking business, according to Paul and Lehrman, was the subtle pressure exerted on banks to invest in state government securities that then could be utilized as capital. These state government bonds became the reserve base upon which banks expanded their deposits and issued notes. "This provision deliberately tied banks and bank credit expansion to the public debt," Paul and

Lehrman note. "It meant that the more public debt the banks purchased, the more they could create and lend out new money."[143] The effect of this unholy alliance was that state governments found it easy to go into debt, private banks had strong incentives to monetize the public debt, and hence "government and bank inflation were intimately linked."[144]

Whether or not free banking and the existence of competitive private currencies served the public's interest, then, is still open to debate. But in every case mentioned, the practice of free banking was brought to an end by government. The U.S. free banking era concluded with the National Bank Act of 1863, which prohibited the issuance of any state bank notes and granted a monopoly to the federal government to control the nation's monetary system through the exercise of regulatory authority over commercial banks. The goal of the bill was to ensure sound currency in the face of financial chaos and to provide funding for the Civil War, because the new nationally chartered banks were compelled to hold a substantial portion of their reserves in the form of U.S. government debt.

Free banking episodes similarly were brought to a close in China, Sweden, and Scotland. Governments typically rewarded those bankers willing to provide public debt financing by granting them regulatory concessions or monopolistic privileges that effectively eliminated private competition; if governments did not act directly by imposing decrees, than they used more subtle means, such as designating "legal tender" in exclusive terms. The bottom line is that governments everywhere have found it irresistibly tempting to insinuate their own fiscal interests into the business of supplying money. And, often enough, powerful banking interests have found it equally lucrative to accommodate government financing requests in exchange for the rewards of a protected market environment.

5

The Solid Choice

For all the references that one hears to the global economy, it is sometimes difficult to determine whether the concept suggests a threat or an opportunity. Many portray the global economy as a battlefield where the United States, Japan, and Europe struggle for market share and financial dominance. Others focus on the possibility of losing high-paying jobs in developed countries to poorer nations with lower labor and environmental costs. If one views the world's resources with a zero-sum mentality, which see's one nation's gain as another nation's loss, the prospect of a global economy where jobs and markets are not protected and competition knows no boundaries is indeed a threatening vision.

But others take a different view, recognizing expanded opportunity and potential for growth in an integrated global economy. They reject the notion that the enrichment of an individual or an entire nation comes at the impoverishment of another. Instead, they embrace international competition as the means to achieving lower production costs and ultimately higher living standards; they are only too delighted to see protectionist barriers removed. Proponents of an open global economy believe that free markets and free trade work to the benefit of all participants.

Depending on which view one takes, the international monetary system is either yet another protectionist tool that should be exploited by governments as necessary or it is something not to be tampered with—the pure language of international commerce. If the latter view is taken, the objective of the international monetary system should be to provide a clear, concise language that communicates accurate price signals to all participants in the international marketplace. A common monetary language is the key to maximizing the returns from global free markets.

But even if one accepts the idea that money should work on behalf of people to facilitate trade and business and not be subject to government distortions that create false signals, there is still the matter of figuring out how to set up a system that delivers sound money for the global economy. Humans have yet devised only so many ways to coordinate currencies; the advantages and shortcomings of four basic approaches were presented in the previous chapter. Beyond the theoretical appeal of various schemes for producing good money is the practical aspect of human behavior. What do people want? Conceivably, it would be possible to design and operate a world currency. The fact is, though, that people live in nation-states and most citizens would be justifiably reluctant to turn over their countries' monetary reins to a group of supernational central banking officials. Who would be chairman—someone from the moon?

While people are suspicious generally of governments, it doesn't necessarily follow that they would prefer to have a money issuer other than government. If that is the case, the goal is to place governments under proper restraints so that they do not abuse the privilege of monetary sovereignty. Moreover, any domestic mechanism for regulating the issuance of money must be in conformance with an overall global approach to currency relations. Whether one fears or welcomes the global economy, it is not to be denied; a monetary system that does not somehow reconcile internal and external economic realities in the end will be ripped apart in the threshing pits of integrated global financial markets.

In short, the future success of the global economy depends crucially on the integrity of the international monetary system. If you can't evaluate competitive goods and services across borders in terms of their prices, you cannot have a functioning free market. If prices cannot be compared on the basis of a common monetary unit, the forces of supply and demand do not come into proper play. In a global economy ostensibly dedicated to free trade, buyers and sellers must have access to an honest and reliable international monetary system so they can find each other and transact business anywhere in the world.

Is it possible to create and implement such a system? Are powerful, automatic mechanisms required to preserve it? What is the proper role for governments in maintaining orderly currency relations? Should private markets determine the relative values of competing monies?

COMPARING THE OPTIONS

The objective here is to summarize the key ideological and practical features of the various approaches discussed earlier and to ascertain which one offers the most appropriate form of international monetary system to serve the needs of a global economy.

The most important point to be made about the prevailing regime of floating rates is that it has not performed as advertised. Instead of delivering smooth adjustments through constantly changing market prices for currencies, floating rates have exacerbated diverging economic paths among nations. The foreign exchange rate market is ruled more by speculative hunches and rumor-driven efforts to divine the motives of finance ministers and central bankers than by any underlying economic rationale.

The problem of applying market solutions to the fundamental question of defining the value of money is that the forces of demand and supply that dictate the profitability of taking a certain market position—shorting a currency perceived to be weak, for example—overwhelm the interplay of demand and supply for money for its own sake—that is, for what it will buy. As economist and Nobel laureate James Tobin noted in 1980:

[F]oreign exchange markets are necessarily adrift without an-chors. . . . In these markets, as in other markets for financial instruments, speculation on future prices is the dominating preoc-cupation of the participants. In the ideal world of rational expecta-tions, the anthropomorphic personified "market" would base its expectations on informed estimates of equilibrium exchange rates. Speculation would be the engine that moves actual rates to the equilibrium set. In fact no one has any good basis for estimating the equilibrium dollar-mark parity for 1980 or 1985, to which cur-rent rates might be related. That parity depends on a host of incal-culables—not just the future paths of the two economies and of the rest of the world, but the future portfolio preferences of the world's wealth owners. . . . In the absence of any consensus on fundamen-tals, the markets are dominated—like those for gold, rare paint-ings, and—yes, often equities—by traders in the game of guessing what other traders are going to think.[1]

Kenichi Ohmae confirms the view that foreign exchange mar-kets are driven by traders' efforts to outsmart each other in inter-preting the utterances of G-7 finance officials that may contain veiled references to shifting policies. "On a real-time basis," Ohmae writes, "traders pay more attention to announcements (or hints) about fundamentals than to the fundamentals themselves."[2] Ohmae suggests that, with a saturated real estate market in Tokyo and golf memberships (which can be traded) at the Kasumigaseki Country Club running at about $2 million, investors need some other bucket in which to dump their money. The hottest bucket turns out to be the foreign exchange market, which is a specula-tor's paradise offering high volatility and, hence, exciting opportu-nities to make quick profits.[3]

Those profits depend, though, on out-smarting governments. Currency markets are supposedly private and free, but the biggest players, the central banks, can rig them whenever so directed by treasury officials. When jobs are seemingly at stake, or foreign competition threatens to hurt domestic sales, or exports appear to be suffering, the temptation to execute adjustments through for-eign exchange markets holds irresistible allure for governments. There are no regulations to protect the little guy from price-fixing actions taken by government cartels to move the market. Nor does an average business manager have the minute-to-minute information necessary to guess right on currency movements. In short, between the central bankers and the speculators, the individual entrepreneur who wants to sell products in another country is at the mercy of uncontrollable forces. People in this position can always pay a specialist to construct a "currency hedge" to cover the transaction, or they can just forget the whole idea.

If it were possible to have a truly market-determined system of freely floating rates, along the lines envisioned by Milton Friedman, then it might make sense to let demand and supply for various currencies determine their prices. Not knowing how gyrating currencies would affect their profits, people wanting to engage in international trade would have one more element of uncertainty to factor into their general business risk, but at least they would know that exchange rates at any given moment were an honest reflection of the market's assessment of currency values.[4]

However, this is not the way the floating rate system actually works. Even Friedman acknowledges that he has become increasingly skeptical that a system of freely floating exchange rates is politically feasible. "Central banks will meddle," he notes, "always of course with the best of intentions."[5] The floating rate monetary system in effect today thus is irredeemably tainted by the presence of powerful government players who do not hesitate to influence the market value of the currency over which they exercise monopolistic influence.

Following the breakdown of the Bretton Woods system, the move to floating rates was widely hailed as advantageous because it liberated nations from having to bring their domestic monetary policies into alignment with international economic and financial flows. But as Lester Thurow observes in his 1992 book *Head to Head*, the violent and seemingly irrational swings in exchange rates that have occurred in the past two decades have severely reduced economic efficiency and taken their toll on world growth. "Nobody knows where economic activity should be located; nobody knows the cheapest source of supplies," Thurow notes.[6] Risk and uncertainty are needlessly increased when firms are unable to discern the real costs of production or estimate potential rewards from investment because they operate in a global economic environment characterized by unpredictable currency values. Says

Thurow: "Flexible exchange rates are an area where members of the economics profession, myself included, were simply wrong."[7]

So how do we get it right? If the goal is to maximize global trade and opportunity, individuals around the world must be able to assess world markets in terms of a common unit of value. The first step, then, is to fix the money—fix it in the sense of making it solid and reliable, not subject to deterioration over time, and in terms of a global standard of value, so that national currencies are convertible into each other at specified rates of exchange. It is not necessary to have a world currency in order to have a common money. As long as different currencies can be converted into each other at a stable exchange rate, it is functionally the same as having a common form of money.

Fixed rates thus deliver what the entrepreneurs of the world need to compete on the basis of genuine merit and comparative advantage without having to worry about currency risk. The problem, though, is what to fix these rates *to*. Is it enough for governments merely to declare that a matrix of exchange rate parities has been established by decree to serve as a semipermanent formula for converting monies across national borders? What happens when domestic economic pressures build up, as they inevitably do, in one of the participating countries? Suddenly the government officials of that country insist they can no longer maintain the established fixed rate, so they want out of the system. Or, more likely, they want the other members of the system to recognize the existence of a "fundamental disequilibrium" and accommodate them accordingly.

Once a group of nations has decided to coordinate exchange rates among themselves, an escape hatch for weaker members tends to become an institutionalized part of the monetary system. The exchange rates are fixed, yes, but only temporarily. If that seems a contradiction in terms, it is because the governments of nations that sign on to such an arrangement have contradictory motives. They want to reap the advantages of fixed rates, which everyone admits are a boon to international trade and investment, but they don't want to give up their flexibility. That is, they don't want to lose their ability to use monetary policy as a convenient way to absorb a multitude of fiscal sins.

While fixed rate systems are officially described by members in the most egalitarian terms, in reality they are dominated by a single country. During the Bretton Woods era, that country was the United States. More recently in Europe, that country has been Germany. Germany's central bank, the Bundesbank, effectively set the monetary policy for all the other member countries of the European monetary system. This arrangement was fine as long as the other governments were comfortable with the level of fiscal restraint and monetary prudence exercised by the Germans.

But what happens when the anchor country for a fixed rate system puts its own domestic economic priorities ahead of its responsibility to maintain international monetary stability—if it ever agreed to take on such a responsibility? While German officials increasingly are fixated on the economic and financial problems of their newly-unified country, the rest of Europe is left to wonder whether the anchor is adrift or merely temporarily sidelined. Since the breakdown of the exchange rate mechanism, the nations of Europe have had occasion to pause and reflect on the implications of giving up monetary sovereignty to a faceless bureaucracy in Brussels that likely would be taking its marching orders from the Bundesbank. Private fuming about German attitudes toward European unity has taken on a most uncharitable tone.

This case illustrates precisely the problem with a fixed rate system that requires member countries to answer to each other on sticky financial issues rather than relying on an objective monetary point of reference. The anchor for a fixed rate exchange system should never be a single country. While reasonable people can agree to set up rules for monetary cooperation among their nations, raw emotion comes to the forefront when the pivotal nation suddenly becomes preoccupied with its own destiny and ignores the nations that have come to rely on its stalwart policies. A fixed rate system that designates no outside anchor inevitably will come to depend too much on the strongest country, and no country is immune to pursuing its own national economic interests. The threshold for one nation might be a certain level of unemployment; for another, it might be the threat of a painful recession. For Germany, it was the costs associated with the opening of the Berlin Wall and the potential for domestic inflation.

Without an outside anchor, fixed rate systems soon become mere economic points of departure for aggressive bargaining among the finance ministers of powerful nations. At best, they supply a mechanism for communal monetary drifting; at worst, they feed national resentments. The main operating feature of a pegged exchange rate system is not the internal fiscal discipline exercised by its members, but intimidation: central banks stand prepared to intervene as necessary to thwart market pressures that threaten to alter the relative prices of currencies. Access to vast financial resources was always their ace in the hole—until the big-time currency speculators came along with even greater access to financial resources.

The message is that the anchor for a fixed rate system must be outside that system. It must be beyond nationalistic suspicions and beyond the ability of any government or private party to manipulate for personal advantage. Good fences make good neighbors. As long as everyone recognizes the cold, hard reality of an objective monetary standard, economic frustrations are less likely to turn into dangerous provocations.

If it is not enough simply to designate an accounting abstraction, such as the ecu, as the international standard of value, and if it is a mistake to depend on a single nation to supply the anchor currency, then how do you set up a global monetary system with fixed rates? One way is to define the common monetary unit for all currencies in terms of real assets. When money is backed by commodities, it assumes intrinsic worth. No longer just a marker for some vague affirmation of government responsibility, money takes on the quality of a financial claim to something of real value—the money represents the goods themselves. In the most basic sense, it is sound. At the option of the holder, such money can be converted into material wealth. Fiat money, in contrast, has value only as long as the next person accepts it in payment for goods and services. When a monetary Ponzi scheme reaches its limits, the last person stuck with the paper currency loses.

If commodity-backed currency has so much to offer in terms of transcending politics and furnishing sound money, what are the arguments against it? What is the downside of a commodity-backed monetary system? To keep the case succinct, let us assume we are talking about a monetary system backed by a single commodity: gold.

Aside from the obvious point that a gold standard prevents government from controlling key economic and financial variables, such as interest rates (which might strike many as a significant virtue), the fact is that a gold standard links the money supply to the supply of gold. Or, rather, it links the rate of growth in the money supply to the rate of growth in the gold supply. So when the supply of gold grows at a rate that is higher or lower than the rate of economic growth, inflation or deflation can result.

The smooth functioning of a gold standard does depend on a stable growth rate in the supply of gold, one roughly equivalent to the growth in the demand for money, which in turn is a function of the rate of growth in economic productivity and the population. All of these rates ideally converge at around 3 to 3.5 percent per year. When the gold supply is increasing at that rate, along with economic growth and population levels, the natural result is zero inflation.

What happens when the rate of growth in the supply of gold is dramatically increased by the discovery of a new source or a breakthrough in gold production techniques? Much of the reliance on gold as a stable monetary base stems from the fact that traditional methods of extraction have relied on a remarkably consistent combination of human labor and physical capital. When chemical leaching or another new process changes that formula, the cost of adding a new unit of gold to the world's supply is likewise altered. If gold becomes more plentiful or cheaper to produce while the world is on a gold standard, people turn in gold for money and expand the supply of paper claims. Money becomes inherently less valuable—that is, the impact is inflationary.

But is this disadvantage serious enough to preclude moving to a gold standard? Consider the following: The annual new production of gold represents a tiny proportion of the existing stock of gold in the world. Gold is a highly durable metal and has been accumulated by people since the beginning of history. As long-time gold standard advocate Lewis Lehrman points out, total new gold production in any single year has amounted on average to only about 2 percent of the total supply of gold in existence:

Even huge gold discoveries never resulted in sustained, high inflation. The vast expansion of gold money in Europe during the six-
teenth century and the nineteenth century never caused the price
level to rise in excess of an average of 3 percent over a long period.[8]

The potentially destabilizing impact of changes in the rate of
new gold production on the soundness of a gold-backed money
thus pales in comparison to the fiscal offenses that are carried out
by profligate politicians in the absence of the discipline inherent in
a gold standard. When citizens have the right to redeem money
for gold whenever they suspect its value is being compromised by
government policies, such as expanding the money supply to finance a federal budget deficit, they hold an ax over the necks of
politicians. Not that legislators would be prevented from spending
vast amounts of taxpayers' money just because a gold standard
was in effect; there is nothing implicit in a gold standard insofar as
demanding low taxes or minimal redistribution of national wealth
by government. It's just that under a gold standard, the government could not monetize a budget deficit. Whether tax revenues
were high and government spending was high, or whether tax revenues were low and government spending was low, the decision
would be up to the citizens who elect representatives to carry out
their socioeconomic will. All a gold standard does is ensure that
the government spends at the level explicitly authorized and paid
for by taxpayers.

Internationally, a gold standard would provide the mechanism
for reconciling domestic and global finances and create a level
monetary playing field for international competition and trade.
Mutually beneficial economic links among trade partners would
erect a hedge against potentially hostile national rivalries, and adherence to an international gold standard would ensure the proper monetary foundation for such peacekeeping arrangements. Not
only would a gold standard prevent powerful trading nations from
being in a position to deliberately exploit their neighbors by or-
chestrating movements in exchange rates, it would lift such potentially incendiary practices out of the realm of government
influence. It would make the ground rules for international trade
subject to the rule of law, not of men.

Some would argue at this point that even a gold standard leaves money too vulnerable to the actions of government officials. Better to avoid the monopoly syndrome, Friedrich Hayek and others have suggested, and open up the money business to private suppliers.

The idea of competing private currencies is theoretically appealing because it embraces free market doctrine to advance the notion that the best money would come about as the result of having to satisfy consumer desires. But the concept leaves aside the fundamental question of whether consumers want to have a choice when it comes to money. Is the public eager to take on the task of constantly having to evaluate the relative features of one brand of money versus another and be ready to switch at a moment's notice?

Irrational or not, history has shown that people have a remarkable loyalty to money that offers familiarity, even long after that currency has been debased by government and even when alternatives are available. Some of this reluctance to move to unfamiliar currencies is not irrational at all; there are information costs associated with accepting a new medium of exchange. There is always the risk, too, that the next person may not be willing to accept the new currency—a possibility that detracts from the seeming superiority of an alternative form of money. And what about counterfeiting? With many different brands of money floating around, the potential for counterfeiting increases.

Unquestionably, there is psychological discomfort associated with having to deal in an unfamiliar medium of exchange. Anyone who has traveled to a foreign country knows the sense of insecurity one feels when forced to make mental calculations under pressure to judge the value of goods or services in a different currency. Herbert Stein, who served as chairman of the Council of Economic Advisers under both presidents Nixon and Ford, admits to being "traumatized by exchange rates" and provides a painfully humorous account of his own experiences while traveling from one country to another:

> Leaving Israel to fly to Paris I had a handful of leftover shekels. I decided to exchange them for francs. Going from the exotic shekel to the romantic franc without passing through the humdrum dollar made me feel like a sophisticated jet-setter.

I received 279 francs, which somehow seemed enough for taxi fare from Charles de Gaulle Airport to my Paris hotel. I also got a printout saying that the rate was .39. Since I thought that the shekel was worth about 50 cents and the franc about 20, it seemed reasonable enough that a figure like .39 would appear somewhere, although I wouldn't have bet on doing the algebra right the first time.

Five hours later I am speeding along in a French taxi and the taximeter is clicking off two francs at an even more furious pace, alongside a sign saying "No checks accepted." I worry about whether my 279 francs are going to survive this race, at the same time trying to remember whether I should multiply the francs by .2 or by five to get them into my native currency.

To my relief, the taxi and the meter slow down as we enter the XVI Arrondissement, and the meter says only 132 when we stop in front of the hotel. "One hundred and sixty," says the driver. (All this is a blur in my mind now, and I'm not sure what language we were using. I suppose English.) "Why?" I ask. "Luggage," he explains. I am so annoyed and angry about this, as well as by his general manner, that I determine to give him no tip. I had barely reached the sidewalk, however, when I realized that I had only 19 francs left. I had given the driver 260. But he assured me that I was mistaken. He showed me that in one pocket he had a lot of money, which was his, and in the other pocket he had a little, which was what had been mine. Before we could pursue the subject he drove off. . . .

All the money amounts are trivial. This story is not about the amounts; it is about confusion, mental anguish, humiliation. It is about states of mind, which is, after all, what economics is all about.[9]

One of the important features of money is the sense of confidence it imparts as a measure for evaluating other goods and services. A monetary regime of competing private currencies likely would raise the stress level an individual already experiences in making economic and financial decisions. To the extent that there is this negative aspect of having to choose among currencies, a dominant producer probably would arise as consumers rallied around the most familiar form of money. Indeed, the more popular a certain brand of money became, the more it would take over the market, until eventually it would become the only readily accepted form of money. Then the supposed advantages of private competitive currencies would disappear as the most successful money producer attained a monopoly.[10]

If the ultimate outcome of a private market for money is a monopoly, does it make much difference whether the monopoly is run by a private company versus a public entity? As long as people are confident that the currency is redeemable into real assets on demand, they might be willing to grant government the power to issue the money.

GOING FOR GOLD

It is difficult to argue with Ludwig von Mises's assertion that the ultimate goal of any approach to monetary issuance should be to provide sound money. Whatever the presumed benefit of inflation (a spur for growth?) it relies on tricking the public into thinking prices are increasing and profits are rising faster than they truly are—that is, faster than they would on the basis of real increase in demand. Surely money should not be used to delude producers and laborers into taking actions they otherwise would not take for the sake of artificially stimulating the economy. Businesspeople are not children who can be enticed with candy; rational decision making should not be undermined by holding out alluring paper profits. Aren't citizens capable of making economic choices and conducting financial transactions in response to accurate price signals, without phoney monetary inducements?

It was John Maynard Keynes, after all, who believed that artificial profits gained through inflation eat away at the moral fiber of the entrepreneur:

> But if the depreciation of money is a source of gain to the business man, it is also the occasion of opprobrium. To the consumer the business man's exceptional profits appear as the cause (instead of the consequence) of the hated rise of prices. Amidst the rapid fluctuations of his fortunes he himself loses his conservative instincts, and begins to think more of the large gains of the moment than of the lesser, but permanent, profits of normal business. The welfare of his enterprise in the relatively distant future weighs less with him than before, and thoughts are excited of a quick fortune and clearing out. His excessive gains have come to him unsought and without fault or design on his part, but once acquired he does not lightly surrender them, and will struggle to retain his booty. With

such impulses and so placed, the business man is himself not free
from a suppressed uneasiness. In his heart he loses his former self-
confidence in his relation to society, in his utility and necessity in
the economic scheme. He fears the future of his business and his
class, and the less secure he feels his fortune to be the tighter he
clings to it. The business man, the prop of society and the builder
of the future, to whose activities and rewards there had been accorded, not long ago, an almost religious sanction, he of all men
and classes most respectable, praiseworthy and necessary, with
whom interference was not only disastrous but almost impious, was
now to suffer sidelong glances, to feel himself suspected and at-
tacked, the victim of unjust and injurious laws,—to become, and
know himself half-guilty, a profiteer.[11]

For Keynes, the presence of inflation threatens the tranquility
of capitalist society because it calls into question fundamental issues of economic justice and opportunity; it could destroy the necessary "psychological equilibrium" that preserves social peace
across various wealth classes. If people believe others have gained,
not through honest effort but through unearned profits obtained
through inflated prices, they grow resentful. "The economic doctrine of normal profits, vaguely apprehended by every one, is a
necessary condition for the justification of capitalism," Keynes
noted. "The business man is only tolerable so long as his gains can
be held to bear some relation to what, roughly and in some sense,
his activities have contributed to society."[12]

Why should people tolerate monetary policies that seek to lure
them into responding to false profit signals or false wage increases? Why should they be pawns of politicians or economists trying
to influence their behavior to achieve short-term "feel good" economic objectives? Most people, it's safe to say, do not appreciate
being toyed with by government officials; they would prefer to
take their money straight.

Keeping Government Honest

Just as Mises was correct in designating sound money as the ultimate policy goal, he also saw that governments could not be expected to deliver sound money in the absence of some
enforcement mechanism. Mises was extremely suspicious of the

motives of politicians and pressure groups. For Mises, the only way to guarantee the soundness of money in the face of ambitious government inclinations was to adopt a gold standard. Only a gold standard, Mises asserted, could keep the purchasing power of money independent from such compromising influences.[13]

Could that same logic apply today? Could it be that the optimum approach for structuring a new global monetary order would be to implement the classical international gold standard? A gold standard is not perfect, as noted previously, because it depends on steady increases in the rate of growth of world gold supplies that accord with increases in real economic growth. But given the disadvantages of other systems—the corruptness of floating rates, the superficiality of pegged exchange rates, the confusion of competitive private currencies—an international gold standard emerges as the most attractive option. Even if that conclusion is derived through the process of elimination, it still stands that a gold standard offers the least imperfect system. Certainly, it provides the strongest mechanism for guarding against tinkering by self-serving governments—and that is no small consideration.

Not the least of the problems associated with the other approaches is their complexity. Money is the most basic economic tool, the standard for evaluating goods and services around the world. How many members of the public comprehend or feel comfortable dealing in foreign exchange markets today? Trading currencies is seen as some kind of specialist activity better left to the experts who operate on behalf of huge mutual funds and international banks. A gold standard offers a straightforward monetary rule that requires no expertise or arcane knowledge to understand. The money can be redeemed for gold. Period. And while gold-backed money could conceivably be provided through private enterprise, most people don't want to have to second-guess the integrity of an array of money manufacturers competing to appeal to consumers.

Thomas Jefferson, for one, felt that the power to issue currency and credit is too great to be entrusted to private business interests. In a letter to John Wayles Eppes in 1813, Jefferson bemoaned the ruinous practice of allowing "self-created money lenders" to issue excessive levels of monetary claims. He wrote:

> The unlimited emission of bank paper has banished all [Great Britain's] specie, and is now, by a depreciation acknowledged by her own statesmen, carrying her rapidly to bankruptcy, as it did France, as it did us, and will do us again, and every country permitting paper to be circulated, other than that by public authority, rigorously limited to the just measure for circulation. Private fortunes, in the present state of our circulation, are at the mercy of those self-created money lenders, and are prostrated by the floods of nominal money with which their avarice deluges us.[14]

Jefferson was suspicious of the motives of private banks and concerned about their ability to depreciate the value of money through "demoralizing" lending practices.[15] Writing to John Taylor in 1816, Jefferson noted, "And I sincerely believe, with you, that banking establishments are more dangerous than standing armies; and that the principle of spending money to be paid by posterity, under the name of funding, is but swindling futurity on a large scale."[16] In the latter part of this comment, Jefferson makes it clear that although the power to issue money should be vested in government, strict controls should be put into effect at the same time to prevent government from abusing the public trust. In the debate over the government's proper monetary role in 1784, Jefferson asserted, "If we determine that a dollar shall be our unit, we must then say with precision what a dollar is."[17]

As soon as you define with precision what a dollar is, you remove the capacity of a financial authority or central bank to exercise discretion over the money supply and alter the value of the monetary unit. Once a dollar, say, is defined in terms of so many grams of gold, it cannot be redefined as the result of unwarranted growth or restrictions in the money supply; instead, the money supply contracts or expands in response to public demand for use of dollars of unyielding value.

For all the worldly sophistication that has been brought to bear on what constitutes a viable monetary system, it seems hard to refute the notion that the supply of money should be a function of the natural demand for it. While monetarists may insist that it is possible to calibrate the supply of fiat money to the economic and financial needs of the population, their arguments, in light of experience, are not convincing. It is as impossible to manage the money supply to accommodate the complex needs of society as it is to run the economy of a large nation through central planning. No individual is that smart; no econometric formula is that comprehensive. Better to let the actions of hundreds of millions of individuals seeking to improve their personal economic welfare be regulated by Adam Smith's "invisible hand." Just tell people what the rules are—they can take it from there. One of the primary rules should be this: Money is defined in precise terms so that it is worth something.

As the global economy increasingly becomes a reality with improved communications throughout the world, individuals in different countries will have less tolerance for the discretionary actions of fallible central bankers that undermine the value of money. Producers and consumers will want to deal directly with each other. A gold standard provides the common denominator for conducting business across national boundaries—a sort of monetary Esperanto. National currencies function as dialects of the same root language, gold-backed money.

But people who might be willing to concede that sound money is the desirable objective of international currency relations and who acknowledge that humans are incapable of anticipating the diverse and constantly changing monetary needs of populations may still have qualms about moving to a gold standard. The constancy and rigidity of a gold standard can be seen as a disadvantage. Flexibility for so long has been hailed as a vital element in conducting economic policy that governments are averse to any mechanism that might constrain their actions in the realm of policy initiatives. But that aversion to constraints is cause for alarm. What do government officials mean when they insist on preserving monetary flexibility? Flexibility to do what?

Granting monetary autonomy to governments in the absence of built-in discipline rarely serves the interests of private citizens. As *The Economist* has observed:

> Historically the most popular use of monetary independence has been to finance, by means of printing money, budget deficits that cannot be financed any other way. The result is always inflation—but this has generally failed to deter the spendthrift, perhaps be-

cause they hope the effects of their policies will be their successors' problem not theirs. All of which suggests a simple rule: a government that insists on access to the printing press cannot be trusted with it.[18]

Not surprisingly, the countries that enjoy the lowest levels of inflation are those where the central banks enjoy the most independence from governmental coercion. One of the most interesting examples of an autonomous central bank is New Zealand's Reserve Bank; the chairman operates under a five-year contract to keep inflation between zero and 2 percent. The chairman can utilize any instrument of monetary management deemed necessary but can be fired if the contract is not adhered to.[19] By contrast, the Bank of England has operated since the end of World War II under the control of the chancellor of the Exchequer, so that Britain's monetary policy is effectively administered by the Treasury—an arrangement praised by some as "democratic." But permitting money supply growth to be responsive to political pressures is anathema to achieving soundness. Germany's Bundesbank was thought to enjoy considerable independence from political pressures; indeed, this earlier reputation contributed to the perceived integrity of the deutsche mark. But when the Bundesbank was instructed to carry out monetary unification with East Germany on terms that meant future inflation, German monetary authorities had to succumb.

Because autonomy is an advantage when it comes to delivering stable money, why not institutionalize monetary independence by completely removing it from the realm of internal politics and managerial error? Going on a gold standard constitutes the ultimate manifestation of central bank independence.

Yet even those who disdain the use of discretionary monetary authority, such as Sir Alan Walters, express opposition to a gold standard. Walters derides the notion of physically accumulating gold to serve as backing for government-issued currency and notes that "it seems quite absurd for scarce resources to be devoted to digging a hole in the ground to extract gold, only to return that gold again to the deep vaults of the world's central banks."[20]

But an effective counter to that argument was put forward by Jack Kemp in a 1982 speech before an audience that included representatives of the Federal Reserve system:

> It is true that when gold convertibility is working best, the system appears most absurd. The gold just sits there in vaults, because people generally prefer holding convertible paper dollars, which earn interest, to holding gold, which does not. By the same token, national defense is working best when our expensive and sophisticated weapons are just sitting there, looking useless, because our adversaries don't dare to threaten us. And the same is true, I guess when you buy life insurance but don't die. It is only when we convince ourselves that these reserves are wasteful, and can therefore be dispensed with, that we find out, too late, how wrong we were.[21]

It is neither absurd nor wasteful, but entirely prudent, to expend the resources necessary to make gold convertibility a reality, to back up government-issued money with collateral that people can see and touch. Not to maintain sufficient inventory to preserve the integrity of the currency is an act of fraud.

Power Corrupts

A gold standard operated by the government provides a monetary mechanism with all the advantages of commodity-backed currency to protect citizens from potential debasement, and yet at the same time recognizes money issuance as a legitimate government function. To choose a gold standard is to insist on outside discipline to ensure the long-term integrity of the value of money. But it also is to acknowledge that people are not entirely comfortable with turning over the issuance of money to private suppliers. Certain responsibilities are granted to government because citizens believe their needs can be met best by a recognized central authority, whether for defending the nation or preserving private property rights.

The framers of the Constitution were well aware, however, that when powers are knowingly granted to central government, those powers must be precisely defined and limited. One axiom has proved true through the ages: power corrupts. Therefore it is necessary to stipulate limits to power to curtail the inevitable push toward exercising greater levels of authority once government is empowered. A gold standard represents the embodiment of this thinking applied to monetary sovereignty. While Jefferson and others were willing to grant to government a central role in defining the value of the monetary unit, they just as vehemently argued for the imposition of constraints that would prevent government from using its monetary powers to enrich itself.

Jefferson was horrified at the prospect that the government would issue debt that ultimately would have to be paid by overtaxed citizens. Jefferson offered a brilliant argument against Keynesian economics (long before Keynes was born) when he declared that it would be much better for the United States to grow solidly at a pace it could afford than to have the government borrow heavily to artificially stimulate the rate of growth of the economy. For Jefferson, the evil was not only that citizens would be excessively burdened by taxes associated with high levels of public debt. He was even more upset that the role of government in peoples' lives would become oppressive and that citizens would turn against each other in mutual frustration and misery. In a letter to Samuel Kercheval in 1816, Jefferson wrote:

> We must make our election between *economy or liberty*, or *profusion and servitude*. If we run into such debts as that we must be taxed in our meat and in our drink, in our necessaries and our comforts, in our labors and our amusements, for our callings and our creeds, as the people of England are, our people, like them, must come to labor sixteen hours in the twenty-four, give our earnings of fifteen of these to the government for their debts and daily expenses; and the sixteenth being insufficient to afford us bread, we must live, as they now do, on oatmeal and potatoes; have no time to think, no means of calling the mismanagers to account; but be glad to obtain subsistence by hiring ourselves to rivet their chains on the necks of our fellow-sufferers. . . . This example reads to us the salutary lesson, that private fortunes are destroyed by public as well as by private extravagance. And this is the tendency of all human governments. A departure from principle in one instance becomes a precedent for a second; that second for a third; and so on, till the bulk of the society is reduced to be mere automatons of misery, and to have no sensibilities left but for sinning and suffering. Then begins, indeed, the *bellum omnium in omnia*, which some philoso-

phers observing to be so general in this world, have mistaken it for the natural, instead of the abusive state of man. And the fore horse of this frightful team is public debt. Taxation follows that, and in its train wretchedness and oppression.[22]

Jefferson's farsightedness is validated in today's newspapers as the issue of fairness is increasingly invoked to justify higher taxes on the wealthy. Fairness is seldom discussed in terms of what is the proper amount to require taxpayers to remit to government for redistribution; rather, the concept is aimed at making sure the chains of public debt are riveted on the necks of our fellow sufferers as securely as they are fastened around our own necks. This, surely, is not the American Dream. It conjures up feelings that contrast sharply, tragically, with the idea of a nation dedicated to every individual's inalienable right to life, liberty, and the pursuit of happiness. No wonder Jefferson was so deeply concerned about excessive government spending and the eventual depressing effect it would have on the spirit of the people. "I place economy among the first and most important virtues, and public debt as the greatest of the dangers to be feared," he wrote.[23]

Latter-day supporters of honest money often echo Jefferson's fear of public debt and its debilitating impact on personal freedom. In their book *The Case for Gold*, Ron Paul and Lewis Lehrman make the following observation:

> Gold money is always rejected by those who advocate significant government intervention in the economy. Gold holds in check the government's tendency to accumulate power over the economy. Paper money is a device by which the unpopular programs of government intervention, whether civilian or military, foreign or domestic, can be financed without the tax increases that would surely precipitate massive resistance by the people. Monetizing massive debt is more complex and therefore more politically acceptable, but it is just as harmful, in fact more harmful, than if the people were taxed directly.
>
> This monetising of debt is literally a hidden tax. It is unevenly distributed throughout the population, one segment paying much more than another. It is equivalent to a regressive tax, forcing the working poor to suffer more than the speculating rich.

Deliberately debasing the currency for political reasons, that is, paying for programs that the politicians need in order to be reelected, is the most immoral act of government short of deliberate war.[24]

The most damning aspect of paper money—the one in keeping with Keynes's analysis of bloated profits—is that it leads to class warfare. Money should perform the same way for everyone. Members of society should not be divided on the basis of those who seemingly benefit from inflation and those who do not. Borrowers are unduly enriched if inflation enables them to pay back their debts in less valuable money. So what do creditors do? They start charging a premium to protect themselves from this risk. Eventually everyone bears the extra cost of investment and society at large incurs the net loss—all because the government is not held accountable for carrying out its fundamental responsibility to keep the money sound.

If it is important to Americans that government be restrained from putting burdensome economic chains around the necks of the people, if honest money is seen as going hand-in-hand with free markets and democracy, then the adoption of an international gold standard represents an extension of American ideals to the global economy. Certainly it must strike other nations as hypocritical that the United States talks up the benefits of eliminating tariffs and other barriers that compromise free market mechanisms and then engages in behind-the-scenes tactics to influence the currency prices of its major trading partners. If governments should not be allowed to interfere in voluntary business transactions among individuals around the world, they surely should be prevented from subverting the value of money, which, after all, permits individuals around the world to make meaningful market decisions.

BACK TO THE FUTURE

The most appealing, and most demanding, aspect of going on a gold standard is that such a move would require that domestic monetary policies be brought into line with international economic verities. To adopt a gold standard would be to accept the fact that economic and financial transactions and the market forces that shape them do not stop at national borders. Professor Robert Mundell was correct: the only closed economy is the world economy. Once the reality of the global economy is acknowledged, it is clear that manipulating the money supply to create artificial price signals as the means to counter recession or relieve unemployment is futile in the long run—not only futile, but selfish.

The United States is the most powerful nation in the world, and while it may not dominate the international economy to the extent it did in the past, it still plays a formidable role in determining global economic growth. One overarching statistic: the United States is the world's largest exporter. Moreover, much of the economic growth the United States has experienced in recent years has come from exports. So if any nation should be trying to reconcile its domestic economic, financial, and monetary profile with the larger contours of the global trade community, it logically should be the United States. The greater the conformance between internal policies and global practices, the less distortion and inefficiency to detract from the benefits of free trade—presuming that the United States truly is devoted to free trade.

A House in Order

What would it mean for the United States to go on a gold standard? What kinds of domestic financial issues would be affected? How would moving to a gold standard affect the federal budget process, borrowing and lending activities, and price levels?

In terms of the federal budget deficit, the impact would be straightforward. Under a gold standard, the government would be put under extreme pressure to balance the budget. If government expenditures exceeded government revenues, the difference would have to be financed—the government would have to borrow to cover the shortfall. When the government borrows, it does so by creating debt instruments that provide purchasing power to their holder. People pay money to the government in exchange for the debt instruments and the government spends the money it receives; at the same time, it issues additional money claims that can be sold for funds today or redeemed in the future. Out of nothing more than a gap in the budget, the government creates purchasing power by obligating itself—or, rather, U.S. taxpayers—to pay back money in the future (which might be defined as three months away). This process is known as "monetizing" the debt.

Under a gold standard, citizens can resist this monetizing process, which they rightly see as diluting the value of their money, because it increases purchasing power without adding to the productive output of the economy. All they have to do is exercise their right to redeem their money in gold. The redemption of dollars for gold in response to excess credit creation by the federal government would furnish a strong political signal, as suggested by Alan Greenspan in 1981 in a *Wall Street Journal* op-ed piece.[25] Indeed, it would surely have a curtailing effect on the congressional spendthrifts, who would be held accountable for undermining the integrity of U.S. money; the more citizens began turning in their money for gold, the more reproach would be directed at those who were deemed responsible for profligacy.

Going on a gold standard would force the legislators who exercise control over federal spending to suffer the consequences of their decisions. The whole budget process would be made transparent. Ordinary citizens would be empowered to fully comprehend how their tax money was being spent and to register their approval or disapproval accordingly. Federal spending goes to the heart of the government's proper role in society and the economy, and a gold standard would force the issue into the light of public scrutiny. (In his earlier writings during the 1960's, Greenspan elaborated on this more ideological point, noting that a gold standard is incompatible with chronic deficit spending and redistributionist government.)[26]

The government's ability to borrow money to resolve fiscal imbalances, while at the same time using monetary policy to influence interest rates, is an obvious conflict of interest and has led to tremendous financial losses in the private sector. Could a thrift crisis, such as the one Americans are still paying for, occur under a gold standard? The financial environment that accompanies a gold standard—stable purchasing power, stable interest rates—all but eliminates the possibility. In contrast, the recent U.S. savings-and-loan debacle can be traced directly to the discretionary monetary policies that were practiced by the Federal Reserve under the stewardship of Paul Volcker. Interest rates seesawed violently at the beginning of the 1980s as the Fed sought to wring inflation out of the domestic economy by imposing punishing rates. Productivity and growth fell victim to the tight money policies; innumerable business opportunities were lost forever.

When prices for real estate increase steadily for years, as they did during the late 1970s, people are lulled into thinking the trend will never change. Bankers and savings-and-loan officers believe it, too; making real estate loans, whether in the form of thirty-year home mortgages or commercial property deals, seems like a sure bet. The value of the collateral strengthens behind the face value of the loan, and the owner has the money to easily pay back the loan when the property is sold at some future date. At least, the situation appears that way when inflation is creating artificial signals of the sort alluded to by Keynes, the ones that prompt businessmen to "lose their conservative instincts" and concentrate on reaping the nominal gains from inflation rather than the normal profits of business.

But when normal supply and demand assert their more legitimate claim to economic growth and the policy of trying to peg money supply and interest rates begins to unravel, the effect is to wreak havoc on peoples' lives and punish them for having responded to false stimuli. William Greider, in his book *Secrets of the Temple*, writes:

> Housing, automobiles and other interest-sensitive sectors—where both the buyer and the seller rely heavily on borrowed money—never really recovered from the roller-coaster recession of the previous year. Early in 1980, the combination of high interest rates and credit controls had forced the economy into a sharp but brief contraction. When the Federal Reserve eased money rapidly in the spring, however, interest rates fell dramatically—from a high near 20 percent to below 9 percent—and the economy turned around abruptly. By fall, however, the Fed was progressively tightening again and driving interest rates to a new peak. The Federal Funds rate rose past 12 percent in October and by January it crested at 20 percent.[27]

Greider concludes that the Federal Reserve's ability to determine the price of money gives it unique power to convey the trappings of success or failure on individuals without regard to their actual performance in their chosen profession:

> By the summer of 1981, the real price of money was higher than it had been in fifty years and it would go still higher.
>
> Whether people profited or lost from these new terms depended, in large measure, on where they stood in the spectrum of economic interests, less on their personal skills or energy. A farmer, after all, could not simply stop being a farmer and decide to be a bond investor. A home builder or an auto worker could hardly quit and go into banking. Many of them would be ruined, and after the fact, their failure would be blamed on their own miscalculations. American finance, meanwhile, would enter its most profitable cycle of the century.[28]

If people cannot reasonably count on stable interest rates and stable purchasing power as they endeavor to achieve economic self-sufficiency over their lifetime, they can hardly embrace the notion that it is worthwhile to sacrifice immediate gratification for the sake of future consumption. It makes no sense to put away funds for tomorrow if the value of savings is up for grabs in Washington. Humans display behavior at its most rational when, having experienced first-hand the ravages of inflation, they decide not to save money—especially when interest rates are not sufficient to compensate for the expected decline in the value of money. In July 1993, Greenspan noted in his testimony before Congress that the short-term interest rate adjusted for current inflation was close to zero.[29] When there is no proper compensation for saving money, individuals have little reason to sacrifice any portion of their current consumption.

Mises instructs us that capitalism cannot exist without savings. "When a man has accrued a certain amount of money—let us say, one thousand dollars—and, instead of spending it, entrusts these dollars to a savings bank or an insurance company, the money goes into the hands of an entrepreneur, a businessman, enabling him to go out and embark on a project which could not have been embarked on yesterday because the required capital was unavailable."[30] But the sad reality is that Americans' savings rate today is the lowest among industrial countries. The citizens of the nation representing capitalism at its best are showing widespread resistance to accumulating capital. In less than a generation, the savings rate in the United States has fallen from a solid 9 percent to less than 3 percent.[31]

What a gold standard can do is restore peoples' faith in the merit of saving money. That is, it can resurrect the idea that saving is a virtue, as opposed to being naive, ill-considered, and stupid. A psychological adjustment is needed, because under inflation, the smart borrowers are rewarded and the dumb savers are hurt. As George Goodman, alias "Adam Smith," explains in *Paper Money*:

> How do I beat inflation, how do I stay ahead? Hedging depends on a continuous supply of gulls, of suckers, of greater fools, of people who haven't gotten the word. Think a minute: somebody has to sell you that "inflation hedge," somebody who already owns it. Why should he? Why should I sell my house for your depreciating dollars? The advice that tells you to go out and borrow, buy *things*, that's the way to beat it, presumes that the lender hasn't heard what's happened to the money. Maybe the lenders are the foolish children with the 5-percent bank passbooks and the 6-percent $50 Treasury E bonds. When the foolish children find that the skates they were saving for have doubled in price while they were saving, when all the foolish children together find they lent you the money through their savings bank for a condo that's gone way up and they still don't have their skates, they will say the hell with it. When they get old enough to vote, they're going to remember what fools they were and come looking for you with a candidate who has blood in his eye.[32]

If people have memories as long as Goodman suspects, it suggests why so much animosity has been directed at the late 1970s and early 1980s as an era of greed, a time when Wall Street financial interests somehow rode roughshod over the rest of the country. And why, in the 1990s, the emphasis is on getting the wealthy to "pay their fair share."

A monetary standard that delivered sound money would certainly help alleviate the social tensions that divide people into classes—creditors versus debtors, wage earners versus financial speculators—on the basis of how much they are helped or hurt by unanticipated changes in the value of money. Price distortions associated with inflation or deflation are largely avoided under a gold standard. Business may be good or bad, profits may be high or low. But when the currency is backed by gold, individuals do not have to tally their performance against a moving monetary target.

A Boon to Trade

The emergence of a standard definition of monetary value would serve as a tremendous contribution to the cause of global free trade. Not just free but also fair trade would be enhanced, in the sense that governments would be precluded from using their currency as a trade weapon to grant an unfair price advantage to exports. The concept of fairness in trade, ironically, has become a euphemism for justifying various acts of protectionism, such as imposing quotas or punishing competitors for alleged dumping. Yet the area where it makes sense to insist on fairness—designating a standard monetary unit so people can accurately assess value in the international marketplace—does not receive attention.

A gold standard would be particularly helpful for developing countries that desire to participate in global markets on the basis of their legitimate capacity to compete, rather than through succeeding rounds of debilitating currency devaluations. Stable money is an extremely attractive feature in a national economy. The confidence required to entice potential entrepreneurs and outside investors to put their personal capital at risk depends crucially on a stable money environment. It is when investors must consider the possibility that profits will be cut by unforeseen devaluations that the costs of doing business become prohibitively high.

Whereas Latin America used to be considered an economic basket case, it is today one of the most promising areas in the world for sustained growth. The secret to success for such countries as Mexico, Argentina, and Chile has been a combination of intensive efforts to privatize government-owned industries, reduce tariffs, lower taxes, and stabilize money. Painfully aware of the economic and social damage inflicted during preceding years of hyperinflation, the leaders and finance ministers of these countries have worked diligently to slash inflation. Mexico and other

Latin American countries are now running budget surpluses. In Argentina, where the money is backed by gold and foreign reserves, the emphasis has moved away from protecting financial assets against inflation to manufacturing competence. "I hear Argentines talking about quality now," said a Santiago banker in *Business Week*. "Used to be, they only talked about interest rates on yen."[33]

When people no longer have to concentrate their creative energies on being sufficiently nimble in currency markets to not lose money, those energies are freed to be genuinely productive. Wealthy, industrial nations may have the luxury of being able to waste the human resources that go into playing the currency markets, but developing countries simply cannot afford it. Their citizens need to be able to quit worrying about monetary policy, domestic or international. The greatest economic favor the United States could do for developing countries would be to back its money in gold, so they could do the same. Even if these countries chose not to establish their own gold standard, at least they could link the value of their money to the dollar.

Clearly, among the countries most vulnerable to monetary shock and breakdown in the world today are the former republics of the Soviet Union, particularly Russia. Yet the measures enacted thus far to put Russia on a solid monetary footing have been woefully inadequate, if not downright damaging. The Group of Seven major industrial nations granted the International Monetary Fund the leading role in transforming the ruble into a valid currency. But IMF officials have taken the approach that by floating the ruble against hard currencies, the value of Russian products will become equilibrated with the prices of goods and services offered in the global economy. They are mistaken. At least, by the time the equilibration has fully taken place, the Russian economy will be largely destroyed. The disintegrating value of the hyperinflating ruble guarantees that there will be infinite demand to convert it into Western currencies. Economic and financial distortions caused by the debasing of the ruble by the central bank, first under Soviet control, then under Russian control, are far too vast and deeply ingrained to be reconciled with world market prices through floating rates.

In the meantime, Russian citizens are left with money that loses value every day. In a country where the need for investment capital is desperate, few bother to accumulate funds. Indeed, only the ignorant save their rubles. "Almost everything I earn I spend," a Moscow resident, Natasha Stepanov, told a *New York Times* reporter, "because I'm afraid to keep money at a time like this."[34] After the fiasco perpetrated by Russia's central bank chairman, Viktor Gerashchenko, in July 1993, when citizens were bluntly informed they had only a short time to trade in a limited amount of old ruble notes before the currency would be declared invalid, Russians have even less reason to trust their money.

In the countries of Eastern and Central Europe, the earlier enthusiasm for joining the global economy has been dampened by the muted response of their neighbors in the European Community. Plans for a single European currency have been delayed if not permanently sidetracked by the effective collapse of the exchange rate mechanism. The East Europeans can hardly expect to exert much influence over monetary arrangements negotiated by the finance ministers of the strongest industrial countries; a future European monetary system managed by a network of central banks would assuredly cater to the demands of the dominant member countries rather than the needs of the newcomers. It is difficult to imagine Germany having much interest in a monetary system that was not sensitive to the will of the Bundesbank.

A gold standard, in contrast, would establish objective criteria for participating in international trade and finance. It would not distinguish between well-established industrial powers and poorer developing nations. Europe's purported goal in seeking monetary union is to eliminate the unnecessary costs of currency hedging and the problems of exchange rate fluctuations. So one might expect a good reception to a proposal for an international gold standard. If it makes sense for the nations of Europe to use the same monetary unit so that goods and services, along with financial and human resources, all have the opportunity to flow freely toward their most productive use, why shouldn't these same benefits be extended to the world? And to the extent that the unacknowledged European agenda is to get out from under American hegemony in currency markets, again, it makes sense for Europe to embrace the kind of international monetary order that would obtain through a classical gold standard. In short, European leaders should enlarge the conceptual framework of the debate over European monetary union. They should be prepared, not merely for their own interests but for the sake of struggling nations only recently freed from communist domination, to transcend the current discussion and transform it into a call for full-scale international monetary reform.

What would it mean for Japan if the global community moved to a gold standard to define the monetary unit for international trade? If one considers the extent to which Japan has been the victim of targeted efforts by the United States and other G-7 nations to manipulate exchange rates, there is no question that Japan has much to gain. Instead of having to contend with efforts by U.S. finance officials to revalue the exchange rate between the yen and the dollar whenever Japanese exports become too popular with American consumers, Japan could be assured that competition with U.S. products would be conducted on a legitimate cost basis.

Put at a price disadvantage through no fault of their own after the Plaza Agreement in 1985, Japanese exporters were forced to become more efficient; to the extent they were successful, the deliberate devaluation of the dollar against the yen may have helped them grow even more competitive and offer more value to the American consumer for the money. Business journalist Hobart Rowen speculated in the *Washington Post* that *endaka*, the Japanese word for a high yen, "could have been more beneficial to Tokyo than Washington."[35] But when the yen began to climb again in 1993, Japanese manufacturers were clearly pressed to the limit. After Japan's new government urgently notified its trade partners in August that the high yen was seriously damaging economic performance, the Federal Reserve (at the direction of the Treasury) intervened heavily in currency markets, purchasing dollars and reversing the momentum that had driven the yen to near-parity with the U.S. penny.[36]

Level Playing Field

Because efforts to manipulate exchange rates by intervening in currency markets can lead to unexpected and unwanted outcomes, the case for an international gold standard is made all the stronger. It would protect nations from the foibles of their own finance ministers. It would assure private citizens that their purchasing power—for domestically-produced goods as well as imports—could not be manhandled by ambitious government officials all too eager to correct for "market imbalances" that were likely the result of their own misguided economic policies.

A global gold standard would provide monetary stability across borders and through time. Decisions made by individuals to conduct trade with people in other nations, to purchase goods and services, to invest at home or abroad, to forgo consumption and save money for future use—it should be possible to contemplate and carry out all these choices on the basis of a consistent monetary unit. A gold standard guarantees the constant value of money so that people can focus on the merits of economic and financial opportunities without being distracted by the risk of unanticipated changes in future purchasing power caused by inflation or deflation or fluctuations in the relative prices of national currencies.

A gold standard would close governments' option to practice protectionism against trading partners through the deliberate devaluation of their domestic currency. That the United States would resort to such tactics, given its size and power in the global economy, seems particularly unseemly. Yet the United States is one of the worst offenders because it not only chooses on occasion to run down the dollar but it also uses its influence to get powerful economic allies to cooperate in moving the foreign exchange markets.

Some economists, such as Ronald McKinnon, have put forward proposals for establishing a partnership among the United States, Japan, and Europe to jointly manage a monetary base defined in terms of the dollar, yen, and deutsche mark. In McKinnon's view, returning to a gold standard would not be necessary to guarantee the integrity of the system; monetary cooperation and conscious management of the aggregate monetary base by the central banks of Japan, the United States, and Germany (representing Europe) could prevent worldwide inflations or deflations.[37] But others are sensitive to the negative implications of an alliance among the big three economic powerhouses. Johei Kono, chairman of the Research Commission on Foreign Affairs of Japan's Liberal Democratic Party, cautions that cooperation among Japan, the United States, and the European Community "should never resemble a cartel protecting the interests of the advanced nations at the expense of poorer nations."[38]

It is difficult to imagine how lesser nations could avoid the impression that when it comes to foreign exchange markets, where selecting the best currency is akin to playing roulette, the wheel is rigged against them. Under the present system, the United States can enlist the support of the central banks of its economic partners to counter market trends that threaten to undermine exchange rates calculated to protect U.S. interests in world trade. But if the global monetary order were determined in accordance with a classical international gold standard, no country, not even the most powerful, could dictate exchange rates by prevailing on its allies to manipulate foreign exchange markets. No Group of Seven inner circle of central banks could conspire to buy and sell each others' currencies to change the natural course of trade flows.

A gold standard, in short, would prevent governments from using their currencies as tools of short-term economic policy, trading the temporary advantage of cheaper exports against the longer-term problems of decreased purchasing power for their citizens in the global economy. The emphasis among participants in the international marketplace would rightly turn to comparative advantage and genuine competence. As Robert Hormats, vice-president of Goldman Sachs and former State Department economic policy official, observes: "The real answer is not to lower the dollar. The real answer is to boost competitiveness."[39]

In the global economy, there is no rationale for a monetary system that can be exploited by a powerful nation for its own advantage. To discourage protectionism and to foster more international trade, a global gold standard should be put into place. It would effectively provide a common world money in the sense that currency risk would no longer be a factor in international trade. At the same time, it would permit individual nations to exercise monetary sovereignty, but not monetary abuse; they would have to abide by the discipline inherent in a gold standard. Nations would maintain their own national currencies, but they would not have the latitude to indulge in spendthrift fiscal habits.

Whether government revenues and government expenditures comprised a high proportion of the domestic economy, or whether they constituted a low proportion, the choice would be up to citizens of that nation. A gold standard would simply require that a government's decision to redistribute resources, whether in accordance with socialist doctrine or laissez-faire principles, be recognized explicitly. Its budget would have to be balanced.

Most important, the implementation of a global gold standard would establish objective monetary criteria for successful participation in the global economy rather than bestowing special benefits on countries that, either through their own efforts or through the efforts of powerful allies, attempt to reap the rewards of favoritism in currency markets.

DEMOCRATIC MONEY

In discussions of international monetary reform, much of the emphasis is directed toward how much individual nations would gain or lose under various systems. Nations are presumed to be the primary players in the global economy. Nations have currencies that are valued high or valued low in terms of their level of international competitiveness; governments take action in foreign exchange markets when they wish to strengthen or weaken their money compared to other trading nations' money.

But as George Gilder explains in his book *Microcosm*, the world is changing dramatically because of the technological revolution in computers and telecommunications. Gilder sees a direct analogy between what he describes as a "quantum" revolution in technology and its impact on economic developments. For Gilder, the technological move away from material resources and toward the exploitation of knowledge has a liberating effect on humankind— not people in the aggregate sense, but individuals. Individuals can utilize computers and an expanding communications network to maximize their personal productive output. Instead of being held back by the physical limitations of material wealth (think of huge manufacturing plants that must have proximity to iron and coal mines), economic development can now come from the brain of a software genius who creates a useful new computing program.

Whereas national wealth has historically been determined on the basis of physical resources located within territorial boundaries, the new sources of wealth in the global economy dwell inside the minds of creative entrepreneurs who devise new services or new ways to improve productivity.

What does the quantum age of technology and economics require in terms of global monetary arrangements? In one sense, Gilder might be the last to advocate the use of gold—the classic material asset, the ultimate commodity—to facilitate the movement to a global economy. And yet, Gilder recounts ideological arguments that dovetail perfectly with the philosophical leanings of Mises and others who would elevate the individual over the government, and business over bureaucracy:

> The central conflict in the global economy pits the forces of statism against entrepreneurs using the new microcosmic technology to integrate world commerce. Defying national boundaries, entrepreneurs have knitted together a dense global fabric of manufacturing suppliers with near just-in-time delivery commitments. They have ferreted out the world's best human resources without regard to nationality, setting up factories and laboratories in foreign countries, and they have brought in the immigrant engineers and researchers who are revitalizing the best American firms. They have summoned an explosive expansion of international investment ties that leaves the entire history of national economies in its wake. . . .
>
> In their most deadly assault on U.S. high technology, the bureaucrats destroyed the value of their dollars in order to favor increasingly uncompetitive heavy industry. The result was to strengthen Japanese electronics firms vastly by nearly doubling the value of their capital, profits, and market share without in any way helping innovative U.S. companies. The majority of high-tech products offer unique functions rapidly moving down the learning curve with heavy investment in both R & D and capital equipment. A one-time drop in price is worthless when it comes at the expense of skewing investment away from American innovation and strengthening foreign rivals.
>
> As the driving force in the rise of the world's central strategic technology, the U.S. upsurge in computers in the early 1980s was a major factor in the rise of the dollar. The U.S.-led devaluation of the dollar, at the behest of farmers and uncompetitive commodity producers, showed a complete incomprehension by the U.S. government of the

true sources of competitiveness. A fruitless mercantilism, worshipping trade gap totems, threw away the fruits of American high-tech entrepreneurship and allowed the Japanese to buy at bargain rates what they could not create. A revolt against the microcosm allowed textiles and timber firms to export material goods against third world rivals while devaluing the creativity of American innovators on the frontiers of the global economy of the mind.[40]

Though Gilder does not specifically advocate an international gold standard or other monetary regime, he does display a clear bias in favor of the entrepreneurs whose personal efforts are the building blocks of the global economy. Gilder shows an equally clear disdain for the kind of bureaucratic thinking that attempts to stifle international competition in the name of protecting the national interest. He is vehemently opposed to protectionist measures that choke trade with quotas, spurn foreign investors, burden producers with new taxes, and "wage war in general against the key sources of growth in world capitalism."[41]

One thing Gilder makes clear is that it is a mistake to allow the government to destroy the value of money in pursuit of misguided trade advantages of a temporary political nature. He believes that, with the advent of the global economy in the quantum age, individuals will be less willing to subordinate their own economic interests to the interests of the state. Gilder is quite hopeful in this respect, despite his regret over losses already incurred as the result of government meddling:

> Nonetheless, barring war or other catastrophe, the bureaucrats will inevitably lose in the end. The global microcosm has permanently shifted the world balance of power in favor of the entrepreneurs. Using the planetary utility, they can avoid most of the exactions of the state. Without their fully voluntary cooperation a government cannot increase revenues, enhance military strength, provide for the public welfare, or gain economic clout.[42]

If Gilder is right, the rise of entrepreneurs throughout the world may prove the driving force for the enactment of a new global currency order. People may increasingly balk at having to submit the fruits of their labor to the monetary machinations of central bankers and finance ministers. They will start to object to the government's assumed right to alter the monetary terms of international transactions at its own discretion. They will insist that the money be left alone; they will no longer permit its value to be tossed about by wily speculators or currency specialists at international banks. They will not allow it to be moved at will by G-7 officials working the markets in concert. They will insist that money be simply left alone to retain the value assigned to it from the start—across borders and through time.

In a sense, most people are already participants in the global economy. Even if they never conduct business deals with foreigners or never step beyond the borders of their own country, people still suffer a decline in their purchasing power when the government devalues their money in foreign exchange markets. As Paul Volcker observes in *Changing Fortunes*: "Certainly a depreciating currency ordinarily means that imports cost more and that exports earn less foreign currency. In other words, the nation is poorer, not richer, and that's not something to jump with joy about."[43] When the government attempts to move the market in the other direction, driving up the value of its currency against the currencies of other nations, it causes damage of another sort; domestic exports are suddenly priced too high relative to the international competition. Imports become artificially cheap, shifting markets away from domestic suppliers.

Thus, whenever government gets involved in manipulating the value of its currency relative to other currencies, the people lose. Just as inflation proves to be an artificial stimulus that distorts the normal rewards of investment and lures people into making wrong business decisions, devaluing currency in foreign markets likewise creates false signals that disrupt normal economic processes and thwarts the gains that might otherwise have been achieved through legitimate competition. Whether citizens are seemingly on the upward side or the downward side of government intervention in monetary markets, whether their currency is strengthening or weakening in foreign markets, they inevitably suffer the consequences of distortion. In the end, they pay the price for the bureaucratic bungling that takes place at the expense of free market solutions in the world trade arena.

Gold Has No Politics

In the new global economy, there should be no room for political maneuvering by governments and no tolerance among individual economic competitors for the unfair advantages—temporary though they may be—that are sought through currency market intervention. Sound money should be the rallying cry of the entrepreneurs who are rapidly turning the vision of a global economy into reality. They should demand it from their governments. Sound money is the only proper foundation for free trade and the successful operation of an open international marketplace. A global gold standard would be the means to achieve the monetary system that would best serve the requirements of the global economy simply because it would provide common money with permanent integrity beyond the realm of governmental tampering. A classical gold standard ensures that government officials remain true to the economic interests of their own citizens. At the same time, it defines currency values in consistent terms across national borders so that the world captures the benefits of a unified monetary system.

Demand for sound money and proclamations about the virtues of a gold standard are sometimes dismissed as pet conservative causes. Could it be that more liberal types are not concerned about the value of their money or that they believe uncertain currency values in world markets accomplish something useful? If political stereotypes are stripped away from the issue of sound money, it becomes clear that the interests of all citizens are served when stable purchasing power enables them to make their own decisions regarding their future economic welfare and to maximize their opportunities in world markets. If a gold standard furnishes the best mechanism for preserving a sound money regime, it should appeal to citizens of all political stripes. Quoting William Rees-Mogg, former editor of the London *Times*, Jack Kemp has made the statement:

> A gold system works through the money supply and does not require an elaborate system of controls; it should appeal to the political liberal. Gold is international; it is in the world's money supply; it is natural for a man who believes in gold to be internationalist

rather than nationalist in outlook. Gold is stable; it not only represents order, it imposes order by a quasi-automatic mechanism; it should appeal to the institutional conservative. Gold is just; it deals equally between one man and another, between past, present, and future; it does not take from the weak and give to the strong; it should appeal to the seeker of social justice, to the social democrat.[44]

By the rationale invoked by Rees-Mogg, advocates for a gold standard might well define themselves as being "institutional conservatives" and "social democrats." Certainly, the desire for monetary stability and fiscal discipline translates into support for a gold standard; in that sense, supporters might be labeled financial conservatives. But the idea that individuals should take measures to protect themselves from the potential abuses of government is distinctly liberal in its outlook. Under a gold standard, the people retain control over both the quality and the quantity of the money. The two aspects are inviolably linked, because citizens can redeem their money in gold if they believe too many paper claims have been issued, and to the extent that they do, the quantity of currency in circulation automatically decreases. "A gold-based currency is in fact democratic money," notes Lehrman. "It is a populist institution beyond the reach of a guardian elite."[45]

Distrust of a guardian elite stems from the philosophy that overarching government solutions to economic problems may not be solutions at all. Indeed, government most often is the problem when it comes to monetary, financial, and economic difficulties. The precipitous decline of communism and the disintegration of the Soviet Union have underscored the futility of central economic planning. Armies of bureaucrats, no matter how well armed with complex formulas and statistics, simply cannot compete with the invisible hand. When they attempt to do so, they inevitably distort natural economic processes by injecting the government into the market as a player when the government's role should be strictly limited. The government's role should be to see that no outside forces restrict or encumber the market, and it should strive to ensure that the legality of contracts is honored. Government that functions as a guardian elite violates the concept of democratic rule; money controlled by a small group of central bankers and finance ministers is likewise anathema to the principles of democracy and free markets.

Asking who should control the money is the same as asking who should control the market. It suggests a lack of faith in the basic notion that supply and demand, as determined by the voluntary economic activities of free individuals, ultimately furnish the right amount of goods at the right price. The desire to grant discretionary monetary authority to a small group of government officials indicates a basic hesitation to trust the market to properly allocate goods and services among producers and consumers. Certainly, this stance goes against the classic liberal position as outlined by Hayek in his essay: "Why I Am Not a Conservative." Hayek explains that a key characteristic of the liberal attitude is its confidence in the assumption that the self-regulating forces of the market will bring about whatever adjustments are required to adapt to new conditions, even when no one can foretell how exactly these adjustments will take place.[46] Hayek contrasts this sharply with the attitude of conservatives who prefer powerful centralized authority over diffused and spontaneous market processes:

> There is perhaps no single factor contributing so much to people's frequent reluctance to let the market work as their inability to conceive how some necessary balance, between demand and supply, between exports and imports, or the like, will be brought about without deliberate control. The conservative feels safe and content only if he is assured that some higher wisdom watches and supervises change, only if he knows that some authority is charged with keeping the change "orderly."[47]

For Hayek, conservatives are much too prepared to turn over the reins to some higher human authority for the sake of preserving order, even when it means sacrificing the gains that arise from more organic economic processes. Hayek derides conservatives for their lack of faith in the wisdom and competence of common people and for their eagerness to grant special privileges and monopolies to those "recognizably superior persons" who, the conservatives are willing to concede, "should have a greater influence on public affairs than others."[48] Hayek does not accept the conservative view that arbitrary power is not necessarily bad as long as it is exercised by decent people in pursuit of what conservatives consider to be the right purposes; he rejects the idea that a select group of authorities should be allowed to do whatever they believe is required by a particular set of circumstances.[49] Instead, Hayek extols the attitude of the liberal who is opposed to unlimited government and who believes that nobody is qualified to wield unlimited power.[50] Hayek points out, too, that "conservatives are usually protectionists" and can match the efforts of socialists at times in their attempts to discourage and discredit free enterprise.[51]

To sum up: Those who might try to trivialize the idea of achieving sound money through a gold standard by branding it as a conservative fetish reveal a fundamental misunderstanding of the philosophical underpinnings of the central issue in economic and political debate. Moving to a gold standard is a radically liberal proposition because it means turning over the reins of monetary power to the people. This is no small concession to ask of government given its prior hold on power. Gold-backed currency goes to the heart of the issue of who should control the money and how the process should be managed—by a human authority with discretionary powers or through an organic process that evolves as the result of spontaneous actions by individuals engaged in free market pursuits. In the latter case, the government's role changes from managing the money supply to ensuring that contractual obligations are honored—chief among them the right to convert currency into gold.

The implementation of a gold standard on a worldwide basis would signify the recognition of the priority status of productive individuals, as opposed to governments, in the new global economy. Relinquishing control of the money to the people who earn it and use it would mean fully embracing the validity of Adam Smith's argument that individualism provides the greatest benefits to society. Such a proposition can only be viewed as profoundly liberating.

Fixing What Broke

In attempting to lay out a new global monetary order to meet the needs of the global economy, it makes sense to reexamine the experience under Bretton Woods, which was, at its heart, a gold-based system for international monetary stability. Bretton Woods clearly ran into problems, and identifying and fixing what went wrong presents a formidable task. But there can be no disputing that much was right about the Bretton Woods approach. The United States flourished under the system, as did Europe, Japan, and developing countries around the world. "Looking back," says Paul Volcker, "the performance of the world economy in the first twenty-five years after Bretton Woods was exceptional."[52]

Given that Volcker was one of those present at Camp David in August 1971 when the decision was made to close the gold window and effectively dismantle the Bretton Woods system, one might find it curious that now, over twenty years later, Volcker expresses nostalgia for the old gold-based approach. But Volcker suggests in *Changing Fortunes* that he had misgivings at the time; indeed, he says he felt a certain anguish when the decision was made by the United States to suspend gold payments. Volcker had spent much of his career defending the Bretton Woods system and was concerned that the Camp David initiative would be seen as a humiliating change in U.S. domestic policy and a derogation of duty in the international monetary arena. Even though, as Volcker explains, he believed the immediate crisis could only be solved by announcing the suspension of gold payments by the United States, he worried about the long-term implications of such a move and was eager to proceed to meaningful reform of the international monetary system.[53]

What impressed Volcker most about the August 1971 experience was how an embarrassing defeat for U.S. financial leadership was presented as a bold new initiative by giving it a clever political and rhetorical spin. He observes:

> After the speech was delivered, on the night of Sunday, August 15, I learned a good lesson about what masterful politicians can do. I had feared that suspension of gold would be seen by Americans as a humiliation: that the United States had been done in by foreigners, that the dollar that Americans loved and treasured was being trashed, and that we ought to turn inward, put up tariffs, cut off aid, and bring back the troops. But Mr. Nixon's performance, followed up with enormous panache by Secretary Connally's news

conference on Monday, played it all as more of a triumph and a fresh start. And, as it all worked out at home, it *was* a fresh start. Stronger economic growth and reduced inflation made for a powerful campaign platform in 1972.

Now, twenty years later, I wonder. It was, after all is said and done, in some ways a defeat. The inflationary pressures that helped bring down the system did not abate for long; they got much worse as the controls came off and plagued the country for a decade or more. The monetary system has not been put back together in a way that really seems to satisfy anyone. And somehow we are still complaining about unfair military, aid, and trade burdens.[54]

Still, there is no denying that the Bretton Woods system, as originally structured, was unsustainable. Now the question is: Can the flaws of Bretton Woods be redressed and the basic system reinstated?

One of the fatal errors, it seems in retrospect, was the preoccupation of the framers of the original Bretton Woods agreement with satisfying foreign central banks rather than individual citizens. Both Keynes and Harry Dexter White were inordinately impressed by those great bastions of government power—the central banks and the treasury departments—to which they were both drawn professionally. It must have seemed natural that a new world monetary order rising out of the ashes of World War II would be geared toward mighty government institutions managed by the world's financial elite rather than toward the rights of average citizens.

Hubris often proves a poor basis for social engineering, but it clearly engendered the thinking of the day. As Volcker notes, there was a strong sense of mission and a recognition that international leadership was required to move the world to a higher plane, away from its painful experiences with depression and war. Concern for improving the economic lot of humankind was prevalent among the intellectual political crowd. As Volcker recounts, the label "elites" was not considered so bad in those days.[55]

The focus on coordination among central banks and the idea that it was necessary to offer gold convertibility only to foreign central banks reflected an attitude that ordinary citizens should not manage the world's money supply. Such complex and consequential functions were better left to the monetary authorities who held the currency reins. Within that exclusive clique of central bankers and treasury officials, disputes could be resolved in a gentlemanly fashion without alarming the general public. Money was too far important to be influenced by the collective actions of freewheeling individuals.

So the Bretton Woods system granted to foreign central banks the privilege of redeeming U.S. dollars for gold at a prespecified rate. Private citizens had no such right, including U.S. citizens. Indeed, they were prohibited by law from owning gold for monetary purposes; since the 1930s it had been illegal for individuals in the United States to have gold in their possession except for industrial or numismatic use.[56] By ordaining that foreign central banks would have exclusive rights to sound dollars, the United States limited its exposure to criticism on monetary policy in significant ways. First, any doubts among foreign central banks about the integrity of U.S. money would only be expressed after the fact as dollars were accumulated through trade imbalances; in contrast, domestic users of dollars with the right to convert on demand would immediately register their suspicions. Second, foreign central banks, while professing to be independent, are still entities of their governments. Political considerations enter into a decision to request that dollars be converted into gold. In short, the nature of central banks as cautious, bureaucratic organizations compromises both the timing and clarity of their response to U.S. monetary policy.

One major way, then, to improve the old Bretton Woods system is to extend the right of convertibility to private citizens. Had private citizens enjoyed the same convertibility rights as foreign central banks under the Bretton Woods agreement, their individual actions would have brought about a more diffused adjustment to changes in the U.S. money supply and alerted officials to dangerous developments long before the integrity of the entire system came under threat. Continuous "real time" responses to incremental monetary signals would have prevented anchor currency imbalances from reaching untenable levels. The potential dislocations that undermined the old Bretton Woods system thus could have been avoided.

The other serious flaw in the original Bretton Woods approach was its reliance on a single anchor currency. Monopoly power has an inherent tendency to be abused; this fact is no less true for the key currency issuer than for suppliers of other economic goods. The United States controlled the value of the dollar. The rest of the world, meanwhile, was left with no alternative source of reserve currency in the event the dollar proved less than reliable. The other participants in the Bretton Woods system were at a loss when the United States began to inflate its currency to accommodate excessive domestic spending. The sense of vulnerability they experienced at that time still taints their approach to monetary relations with the United States. As much as the leading nations of the world might like to halt the momentum toward competitive devaluations and implement some kind of coordinated international monetary system, they are understandably leery of returning to a Bretton Woods approach. Would Germany, Japan, France, or Britain ever again agree to link its monetary fate to the sworn good fiscal intentions of the United States? Not likely. Not after the United States so thoroughly abused its monopoly position as the world's key currency nation.

But what is to prevent a core group of economically powerful countries from agreeing to go on a gold standard jointly, thus setting up a critical mass of nations willing to convert their currencies into gold on demand? That would rectify the monopolist dilemma inherent in the original Bretton Woods system. The United States could be the leading force behind a global gold standard initiative and, indeed, it *should* be the leading force given its vital growing role in the global economy and its traditional support for free trade and open competition. A move by the United States to guarantee the integrity of its currency would be a global confidence booster because other nations would be compelled to follow suit. Such a move would also provide the necessary assurances to the world that the United States was finally willing to exercise the fiscal discipline required to maintain a gold standard—namely, to bring its budget into balance.

Why should it fall to the United States to take the first step? Mises once made the observation that people in other nations look to the U.S. example in economic matters and say to themselves: why shouldn't we engage in the same policies of deficit spending and manipulating the money supply?

> To these people one should answer first of all: "One of the privileges of a rich man is that he can afford to be foolish much longer than a poor man." And this is the situation of the United States. The financial policy of the United States is very bad and is getting worse. Perhaps the United States can afford to be foolish a bit longer than some other countries.[57]

In the 1990s, time has run out as the United States' past financial policies have caught up with it, taking their toll on the domestic economy and threatening its leadership role in the world. The United States no longer can afford to be foolish. Nor can the world afford to permit monetary meltdown to bring about a more serious rupture in global relations.

6

Agenda for a New Bretton Woods

T he next effort to build a new world monetary order should reflect an appreciation for what has worked well in the past. It should start with the same basic framework laid out in the old Bretton Woods approach: fixed exchange rates among national currencies anchored by a government commitment to redeem in gold. Only this time, the weaknesses of the original Bretton Woods system should be remedied to prevent the system from falling apart under pressure.

Specifically, the next Bretton Woods should be oriented toward the needs and rights of private citizens, as opposed to central banks, to ensure that the integrity of money is maintained on a continuous basis subject to the assessment of the people who use it daily. The next Bretton Woods, too, should designate a core group of countries to offer gold convertibility rather than setting up a single dominant country to exercise a monopoly over the world's anchor currency.

If these two failings of the original Bretton Woods system are corrected, the next Bretton Woods has the potential to reinstitute monetary and trade conditions on terms as favorable as those that provided the foundation for spectacular economic growth in the post–World War II era. Moreover, by learning from past mistakes and using the experience to design a superior system, the builders of the next Bretton Woods can expect to establish a more permanent international monetary order, one that will deliver stable currencies and fixed exchange rates far into the future. One that will provide the appropriate monetary regime—a unified global monetary system—for the global economy.

By offering gold convertibility privileges at the level of the individual and by enlarging the key currency base to include numerous countries, the next Bretton Woods could avoid the inherent flaws of its predecessor. It could explicitly confront the logical inconsistencies of that earlier system. Under the old Bretton Woods, nations were somehow presumed to be able to enjoy domestic economic autonomy even when it flew in the face of international pressures. The role of an international monetary fund under the old system was to permit the accumulation of currency imbalances to give an offending country sufficient time to adjust; rather than forcing nations to immediately deal with the consequences of their economic failings, distortions were tolerated for prolonged periods. But while patience is a virtue, tolerance carried to excess can have negative results. In the absence of punitive measures, governments have little incentive to improve policies or performance.

The old Bretton Woods system reflected John Maynard Keynes's theory that government could play a useful role in the economy by stimulating it during times of recession to make up for inadequate consumer spending, even when that policy meant running a budget deficit. Yet deficits caused by government fiscal stimulus invariably lead to excessive money creation, which in turn means that a nation's currency becomes out of sync with the currencies of other nations. How could any government reserve the right to devalue its money as part of an aggressive set of economic policies at home and still pay homage to the doctrine of international monetary stability to preserve free trade? Logically, this situation is not possible. Keynes wanted it both ways because he had dazzling theories on two particular subjects: domestic economic spending and global monetary coordination. Unfortunately, his theories could not be successfully merged.

A similar lesson can be drawn from the world's recent experience with floating rates. While the ostensible goal at the outset was to insulate domestic monetary policy from the effects of international economic integration, the result was to destroy any notion of system. Floating rates have delivered monetary chaos by destroying the validity of price signals across borders and turning international trade into a game of chance. Attempting to isolate the fiscal and monetary behavior of a nation from its impact on the global economy has proved impossible; the results of misguided policies inevitably show up, sometimes in bizarre ways. Floating rates do not alleviate the consequences of irresponsible fiscal decisions but rather compound them in foreign exchange markets distorted by capricious central bank interventions.

Much of the experience of the last two decades can be seen as a slow-motion effort to recoup the advantages of the Bretton Woods system, as governments move steadily away from the vacuum of floating rates to the managed currency approach of more recent years. It is almost as if finance officials and central bankers desire to capture the virtues of stable money yet remain tentative about being locked into any official arrangement that might impose disciplinary measures for violating the conditions that guarantee stable money on a permanent basis. But there is no getting around the fact that commitment (whether on a personal or government level) is most convincing when it is publicly acknowledged. The best intentions of the government are no match for a concrete mechanism that provides ordinary citizens with an escape clause in the event of monetary breach of contract.

If the two major failings of the old Bretton Woods system were corrected, the resulting monetary system would effectively be a classical international gold standard. Given that the original Bretton Woods system, a gold exchange standard, was a variant of the gold standard, it makes sense that once the embellishments introduced by Keynes and Harry Dexter White were removed, the tenets of a gold standard would come into full force. Because Keynes and White sought to mitigate the disciplinary aspects of gold convertibility by limiting the redemption privilege to central banks, and because they were willing to relegate the integrity of the entire system to a monopoly key currency supplier, much of their personal imprint on the design of the original Bretton Woods system would be erased by reverting back to the more democratic classical international gold standard.

At the same time, the inconsistencies that plagued and ultimately destroyed the old Bretton Woods system would be neatly avoided under a classical gold standard. Domestic economic policies cannot be divorced from their international monetary implications. An international gold standard would force near-instant reconciliation of national fiscal policies with global economic imperatives. In that sense, the classical gold standard was ahead of its time. A gold standard explicitly recognizes the primacy of the individual and demands budgetary responsibility from the government on behalf of the nation-state within an integrated global community.

AMERICA: HEAL THYSELF

The United States, not without a sense of déjà vu, today finds itself the leading economic power in the aftermath of a world war. It was a cold war, fortunately. Nevertheless, the conflict left a once-powerful nation and its wards struggling to overcome the damage caused by running their economies on a military footing at the expense of the peoples' standard of living. Unlike World War II, the Cold War did not leave physical destruction in its wake as much as social and political collapse. Russia's economy is in shambles; former Soviet republics are struggling to survive as sovereign nations, inspired in varying degrees by the promise of democracy and free markets but thwarted by the legacy of central planning and communist control.

The United States paid a heavy price to win the Cold War. The requirement of heavy military spending to match the priorities of the Kremlin left the United States with financial problems of its own. A bloated government budget still acts as a drag on the national economy, even as defense spending is steadily reduced. Social spending continues to rise, and as deficits accumulate year after year, the total volume of national debt accumulates with depressing predictability. The cost of paying interest on U.S. government debt obligations has become a significant expenditure, now requiring about eighteen cents of every dollar collected in tax revenues; in 1980, interest payments took ten cents of every tax dollar.[1]

For a long time, economists promoted the notion that money paid by the U.S. government on its own debt should be seen as a payment *to* Americans rather than a payment *by* Americans; there was no need to get excited about either the amount of national debt or the cost of paying interest on it because the debt was owed to "ourselves" and the interest was received by us. But in fact, much of U.S. debt is held by foreigners, particularly Japanese. Americans should be grateful, because U.S. domestic savings have not been sufficient to meet private investment needs and finance the huge public sector deficits that have been mounting since the mid-1980s. At the same time, though, this development confounds the theory that the money is owed to "us." As Paul Volcker observes in *Changing Fortunes*, reliance on foreign capital is a two-edged financial sword:

> We were dependent on the money, but there was also something ironic in the fact that Japanese workers producing all those exports for the U.S. market would be supported in their old age by interest payments on thirty-year U.S. Treasury bonds.[2]

In the context of the global economy, of course, there should be no sense of us or them. Individuals around the world should be free to invest their savings wherever they choose; that is the best way to maximize the use of capital and achieve the optimal return from investment. However, when national currencies substantially change in value relative to one another over a short time period, investment flows deviate from their normal path. Suddenly foreign investors are attracted to U.S. securities, not because they offer the best underlying trade-off between risk and reward, but because a cheap dollar enhances their appeal. Just as the exceptional profits gained by entrepreneurs during times of inflation are due to skewed prices, investment returns from foreign bonds are distorted by skewed currencies.

The United States seemingly has learned the hard lesson of inflation after having suffered through brutally high interest rates in the late 1970s and a punishing shake-out in real estate and other key sectors of the economy in the late 1980s. The savings and loan crisis of the early 1990s still stands as a reminder of the financial and economic pain that results when distorted prices and interest rates create false expectations about future profits. The key to avoiding such roller-coaster results is to ensure that the signals engendered in prices and interest rates serve as unimpaired beacons rather than false lures to suppliers and investors. Sound money is the answer. But is the United States government ready to face the question? Can Washington finally balance its budget, accept the discipline of gold convertibility, and rise to the challenge of serving as a model of fiscal and monetary integrity for the world?

A Balanced Budget

The United States must resolve its chronic problem of domestic budget deficits in order to guarantee the long-term validity of its currency. Fiscal discipline is a prerequisite to offering sound money. So long as government spending exceeds government revenues, the budgetary shortfall must be financed. Government borrowing leads to excess money creation, which inevitably translates into inflationary pressures. Even when prices and interest rates are not manifestly higher (because of widespread hesitation among consumers and borrowers, who see grim economic prospects), the effects of government deficit spending and government borrowing lie latent in the economy, waiting to make their appearance at the first sign of recovery.

The practice of deficit spending, as entrenched as it seems, does not have to go on forever. As Ludwig von Mises reminds us, "inflation is not an act of God" or some unavoidable disease that descends like the plague:

> Inflation is a policy. And a policy can be changed. Therefore, there is no reason to give in to inflation. If one regards inflation as an evil, then one has to stop inflating. One has to balance the budget

of the government. Of course, public opinion must support this; the intellectuals must help the people to understand. Given the support of public opinion, it is certainly possible for the people's elected representatives to abandon the policy of inflation.[3]

The time may finally be ripe to garner sufficient public support in the United States to insist on putting an end to deficit spending and eliminating the government's access to the U.S. money supply as its financing vehicle. Dissatisfaction with economic policy making in Washington and cumulative disgust over a budget process gridlocked by political interests has now reached levels that demand nothing short of radical change and bold action. This pouring forth of intellectual energy should include calls for a new round of international monetary reform spearheaded by a morally rejuvenated United States prepared to right the mistakes of the past. The agenda for the next Bretton Woods should start with a fundamental decision by the American people to put their own financial house in order. It should be fueled by a collective recognition that manipulating interest rates is not the proper remedy for unemployment or recession; stimulation of the economy under false monetary pretenses is ultimately self-defeating. Once and for all, Thomas Jefferson's admonition to live within our means and avoid the debilitating shackles of public debt must be taken to heart—and taken to Washington.

Choosing to end deficit spending and live within our means should not be taken as a rationale by politicians in Washington to impose austerity measures against the American people. Living within our means does not preclude *expanding* our means. The overarching goal of fiscal reform should be to encourage growth of the private sector while holding down government spending. Instead of shrinking the nation's level of productive economic activity by imposing higher tax rates in a misguided attempt to raise government revenues, private business activity should be spurred through lower tax rates. Despite the drubbing supply-side economics has been subjected to, lower marginal tax rates can lead to higher overall levels of tax revenue as individuals respond to opportunities to reap greater personal rewards from their entrepreneurial activities. No less a symbol of stringent monetary discipline than former Federal Reserve Chairman Volcker himself, defending a tax-reduction program while still a young Treasury official during the early 1960s, argued that "most or all of the revenues lost by lower tax rates could be recovered as a result of triggering greater investment and growth."[4] Volcker is quick to point out, though, that tax cutting "should be paralleled by expenditure reduction."[5]

In balancing the budget, the emphasis should be on limiting the amount of federal government spending rather than on imposing increases in the tax rates paid by individuals. Indeed, a progrowth strategy aimed at increasing the aggregate tax base by expanding the domestic economy—and, with it, national income—is not only the most promising, but also the least painful, route to balancing the budget. If the net result of holding down public spending in the face of private sector growth is to shrink the federal budget's share of gross domestic product, so much the better. The federal budget's share now stands at about 25 percent of the nation's economy. The size of government today is at odds with basic American principles that favor limited government intrusion into private sector activities.

What is the best way to force Washington to bring the federal budget into balance within a reasonable time frame and then continue to keep it in balance year after year? After the failed attempt to curb government spending through the Gramm-Rudman-Hollings legislation, it's clear that more severe measures must be imposed and closer surveillance must be executed to achieve compliance. A balanced budget amendment to the Constitution holds out the best prospects for moving substantively toward achieving fiscal responsibility. Such an amendment might be enshrined in a larger provision to provide guarantees concerning those areas of budgetary, fiscal, and monetary governance where the potential for government abuse poses a threat to the perpetuation of the American economic system. As Martin Anderson, former chief domestic economic policy adviser to President Reagan, has observed:

> The major cause of our economic difficulties is simply that the federal government spends more than we can afford. If we are ever

going to control this spending, we are going to need some new tools. Certain aspects of economic policy are so crucial and fundamental to the proper functioning of a free economy that they cannot be left to the political whims of any particular Congress or administration—whether it be Republican or Democratic. Certain guarantees of economic responsibility should be embodied in our Constitution in the same way that certain personal freedoms are guaranteed by the Bill of Rights. To really ensure that we achieve long-term fiscal control, we have to amend the Constitution; we need an Economic Bill of Rights.[6]

Anderson's proposal would stipulate an outright requirement that the federal budget must be balanced. Moreover, it would explicitly limit the amount the federal government could spend as a percentage of the nation's gross national product; the limit would act as a safeguard against the temptation to impose higher taxes to meet the requirements of a balanced budget in the face of increased government spending. To further dampen excessive government expenditures, Anderson would require more than a majority vote of the Congress on all spending bills and he would also seek a constitutional guarantee to secure line-item veto power for the president to enhance the executive's budgetary authority to eliminate unnecessary spending.[7]

Even when public opinion supports the general notion of balanced budgets and there exists strong political resolve, technical and timing details can still derail serious efforts to implement effective constraints. In recent years, Britain adopted a balanced budget measure aimed at balancing the national budget over the economic cycle. The basic idea behind the approach was that deficits accumulated during times of recession would be offset by the surpluses achieved when the economy was booming. The strategy went to the heart of Keynes's rationale for deliberately running a deficit in the first place; what Keynes sought was to smooth out business cycles by having the government pick up the spending slack when necessary and be equally prepared to absorb excess demand during high growth periods to avoid overheating. (That Keynes's ideas have been used to justify chronic deficit spending shows the extent to which economic proposals are often bastardized to serve political objectives.)

But then-Chancellor of the Exchequer Norman Lamont was forced to acknowledge in August 1992 that capturing a budget surplus is not nearly as easy as running a budget deficit.[8] Somehow the projected boom years never seem to provide enough revenues to offset the huge and rising public sector deficits. As the day of reckoning approaches, finance officials are pressured to submit to legislators, who expound increasingly on the virtues of flexibility versus rigid budgetary targets. The relaxation of earlier commitments is given further impetus, not surprisingly, when elections loom on the horizon.

There is a simple solution: Budgetary timing problems could be eliminated by lagging revenues and expenditures by one fiscal year. For example, government budget expenditures for the current year should be strictly limited to the revenues received the year before; funds could not be spent that had not already been collected. Not only would this strategy prevent accusations of employing a rosy scenario to justify high levels of spending—and then discovering that the tax money was not flowing in as projected—it would also smooth out economic cycles without opening the door to government intervention. Going into a recession, tax revenues from the prior more robust year would be modestly stimulative, exerting economic effects consistent with Keynes's original thesis. Conversely, going into a boom year, government spending would be modestly restrained by the lower receipts of the weaker prior year and would exercise a dampening effect.

To expedite the achievement of a balanced budget, the government also should initiate a special privatization program to sell assets to the public; the extra revenues would be taken in as extraordinary income. (France is setting an excellent example of privatizing state-owned companies under Prime Minister Edouard Balladur.) For the United States, assets slated for privatization might include the postal service and Amtrak, along with numerous federal land holdings. Such a move would underscore the resolve of politicians to take bold action to eliminate the deficit as quickly as possible. It would also help to limit the absolute scale of government.

Gold Price Target?

When it comes to defining the ultimate objective of monetary policy, there are variations about how to achieve soundness, even among those who favor a strong role for gold. Proponents of gold price targeting, for example, have much in common with strict monetarists. Both groups wish to eliminate the discretionary factor in determining the money supply. Monetarists would designate their preferred money supply target, whether M1, M2, or some other definition of money, and then charge the Federal Reserve to meet that target. Gold advocates, on the other hand, focus on the price level as an indicator of whether monetary policy is accommodating peoples' demand to hold money. For both groups, the main goal is to impart stable purchasing power to the currency.

While it might be possible to establish a broad index of goods and services to reflect the general price level, the simplicity and straightforwardness of using the price of gold as a surrogate for changes in the purchasing power of money clearly has advantages. Gold proponents have long expressed their wish for an explicit price rule that would require the Federal Reserve to direct its monetary policy toward the goal of achieving a stable dollar price for gold. Deviations from the target price of gold, either higher or lower, would elicit remedial action from central bank officials. In short, the money supply would be expanded or contracted as necessary to maintain the steady value of gold in dollars.

There is reason to suspect that something akin to this policy is already being pursued by the Federal Reserve, yet the long-term credibility of the dollar seems hardly guaranteed. Lawrence A. Kudlow, chief economist for Bear, Stearns & Co., suggested in December 1991 that the Federal Reserve Board under Alan Greenspan was deliberately "running a Bretton Woods style monetary policy anchored by a steady gold price of roughly ten times the old $35 an ounce gold exchange rate" and had thus tacitly accepted the terms of a gold price rule to guide monetary policy. According to Kudlow, Greenspan had "restored low inflation and declining interest rates through a gold-backed dollar," and by doing so had recreated the favorable financial conditions of the 1950s.[9]

It may—or may not—be true that Greenspan's efforts to regulate the money supply are guided by an implicit gold price target. But unless everyone who uses U.S. dollars is privy to the rules that effectively govern monetary policy, advocates of sound money scarcely have reason to rejoice. Suspicions concerning the factors that perhaps influence the United States' chief central banker might provide additional insights about future likely actions to control the money supply, but they do not represent a change from the fundamentally discretionary behavior of the Federal Reserve Board. Even if it were Greenspan's personal desire to manage the money supply in conformance with a dollar price target for gold, there is no reason to assume that the next Fed chairman would choose to target the price of gold versus interest rates or another particularly favored monetary aggregate. Fed chairmen do change from time to time; moreover, the chairman is free at any time to change the criteria used to dictate the direction of monetary policy.

The unacknowledged private commitment of a Federal Reserve Board chairman, therefore, is not sufficient to guarantee the integrity of dollars through some implicit connection to gold. What if a formal rule were publicly adopted? What if it were stated in explicit terms that monetary policy would be loosened or tightened in direct correspondence to a specified target price for gold? If that price, for example, happened to be $350 per ounce of gold, and gold was presently fetching $355, everyone could be assured that the Fed would be aggressively contracting the money supply to bring down the price of gold. Or if gold were selling in private markets for something less than $350, moneyholders could expect to see lower interest rates as the Fed attempted to expand the money supply to raise the level of prices—particularly the price of gold.

The problem with a price rule, however, is that the tools at the disposal of the Fed for controlling the money supply are not nearly as potent as once believed. Raising or lowering the discount rate of interest, changing bank reserve requirements, and engaging in open market operations are the traditional instruments utilized by the governors of the Federal Reserve Board. But the expected correlation between lower interest rates and higher economic growth has failed to materialize in recent times. Indeed, Clinton administration officials have been disappointed by the lack of economic response to low interest rates, which they were counting on to compensate for the dampening effect of tax increases and spending cuts. Alan Blinder, a member of the president's Council of Economic Advisers, suggested in *The New York*

Times in August 1993 that a "pervasive insecurity" about layoffs and salary prospects may partly explain why the economy has failed to grow more robustly as the result of enticingly low rates.[10] Few private borrowers have the confidence to take on the burden of personal loans in the face of economic uncertainty.

The Fed thus finds itself in the position of being relatively ineffective with regard to influencing economic growth using the monetary tools at its disposal. Whether or not Greenspan has been taking cues from the dollar price of gold about how far to go in attempts to expand the money supply, it is clear that achieving a gold price target is subject to all the problems of achieving any other target, such as the monetary aggregates. The impact of Fed actions is at best difficult to measure. At worst it is unpredictable and subject to timing lags that may exacerbate cyclical variations rather than smooth them out.

All of these problems argue for implementation of a solid mechanism for converting dollars into gold rather than relying on a weak price link or an even weaker discretionary preference. As economist Phillip Cagan has summarized:

> I see no escape from the conclusion, inherent in the position of the advocates of gold, that only a convertible monetary system is sufficiently free of discretion to guarantee that it will achieve price stability. The operation of any inconvertible monetary system introduces a discretion in management that cannot guarantee price stability despite the efficacy of its monetary controls. Of course, no system can guarantee that the system itself will not be tinkered with or abandoned. But if one is looking for some kind of long-lasting commitment of a constitutional nature, a convertible monetary system seems to be the only practical possibility.[11]

Cagan's argument in favor of a monetary system offering convertibility, as opposed to one that operates on the basis of discretionary management, such as the Federal Reserve system, is only strengthened by the fact that the "efficacy of its monetary controls" has come into serious question.

Gold Convertibility

What would it take to set up a genuine gold standard with a working mechanism for converting U.S. dollars into gold on demand?

The first step would be to repeal all current federal legal tender laws. These laws now require that people must accept paper currency issued by the Federal Reserve as lawful money. Indeed, U.S. currency bills today carry the declaration: "This note is legal tender for all debts, public and private." Earlier notes had a somewhat different inscription: "Redeemable in lawful money at the United States Treasury, or at any Federal Reserve Bank." Still earlier forms of U.S. paper money, such as the gold certificates issued in the 1920s, stated: "This certifies that there have been deposited in the Treasury of the United States of America twenty dollars in gold coin payable to the bearer on demand."

But an individual seeking to convert a Federal Reserve note into lawful money by submitting it to the U.S. Treasury or a branch of the Federal Reserve system would today have his paper money returned to him with the tautological explanation: the note itself is, by definition, lawful money. Revoking the government's right to force people to accept its paper notes as legal tender would mark the beginning of the transition toward solid money convertible on demand into a fixed weight of something valuable.

It should be seen as more than a residual benefit, too, that repealing existing federal legal tender laws would put an end to a government practice that is viewed by many legal scholars as distinctly unconstitutional. Citing Article I, Section 10 of the U.S. Constitution, which prevents the states from having the power to "emit Bills of Credit" or to "make any Thing but gold and silver Coin a Tender in Payment of Debts," monetary historian Richard Timberlake notes that the Founding Fathers regarded the states as political entities whose standing should be equal or superior to that of the federal government of the United States. "Therefore," he notes, "any power denied the former was also denied the latter by the Tenth Amendment, unless specifically granted by the Constitution."[12]

The next major step toward achieving gold convertibility would be to define the U.S. dollar as a fixed weight of gold. Legislation to bring this about should be acted on by Congress with the objective of securing a description of the term dollar that accords with a measurable quantity of gold of a certain fineness, thus defining a meaningful unit of account for monetary purposes. The period of time between an announcement by the U.S. government that it intends to establish, by statute, a weight unit of gold as the dollar monetary standard and the time the actual parity would be officially stipulated could be two years. During that period, the appropriate dollar price of gold would be determined by tracking the value of gold on world markets and estimating the potential impact on price levels as the United States prepared to go on a gold standard. It is an important calculation. Fixing the dollar price of gold too low could bring on deflation as individuals sought to convert their dollars into gold at what seemed a bargain rate, thus contracting the money supply. By contrast, establishing too high a parity between dollars and gold would prompt people to turn in gold for dollars, expanding the money supply and causing inflation.

To ensure that the free market dollar price for gold is evaluated properly, Ludwig von Mises suggested that the government be precluded from participating in the market during the stabilization period following public announcement of the intention to go on a gold standard:

> In this first period of the reform it is imperative that the American government and all institutions dependent upon it, including the Federal Reserve System, keep entirely out of the gold market. A free gold market could not come into existence if the administration were to try to manipulate the price by underselling. The new monetary regime must be protected against malicious acts by officials of the Treasury and the Federal Reserve System. There cannot be any doubt that officialdom will be eager to sabotage a reform whose main purpose is to curb the power of the bureaucracy in monetary matters.[13]

Mises was confident that once the market price attained some stability, it would be possible to designate the new legal gold parity of the dollar. The next step would be to secure the unconditional convertibility of the dollar into gold at the established parity. While Mises would insist on setting up a special conversion agency to execute the task of converting dollar bills into gold (and gold into dollars), Lehrman and others have indicated a willingness to entrust this responsibility to the U.S. Mint, while at the same time imposing strict limits on the scope of allowable actions that might be taken by the Federal Reserve system. For example, the Fed would no longer be permitted to engage in open market operations involving U.S. government debt securities. Existing federal government debt held by the Fed would not be replaced when it matured. In short, the Federal Reserve would be prevented from accommodating the fiscal improprieties of the U.S. government by monetizing the budgetary gap between federal revenues and federal expenditures. Instead, the new mandate of the Federal Reserve would be to maintain the value of the monetary standard of the United States.

As a further protection that the link between the dollar and gold would be upheld, the monetary transition should include a new coinage of gold pieces to be freely exchanged for commonly used denomination notes such as the hundred-dollar bill. Putting gold coins into the hands of individuals for use in carrying out daily transactions would help to make the concept of sound money more concrete, more real, and thus more imperative to all citizens. No individual can handle a printed piece of paper and a hard gold coin and deem one as valuable as the other unless an ironclad arrangement exists for converting the paper into gold on demand. "Gold must be in the cash holdings of everybody," Mises insisted. "Everybody must see gold coins changing hands, must be used to having gold coins in his pockets, to receiving gold coins when he cashes his paycheck, and to spending gold coins when he buys in a store."[14]

Unlike a pseudo gold standard approach, such as a gold price target rule meant to provide guidance for actions taken by the Federal Reserve, or a gold exchange standard that grants convertibility privileges only to foreign central banks and is compromised by diplomatic considerations, an authentic gold standard that puts gold coins into public circulation would provide citizens with a credible safeguard against the abuse of monetary authority by government. As monetary economist Donald Kemmerer observed in *Human Events*:

> The gold coin system has this little-realized advantage: once the coins are circulating widely, it is difficult, embarrassing and costly to call them back. This obliges the government in office to reflect carefully before letting itself get into a situation where a planned devaluation would necessitate recalling the gold coins.[15]

If the United States were to announce its intention to go on a gold standard two years hence, and during the interim enacted a balanced budget amendment to the Constitution, and if it were to repeal the legal tender laws, reform the Federal Reserve system, and permit world gold markets to determine the dollar price of gold, it would then be possible to announce at the end of the transition period a statutory gold weight for the dollar—that is, an official dollar price for gold. After congressional acceptance of all the necessary legislation that would be submitted on behalf of an appropriately structured gold standard act, the banknotes issued by the Federal Reserve would be convertible into gold at the established parity at the option of any individual holding those notes. The U.S. Mint would also be obliged to coin bullion or issue paper dollars in exchange for gold as demanded. It would also be asked to initiate a broad gold coinage to heighten the presence of gold in the money supply of the United States.

Because the issue of sound money inevitably is caught up in the issue of credit, reform of the U.S. commercial banking system would have to accompany the move to a gold standard. The government cannot be held liable for the soundness of financial instruments created by commercial banks and thrifts that function effectively as money, such as checking accounts and credit cards. Banks must be responsible for upholding the value of the monetary obligations they issue on the basis of held reserves or viable, well-managed loan portfolios. The existence of federal deposit insurance schemes that serve to insulate bank management from the discipline required to properly manage deposited resources against investment assets undermines the integrity of the banking industry in the United States by steering it in the direction of excessively risky loan portfolios (as taxpayers, not the equity-holders of the bank, bear a substantial part of the cost of fiduciary mismanagement). Depositors must come to the realization that their concept of saving as defined by the act of putting money in a banking institution is erroneous. Deposited funds are not held inert in vaults but are loaned out. They function as investment capital; accordingly, they are at risk. Depositors are entitled to receive interest on the funds they place with a bank precisely because their money is at risk. If the money they place in the bank were being safeguarded rather than invested, depositors would more appropriately be required to pay a fee for the service.

Banks earn profits, of course, by taking a cut of the difference between the interest they receive on loaned funds and the amount they remit back to the suppliers of those funds—that is, the depositors. Banks effectively are compensated by depositors for their expertise in selecting profitable, yet prudent investment opportunities. However, when government insurance exists, the fundamental arrangement between the furnishers of investment capital and the loan experts is grossly altered. Depositors no longer have to make judgments about the competence of bank management or the characteristics of the loan portfolio. When the government agrees to insure the safe return of deposited funds, it takes on the risk inherent in every investment opportunity and perpetuates the mistaken notion that funds deposited in interest-bearing accounts at banking institutions can be thought of as being safe.

Eliminating federal deposit insurance would restore the essential character of banking as a vehicle for channeling financial capital into productive investments while striving to meet the risk and timing preferences of depositors. Government should not intervene in that private business activity any more than it should guarantee the return of money invested through the stock market. Given that taxpayers ultimately bear the burden of government deposit insurance as the costs of bailing out insolvent banking institutions swell the level of government spending, it makes eminent sense to limit government liability to guaranteeing only the value of its own financial obligations—the notes it issues directly—and that by means of gold convertibility.

CRITICAL MASS

A decision by the United States to balance its budget and provide sound money through gold convertibility would set the stage for establishing a global gold standard. The resurrection of U.S. financial integrity would constitute a necessary, though not sufficient, condition for building a new world monetary order to serve the needs of an integrated global economy. Given that the United States is no longer in a position to dictate economic or monetary policy to Japan or Germany, it is imperative that these and other powerful member nations of the international trade community support the U.S. decision to accept fiscal responsibility by themselves committing to abide by the same set of monetary rules.

To suggest that the United States should work in cooperation with its global partners is to recognize that the U.S. economy is only part, albeit a very important part, of the larger world economy. The idea that the United States is a participant in a larger system is not some vague macroeconomic observation; the U.S. economy *is* integrated with global economic and financial developments. The connections have impact at the most microeconomic level, as U.S. producers compete directly with foreign producers for the same consumer markets. While it is sometimes useful to distinguish between the U.S. domestic economy and its position among foreign trade partners, it is becoming increasingly difficult to separate the domestic effects of U.S. monetary policy from the implications they carry for the global economy. It is also becoming impossible for the United States to protect itself from the repercussions of its own financial foibles. During the 1960s, the United States could painlessly export its inflationary excesses overseas by dumping devalued dollars at the doorstep of its allies; today the refuse of bad economic policy is dumped right back on its own doorstep. Indeed, the advancing technology of the quantum age makes for nearly instant economic justice as foreign exchange markets register the aggregate global response to U.S. financial developments with the speed of a ricocheted bullet.

When the Federal Reserve opts to lower interest rates to spur the economy, for example, and thus flies in the face of a Bundesbank decision to tighten monetary policy to stave off inflation, the value of the dollar in foreign exchange markets reflects the impact. Low interest rates in the United States may be comforting, if not necessarily compelling, to American businesses, but low rates are decidedly uninspiring to foreign investors, whose fickle currency preferences are largely driven by the projected rates of return on deposited funds. When dollar deposit accounts offer a meager 3 percent return while accounts denominated in deutsche marks yield closer to 9 percent, as was the case in August 1992, it is difficult to convince foreign suppliers of capital that their decision to assist in funding the U.S. budget deficit is well-founded. At some point, the need to retain foreign capital by offering attractive interest rates comes into direct conflict with domestic pleas for lower rates and further loosening by the Federal Reserve. The United States ignores the need to satisfy foreign financial suitors at its own economic peril.

The day after then-President Bush, in his acceptance speech at the Republican convention in Houston in August 1992, asserted his intent to cut taxes while simultaneously cutting government spending, the dollar went into a tailspin in foreign exchange markets. A journalist for the *Financial Times*, Patrick Harverson, speculated that markets were concerned over the lack of specifics in the speech. Bush had offered no concrete explanation of how he would manage to cut taxes and spending, create jobs, and reduce the deficit all at the same time—with a Democratic congress.[16] So even as partisan crowds in Houston whooped and cheered for their nominee, observers around the world were assessing the economic, financial, and monetary implications of Bush's utterances in coldly objective terms. Their mass decision to dump the dollar prompted concerted intervention efforts by the world's central banks and spawned headlines in European business newspapers the next morning with titles such as "D-Day for the Dollar."[17] Portraying the prior day's flight from the dollar as a global verdict on the United States' economic future, Harverson suggested:

> It must have been embarrassing for the White House to see the world's central banks stampeding into the currency markets to save the plummeting dollar the day after a supposedly triumphant appearance before the nation by the President.
>
> Luckily for Bush, the US electorate pays no attention to the dollar.[18]

In the wake of the continuing international currency turmoil since September 1992, and considering the United States' increasing reliance on its ability to export goods and services to foreign consumers, one thing is clear: It is high time the American electorate started paying attention to the dollar. U.S. financial integrity must be restored, not only to put its domestic economy on a solid footing, but to assert a strong American presence in the global economy. Even if the United States can no longer exhort other nations to do its economic bidding on the basis of sheer dominance, it can still play an important global leadership role. It would be more convincing than any campaign rhetoric if Washington demonstrated its resolve by taking the necessary steps to achieve a balanced budget and offer gold convertibility, thus literally putting its money where its mouth is. In short, the United States can best lead the world by example.

At the same time, recognizing the quicksilver nature of financial developments in the world today, the United States' program for going on a gold standard should seek to garner global cooperation. If the motivation behind the original Bretton Woods conference included a certain amount of charitable sentiment to assist those nations devastated by war, the U.S. incentive for international cooperation today should be driven by its own basic instincts for economic survival. The United States needs a healthy Europe, an economically robust Japan, and a thriving Latin America to boost its economy. Just as U.S. policy mistakes quickly come back to haunt its economy, meaningful steps to correct past mistakes and build a solid monetary foundation would rapidly provide direct benefits to its domestic economy, even as they would improve international financial conditions and the prospects for increased trade and prosperity around the world. The important task is for the United States to convince its trading partners that it is serious about monetary reform and that its efforts to restore the credibility of the dollar at home are meant to strengthen the integrity of the global financial system.

A Global Conference

If the United States shows genuine resolve in moving toward a gold standard, other major countries will be compelled to evaluate their own policies governing money issuance with an eye toward maintaining the value of individual currencies in the presence of a gold-backed dollar. Calling for an international monetary conference would reassure the United States' trading partners that their cooperation is welcomed, even solicited; at the same time, it would be seen as an important step toward achieving radical international monetary reform—so important, in fact, that raising the possibility of holding such an event would prompt anxious speculation about its potential outcome. When then-Treasury Secretary Donald Regan suggested in late 1982 that it might be time to call for a "new Bretton Woods" conference to discuss potential changes in the international monetary regime, observers around the world were concerned and not a little confused.[19] Regan had been viewed as a champion of laissez-faire markets who favored floating rates. Was he now turning into an advocate of fixed exchange rates?

Clearly, a meeting alone would not be sufficient to convince participants to cooperate in building a new international monetary system—not unless they already had recognized the virtue, in principle, of adopting a new global monetary regime and were prepared to make the necessary internal adjustments. The purpose of having an international conference would be to ratify proposals that already had been well circulated, refined, and largely accepted. But the act of proposing a conference and determining when and where it should take place would provide the proper focus and impart seriousness and expediency to the process of comprehensive and coordinated international monetary reform.

Not all monetary scholars accept the notion that international conferences play an important role in the transition to fundamentally different monetary regimes. Giulio Gallarotti notes that four major international monetary conferences were held during the latter part of the 1800s (specifically, in 1867, 1878, 1882, and 1892) to create an international monetary union that would integrate the various currencies of participating nations.[20] The first one, the Conference of 1867, initiated by Napoleon III, was aimed at creating an international union based on gold with the franc playing a central role in the system. The subsequent conferences were less oriented toward forming a gold union and more eager to support the monetary role of silver by forming a bimetallic system.[21]

According to Gallarotti, all these conferences should be considered failures or, at best, irrelevant exercises. Gallarotti contends that the success of the classical gold standard from 1880 to 1914 was the result of "spontaneous order" and not the calculated efforts of political operatives from powerful nations seeking multilateral collaboration on monetary relations. "The international gold standard was no more the creation of an international consciousness than markets are the creation of social consciousness," Gallarotti notes. The classical gold standard came into being, he explains, because individual nations accepted the principles and rules necessary to keep their own domestic monetary policies well disciplined:[22]

> The international character of the regime was simply an unintended consequence of the convergence of monetary policies across nations. An orderly and stable system of exchange rates, international interconvertibility, and capital mobility were natural outcomes of nations fixing the price of national currencies to gold, monetary authorities standing ready to buy from and sell gold to anybody, and low restrictions on the importation and exportation of precious metals. Things equal to the same thing are equal to each. And to the extent that nations practiced gold monometallism in a responsible way, which they did, international confidence remained high, as convertibility and exchange risk continued to be perceived to be low. A German monetary official of the period put it best: "Who needs an international monetary union if everyone is on gold?"[23]

Certainly it is true that the success of a global gold standard depends on each participating nation's adherence to enforcing the fiscal and monetary discipline in their domestic economic policies necessary to maintain the viability of the system on an international basis. If every major nation maintains gold convertibility to ensure the credibility of its own currency, the world is de facto on an international gold standard. Even though every nation exercises individual monetary sovereignty in terms of protecting its own citizens from debasement of the national monetary unit, the overall result is the creation of a unified global monetary system.

While Gallarotti is correct in pointing out that a viable international monetary system such as the classical gold standard can come about only when nations individually are willing to abide by the discipline of gold convertibility, he perhaps underestimates the potential usefulness—certainly in the global communications era of the 1990s—of holding an international monetary conference. There can be no doubt that if the United States put forth a solid proposal to hold such a conference, and at the same time took convincing steps to adopt gold convertibility at home, it would have a profound impact on the United States' trade partners, particularly the other members of the Group of Seven.

Even though a functioning international gold standard may be seen as the result of spontaneous order rather than an artificial design imposed by social engineers, it is still very important—in psychological terms, certainly—to achieve a consensus among the nations of the world that global monetary reform is a vital and worthy objective, the indispensable corollary to global free trade. Calling for an international conference emphasizes the notion of integrated markets and reinforces the concept of a global economy. It suggests that while the classical gold standard may have occurred as the result of spontaneous order, a new global gold standard can be efficiently enacted through the deliberate efforts of leading nations seeking to reconcile their domestic and international economic responsibilities.

For all of these reasons, the agenda for the next Bretton Woods should start with a commitment by the United States to get its own fiscal and monetary house in order. Such a commitment will come about when American citizens collectively insist that Washington balance its budget and offer gold convertibility as a guarantee against future attempts by the government to finance its spending indulgences with diluted dollars. But along with that intentional effort by its citizens to restore soundness to the nation's currency, the United States should put forth an official call for a global monetary conference.

Contrary to the original Bretton Woods conference, to which participants from some forty-five countries were invited, the next monetary conference should go beyond the definition of international to include representatives from every nation in the world. The distinction between "international" and "global" might seem rhetorical, but it is in fact significant. The conference held at the Mount Washington Hotel in Bretton Woods, New Hampshire, in July 1944 was aimed largely at rebuilding the economies of the nations of Western Europe that had been devastated by World War II. The meeting allocated central roles to the United States and its chief partner, Great Britain, to balance financial and trade flows so as to maximize the returns to both the suppliers of capital and its users. The next Bretton Woods would be dealing with devastation of a different sort—the devastation wrought by communism. The economic legacy of the Cold War is not limited to those countries that were the direct victims of central planning. It also extends to the United States, and to a lesser extent its military allies, who were forced to spend inordinately high levels of national revenues to defend against potential attack by the former Soviet Union.

At the next Bretton Woods, the conference participants would not divide up so easily into winners and losers; nearly all nations lost something as the result of the prolonged enmity between West and East. This time around, former divisions among superpowers, as well as the developing nations that fed off the rivalry between them, should be subsumed by a larger sense of global community and mutual economic interests. Where international prestige was once determined by a nation's capacity to destroy the world, it should now be reckoned in terms of a nation's ability to maximize the welfare of its people and contribute to global prosperity.

Just as important, the next Bretton Woods should be dedicated to reforming the world's money so as to meet the needs of individuals around the world rather than governments. Where huge supernational organizations such as the International Monetary Fund and the International Bank for Reconstruction and Development (World Bank) once seemed necessary to manage world financial and economic flows, an age has dawned where individuals empowered by technological advances in computers and communications increasingly are capable of dealing directly with one another. Why should their money be subject to governmental interference and manipulation? Why should their competitive achievements be undermined by unforeseen exchange rate shifts among the world's currencies? The message of the next Bretton Woods should be that the successful efforts of individual producers—not finance ministers negotiating behind closed doors, not exchange market speculators—should determine profits in the global economy.

Core Group Support

If the United States were prepared to pursue an agenda for putting global trade on a sound money basis, in a sense giving up its current franchise on manipulating currencies in foreign exchange markets, would the other major industrial countries in the world be willing to go along? Could the United States count on its G-7 partners to support a move away from floating rates and toward a global gold standard?

The question is ironic in some ways, given that most of those G-7 nations would be quick to point out that they have been arguing for years that a more stable international currency system is desirable and that it has been the United States that has consistently refused to make the necessary fiscal and monetary adjustments to permit such a system to evolve. France, in particular, has championed the cause of fixed rate "reference zones," if not actual targets. Yoichi Funabashi, in his book *Managing the Dollar*, describes an incident involving then-Treasury Secretary Baker that took place two weeks after the Plaza meeting of September 1985:

> During a discussion among the G-5, French Finance Minister Pierre Beregovoy passed a note to Baker, who was sitting next to him, which said, "the Plaza looks like it was an agreement for a reference zone." Baker read the note and scribbled a reply. "Reference zone, no. Reference range, yes." The French were heartened to know that the United States was leaning toward some kind of range system and dared to push their position further, although the French had to guess what Baker really meant by making a distinction between zone and range.[24]

When government officials take care to define their policy leanings in such precise terms, it is a clear signal that delicate international political sensitivities are present. Innuendo becomes the order of the day. In suggesting, or even hinting, that the time has come to quit pretending that there is any kind of a free-floating rate market for currencies, the danger lies in being accused of betraying the principles of laissez-faire economics. As soon as the discussion turns to the possibility of reintroducing fixed rates, even if the transitional euphemism "target zone" is used, the lines are drawn among the ideologues and pragmatists. This time the battle is not between free market "floaters" versus those who would fix exchange rates among the world's currencies; instead, the argument centers around whether the relative value of currencies should be determined on the basis of their constant convertibility into gold or whether governments should take upon themselves the task of maintaining stable exchange rates through their intervention efforts in exchange markets. By advocating target zones (or ranges) for currency exchange rates, governments keep their ideological options open. Target zones can be seen as an interim step toward adopting a gold standard. Or they can be sold to those who favor activist government as a mechanism for achieving desired rates of exchange among currencies.

The difference, of course, boils down into the fundamental debate over whether people want to live according to the rule of law or the discretionary authority of individuals. When speaking of international monetary reform, the distinction is more often phrased in terms of favoring "consultation" and "cooperation" over automaticity. There is either the continuing coordination process, replete with secret meetings and behind-the-scenes staging efforts, whereby financial ministers from the world's most powerful countries endeavor to coerce each other into supporting their own government's monetary and trade agenda, or there is the simple rule of gold convertibility.

How would central bankers responsible for the monetary policies of those nations at the core of the global economy—Germany, Japan, and the United States—respond to a proposal for international monetary reform that had as its primary goal the objective of achieving sound money? Here one might begin to discern a subtle difference between the priorities of central bankers as opposed to the objectives of finance ministers. Central bankers believe (and it is almost a matter of moral philosophy) that their chief responsibility is to ensure the soundness of money. Finance ministers may concede the appeal of stable price levels, but they are much more apt to sacrifice that particular benefit in pursuit of what they consider more pressing economic objectives, such as reducing unemployment or increasing exports. Stimulating the economy through government fiscal measures is considered well within the range of acceptable actions that might be exercised by a treasury official, whereas a central banker is likely to be more concerned not just about the monetary effects themselves but also their implications concerning the ethics of government. Asked to explain why the Bundesbank persisted in its efforts to battle inflation, even in the face of considerable political pressure, one member of the German central bank's policy-making council told a group of sympathetic Federal Reserve officials in August 1992 that Germany had no other choice. A central bank that would attempt to ignite economic growth by accelerating inflation was engaging "in a strategy . . . built on deception."[25]

Central bankers around the world seem to share a collegial respect for the virtue of maintaining steady prices and for not disturbing global monetary equilibrium just for the sake of achieving a temporary uptick in national growth statistics. According to Mikio Wakatsuki, deputy governor of Japan's central bank, "Our duty is to maintain a non-inflationary, sustainable growth led by domestic demand and not look for short-term boosts of demand."[26] In using the word *duty*, Wakatsuki perhaps provides a glimpse of the inner sense of responsibility that gives central bankers the strength to resist pleas from politicians and finance ministers to prime the economic pump with low interest rates and excess money. "We must do nothing that disturbs the global balance," he solemnly explained to *Washington Post* columnist Jim Hoagland in April 1992.[27]

To the extent that German and Japanese central bankers have already embraced the doctrine of stable currencies as the motivating principle behind their actions, one would expect them to welcome the United States' late conversion to their monetary camp. The United States finally seems ready to accept the lessons from its own experiences. Quick financial fixes are no substitute for fundamental economic reform to enhance long-term productivity. And manipulating the money supply, at home or abroad, merely camouflages problems. As Paul Volcker notes: "Repeated time and again, devaluations represent in effect a kind of abdication from necessary policy decisions, and in the end only complicate the job of maintaining growth and stability."[28]

But favoring sound money is not the same as being willing to go on a global gold standard—or is it? If one accepts the teachings of Mises, the only way to achieve sound money is to make it convertible into gold on demand. Only a gold standard, Mises believed, could ensure that the purchasing power of money would be kept separate from the "ambitions" of governments, political parties, and pressure groups. But can the ambitions of governments be so easily dismissed? Most governments would insist that their actions are guided by the desire to improve the welfare of their citizens. Most would further argue that they support international free trade and the prospect of an open integrated global economy. The question remains: Are economic processes better managed by government officials (those "recognizably superior persons" looked on with such suspicion by Hayek)? Or can we reliably depend on the forces of supply and demand in a free market to properly equilibrate trade and financial flows?

When gold serves as the universal standard of monetary value, the world enjoys the benefits of maximum economic and financial integration. Even though the units of exchange (the dollar, the yen, the deutsche mark) vary from country to country, their common link to gold ensures the most efficent allocation of capital, both human and material.

But the vision of a global economy characterized by rational decision making and confidence achieved through the automaticity of a gold standard conflicts with the reality of an international monetary system subject to government exploitation. As columnist George Melloan observed in the *Wall Street Journal* in August 1992: "The U.S. today—with its efforts to use monetary policy to manipulate the economy—is following a modern equivalent of the Keynesianism that came into vogue in the 1930s."[29] The essence of Keynesianism is, of course, government intrusiveness into economic processes. Melloan argues that monetary policy is being used as an active instrument of Keynesian economics for the purpose of stimulating growth. Contrary to a scenario wherein the United States provides the ideological leadership among its major trade partners to move toward sound global money by accepting the discipline of a global gold standard, Melloan asserts that a divide has opened up between Europe and the United States with regard to monetary theory and practice. The United States retains its attachment to Keynesian practices, Melloan suggests, because officials in Washington are loath to give up their ability to manipulate monetary and financial variables. "But today's Europe, under the leadership of the Bundesbank, is pursuing something that might be called steady state money management," Melloan notes.[30] He continues:

> So far as monetary policy is concerned, Europe today is closer to the philosophy that has for many years been the opposite of Keynesianism, the noninterventionist "Austrian school" of Friedrich von Hayek and Ludwig von Mises.[31]

How is it possible to explain the glaring discrepancy between sound money policies and irresponsible fiscal policies that reigns among the world's top industrial powers? It would almost seem that central bankers are engaged in a silent battle of wills against finance ministers who would sacrifice sound money to achieve short-term political objectives. Consider the following: Europe's leading central bankers have apparently embraced the monetary philosophy of Ludwig von Mises as they concentrate on providing sound money rather than attempting to influence economic performance. Moreover, the chairman of the U.S. Federal Reserve Board, in his past writings, ans expressed a philosophical reverence for the classical gold standard. Additionally, the deputy governor of Japan's central bank has declared: "In the 1990s, the world is chasing sound money. That is the right direction."[32] If all of these central bankers, representing the most powerful economies in the world, can agree on the importance of providing sound money, what is the obstacle preventing a move to a global gold standard?

In a word: politicians. Finance officials who are quick to latch onto theories calling for activist government participation in the economy and who attempt to jawbone monetary authorities into "loosening" the money supply by lowering interest rates in the mistaken notion that government can create jobs or contribute to economic productivity—these officials constitute a small but powerful contingent among the larger group of politicians who refuse to exercise the necessary discipline to restore basic fiscal integrity. Introducing a gold standard requires a nation to achieve a certain level of financial stability. The task is then to ensure that the discipline will be maintained in the future. In the case of the United States, the solution lies in creating a fiscal and monetary environment which in effect makes the dollar as good as gold in terms of the general price level and the dollar price of gold itself. But that very requirement poses a tautology of sorts: Stable financial conditions, which are necessary for a nation to successfully go on a gold standard, are precisely what a gold standard is meant to bring about. Why is it necessary to adopt a gold standard if its objectives have already been achieved?[33] The answer, of course, is that gold convertibility ensures that fiscal discipline is no temporary monetary aberration but, rather, a permanent condition. If politicians are sincere in insisting that a balanced budget is part of their new commitment to fiscal responsibility and that they will never again resort to inflating the money supply to cover deficit spending, there should be no resistance to implementing a gold standard—even if it hardly seems necessary at the time—to provide citizens with a solid guarantee that their purchasing power will not be abused in the future. Call it money insurance.

The United States can be the catalyst for putting the global economy on a gold standard. German monetary authorities are living up to their reputation for resisting inflation, even when it means incurring the wrath of their European neighbors. Japan has succeeded in running its domestic budget so as to make available huge sums to invest in the economy. If only the United States could rectify its budgetary and monetary failings, there is no reason a global gold standard could not be pursued with the solid support of the core members of the major industrial nations of the world. An initiative for a global gold standard would certainly dovetail with the purported fiscal and monetary objectives of other European nations as well. The collapse of the European rate mechanism into meaninglessly wide bands should not be seen as negating the benefits of a unified currency; rather, it merely demonstrated that a pegged rate system could not sustain the integrity of fixed exchange rates among individual nations. A global gold standard would encompass and broaden the goals of European monetary union by providing exchange rate stability for a unified currency region that extended not merely across a continent, but throughout the world. Moreover, a gold standard would not subject British or French citizens, or the citizens of any country, to the tyranny of a monetary elite, whether located in Frankfurt, Washington, or Tokyo. National monetary authorities would be answerable to the discipline of an inanimate and nonpolitical standard and, hence, to the needs of private individuals.

In the wake of the Cold War, as the ostensible winners wrestle with the economic fallout of bloated defense budgets and a prior reliance on inflationary monetary policies, it is crucial to set the right example for developing countries. For newly emerging democracies, the futility of central planning is best illustrated by the success of Western nations where capitalism is practiced and free markets are promoted. The monetary corollary of Adam Smith's invisible hand is the gold standard, and by resigning themselves to abide by the tenets of a sound global monetary system, the governments of the world's most powerful countries could demonstrate their commitment to free market ideals. Perhaps even more importantly, they could prove their allegiance to the fundamental principle of democracy—rule of the people—by adopting a monetary mechanism that not only delivers sound money but in the process conforms with the requirements of representative government. As Mises notes:

> The excellence of the gold standard is to be seen in the fact that it renders the determination of the monetary unit's purchasing power independent of the policies of governments and political parties. Furthermore, it prevents rulers from eluding the financial and budgetary prerogatives of the representative assemblies. Parliamentary control of finances works only if the government is not in a position to provide for unauthorized expenditures by increasing the circulating amount of fiat money. Viewed in this light, the gold standard appears as an indispensable implement of the body of constitutional guarantees that make the system of representative government function.[34]

Open Membership

Going on a global gold standard would provide a much more democratic international monetary system than the one that exists today in the sense that less powerful developing countries would have a chance to participate on an equal footing with members of the Group of Seven instead of being shunted aside by elitist finance ministers who are only interested in negotiating exchange rates among the world's leading currencies. There would be no leading currency per se under a global gold standard; there would be only the credibility of the individual nation's promise to redeem its currency in gold on demand. Every nation, large or small, that complied with this basic requirement could participate as a full-fledged member of a unified global monetary system.

Compliance would not require having physical possession of vast hoards of gold. A government could buy gold if necessary to fulfill its obligation to redeem its currency. In considering whether or not it will have sufficient gold to meet the demands of currency holders who wish to convert paper claims into gold, the government of every potential gold standard participant should keep in mind that citizens have no incentive to exchange paper currency for gold *unless they believe the value of the paper money has been debased*. That is, people will choose to hold the far more convenient paper money, which can also be invested to earn financial returns, rather than possess large amounts of gold, which impose high costs for storing and safeguarding.

To the extent that an individual nation followed prudent fiscal policies, maintaining a balanced budget and refraining from inflating the money supply by monetizing government debt, it would remain a member in good standing of the community of nations voluntarily succumbing to the discipline of gold to uphold the value of their currencies. If any particular nation, even one of the core group members, began to fall away from its commitment to monetary integrity by inflating its currency, other members would not have to suffer negative economic or financial consequences, nor would they find themselves embroiled in political or diplomatic attempts at intimidation. Under a gold standard, the offending nation automatically would be censured as holders of its currency turned in their claims for gold (or exchanged it for other currencies and the central banks of the receiving nations then redeemed the currency for gold from the issuing country's central bank). Without inciting ugly nationalist rivalries, without resorting to political battles, the existence of a gold standard would quietly resolve the matter. Moreover, in the process of correcting for the actions of the offending nation, the problem would be solved; as people turned in the debased currency for gold, the money supply of the issuing country would shrink until equilibrium was once again achieved between the perceived value of the currency and the value of gold. When a country's money supply is in alignment with the terms of the gold convertibility it offers, balance is restored.

The driving mechanism of a global gold standard is that it makes each individual nation responsible for its own fiscal and monetary behavior. Nations that exercise proper discipline earn the right to participate fully in an open and integrated global monetary system. Nations that do not behave responsibly incur the consequences directly and automatically and can blame only themselves. In any case, citizens are protected from the financial misbehavior of government because they always have the option of turning in their currency for gold.

Compared to the existing system of managed floating rates, where the economic interests of lesser nations hardly figure into the intense negotiations among the leading finance ministers, a global gold standard offers substantially more benefits for developing nations attempting to break into global markets. When the United States devalues its currency to "enhance exports," for example, the efforts of individuals from competing nations are hopelessly undercut. Unless their own governments likewise choose to devalue their currencies in foreign exchange markets, the monetary differential may utterly swamp any benefits from comparative advantage. Less industrialized countries are particularly hurt when their exported commodities, which are sensitive to world market prices, suddenly are seen as more expensive in comparison to prices of U.S.-supplied commodities strictly as a result of a drop in the relative value of the dollar against other currencies.

It is often pointed out that if a critical mass of nations were to go on a gold standard in the interests of creating a global monetary system, the major gold-producing nations would receive excessive benefits. Two of the two largest gold producers in the world are Russia and South Africa. While both nations have seen much of their gold wealth depleted—in Russia's case, huge amounts of gold bullion were illegally transferred out of the country by corrupt communist officials—they still have substantial reserves yet to be mined within their borders. Ironically, the old political arguments that once served the interests of those opposed to going on a gold standard have now been turned around; Russia and South Africa are trying desperately to overcome the economic and social damage suffered as the result of former oppressive and immoral regimes. If any countries in the world today could use an economic windfall as the result of an international decision to utilize gold as the anchor for a new global monetary system, one could hardly come up with two better candidates than Russia and South Africa. The advantage that might accrue to these nations is that one of their major exports would be directly convertible into dollars, deutsche marks, or yen—indeed, any currency of any participating gold standard nation—at a fixed rate. Selling exports is the way other countries gain hard currency as well; the currency earned can then be redeemed in gold if desired. The difference between exporting gold versus other commodities is that the prices of other commodities are subject to the effects of supply and demand. Gold is a unique commodity when it serves as the monetary anchor because its money price is fixed by definition.

If the dollar price of gold, once it officially had been fixed, turned out to be higher than the market price for gold that would have reigned in the absence of a decision by the United States and other major industrialized countries to go on a gold standard, then Russia and South Africa certainly would be in a position to benefit economically. That is, the owners of the gold mines in those countries would benefit. But as economist Murray Rothbard has noted, the prospect that gold miners might receive higher profits because the dollar price of gold increased during the transition to a gold standard should not be a matter of great concern. "I do not believe that we should refuse an offer of a mass entry into Heaven," says Rothbard, "simply because the manufacturers of harps and angels' wings would enjoy a windfall gain."[35]

Moreover, if Russia and South Africa, as major gold-producing countries, were able to offer enhanced credibility in backing their own national currencies with gold and thereby were able to become participating member nations of a global monetary system anchored by gold, so much the better. It otherwise might be years before Russia is capable of competing in world markets with agricultural products or manufactured goods. In the meantime, exports of gold translate into solid purchasing power that can be used to finance the necessary inputs of equipment and technology to build the factories that will generate future revenues. South Africa, too, needs vital Western goods and services to rescue an economy that has been gripped by prolonged crisis in recent years. With unemployment at more than 40 percent, South Africa's ability to attract foreign investment to expand productive output is crucial to carrying out political plans for abolishing the practice of apartheid. Yet investors are put off by the backdrop of social violence that now kills more than eight people each day in South Africa. If the money price of gold is increased somewhat by the impact of moving toward a global gold standard, the world should rejoice at South Africa's good fortune; it is difficult to imagine a nation where extra profits stemming from a natural resource could be put to better use.

More important, though, than the ability of any one nation to benefit from a new world monetary order based on gold would be the ability of all nations to compete in a global marketplace where price signals accurately convey the relative values of goods and services. Less powerful developing countries often feel victimized by rich industrialized countries, particularly by the United States. Speaking in September 1992 at a meeting of the Non-Aligned Movement, an organization of 108 member nations representing more than half the world's population, President Suharto of Indonesia told delegates, "We must insure that the new world order to which leaders of industrialized countries often refer, does not turn out to be but a new version of the same old patterns of domination of the strong over the weak—and the rich over the poor."[36] While there is probably little that Suharto or any other leader of a third world nation can do to make the rich countries poor, there is much that can be gained by ensuring that economically powerful countries cannot use their intimidating presence to capture additional unearned advantages by rigging foreign exchange rates to suit their own domestic needs. Countries, like individuals, are not necessarily endowed equally. Resources are not equitably distributed across national borders. But every nation should assert its right to compete on an equal basis. In a world where monetary policy is dictated by a single powerful nation or by a clique of finance officials representing the interests of the richest nations, less developed countries have no ability to control their own economic destiny. The first step toward taking one's stand in the global economy is to ascertain that the monetary rules are not subject to change and that they are equally applicable to all participants.

In this sense, less developed countries have the most to gain from supporting an initiative for a global gold standard. They are even more eager than advanced countries to expand the productive output of their economies, to raise the standard of living of their citizens, and to attract outside investment for future growth. Not being the largest players, they cannot expect to exert much influence among the finance ministers and central bankers of the world's most powerful countries, yet they are especially vulnerable to the disastrous consequences of core group decisions that change underlying monetary relationships and cause financial capital to flee the borders of poorer nations in search of richer havens abroad, where deposits offer dual returns from interest and currency speculation.

Domingo Cavallo, economy minister of Argentina, has long recognized that the best hope for an underdeveloped country lies in securing a stable currency. As David Asman, editor of the "Americas" column for the *Wall Street Journal*, observed:

> Cavallo's convictions on this point run deep. He recently stated that currency is to an economy as language is to a culture. Without a language whose meaning is clear, well defined, and unchangeable, a culture cannot retain its past achievements or pass on those achievements to future generations. Likewise, an economy cannot function properly without a currency that investors and consumers can count on as maintaining its value. Earners must have confidence in its value if they are to save, and investors must have confidence in its future value if they are to invest in growth bonds.[37]

GLOBAL BREAKTHROUGH

Sound money should not be seen as a luxury that only the most sophisticated, advanced industrialized nations are entitled to use to maximize economic output and growth opportunities. Instead, it should be seen as a necessity for every nation that seeks to maximize the returns from investment and production. The richest nations have already incurred considerable pain in their efforts to achieve sound money. The United States went through years of high inflation in the 1970s and is still suffering the consequences of past distortions in prices and interest rates, as reflected in the diminished portfolios of U.S. thrift institutions. The adjustment back to solid monetary growth and away from the inflationary mentality that takes hold when the prices of real estate and other tangible goods only move upward is wrenching. *So* wrenching that societies often find it tempting to go back to the old self-delusion of rising wages and profits as a temporary economic remedy—only to have the persistent inflationary virus flare up once again.

If the countries with the largest, richest economies must struggle mightily to stave off inflation, the efforts of less developed nations must be even more strenuous. Less powerful economies are often so dependent on the world's strongest nations that they can do little more than absorb the monetary mistakes imposed on them. Countries that link their money to dollars, such as Argentina, are forced to become participants in whatever trade distortions occur as the result of an excessively weak or strong dollar in foreign exchange markets. If a weak dollar raises the relative cost of imports, thus introducing inflationary pressures within any country that depends heavily on imported goods, the results can be much more devastating for the economy of a small dependent country than for the United States. Likewise, if a strong dollar makes exports less competitive in Europe or Japan, export-dependent countries whose own currencies are tied to the dollar are left helplessly vulnerable to currency effects that undermine their own attempts to bring competitive goods and services to the international marketplace.

Even when the most powerful nations manage to keep inflation under control within their own domestic economies—either as the result of recession or by a deliberate policy of imposing high interest rates—the global economy suffers if currency exchange rates are left to absorb the fallout of differential policies for achieving domestic economic goals. The United States may feel it is doing a good job of controlling inflation. Germany may feel it is doing a good job of controlling inflation. But when the value of the dollar in foreign currency markets climbs to 3.44 deutsche marks in February 1985 and then drops to 1.40 marks in August 1992, or goes from 263 yen in February 1985 and plummets to 101 yen in August 1993, a stable monetary foundation for international trade clearly does not exist. For a businessperson, it is impossible to foresee, let alone accommodate, changes of such magnitude in the relative value of leading currencies over a period of only a few years.

The point is, if the global economy is to become a reality, it is not enough for individual nations to pursue price stability within their own borders. The objective should be to obtain price stability throughout the world so that individual citizens are not penalized by currency turmoil. Businesses that attempt to engage in international trade should not be pawns in a contest of currencies where unanticipated gyrations can undermine years of planning and effort. How much more appealing, how much more logical it would be to have an international monetary system that rewarded individuals for offering competitive goods and services, not for guessing right on currencies.

What is the proper role of government in all this? To manage the world's leading currencies in accordance with the domestic agendas of the most powerful players? To play politics with peoples' money and international purchasing power? The more appropriate role, certainly one more in keeping with American principles of limited governance, would be one centered on maintaining order and protecting the rights of individuals. The task of government—all governments—in the context of global monetary arrangements is to *establish and preserve an orderly system* that facilitates international trade and finance and fosters world economic growth.

What is there to be gained? Perhaps the best way to approach the question is to look at what has been lost. Paul Volcker, discussing how the ups and downs of exchange rates have negatively affected growth in trade and economic activity in the last twenty years and thus have dampened productivity and efficiency, notes in *Changing Fortunes*:

> The economic case for an open economic order rests, after all, largely on the idea that the world will be better off if international trade and investment follow patterns of comparative advantage; that countries and regions concentrate on producing what they can

do relatively efficiently, taking account of their different resources, the supply and skills of their labor, and the availability of capital. But is it hard to see how business can effectively calculate where lasting comparative advantage lies when relative swings and prices among countries are subject to exchange rate swings of 25 to 50 percent or more. There is no sure or costless way of hedging against all uncertainties; the only sure beneficiaries are those manning the trading desks and inventing the myriad of new devices to reduce the risks—or to facilitate speculation.[38]

Toyoo Gyohten, who is coauthor of *Changing Fortunes* and who now serves as chairman of the Bank of Tokyo, is even more specific about measuring the costs that have been incurred as the result of unpredictable exchange rates:

> What is wrong with the current non-system is its lack of stability and predictability in exchange rates, which seems to hurt the stable growth of trade and investment. It would be intriguing to analyze technically whether this really is a theoretically valid correlation, but past performance in the real world seems to confirm it in practice. Simply consider the Bretton Woods period from 1960 to 1973, and the period of our non-system from 1973 to 1987. During the Bretton Woods period, the average GNP growth of the OECD countries was 4.8 percent a year; in the second period it declined to 2.6 percent. Annual inflation accelerated from 4.3 percent to 6.8 percent. The export volume of those countries grew by 8.8 percent annually under Bretton Woods, but only by 4.2 percent in the second period, while the annual growth of import volume declined from 9.3 percent to 3.7 percent. Under the present non-system, world economic performance has certainly been poorer, the volatility of everyone's external accounts has been aggravated, and the threat of protectionism certainly has increased.[39]

If these two highly respected monetary experts have come through the experience of floating rates only to conclude that the lack of order and predictability in international monetary relations has cost the world a great deal in terms of lost economic opportunities, one can only feel a greater sense of urgency to put an end to the current approach (or, as Gyohten calls it, the nonsystem) and take solid steps to implement a new, improved Bretton Woods system, a global gold standard, to maximize the prospects for world economic prosperity in the future.

Poised for an Initiative

It is commonplace to assert, whenever it seems useful, that the world stands at some sort of crossroads. Politicians are apt to invoke the metaphor as a way to impart historical relevance to whatever cause they are promoting. And yet, in terms of the prospects for global monetary reform—more importantly, in terms of the necessity for global monetary reform—there can be no refuting that the international community has arrived at that point where it must either chart a new course or continue to risk the survival of free trade by drifting along with an approach that has failed. The era of floating rates represented an impossibly purist theoretical approach to letting the free market establish the value of competing government-issued brands of money. Managed floating rates have turned out to be far worse; they subject the value of peoples' purchasing power to the negotiating tactics of finance ministers and central bankers operating out of hotel rooms. A managed floating rate system is simply a monetary cartel; like all cartels, it is vulnerable to disputes among the participants. When governments refuse to acquiesce to each other's demands, when they resist pressure to accommodate each other's domestic economic agendas, the system breaks down entirely and precipitates a currency crisis. Then every nation fends for itself, imposing competitive devaluations and enacting protectionist measures in accordance with an economic mindset that seeks to protect "us" against "them."

The reason the world may choose the right road and move forward on the path to global monetary stability is because this particular historical crossroad marks the convergence of more than just economic interests. To the extent that ideas do move the world, it is significant that past policies have been discredited, not only on the basis of experience, but also in terms of behavioral analysis. The theory of devaluation, for example, has been revealed as a policy disaster offering only short-term monetary relief from fiscal responsibility. An interview with Sweden's Prime Minister Carl Bildt published in the *Wall Street Journal* in September 1992 captures the point:

WSJ: Not that long ago, nations were willing to devalue their currencies in times of economic trouble. The IMF has advised nations to devalue. What are the historical lessons of those devaluations?

MR. BILDT: The IMF has changed. We had experience ourselves with devaluations in the early 1980s. There were a number of people who thought that policy was successful for a while. But it was very evident that the policy only contributed to a rise in inflation. During the 1980s, we had inflation that was higher than the European average, and a growth rate that was successively lagging behind.

There is always a short-term boost from devaluing. But it is the easy way out. You don't tackle the long-term problems of the economy. It is like trying to overcome alcoholism. The first morning off the stuff the alcoholic feels bad. If he takes a drink he feels better, but he never gets out of the habit.

WSJ: John Major has been making the same point recently, as has the central banker of Italy today. Would you say that devaluation is recognized to be a bankrupt policy all across Europe?

MR. BILDT: Yes. Devaluation is a discredited policy. That lesson is now deep in the European experience.[40]

The theory behind managed floating rates has likewise been called into question. Lady Margaret Thatcher, former British prime minister, told an audience in Korea in September 1992, "If by artificially controlling the exchange rates between countries you try to buck the market, you will soon find the market bucks you—and hard."[41]

So across Europe and throughout much of Latin America, where new financial thinkers such as Mexico's Pedro Aspe and Argentina's Domingo Cavallo expound on the virtues of dependable money, the theory of managed floats and deliberate devaluations has lost credibility. That development helps to set the intellectual stage for a new approach. It would not be enough to introduce new thinking, however, if the financial fundamentals weren't in place to take action to achieve radical international monetary reform. Fortunately, the widespread realization that price stability lies at the heart of genuine, solid economic growth has been reflected in the achievement of relatively low inflation rates among the largest industrialized economies and some of the most promising developing countries. It would be difficult to embark on a new global monetary policy aimed at maintaining sound money through the discipline of gold in the absence of generally low rates of inflation in major areas of the world. But the current emphasis on financial responsibility and budgetary prudence serves as an even more crucial factor in laying the groundwork for achieving global monetary integrity.

In tandem with the prevailing environment of low inflation, the world has reached a political point that also bodes well for initiating fundamental monetary reform. No longer are third world countries seeking to be coddled by superpower benefactors; no longer can they play off communism against capitalism as a means of extracting favors from Cold War rivals. That game is over. What every developing nation seeking to improve its economic standing in the global community now must decide is how best to unleash the energy of its people so as to develop its resources and identify its comparative advantage. The word exploit loses its negative connotation in the absence of perceived imperialist pressures; now the word encompasses the desire of developing nations to put their own strengths to productive use. Most developing countries already have come to appreciate that democratic capitalism offers the best route to prosperity. The most farsighted ones are taking steps to implement the formula of sound money and low taxes that has proven the best way to capture the growth benefits from entrepreneurialism.

Finally, there is a sense of coming to terms with deeper values. Among the most advanced industrial nations, particularly the United States, such traits as responsibility, self-discipline, and integrity are enjoying a new respect, which seems to translate into a new sense of economic morality. As Keynesian "feel good" remedies have been revealed as addictive and ultimately destructive patterns of fiscal behavior rather than economic solutions, there has been a yearning to turn back to tried-and-true methods such as matching expenditures to revenues and striving for monetary stability.

George Goodman, known as "Adam Smith" in his writings on money in modern society, goes so far as to identify a connection between social morals and monetary policies, speculating in his book *Paper Money* that the era of loose money, like the era of loose morals, may be ending:

> We've seen how the deficits under the fixed-rate, key-currency system gave the first push to inflation, and how the system evolved into the floating world of paper money. My suspicion is that this era of infinitely inflatable currencies will not go on forever, and in fact, that it is rather late in the era. My other suspicion is that this floating world, this looseness, reflects the society around it. Its virtues are flexibility and mobility. But we are told that people now are used to instant gratification; capitalism by its very definition is based on some postponed gratification, whether by governments or people, so that the capital can be originated, invested, and compounded. We are told that our respect for institutions is declining, and that those institutions—marriage, schools, courts—are not what they used to be. Yet the smooth functioning of capitalism needs permanent institutions, so that the time can be granted for seeds to be planted, to sprout, and to grow up, for investments to mature.
>
> We shape our houses, and then they shape us.[42]

For some, it may seem a bit of a stretch to connect moral behavior with monetary systems. Pop psychology has no place in any serious plan for initiating global monetary reform. Yet it is surely no coincidence that in explaining his nation's uphill battle to restore its credibility in foreign currency markets, Sweden's Prime Minister Bildt lamented: "There tends to be a slight suspicion against Sweden in the international markets because we have devalued before. They know that we have sinned in the past." But Bildt clearly believes in monetary redemption. "On the other hand," he continues, "it is because we have sinned that we know the consequences of sinning. We are not eternal sinners."[43]

Sunset for the IMF

When the original Bretton Woods conference took place in 1944, the main task was to establish a new international economic order out of the ashes of World War II. Not only were countries physically devastated, their economies and financial systems were likewise in shambles. The United States was the strongest country left standing and the clear victor. But its goal was not to abuse its new-found singular power in the world; if anything, the United States was reluctant to assert its authority over vanquished and weakened nations, instead preferring to get back to its own social and economic priorities.

Still, the United States felt the moral imperative and sensed the strategic necessity for designing and implementing a new system that would avoid a debilitating period of currency chaos and financial isolationism such as the one that had occurred in the aftermath of World War I. Indeed, it was believed that by adopting a new approach, the world could take a huge step forward in the evolution of relations between nation-states; rather than capitalizing on the losses of victims, and rather than turning inward after the horror of international confrontation, nations would this time deliberately agree to cooperate on monetary and financial matters so they could all recover jointly. International trade was seen to be the economic key to revitalization around the world. Countries with money to lend, such as the United States, would put their capital to work in countries that needed to restore their productive capacity for economic growth. All participants would benefit from an open world economic order.

The unifying structure for the plan was to be manifested in the form of a new organization called the International Monetary Fund. Additionally, the plan called for the establishment of an International Bank for Reconstruction and Development to provide long-term financing to help rebuild war-torn Europe and other parts of the world. But the main emphasis, the new twist in international relations, was the artificial structure for regulating monetary flows among nations. The gold standard had taken care of that task in prior years; each nation maintained a gold standard for its own economic purposes and enjoyed stable monetary relations with other trading nations because they also operated on a gold standard within their domestic economies.

But the new system to be run by the International Monetary Fund, according to the claims of its designers, would manage monetary relations better than the gold standard. Adjustments would not be so harsh and immediate as required under the discipline of gold convertibility. Instead, the officials of the International Monetary Fund could smooth those adjustments to suit the needs and individual circumstances of offending nations and help keep the entire network of trade and financial relations in balance so as to best utilize the strengths of creditor nations while attending to the needs of debtor nations.

Many of the goals were laudable. Harry Dexter White's emphasis on the need for stable currency relations was clearly well-founded. Monetary stability across national borders provides the proper environment for free trade because it permits market participants to accurately assess the value of goods and services brought to the international marketplace and because it facilitates legitimate competition. But White's design for injecting an all-powerful International Monetary Fund into the process of international trade by granting it the power to arbitrate monetary relations instead of subjecting them to the automatic law of the gold standard proved to be a failure in the end. Although the connection to gold via the United States' commitment to redeem dollars at a stipulated rate gave solidity to the international monetary system in the decades following World War II, the Bretton Woods agreement ultimately turned out to be fatally vulnerable to power politics. Even an organization so grandiose, so well-financed, and presumably so strongly supported by its founding nations as the International Monetary Fund could not stand up to the abuses of an anchor nation that found itself overwhelmed by domestic economic priorities.

The point is: Why should an organization designed to carry out the objectives of the Bretton Woods agreement continue to exist, continue to make exorbitant demands for additional capital funding from its members, when the system that brought the organization into existence has long since ceased to exist? When Nixon closed the gold window in August 1971, he ended the era of Bretton Woods. Logically, the assets held by the IMF on behalf of all its member nations should have been returned and the organization dissolved at that time. How can the IMF, which was effectively designated to serve as an accounting overseer to ensure that the monetary accounts among trading nations were reconciled in an orderly fashion in terms of a reserve currency convertible into gold, continue to justify its existence when the anchor nation for the system, the United States, has officially gone off gold?

The answer is that the IMF has had no legitimate reason to continue operations since the termination of the Bretton Woods agreement. Yet it does operate. Through the intervening two decades since the United States ended the system, the IMF has stubbornly sought to redefine its mission and perpetuate its survival. In the process, it has transmogrified into various different entities; from a global debt collection agency working on behalf of private commercial banks, to an organization gathering and processing information and offering innumerable scholarly studies and pronouncements to a mostly disinterested public, to a referee for financial disputes among the Group of Seven, and to the voice of authority and potential Western scapegoat for problems arising in the transition to democratic capitalism for formerly communist nations.

Even though the IMF has shown great flexibility in changing its mission to conform to whatever global purpose can be justified given the current economic circumstances in the world, IMF officials have remained fixed in their singular objective of increased funding. In May 1990, after nearly three years of contentious negotiations, the IMF called on its 152 member countries to pump another $60 billion into the organization to "meet the tremendous challenges of the 1990s."[44] It was the ninth time the fund had requested additional funds from its members, and this amount represented the largest infusion. Even so, $60 billion was considerably less than the $120 billion the IMF had first asked for; Michael Camdessus, managing director of the IMF, had initially wanted to double the organization's level of resources.[45]

Rather than continue to pump money into an organization that has moved so far away from its original charter that, at this point, perversely, it would in all likelihood oppose the idea of going on a global gold standard, why not dismantle it and distribute its considerable resources to its member nations, thereby enabling them to pursue currency stability with the kind of single-minded focus in keeping with the intent of the original Bretton Woods agreement? It makes more sense that the next Bretton Woods conference be initiated by addressing the legitimacy of this vestigial heir from that era and by recognizing today's IMF as a pretender to the throne of stable gold-backed monetary relations. If the IMF were true to its original purpose, it would facilitate, rather than block, a move toward a new world monetary order linked to gold.

The army of assorted bureaucrats, economists, and analysts who presently are employed by the IMF would no doubt strive mightily to preserve their jobs. Member nations probably would be forced to exert strenuous efforts to reclaim their share of the $120 billion worth of taxpayer-provided resources now serving as capital for the International Monetary Fund. But the effort could prove well worth it; more than $40 billion worth of IMF resources are held in the form of pure gold.[46]

The IMF has far outlived its original purpose. In the meantime, the world has reached that point where currency chaos now threatens to deter individual governments from living up to the ideals of free trade so vital to the development of an open global economy. The world trading community desperately needs to establish a unified monetary system to maximize the returns from competition in the international marketplace, even as the IMF sits on its gold reserves and extolls the virtues of floating rates and as whole nations succumb to the ravishes of ministerial missteps and currency speculators. Obviously, there is a solution. The first step toward its identification will come when the world acknowledges that the moment has arrived to lay out the agenda for a new Bretton Woods. And this time, we should get it right.

Epilogue:
The Sanctity of
Sound Money

The ideas of economists and political philosophers, both when they are right and when they are wrong, are more powerful than is commonly understood. Indeed the world is ruled by little else. Practical men, who believe themselves to be quite exempt from any intellectual influences, are usually the slaves of some defunct economist. Madmen in authority, who hear voices in the air, are distilling their frenzy from some academic scribbler of a few years back. . . . It is ideas, not vested interests, which are dangerous for good or ill.

—John Maynard Keynes, *General Theory of Employment, Interest and Money* (1936)[1]

Whether Keynes considered himself among those "academic scribblers" whose work found its way into the subconscious minds of "madmen in authority" is hard to say. But no one would deny that Keynes's ideas have exerted a strong influence on major leaders during this century and thus have had a powerful impact on the world. Keynes rightly identified the thoughts put forth by both economists and political philosophers as having the potential to be dangerous; his own ideas melded the two categories.

For Keynes, government was the solution. The more difficult the problems in the economy, the more government was necessary to address them. Keynes's abiding faith in the wisdom of superior beings such as himself and his disdain for free market purists whose theories had in his view been discredited combined to foster his preference for deliberate government intervention in the economic sphere. If the invisible hand could not deliver an adequate level of goods and services, government should step in and manage the economy.

The more one is inclined to turn to government to remedy the perceived shortcomings of free markets, the more one is drawn toward socialism and away from capitalism. Keynes was not alone in recognizing the connection between economic practice and political ideology. The late Nobel laureate Friedrich Hayek likewise made the observation that economic policy prescriptions are inextricably bound up with political philosophy, especially where money is concerned. In his book, *The Constitution of Liberty*, Hayek notes:

> It is no accident that inflationary policies are generally advocated by those who want more government control—though, unfortunately, not by them alone. The increased dependence of the individual upon government which inflation produces and the demand for more government action to which this leads may for the socialist be an argument in its favor. Those who wish to preserve freedom should recognize, however, that inflation is probably the most important single factor in that vicious circle wherein one kind of government action makes more and more government control necessary. For this reason, all those who wish to stop the drift toward increasing government control should concentrate their efforts on monetary policy. There is perhaps nothing more disheartening than the fact that there are still so many intelligent and informed people who in most other respects will defend freedom and yet are induced by the immediate benefits of an expansionist policy to support what, in the long run, must destroy the foundations of a free society.[2]

A contemporary political philosopher of sorts, William Greider, also has noticed the connection between the government's control of money and its control over the destiny of private citizens. In his 1987 book, *Secrets of the Temple: How the Federal Reserve Runs the Country*, Greider refers admiringly to an earlier era when people dared to question the political implications of determining the value of money; what he finds singularly odd is the extent to which modern American culture has repressed the knowledge of money. He cites a "collective blocking out" of rational opinion on the subject, as if people would prefer to accept monetary manipulation as an arcane managerial function of government. "When the money question was alive in American politics," Greider notes, "before its meaning was repressed, before there was a temple called the Federal Reserve, people knew that money was politics and that democracy depended on it."[3]

What role should money play in a democratic society? How should it be used—indeed, should it be used at all? To ask is to pose the more profound question: Is money a tool for redistributing wealth, a lever to be used by government to run the economy? Or does democracy demand that individuals make decisions on the basis of their own preferences for work or leisure, saving or consuming, in which case money should carry no bias or penalties or hidden government agenda that would cause economic behavior to deviate from choices people otherwise would make for themselves.

For those who believe in democratic capitalism, sound money is a prerequisite. Democracy does not convey the right to reward one segment of the population at the expense of another by altering the value of money; when government has the power to depreciate the currency, democracy is severely compromised. President Grover Cleveland expressed as much in 1893:

> Manifestly nothing is more vital to our supremacy as a nation . . . than a sound and stable currency. Its exposure to degradation should at once arouse to activity the most enlightened statesmanship, and the danger of depreciation in the purchasing power of the wages paid to toil should furnish the strongest incentive to prompt and conservative precaution.[4]

Capitalism demands absolute reverence for sound money, not only because free markets need accurate price signals to function properly but because the accumulation of capital occurs only when individuals are willing to forgo current consumption. If the integrity of money is compromised, the virtue of saving is undermined and the validity of capitalism is destroyed. Or as author

George Goodman, alias "Adam Smith," puts it: "The trouble with paper money is that it rewards the minority that can manipulate money and makes fools of the generation that has worked and saved."[5]

AMERICAN PRINCIPLES

If one nation stands for democratic capitalism, surely it is the United States. Even if American citizens fear that the nation's founding principles have been eroded by an increasingly intrusive government presence in society, other countries still look to the United States as the embodiment of democratic values and capitalist opportunity.

What, then, is the appropriate role for the United States in the global economy? The days of unchallenged economic domination are over. The United States is a major player in the world today, but it is not the only player. Moreover, if countries in Europe and Asia take steps to form stronger economic alliances and organize into regional trade blocs, the United States' relative power may decline. Unless, of course, the United States likewise attempts to set up a trade bloc encompassing North and South America.

But instead of creating powerful economic blocs headed by the dominant nation in the region—Germany in Europe, Japan in the Pacific, the United States in the Americas—the goal should be to eliminate trade and monetary barriers that prevent individual nations from participating freely in the global marketplace. The United States should not carve out a fiefdom of its own in response to the perceived threat of a fortress Europe or Asia. Instead, it should strive to live up to free trade principles and practices that promote legitimate competition among all nations and that serve the needs of the entire global economy. By championing the cause of sound money and by eliminating tariffs and other barriers to trade, the United States can provide leadership based on a sense of fair play and other traditional American values.

At the heart of such values is a fundamental respect for the individual. Individuals, not governments, create wealth and initiate business transactions. Therein lies a duality of motivation and purpose that lends a certain tension to the operation of markets. Individuals seek to maximize their personal welfare; to do so, they normally must cooperate with others. The best economic (and for that matter, social) system permits individuals to pursue their personal objectives in the context of an orderly and predictable environment. Community benefits are achieved as the incidental outcome of maintaining a stable regime within which individuals have the opportunity to seek improvements in their economic condition to the extent they so desire, constrained only by the requirement that they do not encroach on the rights of others.

Just as the dual notions of individuality and community must be reconciled in human nature to achieve optimum economic and social benefits, so too must individual nations maximize opportunities for economic growth by cooperating to preserve an orderly framework for global competition and trade. National sovereignty is still a relevant concept in today's world and must be respected. Any attempt to force internationalism down the throats of reluctant nation-states is likely to incite a backlash against global integration. At the same time, individual countries bring different resources and skills to the marketplace; they increase their level of prosperity when they function as part of an integrated global economy.

To be a responsible member of the international trade community, a nation must be willing to conform to a certain standard of conduct even as it maintains its political autonomy. It is neither necessary nor desirable for nations to surrender their monetary sovereignty to an overarching authority, any more than it is desirable for individual citizens to submit to a central planning authority. But to reconcile the desire for national autonomy with the benefits of global cooperation, it is necessary to establish a code of behavior that defines the appropriate terms of cooperation and acknowledges the importance of self-responsibility on the part of participating members.

In defining such a code for international monetary relations, the classical international gold standard offers the best means for maximizing returns to the global community as individual countries pursue their own best economic interests. National sovereignty is preserved under a gold standard because each nation operates its own mechanism for convertibility and each nation is responsible for carrying out fiscal policies in keeping with its obligation to redeem currency in gold on demand. At the same time, because each nation is willing to convert its currency into gold, a unified monetary system is automatically created; it is the byproduct of individual governments' obligation to abide by the recognized rules of monetary conduct.

The most appealing feature of a global gold standard is that no nation is forced to surrender control of its money supply to a supernational organization or global central bank. No nation is asked to conform to a specified budget model or to comply with a universal decree concerning the size of its domestic budget as a percentage of its gross domestic product. One nation might wish to channel a large portion of its economy through the federal budget so that national revenues are largely redistributed by the government. Another nation might wish to carry out libertarian policies, extracting from its citizens only the smallest fraction of revenues to support only the most essential government services. The point is, whether the citizens of a nation choose to operate a welfare state or whether they choose to have limited government, they can still participate in the global economy on a common monetary footing. The only requirement is that they abide by the rules of a gold standard: The government must (1) run a balanced budget and (2) provide for convertibility of its currency into gold on demand.

Adoption of a gold standard changes the nature of the relationship between private citizens and public officials. Government is much more answerable to taxpayers on fiscal issues. The constraint of having to maintain a balanced budget ensures that politicians cannot commit funds without the full awareness and approval of the citizenry. Because governments are not permitted to run deficits under a gold standard, citizens must directly bear the burden of the expenditures they authorize as part of the domestic budget. If they demand high levels of spending for defense or social services, they accordingly must fund those expenses by providing sufficient tax revenues.

While implementation of a gold standard in no way would force government expenditures to be low, it might well have a dampening effect on federal spending, because people who otherwise would be eager to accept the gifts proffered by politicians in the form of subsidies and transfer payments would become more discerning, knowing they would have to pick up the bill. Indeed, one of the great advantages of the gold standard, as Ludwig von Mises notes, is that it offers citizens "a form of protection against spendthrift governments."[6] Mises views the fiscal accountability aspect of the gold standard as an extremely positive feature, one that forces both citizens and politicians to pay more attention to budget decisions and to justify all government spending:

> If, under the gold standard, a government is asked to spend money for something new, the minister of finance can say: "And where do I get the money? Tell me, first, how I will find the money for this additional expenditure."
>
> Under an inflationary system, nothing is simpler for the politicians to do than to order the government printing office to provide as much money as they need for their projects. Under a gold standard, sound government has a much better chance; its leaders can say to the people and to the politicians: "We can't do it unless we increase taxes."
>
> But under inflationary conditions, people acquire the habit of looking upon the government as an institution with limitless means at its disposal: the state, the government, can do anything. If, for instance, the nation wants a new highway system, the government is expected to build it. But where will the government get the money?[7]

When a government is held strictly accountable by its citizens, the principles of democracy are reinforced. The government functions to serve the nation rather than as a separate bureaucratic entity with objectives of its own. Government of the people, by the people, and for the people becomes more than a philosophical ideal; it turns into a political reality with pragmatic applications for controlling the budget. For citizens who long ago dismissed any notion of self-governance, a different mindset is required. Under a gold standard, individuals assume more direct responsibility in allocating resources for the good of their nation. When transparency is restored to the budget process, the level of government spending is approved and anticipated.

Sound money thus goes hand-in-hand with sound government. The guarantee provided by gold convertibility not only assures individuals that their purchasing power is not subject to depreciation, it also serves as protection against a runaway, tyrannical government bent on expanding its own power. When citizens accept responsibility for controlling the federal purse strings and literally control the money, government is constrained in the best Jeffersonian tradition. The United States could hardly provide a better example of its political philosophy than to implement a gold standard and promote the benefits of sound money to a world in desperate search of a rational basis for international monetary relations.

RIVAL DOMAINS

The definition of a bloc, according to the dictionary, is "a group of nations united by treaty or agreement for mutual support or joint action."[8] When people speak of regional trade blocs, they are referring to groups of nations that have chosen to cooperate to form a single economic entity such as the European Community. The North American Free Trade Agreement (NAFTA) constitutes a significant step in that direction by linking the United States, Mexico, and Canada together into a single free trade zone. Whether the arrangement is formalized by treaty or institutional relationship or some other form of agreement, the purpose is to bring together a designated set of nations with perceived joint interests that potentially can be enhanced through mutual action or support.

When the words "free trade" are injected into the official arrangement, the presumption is that barriers to trade have been eliminated among the participating nations. To free trade advocates, that development is positive. But there are disturbing aspects as well. Is the trend toward regional trade blocs an interim step toward achieving a global economy with free trade policies among all nations, or will the gathering of nations into separate blocs result in harder borders encompassing the newly defined regions, repelling outsiders even as barriers within those regions are dissolved? Should free trade proponents rejoice at the emergence of regional zones comprised of nations dedicated to eliminating trade barriers among themselves? Or do such zones threaten to turn into powerful economic domains that become increasingly self-contained and outwardly protectionist?

For the global economy to become a reality, individual nations must be persuaded that it makes sense to orient their monetary, fiscal, and trade policies to a universally accepted standard that serves the interests of all nations in accordance with the doctrine of free trade and open markets. Participation in the global economy should be a matter of direct access; weaker nations should not become economic captives of the local superpower and be constrained by regional rivalries from pursuing direct contacts with prospective outside trade partners. Developing countries may find it tempting to link up with a stronger neighbor to secure certain benefits: increased foreign investment and expanded employment opportunities. At the same time, developing nations must be careful not to sign away the right to seat themselves directly at the international trade table so that they would be forced to stand obsequiously behind the chair of their recognized patron.

Trade blocs are not necessarily bad, because they may initiate the politial process necessary to eliminate tariffs and dismantle long-standing trade obstacles between neighboring countries. Any reduction in trade barriers is to be welcomed. But the formation of trade blocs should not transform major regions of the world into economic enclaves that discriminate against nonmember nations. They should not turn into trade "blocks." The world has scarcely improved its economic prospects if the vision of free trade in a global economy turns out to be a new form of economic imperialism. Regional leaders will be tempted to use protectionist weapons once again as economic rivalries escalate.

The idea of major nations conspiring to solidify such arrangements, and thus tacitly encouraging the breakup of the global economy into separate and identifiable spheres, is an alarming one. There is something ominous about the prospect of the world's most powerful nations attempting to corral their neighbors into trade arrangements that work to further their own economic and political aims. The emergence of trade blocs can only be justified if it constitutes an interim phase, a stepping stone to achieving global free trade. Managed trade—which is likely to occur when the economic interests of weaker nations are subordinated to the objectives of their host—is not the appropriate outcome for a process that was supposed to lead to an open and integrated global economy.

If all nations agree to abide by the same set of monetary and fiscal rules—namely, balanced budgets and gold convertibility of their currency—there will be far less incentive for any individual nation to seek economic shelter. Weaker nations will not be compelled to solicit protection from the local economic power if they are confident of being permitted to interact freely and fairly with nations in general. If access to trade partners is denied through tariffs or distorted through monetary manipulations, however, lesser nations will have little choice but to glom on to hegemonic sponsors who have sufficient economic weight to challenge the leaders of rival trade blocs.

One can easily imagine a future world where the economic battlelines have been drawn to reflect European, American, and Japanese spheres of dominance. Each region would operate as a currency zone defined by the leading nation's money; the operative currencies within the three main trade blocs would be the deutsche mark, the dollar, and the yen. At first, perhaps, the three dominant nations might attempt to coordinate exchange rates and achieve uniform purchasing power across trade zones. But if one of the leading powers were to begin to put domestic economic priorities ahead of the need to preserve international monetary stability, leaving smaller aligned nations to trail along in its monetary wake, trade and capital flows among the blocs could be damaged to the point of collapse.

Certainly the recent experience in Europe has shown how regional dependence on the monetary policies of a single nation can lead to a breakdown in the currency order that can, in turn, undermine trade relations and threaten the political viability of the entire bloc. The lessons of Europe should serve as a warning to a world yearning to define a new global economic order. No single nation can be entrusted with the responsibility for monetary stability beyond its own borders. But every nation can decide to take responsibility for itself to provide sound money for its citizens. The dual objectives of sound domestic currency and international monetary stability are reconciled through a global gold standard.

SOLID FOUNDATION

In the context of monetary discussions, the word "fix" connotes more than just repairing a bad system. To fix the money means also to stabilize its purchasing power, to give it intrinsic value, to make it sound. Contrast this stance with the flexible approach to controlling money. Flexibility is often considered a virtue. Flexibility permits people to change their minds or their objectives; it saves them from being locked into a rigid plan. When it comes to money, though, flexibility is a euphemism by which government planners gain the ability to distort natural economic processes and subvert the intentions of market participants, be they workers or owners, borrowers or lenders.

When the value of money can be altered through government policies against which money holders have no recourse, the economic decisions of private individuals are hostage to the ambitions of politicians. Flexibility in the control of money provides the means for government officials to adjust the purchasing power in the hands of citizens to accommodate budgetary excesses and federal borrowing. If citizens want to reclaim their right to sound money, they must remove the government's ability to exercise flexibility in managing the money supply.

Fixed money in no way implies fixed prices. Prices are determined by the interplay of supply and demand, and these variables continuously reflect changes in labor, technology, consumer preferences, and other factors. Any government that attempted to guarantee fixed prices for its citizens (as in the former Soviet Union) would have to manage virtually every aspect of economic production as it sought to exert total control over the distribution of resources among the population. Obviously, that system is the opposite of capitalism. Under capitalism, the government is expected to ensure legal justice and provide for the physical security of its people, but it cannot guarantee prices without impinging on the economic freedom of individuals.

A gold standard fixes the value of money in terms of a universally recognized commodity so that money holders have the confidence of knowing that their paper claim can be converted to a real asset at a prespecified rate. The gold standard establishes a solid foundation for making rational economic decisions and then enables individuals to exercise personal choice in pursuing their own financial and economic objectives.

Conceivably, the advantages of commodity-backed money could be captured by designating a broad index of products or a basket of consumer goods and services to which the value of currency would be tied. Irving Fisher and, more recently, Sir Alan Walters have recommended such an approach. Currency holders would have the right to convert their money into alternative financial instruments that enabled them to purchase the specified basket of products. But while the concept is clearly an improvement over fiat money, which imposes no real restraint on the government issuer, it seems unnecessarily complicated. Because it functions as a reliable surrogate for changes in the general price level, why not use the more straightforward benchmark of gold? A complex index of goods and services is subject to constant revision and is thus vulnerable to government manipulation.

Certainly, gold has always enjoyed an excellent reputation among central bankers. Central banks that reveal their holdings show impressive stashes of the barbaric metal. According to *The Economist*, they held in their possession some 35,000 tons of gold in January 1993—equal to seventeen years' output from mines. Ironically (or perhaps not) central banks still cling to one-third of all the world's gold, even though it has been more than two decades since the official link between currencies and gold was severed.[9] Although the central banks of Holland and Belgium generated a fair amount of publicity when they sold substantial portions of their gold reserves in 1992, the overall level of gold stocks in central bank vaults has remained remarkably stable since the middle of this century. Statistics furnished by the International Monetary Fund show that the monetary gold holdings of the world's central banks, along with official international organizations (such as the IMF) and other monetary authorities (such as the Saudi Arabian Monetary Authority), amounted to 1,000 million ounces in 1952. Some forty years later, at year-end 1991, gold holdings stood at 1,140 million ounces.[10]

At a market price of $350 per fine troy ounce, these reserves would be worth $400 billion. But the IMF numbers cover no more than 80 percent of the holdings of the official sector, according to the summer 1992 issue of *World Gold Review*, because of the limitations of IMF data, the exclusion of nonreporting nations (such as Iran), and the use of certain accounting methodologies that understate the world's gold reserves.[11] A more accurate figure for estimating the market value of gold held by the official sector for monetary purposes (based again on a $350 price per troy ounce) would be closer to $500 billion.

The United States is by far the world's largest holder of gold reserves; it owns some 260 million ounces, over 20 percent of the total official sector holdings covered by IMF statistics.[12] Most of the U.S. gold stock, which is under the supervision of the U.S. Treasury, is held in vaults at Fort Knox, Kentucky, at West Point, New York, and in Denver, Colorado. The Federal Reserve Bank of New York offers the world's largest gold depository in its subterranean vault, where more than sixty countries store some 10,000 tons of their reserves in gold bars.[13] Interestingly, in China, where there has long been a cultural attachment to gold, individuals have been aggressively accumulating gold as the population becomes increasingly wealthy. Jonie Lai, head of the East Asian office of the World Gold Council, estimates that Chinese gold purchases may account for one quarter of total world gold sales in 1993.[14]

Some might find it difficult to understand why central bankers, who should represent the epitome of monetary sophistication, keep an average 30 percent of their total reserves in the form of non-interest-bearing gold.[15] On the other hand, the keepers of the world's financial system place great emphasis on price stability and sound money. Moreover, they are keen observers of history. Gold provides insurance against economic and political calamity. It is still widely regarded as a "war chest" that can be tapped in the event of global currency chaos. Gold, in that sense, is the bulwark for preserving national financial independence.

If central bankers turn to gold as the ultimate guarantor of monetary integrity, should private citizens be less demanding? Those who demean the monetary use of gold as a provincial vestige of the past underestimate its contemporary appeal among financial sophisticates from Basel to Beijing. No citizen should permit the purchasing power of hard-earned wages to be undermined by fiscal malfeasance or monetary manipulation. The soundness of currencies should be maintained domestically and internationally through a system of fixed exchange rates based on universal gold convertibility. This is no mere academic proposal for international monetary reform; it is a fundamental call for a new approach to financial governance based on balanced budgets, fiscal transparency, and political accountability.

Speaking to a group of monetary specialists and financial officials attending a congressional summit on exchange rates held in Washington in November 1985, Jack Kemp made the connection between the importance of sound money for an individual citizen and the importance of stable exchange rates among nations. Noting that he had "never had any problem explaining this to the average voter," Kemp proceeded:

> We have talked at this conference about the importance of monetary reform for trade among nations. We have talked about its importance for debtor nations and creditor nations. Let's not forget that what is true of nations is also true of individual workers, savers, investors, businesses, and families.
>
> People are creditors when they save for their children's college education or for retirement. They are debtors when they borrow to buy a house or start a business. They deal with exchange rates when they travel or shop for an automobile—or when the local steel plant lays off workers because of imports. They experience the high cost of capital when they take out a car loan. They experience the depreciation of money when they buy food at the supermarket. The monetary issue is anything but remote from people's experience. In my experience, honest, sound, stable money is a popular, blue-collar, bread-and-butter, winning political issue.[16]

No one can doubt that we are moving into an age where citizens are demanding more responsible government. A new level of public scrutiny has replaced a former apathetic acceptance of dubious definitions of the national interest that all too often served as cover for politicians and bureaucrats. Government responsibility begins with sound money. Americans, certainly, should settle for no less. They have endeavored hard and incurred great sacrifice to make democratic capitalism a reality around the world. The United States needs to reaffirm its values and assert its global leadership by taking the necessary measures to restore the integrity of its currency.

The phrase "sound as a dollar" should become meaningful once more—not just at home but around the world. With so many people in developing countries abandoning their own discredited currencies and turning to the dollar, the United States has a moral duty to uphold the integrity of its money. The United States' resolve to put its own financial house in order constitutes the first step toward building a new monetary system to serve an open world economy. The next Bretton Woods conference—aimed at achieving a global gold standard—could mark the beginning of a new era of free trade and economic growth and could lead to new heights of prosperity for all nations.

Notes

Introduction: Losing the Dream

1. William Drozdiak, "Europe Gets Cold Feet on Unification," *Washington Post*, June 14, 1992, p. A25.
2. "The American Dollar's Unhappy Bicentenary," *The Economist*, July 25, 1992, p. 63.
3. Rick Wartzman, "Dollar's Fall Raises Broad Questions on Causes, Outlook for U.S. Markets," *Wall Street Journal*, August 26, 1992, p. A2.
4. Patrick Harverson, "Bush Says Sorry But Stocks Still Slide," *Financial Times*, August 22–23, 1992, weekend FT, p. II.
5. Jodie T. Allen, "The Mark Stops Here: Behind the Euro-Crisis," *Washington Post*, September 20, 1992, p. C1.
6. Richard W. Stevenson, "Europeans' Currency System Shaken as Britain Cuts Free," *The New York Times*, September 17, 1992, p. A1.
7. Ibid., p. D8.
8. Richard W. Stevenson, "Europe's Currencies Wobble On," *The New York Times*, November 23, 1992, p. D5.
9. Peter Marsh, "Storms in ERM Leave Some Currencies Adrift," *Financial Times*, April 19, 1993, p. 2.
10. James Blitz, "All Change in Foreign Exchanges," *Financial Times*, April 2, 1993, p. 15.
11. Barry Rehfeld, "Soros's Alter Ego: Low Profile, Very High Returns," *The New York Times*, April 18, 1993, p. F8.
12. Brett D. Fromson and William N. Drozdiak, "Speculators Take Break from Onslaught Against Franc," *Washington Post*, January 8, 1993, p. F5.
13. See Samuel Brittan, "Black Wednesday's Bill," *Financial Times*, November 30, 1992, p. 10.

14. Fromson and Drozdiak, "Speculators Take Break."
15. Hilary Barnes and Robert Graham, "Speculators Push Danish Krone to Floor in ERM," *Financial Times*, February 4, 1993, p. 1.
16. Fromson and Drozdiak, "Speculators Take Break."
17. William Drozdiak, "France, Germany Pledge Strong Defense of Franc," *Washington Post*, September 24, 1992, p. A20.
18. Hobart Rowen, "Fixed Rates Don't Work in a Free Market," *Washington Post*, September 27, 1992, p. H1.
19. William Dawkins, "Barre Sounds the Alarm over Anglo-Saxon Ambush of Franc," *Financial Times*, February 11, 1993, p. 2.
20. Lionel Barber, "The Pound–Dollar Plot," *Washington Post*, February 28, 1993, p. C5.
21. Steven Mufson, "For Europe, a Body Blow to the Quest for Economic Unity," September 17, 1992, p. A23.
22. Paul Blustein, "Brown Tells Japan to Boost U.S. Purchases," *Washington Post*, April 24, 1993, p. C1.
23. Ayako Doi and Kim Willenson, "Tokyo Woes," *Washington Post*, February 14, 1993, p. C2.
24. Paul Blustein, "Yen's Surge Worries Japanese Industry," *Washington Post*, April 20, 1993, p. D1.
25. Ibid.
26. Michael Prowse, "Clinton Favours a Strong Dollar," *Financial Times*, December 16, 1992, p. 6.
27. Diane Dimond, "Dollar Sags to Low as Bentsen Urges a Stronger Yen," *Wall Street Journal*, February 22, 1993, p. C1.
28. Larry Holyoke, William Glasgall, and Douglas Harbrecht, "The Yen Is Cornering Japan Inc.," *Business Week*, March 8, 1993, p. 50.
29. Blustein, "Yen's Surge."
30. John Bussey and Clay Chandler, "Clinton Pushes Japan to Boost Spending But Tokyo Officials Say, 'No Thanks,'" *Wall Street Journal*, April 19, 1993, p. A6.
31. Craig R. Whitney, "At Eye of Currency Storm, Chief of Bundesbank," *The New York Times*, October 8, 1992, p. D1.
32. Ibid.
33. James F. Clarity, "Dublin Upbraids Its Partners in Currency System," *The New York Times*, February 1, 1993, p. C3.
34. Eugene Robinson, "Major Seeks Curbs on EC's Bureaucracy," *Washington Post*, September 25, 1992, p. A27.
35. Nicholas Denton, "East Europe Quickly Learns the Western Art of Protectionism," *Financial Times*, April 13, 1993, p. 14.
36. Lionel Barber, "Brittan Bangs Drum for E. European Trade," *Financial Times*, April 14, 1993, p. 8.

37. Ibid.
38. Lionel Barber, "East Europe Calls EC's Bluff over Free Trade," *Financial Times*, April 16, 1993, p. 6.
39. Matt Moffett, "Mexicans Anticipate Passage of Trade Pact Will Lift Economy," *Wall Street Journal*, April 20, 1993, p. A1.

Chapter 1. The Legacy of Bretton Woods

1. Anthony Sampson, *The Money Lenders* (Harmondsworth, U.K.: Penguin Books, 1983), pp. 85–86.
2. Ibid., p. 88.
3. John Maynard Keynes, *The Collected Writings of John Maynard Keynes*, vol. XXI (London: Macmillan/St. Martin's Press for the Royal Economic Society, 1973), pp. 334, 144. Quoted in Todd G. Buchholz, *New Ideas from Dead Economists* (New York: New American Library, 1989), p. 211.
4. Robert Kuttner, "Keynes the Able," *The New Republic*, November 6, 1989, p. 62.
5. R. F. Harrod, *The Life of John Maynard Keynes* (London: Macmillan, 1951), p. 50. Quoted in Buchholz, *Dead Economists*, p. 201.
6. W. Carl Biven, *Who Killed John Maynard Keynes?* (Homewood, Ill.: Dow Jones-Irwin, 1989), p. 8.
7. Kuttner, "Keynes the Able," p. 64.
8. Harrod, *The Life* (reprinted in Pelican Books, 1972), p. 190. Quoted in Vincent Bladen, *From Adam Smith to Maynard Keynes: The Heritage of Political Economy* (Toronto and Buffalo, N.Y.: University of Toronto Press, 1974), p. 409.
9. Buchholz, *Dead Economists*, p. 202.
10. John Maynard Keynes, *The Collected Writings of John Maynard Keynes*, vol. I (London: Macmillan for the Royal Economic Society, 1971), p. 70. Quoted in Bladen, *From Smith to Keynes*, p. 411.
11. Keynes, ibid., p. 25. Quoted in Bladen, ibid., p. 409.
12. Keynes, ibid., vol. II, p. 131. Quoted in Bladen, ibid., p. 421.
13. Keynes, ibid., p. 143. Quoted in Bladen, ibid.
14. Kuttner, "Keynes the Able," p. 64.
15. Keynes, *Collected Writings*, vol. XXI, p. 296. Quoted in Buchholz, *Dead Economists*, p. 213.
16. Sampson, *The Money Lenders*, p. 82.
17. J. Keith Horsefield, *The International Monetary Fund, 1945–1965: Twenty Years of International Monetary Cooperation*, vol. I: *Chronicle* (Washington, D.C.: International Monetary Fund, 1969), pp. 14–15.

18. John Maynard Keynes, *Collected Writings of J. M. Keynes*, vol. XXV (London: Macmillan, 1980), pp. 98–99. Quoted in Sampson, *The Money Lenders*, p. 83.

19. John Maynard Keynes, "Proposals for an International Currency (or Clearing) Union," draft dated February 11, 1942, par. 17(3). Reproduced in *The International Monetary Fund, 1945–1965*, vol. III: *Documents*, edited by J. Keith Horsefield, p. 7.

20. Ibid., pp. 6–7.

21. John Maynard Keynes, "Proposals for an International Clearing Union," draft dated April 1943. Reproduced in *The IMF*, vol. III, p. 19.

22. Keynes, "Proposals," draft dated February 11, 1942, par. 51. Reproduced in *The IMF*, vol. III, p. 14.

23. Horsefield, *The IMF*, vol. I, p. 12.

24. Ibid.

25. Ibid.

26. Ibid., pp. 21–22.

27. H. D. White, "Preliminary Draft Proposal for a United Nations Stabilization Fund and a Bank for Reconstruction and Development of the United and Associated Nations," draft dated April 1942. Reproduced in *The IMF*, vol. III, p. 46.

28. Ibid., p. 47.

29. Ibid., pp. 38–39.

30. Ibid., p. 40.

31. Ibid., p. 44.

32. Ibid.

33. Ibid., p. 69.

34. Ibid., pp. 49–50.

35. Ibid., p. 40.

36. Ibid., p. 41.

37. Horsefield, *The IMF*, vol. I, p. 25.

38. Ibid.

39. White, "Preliminary Draft Proposal," *The IMF*, vol. III, p. 41.

40. Horsefield, *The IMF*, vol. I, pp. 39–40.

41. Ibid., p. 33.

42. Ibid., p. 34.

43. Keynes, "Proposals," draft dated February 11, 1942, *The IMF*, vol. III, p. 6.

44. White, "Preliminary Draft Proposal," *The IMF*, vol. III, p. 66.

45. Horsefield, *The IMF*, vol. I, p. 51.

46. Ibid., p. 36.

47. Ibid., p. 79.

48. Ibid., pp. 84–85.

49. *Proceedings and Documents of United Nations Monetary and Financial Conference, Bretton Woods, New Hampshire, July 1–22, 1944* (Washington, D.C.: Department of State, 1948), Alternative C, p. 23. Cited in Horsefield, ibid., p. 93.

50. *Proceedings*, ibid., p. 1088. Cited in Horsefield, ibid., p. 94.

51. Horsefield, ibid., pp. 87–88.

52. John Morton Blum, *From the Morgenthau Diaries; Vol. III: Years of War, 1941–45* (Boston: Houghton Mifflin, 1967), p. 273. Quoted in Horsefield, ibid., p. 92.

53. Horsefield, ibid., pp. 81–82.

54. Ibid., p. 105.

55. Ibid., p. 95.

56. Compare columns (5) and (6) of "Table 2. Suggested Quotas" in Horsefield, ibid., p. 96.

57. Ibid., p. 97.

58. Ibid., pp. 107–08.

59. Ibid., p. 111.

60. "Articles of Agreement of the International Monetary Fund," dated July 22, 1944. Reproduced in *The IMF*, vol. III, pp. 187–89.

61. Horsefield, *The IMF*, vol. I, p. 85.

62. See Henry R. Nau, *The Myth of America's Decline* (New York and Oxford: Oxford University Press, 1990), p. 87.

63. Harrod, *The Life* (New York: Harcourt Brace, 1951), p. 641. Quoted in Thomas D. Willett, *Floating Exchange Rates and International Monetary Reform* (Washington, D.C.: American Enterprise Institute for Public Policy Research, 1977), p. 7.

64. Horsefield, *The IMF*, vol. I, pp. 114–15.

65. Ibid., p. 114.

66. Ibid., p. 116.

67. Sampson, *The Money Lenders*, p. 89.

68. Whittaker Chambers, *Witness* (Chicago: Regnery Gateway, 1952), p. 429.

69. Ibid., p. 383.

70. Ibid., p. 430.

71. Ibid., p. 600.

72. Ibid., p. 737.

73. Horsefield, *The IMF*, vol. I, p. 123.

74. Biven, *Who Killed Keynes?*, p. 12.

75. Horsefield, *The IMF*, vol. I, pp. 159–60.

76. Ibid., p. 132.

77. Ibid., p. 197.

78. Ibid., p. 200.
79. U.S. Department of State, 1947, "European Initiative Essential to European Recovery," remarks by Secretary of State George C. Marshall at Harvard University Commencement, June 5, 1947. Publication 2882, European Series 25, Washington, D.C.: Government Printing Office. Quoted in Nau, *The Myth*, p. 102.
80. Sampson, *The Money Lenders*, p. 93.
81. Nau, *The Myth*, pp. 104–105.
82. Horsefield, *The IMF*, vol. I, p. 225.
83. See Nau, *The Myth*, pp. 112–23.
84. Nau, *The Myth*, p. 115.
85. Michael J. Hogan, *The Marshall Plan: America, Britain and the Reconstruction of Western Europe, 1947–1952* (Cambridge, U.K.: Cambridge University Press, 1987), p. 155. Quoted in Nau, *The Myth*, pp. 115–16.
86. Nau, *The Myth*, p. 116.
87. Ibid., p. 117–18.
88. Henry Wallich, *The Mainsprings of German Revival* (New Haven, Conn.: Yale University Press, 1955). Quoted in Edwin Hartrich, *The Fourth and Richest Reich* (New York: Macmillan, 1980), p. 132.
89. Nau, *The Myth*, pp. 120–23.
90. Based on IMF, UN, and OECD sources; see chart "Performance Indicators (1947–1986)" in Henry Nau's "The U.S. Has Lost Its Economic Policy Compass," *The International Economy*, March/April 1988, vol. 2, no. 2, p. 89.
91. Ibid.
92. "Fix What Broke," *Wall Street Journal*, July 11, 1984, p. 24.

Chapter 2. The Fall from Grace

1. See the chart "War and Prices" (source: Claudia D. Goldin, Harvard University) in Sylvia Nasar, "An Exception to Rule of War: Inflation Threat Is Receding," *The New York Times*, March 10, 1991, p. 24.
2. Hans F. Sennholz, *Age of Inflation* (Belmont, Mass.: Western Islands, 1979), pp. 30–31.
3. Henry R. Nau, *The Myth of America's Decline: Leading the World Economy into the 1990s* (New York: Oxford University Press, 1990), p. 144.
4. Harry Johnson, "The Case for Flexible Exchange Rates, 1969," in *Further Essays in Monetary Economics* (London: Allen and Unwin, 1972), p. 210.
5. *International Financial Statistics: Yearbook* (Washington, D.C.: International Monetary Fund, 1983), see Government Finance Statistics for United States, pp. 524–25, line 80.

6. Paul Volcker and Toyoo Gyohten, *Changing Fortunes: The World's Money and the Threat to American Leadership* (New York: Times Books, 1992), p. 21.

7. Ibid., p. 25.

8. Louis Rukeyser, *What's Ahead for the Economy: The Challenge and the Chance* (New York: Simon and Schuster, 1983), pp. 24–25.

9. See the chart "War and Prices" (Goldin) in Nasar, "Exception to Rule."

10. William Greider, *Secrets of the Temple: How the Federal Reserve Runs the Country* (New York: Touchstone/Simon and Schuster, 1987), p. 323.

11. Ibid., p. 308.

12. Quoted in Greider, *Secrets*, p. 326.

13. Greider, *Secrets*, pp. 340–41.

14. *International Financial Statistics*, 1983, p. 525, line 80.

15. Nau, *The Myth*, p. 156.

16. Volcker and Gyohten, *Changing Fortunes*, p. 21.

17. Robert Kuttner, *The End of Laissez-Faire: National Purpose and the Global Economy After the Cold War* (New York: Alfred A. Knopf, 1991), p. 61.

18. Lawrence S. Ritter and William L. Silber, *Principles of Money, Banking, and Financial Markets* (New York: Basic Books, 1974), p. 485.

19. James Grant, *Money of the Mind* (New York: Farrar Straus Giroux, 1992), p. 284.

20. Nau, *The Myth*, p. 141.

21. Quoted in Grant, *Money of the Mind*, pp. 276–77.

22. Kuttner, *The End*, pp. 63–64.

23. Adam Smith, *Paper Money* (New York: Summit Books, 1981), p. 129.

24. Ritter and Silber, *Principles*, pp. 489–90.

25. John S. Odell, *U.S. International Monetary Policy: Markets, Power and Ideas as Sources of Change* (Princeton, N.J.: Princeton University Press, 1982), p. 263. Cited in Nau, *The Myth*, p. 162.

26. Kuttner, *The End*, p. 65.

27. Herbert Stein, "Remembering the Fifteenth of August," *Wall Street Journal*, August 14, 1981, reprinted in Herbert Stein, *Washington Bedtime Stories* (New York: The Free Press, 1986), pp. 187–88.

28. Herbert Stein, "The Chief Executive as Chief Economist," *Essays in Contemporary Economic Problems: Demand, Productivity, and Population* (Washington, D.C., and London: American Enterprise Institute for Public Policy Research, 1981), pp. 53–78, reprinted in Stein, *Washington Bedtime Stories*, pp. 198–99.

29. Odell, *U.S. International Monetary Policy*, p. 262. Cited in Nau, *The Myth*, p. 157.

30. Volcker and Gyohten, *Changing Fortunes*, p. 81.
31. Ritter and Silber, *Principles*, p. 492.
32. Volcker and Gyohten, *Changing Fortunes*, p. 94.
33. Quoted in Greider, *Secrets*, p. 335.
34. Ronald McKinnon, "The Fixed-Rate Dollar Standard: 1950–1970," unpublished paper, Economics Department, Stanford University, October 1989, p. 26.
35. Milton Friedman and Robert Roosa, *The Balance of Payments: Free Versus Fixed Exchange Rates* (Washington, D.C.: American Enterprise Institute, 1967), pp. 133–34. Cited in Thomas D. Willett, *Floating Exchange Rates and International Monetary Reform* (Washington, D.C.: American Enterprise Institute for Public Policy Research, 1977), p. 15.
36. Margaret Garritsen de Vries, *The IMF in a Changing World: 1945–1985* (Washington, D.C.: International Monetary Fund, 1986), p. 47.
37. Paul H. Douglas, *America in the Market Place* (New York: Holt, Rinehart and Winston, 1966), p. 576. Quoted in Willett, *Floating Exchange Rates*, p. 18.
38. Quoted in Greider, *Secrets*, p. 338.
39. Richard J. Barnet and Ronald E. Muller, *Global Reach: The Power of the Multinational Corporations* (New York: Simon and Schuster, 1974), p. 257.
40. Rukeyser, *What's Ahead*, p. 221.
41. Anthony Sampson, *The Money Lenders* (Harmondsworth, U.K.: Penguin Books, 1983), p. 151.
42. Ibid., pp. 151–52.
43. Darrell Delamaide, *Debt Shock* (Garden City, N.Y.: Anchor Books, 1985), pp. 34–36.
44. Ibid., p. 34.
45. Cited in Sampson, *The Money Lenders*, p. 152.
46. Garritsen de Vries, *The IMF*, p. 111.
47. Ibid., p. 128.
48. Ibid., pp. 128–29.
49. Volcker and Gyohten, *Changing Fortunes*, p. 142.
50. Ibid., p. 143.
51. Rukeyser, *What's Ahead*, pp. 27–28.
52. *International Financial Statistics*, 1983, p. 525, line 80. (Cumulative total budget deficit for years 1970 through 1974 equals $72.38 billion.)
53. Kuttner, *The End*, p. 73.
54. Ibid.

55. Volcker and Gyohten, *Changing Fortunes*, pp. 149–50.

56. Ibid., p. 148.

57. Ibid., p. 162.

58. Greider, *Secrets*, p. 67.

59. Kuttner, *The End*, pp. 75–76.

60. Volcker and Gyohten, *Changing Fortunes*, p. 171.

61. Grant, *Money*, p. 317.

62. Greider, *Secrets*, p. 207.

63. Ibid., p. 218.

64. See chart, "Annual U.S. Consumer Inflation," in Volcker and Gyohten, *Changing Fortunes*, p. 372.

65. Kuttner, *The End*, pp. 78–79.

66. *Washington Post*, April 13, 1985. Quoted in Nau, *The Myth*, p. 265.

67. I. M. Destler and C. Randall Henning, *Dollar Politics: Exchange Rate Policymaking in the United States* (Washington, D.C.: Institute for International Economics, 1989), pp. 22–23.

68. *Wall Street Journal*, April 26, 1986. Quoted in Yoichi Funabashi, *Managing the Dollar: From the Plaza to the Louvre* (Washington, D.C.: Institute for International Economics, 1988), p. 74.

69. Clyde H. Farnsworth, "Democrats Seek Currency Intervention," *The New York Times*, April 25, 1985. Quoted in Funabashi, *Managing the Dollar*, p. 74.

70. Volcker and Gyohten, *Changing Fortunes*, p. 245.

71. Ibid., p. 246.

72. Ibid., p. 256.

73. Funabashi, *Managing the Dollar*, p. 185.

74. Kuttner, *The End*, p. 99.

75. Nau, *The Myth*, p. 281.

76. Destler and Henning, *Dollar Politics*, p. 67.

77. Ibid., p. 69.

78. Volcker and Gyohten, *Changing Fortunes*, p. 246.

Chapter 3. The World on Edge

1. Allen R. Meyerson, "When Soros Speaks, World Markets Listen," *The New York Times*, June 10, 1993, p. D1.

2. Kenichi Ohmae, *The Borderless World* (New York: Harper Business, 1990), p. 157.

3. Peter Norman, "Getting Their Breath Back," survey on foreign exchange, *Financial Times*, May 26, 1993, section III, p. I*.

4. "European Steelmakers Hit Out at 'Trade War,'" *Financial Times*, June 24, 1993, p. 3.

5. David Gardner and Nancy Dunne, "EC Warns of Action over U.S. Trade Threat," *Financial Times*, February 3, 1993, p. 1.
6. Ibid., p. 16.
7. Andrew Pollack, "Look Inward, Tokyo Urges Trade Critics," *The New York Times*, May 12, 1993, p. D2.
8. Paul Blustein, "Taking the Offense on Managed Trade," *Washington Post*, May 21, 1993, p. G1.
9. Andrew Borowiec, "As U.S. Struggles Back, Europe Merely Struggles," *Washington Times*, June 17, 1993, p. A1.
10. Gerald F. Seib, "People Turn More Sour About Clinton in Poll, But They're Willing to Forgive," *Wall Street Journal*, June 10, 1993, p. A12.
11. Quentin Hardy, "Japan Registers Dim Outlook by Business," *Wall Street Journal*, June 14, 1993, p. A11.
12. Barry D. Wood, "America's Commitment to Europe," *Europe* July–August 1990, pp. 14–15.
13. Ibid.
14. Stephen E. Ambrose, "An Early Champion of Unity," *U.S. News & World Report*, October 15, 1990, p. 65.
15. Ibid.
16. Ibid.
17. Malcolm Bradbury, "All Aboard for the New Europe," *The New York Times Magazine*, February 3, 1991, p. 23.
18. Christopher J. Redman, "Interview: How a Superpower Can Avoid Muscle Loss," *Time*, September 30, 1991, p. 11.
19. Eugene Robinson, " 'United' Europe Seen Adrift, in Discord," *Washington Post*, February 8, 1993, p. A15.
20. Robin Knight, John Marks, and Fred Coleman, "Push Comes to Shove," *U.S. News & World Report*, June 14, 1993, pp. 53–54.
21. Ibid.
22. Paul Koring, "Denmark's Vote Doesn't Lift Clouds over European Unity," *Washington Times*, May 21, 1993, p. A9.
23. Ibid.
24. Lionel Barber, "EC Predicts Economic Growth at Zero or Less," *Financial Times*, May 17, 1993, p. 1.
25. Quentin Peel, "State Spending Cuts Planned to Cope with German 'Crisis,'" *Financial Times*, May 28, 1993, p. 1.
26. Knight, Marks, and Coleman, "Push Comes to Shove," p. 64.
27. Alice Rawsthorn, "No Shying Away from the Challenge," *Financial Times*, June 24, 1993, survey: France, p. II*.
28. Ibid.
29. Ewen MacAskill, "Major, in Political Slump, Fires Chancellor of Exchequer," *Washington Post*, May 28, 1993, p. A36.

30. Ibid.

31. Franco Modigliani, "The Year of the Great Opportunity," *Financial Times*, May 5, 1993, p. 12.

32. Knight, Marks, and Coleman, "Push Comes to Shove," p. 61.

33. William Drozdiak, "EC's Executive Body Gingerly Stalls Unity Process," *Washington Post*, May 12, 1993, p. A23.

34. Peter Norman, "Bad Blood as a Relationship Hits Its Floor," *Financial Times*, October 1, 1992, p. 2.

35. Marc Fisher, "Germany's Love Affair with the Mark," *Washington Post*, September 19, 1992, p. A16.

36. Christopher Parkes, "Bundesbank Attack on 'Sham' Proposals for Changes in EMS," *Financial Times*, June 5–6, 1993, p. 2.

37. Marc Fisher, "Denmark Approves European Unity Treaty by 57 Percent Vote," *Washington Post*, May 19, 1993, p. A21.

38. David Marsh and Peter Marsh, "Lessons of the Currency Turmoil," *Financial Times*, April 30, 1993, p. 3.

39. "Complacency on the ERM," *Financial Times*, May 25, 1993, p. 17.

40. Peter Marsh, "Governor Signals Doubts on ERM," *Financial Times*, May 6, 1993, p. 6.

41. Marsh and Marsh, "Lessons."

42. "Germans Make Apparent Snub Toward French," *Wall Street Journal/Europe*, June 25–26, 1993, p. 9.

43. "ERM Remains on Trial," *Financial Times*, April 22, 1993, p. 15.

44. Lionel Barber, "EC Deficits, 'Threaten New Currency Chaos,'" *Financial Times*, June 17, 1993, p. 2.

45. David Marsh and Peter Norman, "System Under Strain Yet Again," *Financial Times*, May 15–16, 1993, p. 9.

46. Edward Balls, "Illusory Gains of Britain's 'Competitive Devaluation,'" *Financial Times*, June 1, 1993, p. 6.

47. "Maastricht Sails On," *The Economist*, May 22, 1993, p. 15.

48. William Drozdiak, "U.S.–European Alliance Plagued by Trade, Security Conflicts," *Washington Post*, February 13, 1993, p. A26.

49. Ibid.

50. Ibid.

51. Bob Hagerty and Timothy Aeppel, "U.S.–German Trade Settlement Hurts EC's Efforts to Present Unified Front," *Wall Street Journal*, June 14, 1993, p. A9A.

52. Daniel P. Galo, "Bush and Clinton Speak Out on Europe," *Europe*, October 1992, no. 320, p. 24.

53. "Excerpts of President Clinton's Speech on International Trade," *Washington Post*, February 27, 1993, p. A8.

54. Ibid.

55. Carla Rapoport, "How Clinton Is Shaking Up Trade," *Fortune*, May 31, 1993, p. 103.
56. Jim Hoagland, "It's Jobs, Remember?" *Washington Post*, May 13, 1993, p. A27.
57. Ibid.
58. Asra Q. Nomani and Masayoshi Kanabayashi, "Kantor Issues Trade Threat Against Japan," *Wall Street Journal*, May 3, 1993, p. A3.
59. Keith Bradsher, "U.S. Partners Say President Shows Two Faces on Trade," *The New York Times*, March 19, 1993, p. D2.
60. "Living with US Trade Policy," *Financial Times*, April 5, 1993, p. 15.
61. Ibid.
62. "Japan Protects Market and Jobs, Clinton Says," *International Herald Tribune*, June 30, 1993, p. 15.
63. Peter Behr, "Japan Told to Cut Trade Edge in Half," *Washington Post*, June 8, 1993, p. A1.
64. "Japan Protects."
65. "U.S. Said to Seek GNP and Trade Targets for G-7," *International Herald Tribune*, June 26–27, 1993, p. 9.
66. Steven Greenhouse, "Paris Rules Out Pact on Trade at Summit," *International Herald Tribune*, June 30, 1993, p. 1.
67. Peter Behr, "OECD Spurns Japan's Trade Policy Pleas," *Washington Post*, June 3, 1993, p. D9.
68. T. R. Reid, "Kohl Defends Japan Against Trade Critics," *Washington Post*, February 28, 1993, p. A25.
69. "U.S. Said to Seek Targets."
70. Peter Behr, "Sanctions Issue Shadows Japan Talks," *Washington Post*, June 19, 1993, p. C6.
71. James Bovard, "The U.S. War on Macedonia," *Wall Street Journal*, June 9, 1993, p. A12.
72. "Living with US Trade Policy."
73. "Losing the Yen Game," *Wall Street Journal/Europe*, June 30, 1993, p. 8.
74. Fred R. Bleakley, "Japanese Firms Raise Prices in U.S., as Yen Stays Strong," *Wall Street Journal/Europe*, June 29, 1993, p. 7.
75. Michael Prowse, George Graham, and Charles Leadbeater, "Yen Dispute Gone But Not Forgotten," *Financial Times*, April 30, 1993, p. 6.
76. Paul Blustein, "Yen's Surge Worries Japanese Industry," *Washington Post*, April 20, 1993, p. D1.
77. Charles Leadbeater, "Bank of Japan Criticises Clinton," *Financial Times*, April 24–25, 1993, p. 3.
78. Ibid.
79. Rich Jaroslovsky, "Washington Wire," *Wall Street Journal*, May 28, 1993, p. A1.

80. Rich Jaroslovsky, "Washington Wire," *Wall Street Journal*, June 18, 1993, p. A1.
81. Elisa Williams, "Addicted to Exports," *Washington Times*, February 28, 1993, p. A13.
82. Jeffrey E. Garten, "Clinton's Emerging Trade Policy," *Foreign Affairs*, summer 1993, p. 183.
83. Ibid.
84. Floyd Norris, "In Washington, the Dollar Has Few Friends," *The New York Times*, July 19, 1992, section 3, p. 1.
85. Lindley H. Clark, Jr., "The Outlook," *Wall Street Journal/Europe*, June 28, 1993, p. 1.
86. Paul Blustein, "High Yen Is Bad News for Japanese Exporters," *Washington Post*, September 26, 1992, p. C1.
87. Bleakley, "Japanese Firms Raise Prices."
88. Blustein, "High Yen Is Bad News."
89. Paul Blustein, "In Japan, Consumption's No Longer Conspicious," *Washington Post*, February 28, 1993, p. H1.
90. Charles Leadbeater, "Bankruptcies Rise in Japan," *Financial Times*, April 17–18, 1993, p. 3.
91. "The Yen Again," *Wall Street Journal*, February 24, 1993, p. A14.
92. Erik Ipsen, "Dollar Skids to Record Lows, Pushing Stock Markets Down," *International Herald Tribune*, August 25, 1992, p. 1.
93. Ibid.
94. Rich Jaroslovsky, "Washington Wire," *Wall Street Journal*, June 11, 1993, p. A1.
95. Michael Prowse, "The Dangers of a Quick Fix," *Financial Times*, February 27–28, 1993, p. 8.
96. David Gardner, "France Sees Dollar Rate as Block to Gatt," *Financial Times*, October 17–18, 1992, p. 2.
97. "Industry Fears Weak Dollar Will Worsen Recession," *Financial Times*, August 25, 1992, p. 7.
98. Robert McGough, "U.S. Investors in European Stock Funds Learn Big Lesson on Vulnerability in Currency Swings," *Wall Street Journal*, September 21, 1992, p. C1.
99. Anatole Kaletsky, "Let's Fall in Love with Falling Currencies," *The Times*, June 30, 1993, p. 23.
100. Leonard Silk, "Head Off a Trade War," *The New York Times*, February 4, 1993, p. A23.
101. James Sterngold, "Japan's New Finance Official Plots an Independent Course," *The New York Times*, August 5, 1991, p. C1.
102. Akio Mikuni, "Behind Japan's Economic Crisis," *The New York Times*, February 1, 1993, p. A13.

103. Ohmae, *Borderless World*, p. 180.
104. Paul Blustein, "Trade Surplus Hangs over U.S.–Japan Talks," *Washington Post*, April 15, 1993, p. D11.
105. Charles Leadbeater, "Japanese Banks Told They Should Write Off Bad Loans," *Financial Times*, February 16, 1993, p. 1.
106. Blustein, "Trade Surplus Hangs."
107. Charles Leadbeater and Michiyo Nakamoto, "The Land of the Rising Surplus," *Financial Times*, June 7, 1993, p. 10.
108. Ibid.
109. Masayoshi Kanabayashi, "Yen's Rise Isn't Likely to Drive Japanese to Build More Plants Abroad This Time," *Wall Street Journal*, May 28, 1993, p. A7.
110. Paul Blustein, "Japan Obsessively Tracks Yen's Climb," *Washington Post*, May 27, 1993, p. B14.
111. "Tokyo's Grim News on Jobs and Output," *International Herald Tribune*, June 30, 1993, p. 18.
112. Ibid.
113. Clay Chandler and Jacob M. Schlesinger, "Japan's Slump Damps Hope in G-7 of Attack on Surplus," *Wall Street Journal/Europe*, July 6, 1993, p. 2.
114. Kenichi Ohmae, "U.S.–Japan Trade Fictions," *Wall Street Journal*, May 27, 1993, p. A12.
115. Tomohiko Kobayashi, "Better, Read the World Trade Rules," *International Herald Tribune*, June 30, 1993, p. 8.
116. R. Taggart Murphy, "Stronger Yen, Weaker U.S.," *The New York Times*, May 1, 1993, p. 15.
117. Blustein, "Japan Obsessively Tracks," p. B13.
118. Quentin Hardy, "Yen Gains Acceptance for Global Use," *Wall Street Journal*, May 18, 1993, p. A2.
119. Ibid.
120. Ibid.
121. Charles Leadbeater and Peter Norman, "Tokyo Pushes to Win Entry to Bigger Security Council," *Financial Times*, July 7, 1993, p. 4.
122. Ibid.
123. Ohmae, "U.S.–Japan Trade Fictions."
124. Ibid.
125. Reginald Dale, "Clinton Is Bull-Headed on Japan," *International Herald Tribune*, July 2, 1993, p. 11.
126. "Land of Rising Sun Turns the Heat on America," *Sunday Times* (London), October 29, 1989, p. B6.
127. "Poll of Europeans Shows Mistrust of Japan on Rise," *International Herald Tribune*, July 3–4, 1993, p. 5.

128. John Lloyd, "Russia Bank Chief Gloomy on Economy," *Financial Times*, July 10–11, 1993, p. 4.

129. O. Kuschpeta, *The Banking and Credit System of the U.S.S.R.* (Leyden and Boston: Martinus Nijhoff Social Sciences Division, 1978), p. 45.

130. Abel Aganbegyan, *Inside Perestroika: The Future of the Soviet Economy* (New York: Harper & Row, 1989), pp. 211–12.

131. Ibid., p. 213.

132. Gerald Nadler, "On the Road to Ruin, Russia Rushes Rubles," *Washington Times*, June 3, 1992, p. A1.

133. Celestine Bohlen, "Economic Furor Growing in Russia," *The New York Times*, June 3, 1992, p. A11.

134. Margaret Shapiro, " 'I Can Hardly Believe in Anything,' " *Washington Post*, July 2, 1992, p. A34.

135. Ibid., p. A1.

136. David Remnick, "Yeltsin Sworn in as Russian President," *Washington Post*, July 11, 1991, p. A1.

137. Bryan Brumley, "Yeltsin Pledges Reform, Human Rights in Russia," *Washington Times*, July 11, 1991, p. A7.

138. Adi Ignatius, "Russia Seeks More Cooperation from West as G-7 Summit Begins," *Wall Street Journal*, July 7, 1993, p. A6.

139. Ibid.

140. Leyla Boulton, "Russia Lurks in the Shadows of G7 Feast," *Financial Times*, July 12, 1993, p. 2.

141. Steve Coll, "Reborn Ukraine Faces Growing Pains in Its Quest for Global Respect," *Washington Post*, June 20, 1993, p. A24.

142. Celestine Bohlen, "Economic Trouble and Nuclear Dispute Deepen Ukraine's Sense of Insecurity," *The New York Times*, June 12, 1993, p. 5.

143. Ibid.

144. Ibid.

145. John Lloyd, "Most CIS States to Get Own Currencies," *Financial Times*, May 22–23, 1993, p. 2.

146. Claudia Rosett, "Kyrgyzstan Is Out from Under the Ruble," *Wall Street Journal*, May 18, 1993, p. A14.

147. Ibid.

148. Ibid.

149. John Lloyd, "IMF Watches as Kyrgyzstan Fights the Battle of the Som," *Financial Times*, May 21, 1993, p. 6.

150. Philippe Legrain, "Estonia Proudly Wears Its Kroon of Thorns," *Financial Times*, June 23, 1993, p. 4.

151. Gail Buyske, "Estonia, Monetary Model for Russia," *Wall Street Journal*, June 29, 1993, p. A18.

152. Ibid.
153. "The European Community," *The Economist*, July 3, 1993, survey, p. 17.
154. Lionel Barber, "Brussels Plan to Speed E. Europe Links with EC," *Financial Times*, May 1–2, 1993, p. 22.
155. Terence Roth, "Recession Holds Back Economic Integration of East Europe and EC," *Wall Street Journal/Europe*, July 1, 1993, p. 1.
156. Ibid.
157. Ibid., p. 6.
158. Craig R. Whitney, "East Europe Still Waits for the Capitalist Push," *The New York Times*, April 30, 1993, p. A7.
159. Nicholas Denton, "East Europe Quickly Learns the Western Art of Protectionism," *Financial Times*, April 13, 1993, p. 14.
160. Roth, "Recession Holds Back Integration," p. 1.
161. Whitney, "East Europe Still Waits."
162. David Marsh and Lionel Barber, "Morsels from a Groaning Table," *Financial Times*, June 7, 1993, p. 11.
163. Lionel Barber, "Commission Opens Doors for E. Europe," *Financial Times*, May 6, 1993, p. 3.
164. Cacilie Rohwedder, "EC Takes Steps to Hasten Lowering of Trade Barriers," *Wall Street Journal/Europe*, July 1, 1993, p. 6.
165. Roth, "Recession Holds Back Integration," p. 6.
166. "Fair Is Foul," *The Economist*, June 26, 1993, p. 56.
167. Alan Riding, "European Community Sets Terms for 6 Former Soviet Allies to Join," *The New York Times*, June 23, 1993, p. A8.
168. "The Challenge to the East," *Financial Times*, September 8, 1992, p. 18.
169. Frances Williams, "Mexico Reaps Benefits of Trade Liberalisation," *Financial Times*, April 21, 1993, p. 6.
170. Stephen Fidler, "Bouncing Back from Disaster in Tigerish Style," *Financial Times*, July 30, 1992, p. 5.
171. "Reforming Latin America," *The Economist*, July 17, 1993, p. 16.
172. Lawrence Malkin, "Investors Return to Latin America," *International Herald Tribune*, July 7, 1993, p. 13.
173. Ibid.
174. Fidler, "Bouncing Back."
175. "Mexico," *The Economist*, February 13, 1993, survey, p. 3.
176. James Brooke, "Latin America's Regional Trade Boon," *The New York Times*, February 15, 1993, p. D1.
177. Ibid.
178. David Goldman, "A Revolution You Can Invest In," *Forbes*, July 9, 1990, p. 50.

179. "President Salinas on Mexico's Economy," interview by David Asman, *Wall Street Journal*, April 4, 1990, p. A24.
180. Nathaniel C. Nash, "Argentina Races to Sell Oil Stake," *The New York Times*, April 16, 1993, p. D1.
181. Tim Golden, "Mexico Sells Off Last of 18 Banks at Big Profit," *The New York Times*, July 7, 1992, p. D2.
182. "Mexico."
183. Damian Fraser, "Mexican Inflation at 21-Year Low," *Financial Times*, July 9, 1993, p. 3.
184. Stephen Fidler, "Venezuela's Central Bank Keeps Its Head," *Financial Times*, June 23, 1993, p. 6.
185. Nathaniel C. Nash, "A New Rush into Latin America," *The New York Times*, April 11, 1993, p. 6.
186. Stephen Fidler, "Breakneck Pace," *Financial Times*, May 27, 1993, survey, p. 12.
187. Ibid.
188. John Barham and Stephen Fidler, "Argentina Turns Down IMF Request," *Financial Times*, May 19, 1993, p. 5.
189. Ibid.
190. Nathaniel C. Nash, "Brazil Seeks to Revive Its Lost Economic Miracle," *The New York Times*, February 16, 1993, p. A4.
191. Ibid.
192. Christina Lamb, "A Rollercoaster out of Control," *Financial Times*, February 22, 1993, p. 8.
193. Ibid.
194. "Brazil Moves on Inflation," *The New York Times*, April 26, 1993, p. D5.
195. Christina Lamb, "A Blind Eye to the Enemy Within," *Financial Times*, April 30, 1993, p. 15.
196. Stephen Fidler and Damian Fraser, "Dark Cloud of Devaluation Gathers over Mexico," *Financial Times*, February 24, 1993, p. 6.
197. "Back NAFTA Now or Lose It," *Financial Times*, June 30, 1993, p. 15.
198. Williams, "Mexico Reaps Benefits."
199. "Mexico," survey, p. 6.
200. Geri Smith and Douglas Harbrecht, "'The Moment of Truth' for Mexico," *Business Week*, June 28, 1993, p. 45.
201. Fidler and Fraser, "Dark Cloud."
202. Sheryl WuDunn, "Booming China Is Dream Market for West," *The New York Times*, February 15, 1993, p. A1.
203. Stephen Brookes, "China on a Slow Boat to Economic Change," *Insight*, January 10, 1993, p. 8.

204. Nicholas D. Kristof, "China, Barreling Along the Capitalist Road, Now Posts Strict Speed Limits," *The New York Times,* July 23, 1993, p. A3.
205. Urban C. Lehner, "Belief in an Imminent Asian Century Is Gaining Sway," *Wall Street Journal*, May 17, 1993, p. A12.
206. Asra Q. Nomani and Robert S. Greenberger, "China Economy Is World's No. 3, IMF Calculates," *Wall Street Journal*, May 21, 1993, p. A5A.
207. "China at Boiling-Point," *The Economist,* July 10, 1993, p. 15.
208. "China Belongs to Me," *The Economist*, May 29, 1993, p. 13.
209. WuDunn, "Booming China."
210. Brookes, "China on a Slow Boat."
211. Lena H. Sun, "Counting Cash Is What Counts to China's New Entrepreneurs," *Washington Post*, April 11, 1993, p. A1.
212. Tony Walker, "'Money Is Not Everything, But Having No Money Is Worse,'" *Financial Times*, July 6, 1993, p. 7.
213. Sun, "Counting Cash," p. A26.
214. Lena H. Sun, "China's New Ideology: Make Money, Not Marxism," *Washington Post*, July 27, 1993, p. A1.
215. Sun, "Counting Cash," p. A.26.
216. Garth Alexander, "Chinese Shoot 'Economic Saboteurs,'" *Sunday Times* (London), July 4, 1993, business, p. 11.
217. Lena H. Sun, "Illegal Chinese Migrants Arrive Home; Punishment Unlikely," *Washington Post*, July 20, 1993, p. A13.
218. Tony Walker, "Lure of the Billion-Buyer Market," *Financial Times*, June 14, 1993, p. 2.
219. Robert B. Oxnam, "The Hidden Foundations of Chinese Democracy," *CEO International Strategies*, vol. 6, no. 3, June–July 1993, p. 27.
220. Tony Walker, "Lure."
221. Clive Crook, "The Third World," *The Economist*, September 23, 1989, survey, pp. 39–40.
222. Haroldo J. Montealegre, "Prescriptions for Latin Growth That Won't Kill the Patient," *Wall Street Journal*, June 29, 1990, p. A13.
223. Crook, "The Third World," survey, p. 16.
224. Ibid., survey, p. 21.
225. Nash, "A New Rush."
226. "Poor Nations Seek Exports to Rich Nations," *The New York Times*, September 20, 1992, international, p. 14.
227. Ibid.
228. Alan Greenspan, remarks before a management briefing of the Edwin L. Cox School of Business, Southern Methodist University, Dallas, Texas, May 25, 1993.

229. Stuart Auerbach, "Europe Crisis Likely to Hurt 3rd World Aid," *Washington Post*, September 25, 1992, p. F1.

230. "While the Rich World Talks," *The Economist*, July 10, 1993, p. 11.

231. Joanna Pitman, "Yeltsin Stakes Claim for Full Seat in Economic Grouping," *The Times* (London), July 10, 1993, p. 10.

232. Roger Thurow, "Gold Bust Strains South Africa Transition," *Wall Street Journal*, July 8, 1993, p. A6.

233. Jerelyn Eddings, "Facing an Economic Meltdown," *U.S. News & World Report*, July 5, 1993, p. 37.

234. "While the Rich World Talks," p. 12.

235. Lawrence Malkin, "Developing World Takes Growth Lead," *International Herald Tribune*, June 25, 1993, p. 11.

Chapter 4. Theory Versus Reality

1. Adam Smith, *The Wealth of Nations*, 1776, vol. I, book I., chapter IV, ed. James E. Thorold Rogers (Oxford: Clarendon Press, 1869), p. 28.

2. Quoted in David Smith, *The Rise and Fall of Monetarism* (London: Penguin Books, 1987), p. 15.

3. Milton Friedman, "Quantity Theory of Money," *The New Palgrave: Money*, ed. John Eatwell, Murray Milgate, and Peter Newman (New York: Norton, 1989), p. 28.

4. Ibid., p. 32.

5. Milton Friedman, "Monetary Policy for the 1980's," excerpted and adapted from *To Promote Prosperity*, ed. John H. Moore (Stanford, Calif.: Hoover Institution Press, 1984). Adapted and published as "Monetary Policy : Tactics versus Stategy" in *The Search for Stable Money*, ed. James A. Dorn and Anna J. Schwartz (Chicago and London: University of Chicago Press, 1987), p. 362.

6. Friedman, "Quantity Theory," p. 16.

7. Quoted in D. Smith, *Rise and Fall*, p. 148.

8. Friedman, "Monetary Policy," *Search for Stable Money*, p. 381.

9. Ibid., p. 382.

10. Milton Friedman and Rose Friedman, *Free to Choose* (New York: Harcourt Brace Jovanovich, 1980), p. 308. Quoted in Friedman, "Monetary Policy," *Search for Stable Money*, p. 368.

11. Friedman, "Monetary Policy," *Search for Stable Money*, pp. 377–78.

12. Ibid., p. 371.

13. Smith, *Rise and Fall*, pp. 149–50.

14. Owen Ullmann, "How Long Can the Fed Steer Without a Map?" *Business Week*, August 2, 1993, p. 32.

15. Owen Ullmann, Pete Engardio, Peter Galuszka, and Bill Hinchberger, "The Global Greenback," *Business Week*, August 9, 1993, p. 40.
16. Paul Volcker, excerpts from speech delivered in Geneva on the fortieth anniversary of the General Agreement on Tariffs and Trade, published in the *Wall Street Journal*, "Don't Count on Floating Exchange Rates," November 28, 1988, p. A12.
17. Yoichi Funabashi, *Managing the Dollar: From the Plaza to the Louvre* (Washington, D.C.: Institute for International Economics, 1988, 1989), p. 83.
18. Ibid., p. 77.
19. Ibid., p. 24.
20. Ibid., p. 80.
21. Robert Kuttner, "Jim Baker Remakes the World," *The New Republic*, April 21, 1986. Quoted in Funabashi, *Managing the Dollar*, p. 85.
22. Kenichi Ohmae, *The Borderless World* (New York: Harper Business, 1990), pp. 163–64.
23. International Monetary Fund, *The Exchange Rate System: Lessons of the Past and Options for the Future*, occasional paper no. 30 (Washington, D.C.: IMF, July 1984), p. 9.
24. International Monetary Fund, Articles of Agreement (IMF (1978)), article IV, section 1 (iii). Cited in International Monetary Fund, *The Exchange Rate System*, p. 4.
25. International Monetary Fund, *The Exchange Rate System*, ibid.
26. "As Good as Gold: A Symposium," *National Review*, June 11, 1990, p. 34.
27. I. M. Destler and C. Randall Henning, *Dollar Politics* (Washington, D.C.: Institute for International Economics, 1989), p. 42.
28. Henry Nau, *The Myth of America's Decline: Leading the World Economy into the 1990s* (New York: Oxford University Press, 1990), p. 276.
29. George P. Shultz, "National Policies and Global Prosperity," address before the Woodrow Wilson School of Public and International Affairs, Princeton University, Princeton, New Jersey, April 11, 1985. Released by the Bureau of Public Affairs, Department of State, Washington, D.C., Current Policy no. 684. Quoted in Nau, *The Myth*, p. 251.
30. Destler and Henning, *Dollar Politics*, p. 54.
31. Robert Kuttner, *The End of Laissez-Faire: National Purpose and the Global Economy After the Cold War* (New York: Alfred A. Knopf, 1991), p. 104.
32. Ibid.
33. See Ohmae, *Borderless World*, p. 164.

34. R. Taggart Murphy, "Stronger Yen, Weaker U.S.," *The New York Times*, May 1, 1993, p. 15.

35. Ohmae, *Borderless World*, p. 167.

36. Quoted in Hobart Rowen, "Reflections on World Cooperation," *Washington Post*, February 21, 1988, pp. H1, H10.

37. See "Agreement of 13 March 1979 Between the Central Banks of the Member States of the European Economic Community Laying Down the Operating Procedures for the European Monetary System," reprinted in *Compendium of Community Monetary Texts* (Brussels: Monetary Committee of the European Community, 1989), p. 50.

38. Ibid.

39. Anne Bagamery, "Toward a Common Currency," *Investment Vision*, February–March 1991, p. 73.

40. Paul Krugman, "Europe's Monetary Day of Reckoning," *CEO/International Strategies*, May–June 1991, vol. 4, no. 3, pp. 25–26.

41. Ibid., p. 25.

42. Peter Norman, "E.C. Studies Ways Toward Monetary and Economic Union," *Europe*, March 1989, p. 19.

43. Marc Fisher and David Hoffman, "Behind German Unity Pact: Personal Diplomacy from Maine to Moscow," *Washington Post*, July 22, 1990, p. A26.

44. "The Great Money Swap," *The Economist*, June 30, 1990, survey: The New Germany, p. 10.

45. Ibid.

46. Leonard Silk, "Economic Scene: The Huge Costs of German Unity," *The New York Times*, July 6, 1990, p. A5.

47. David D. Hale, "Deutsche Mark uber Alles," *Washington Post*, July 1, 1990, p. B4.

48. Sheila Rule, "A British Official, Stirring Outcry, Says Germans Are Taking Over," *The New York Times*, July 13, 1990, p. A5.

49. Ibid.

50. John Ridding, "Balladur Blames Crisis on High German Rates," *Financial Times*, August 3, 1993, p. 3.

51. Ferdinand Protzman, "Kohl Sees Delay in Currency Union," *The New York Times*, August 10, 1993, p. D2.

52. Ibid.

53. David Smith and Iain Jenkins, "Meltdown for the D-Mark as Bundesbank Dithers," *Sunday Times* (London), June 27, 1993, section 3, p. 3.

54. Peter Marsh, "Warning for Central Bankers," *Financial Times*, June 15, 1993, p. 4.

55. Ibid.
56. Michael Meyer and Anne Underwood, "What Currency Crisis?" *Newsweek*, August 16, 1993, p. 65.
57. Christopher Parkes and John Ridding, "Newspapers Wage a War of Words," *Financial Times*, August 2, 1993, p. 4.
58. Ibid.
59. David Lawday and Warren Cohen, "Capsizing Currencies," *U.S. News & World Report*, August 16, 1993, p. 45.
60. John Ridding and James Blitz, "France Resists Rate Cut After Sharp Decline in Reserves," *Financial Times*, August 6, 1993, p. 1.
61. Mary Beth Sheridan, "Speculators Pose Threat to Europe's Central Banks," *Washington Times*, July 27, 1993, p. C3.
62. Michael R. Sesit, "Europe's Stormy Currency Markets Turn Calm," *Wall Street Journal*, August 3, 1993, p. C1.
63. Glenn Whitney, "Currency Traders Welcome Upheaval," *Wall Street Journal*, August 5, 1993, p. A4.
64. Ibid.
65. Saul Hansell, "Europe's Turmoil Aids U.S. Banks," *The New York Times*, August 4, 1993, p. D1.
66. Allen R. Myerson, "Turmoil in the Currency Markets," *The New York Times*, September 17, 1992, p. D1.
67. "George Soros: Talkative," *The Economist*, August 7, 1993, p. 67.
68. James Blitz, "Franc Could Be the Death of Him," *Financial Times*, August 7–8, 1993, p. A4.
69. Meyer and Underwood, "What Currency Crisis?"
70. Lawden and Cohen, "Capsizing Currencies."
71. Hans F. Sennholz, *Age of Inflation* (Belmont, Mass.: Western Islands, 1979), p. 148.
72. Philoeunomos (Roger Sherman), "A Caveat Against Injustice, or an Inquiry into the Evil Consequences of a Fluctuating MEDIUM OF EXCHANGE," (1752). Quoted in Edwin Vieira, Jr., *Pieces of Eight: The Monetary Powers and Disabilities of the United States Constitution* (Old Greenwich, Conn.: Devin-Adair, 1983), p. 7.
73. Ibid., pp. 7–8.
74. *Webster's Ninth New Collegiate Dictionary* (Springfield, Mass.: Merriam-Webster, 1986), p. 459.
75. Friedrich A. Hayek, "Toward a Free-Market Monetary System," reprinted in *Search for Stable Money*, ed. Dorn and Schwartz, p. 384.
76. Ibid.
77. Ibid.
78. "A Stronger Dollar, a New Money Order," interview with Edouard Balladur, *Wall Street Journal*, December 5, 1990, p. A16.

79. Ludwig von Mises, "Monetary Stabilization and Cyclical Policy" (1928) in *On the Manipulation of Money and Credit* (Dobbs Ferry, N.Y.: Free Market Books, 1978), p. 84. See Richard M. Ebeling, "Ludwig von Mises and the Gold Standard" in *The Gold Standard: An Austrian Perspective*, ed. Llewellyn H. Rockwell, Jr. (Lexington, Mass.: Lexington Books, 1985), p. 47.

80. Ludwig von Mises, "The Non-Neutrality of Money," an unpublished paper delivered at the Ecole Pratique des Hautes Etudes in Paris (May 1939) and at the Political Economy Club in New York (November 1940). Cited in Ebeling, *The Gold Standard*, pp. 47–48.

81. Ebeling, ibid., p. 48.

82. Hans Cohrssen, "Working for Irving Fisher," *Cato Journal*, vol. 10, no. 3 (winter 1991), ed. James A. Dorn (Washington, D.C.: Cato Institute), p. 825.

83. See Irving Fisher, *The Purchasing Power of Money* (New York: Macmillan, 1911).

84. W. Blackstone, *Commentaries on the Laws of England* (1771–1773). Quoted in Vieira, *Pieces of Eight*, p. 3.

85. Quoted in Ron Paul and Lewis Lehrman, *The Case for Gold: A Minority Report of the U.S. Gold Commission* (Washington, D.C.: Cato Institute, 1982), p. 169.

86. Ibid.

87. J. M. Keynes, *A Tract on Monetary Reform* (London: Macmillan, 1932), p. 12.

88. Ludwig von Mises, "The Gold Problem," in *Planning for Freedom*, 4th ed. (South Holland, Ill.: Libertarian Press, 1980), p. 185. Quoted in Ebeling, "Mises and the Gold Standard," *Gold Standard*, p. 48.

89. Tim Carrington, "A Survivor Shapes Thatcher Europolicies," *Wall Street Journal*, August 29, 1989, p. A10.

90. Walters in "As Good as Gold."

91. Sir Alan Walters, *Sterling in Danger: The Economic Consequences of Pegged Exchange Rates* (London: Fontana, 1990), p. 117.

92. Ibid., pp. 118–19.

93. Ibid., p. 119.

94. Glenn Frankel, "Howe Resigns from Cabinet in Britain," *Washington Post*, November 2, 1990, p. A31.

95. "Flirting with the Hard Ecu," *The Economist*, September 15, 1990, p. 62.

96. Reginald Dale, "Why U.K.'s Wrench Misses the EC Works," *International Herald Tribune*, November 4–5, 1989, p. 1.

97. "Rethinking EMU," *The Economist*, September 15, 1990, p. 14.

98. Ibid., pp. 14–15.

99. David Owen, "Revival of Hard Ecu Plan Tests Tory Unity," *Financial Times*, August 10, 1993, p. 6.

100. Ibid.

101. "Flirting with the Hard Ecu."

102. Walter S. Mossberg and Alan Murray, "Baker Suggests a Role for Gold in Setting World Economic Policy," *Wall Street Journal*, October 1, 1987, p. 3.

103. John Burgess and Hobart Rowen, "Baker Sees Increased Gold Role," *Washington Post,* October 1, 1987, p. A22.

104. Mossberg and Murray, "Baker Suggests a Role for Gold," p. 24.

105. Ibid., p. 3.

106. Edouard Balladur, "Rebuilding an International Monetary System: Three Possible Approaches," *Wall Street Journal*, February 23, 1988, p. 30.

107. Ibid.

108. "A Strong Dollar, a New Money Order," interview with Edouard Balladur, *Wall Street Journal*, December 5, 1990, p. A16.

109. Lewis E. Lehrman, "Full Employment, Four Percent Interest Rates, Stable Prices and a Balanced Budget: The Monetary Standard and Economic Growth," in *Champions of Freedom: The Ludwig von Mises Lecture Series*, vol. 10 (Hillsdale, Mich.: The Hillsdale College Press, 1983), pp. 43–44.

110. Ibid., p. 58.

111. "Report to the Congress of the Commission on the Role of Gold in the Domestic and International Monetary Systems," vol. I (March 1982), p. 19.

112. Ibid., p. 20.

113. "A 'Pre-Williamsburg' Conference on the International Monetary System, Excerpts From Paper by Prof. Robert Mundell on the Need for International Monetary Reform as an Agenda for Williamsburg," *Congressional Record*, Proceedings and Debates of the 98th Congress, First Session, vol. 129, no. 69, House of Representatives.

114. Martin Anderson, *Revolution* (San Diego, New York, London: Harcourt Brace Jovanovich, 1988), p. 146.

115. Robert L. Bartley, *The Seven Fat Years: And How To Do It Again* (New York: The Free Press, 1992), p. 105.

116. Ibid., p. 48.

117. Ralph Z. Hallow, "When Kemp Talks, Now They All Listen," *Washington Times*, May 18, 1992, p. A1.

118. Jack Kemp, "How To Fight Inflation: The Supply-Side Strategy for Lower Interest Rates," remarks before the Federal Reserve

Bank of Atlanta and Emory University, Atlanta, Georgia, March 17, 1982.

119. Ibid.

120. Ibid.

121. Ibid.

122. Hayek, "Toward a Free-Market Monetary System," in *Search for Stable Money*, p. 383.

123. F. A. Hayek, "Denationalisation of Money—The Argument Refined," Hobart paper 70, 2nd (extended) ed. (London: Institute of Economic Affairs, 1978), pp. 116–17. Quoted in James A. Dorn, ed. *The Cato Journal*, vol. 9, no. 2, fall 1989, p. 277.

124 Richard W. Rahn, "Private Money: An Idea Whose Time Has Come," *The Cato Journal*, vol. 9, no. 2, fall 1989, pp. 355–56.

125 Hayek, "Toward a Free-Market Monetary System," in S*earch for Stable Money*, p. 386.

126. Ibid., p. 384.

127. Roland Vaubel, "Competing Currencies: The Case for Free Entry," in *Search for Stable Money*, p. 282.

128. George A. Selgin, *The Theory of Free Banking* (Totowa, N.J.: Rowman and Littlefield, 1988), p. 96.

129. Hayek, "Toward a Free-Market Monetary System," in *Search for Stable Money*, p. 390.

130. Selgin, *The Theory of Free Banking*, pp. 7–8.

131 Ibid.

132. Mary L. King, *The Great American Banking Snafu* (Lexington, Mass.: Lexington Books, 1985), pp. 10–11.

133. Emil Sommarin, Vårt sparbanksväsen. 1834–1892 (Lund: Gleerup, 1942), p. 167. Cited in King, *The Great American Banking Snafu*, p. 11.

134 King, *The Great American Banking Snafu*, pp. 3–4.

135. Lawrence H. White, *Competition and Currency: Essays on Free Banking and Money* (New York: New York University Press, 1989), p. 20.

136. Larry J. Sechrest, "Free Banking in Scotland: A Dissenting View," *Cato Journal*, vol. 10, no. 3 (winter 1991), pp. 799–808.

137. Ibid.

138. C. R. Josset, *Money in Britain: A History of the Currencies of the British Isles* (London: Frederick Warne, 1962), p. 104.

139. King, *The Great American Banking Snafu*, p. 14.

140. Ibid., p. 15.

141. Ibid., p. 14.

142. Paul and Lehrman, *The Case for Gold*, p. 39.

143. Ibid., p. 67.
144. Ibid.

Chapter 5. The Solid Choice

1. James Tobin, *A Proposal for International Monetary Reform*, Cowles Foundation paper no. 495, Cowles Foundation for Research in Economics (New Haven, Conn. Yale University Press, 1980), pp. 157–58. Quoted in International Monetary Fund, *The Exchange Rate System: Lessons of the Past and Options for the Future*, occasional paper no. 30 (Washington, D.C.: IMF, July 1984), pp. 18–19.
2. Kenichi Ohmae, *The Borderless World: Power and Strategy in the Interlinked Economy* (New York: Harper Business, 1990), p. 163.
3. Ibid., pp. 160–61.
4. Judy Shelton, "Gold Mine of Lessons from Europe," *Wall Street Journal*, August 13, 1993, p. A6.
5. Milton Friedman, "As Good as Gold: A Symposium," *National Review*, June 11, 1990, p. 31.
6. Lester Thurow, *Head to Head: The Coming Economic Battle Among Japan, Europe, and America* (New York: William Morrow, 1992), p. 241.
7. Ibid., p. 240.
8. Lewis E. Lehrman, "Full Employment, Four Percent Interest Rate, Stable Prices and a Balanced Budget: The Monetary Standard and Economic Growth," in *Champions of Freedom*, vol. 10 (Hillsdale, Mich.: The Hillsdale College Press, 1983), p. 51.
9. Herbert Stein, "Foreign Travels, Foreign-Exchange Travails," *Wall Street Journal*, August 27, 1990, p. A10.
10. See Richard N. Cooper, "Is Private Money Optimal?" comment in *Cato Journal*, vol. 9, no. 2 (fall 1989), pp. 394–95.
11. John Maynard Keynes, *A Tract on Monetary Reform* (London: Macmillan, 1932), pp. 24–25.
12. Ibid., pp. 25–26.
13. Ludwig von Mises, "The Gold Problem," in *Planning for Freedom*, 4th ed. (South Holland, Ill.: Libertarian Press, 1980), p. 185. Quoted in Richard Ebeling, "Ludwig von Mises and the Gold Standard," in *The Gold Standard: An Austrian Perspective*, ed., Llewellyn H. Rockwell, Jr. (Lexington, Mass.: Lexington Books, 1985), p. 48.
14. Thomas Jefferson, letter to John Wayles Eppes, from Monticello, June 24, 1813. Reproduced in Thomas Jefferson, *Writings* (New York: Literary Classics of the United States, 1984), p. 1285.
15. Ibid., p. 1283.

16. Thomas Jefferson, letter to John Taylor, from Monticello, May 28, 1816. Reproduced in Jefferson, *Writings*, p. 1391.

17. Quoted in Ron Paul and Lewis Lehrman, *The Case for Gold: A Minority Report of the U.S. Gold Commission* (Washington, D.C.: Cato Institute, 1982), p. 1.

18. "The ECU Nationalists," *The Economist*, February 18, 1989, p. 12.

19. Jeffrey Ryser, "Chalk Up Another One for the Monetarists," *Global Finance*, July 1993, p. 67.

20. Alan Walters, *Sterling in Danger: The Economic Consequences of Pegged Exchange Rates* (London: Fontana/Collins, 1990), pp. 117–18.

21. Jack Kemp, "How to Fight Inflation: The Supply-Side Strategy for Lower Interest Rates," remarks before the Federal Reserve Bank of Atlanta and Emory University, Atlanta, Georgia, March 17, 1982.

22. Thomas Jefferson, letter to Samuel Kercheval, from Monticello, July 12, 1816. Reproduced in Jefferson, *Writings*, pp. 1400–01.

23. Thomas Jefferson, letter to William Plumer, 1816, *Thomas Jefferson: His Life and Words*, ed. by Nick Beilenson (White Plains, N.Y.: Peter Pauper Press, 1986), p. 25.

24. Paul and Lehrman, *The Case for Gold*, p. 174.

25. Alan Greenspan, "Can the U.S. Return to a Gold Standard?" *Wall Street Journal*, September 1, 1981.

26. See Alan Greenspan, "Gold and Economic Freedom," reprinted from *The Objectivist*, July 1966, in Ayn Rand, *Capitalism: The Unknown Ideal* (New York: New American Library, 1966), pp. 93–94.

27. William Greider, *Secrets of the Temple: How the Federal Reserve Runs the Country* (New York: Touchstone: 1987), p. 361.

28. Ibid., p. 404.

29. Vivian Brownstein, "The Fed Drops a Yardstick," *Fortune*, August 23, 1993, p. 22.

30. Ludwig von Mises, lecture on "Capitalism," in *Economic Policy: Thoughts for Today and Tomorrow* (Washington, D.C.: Regnery Gateway, 1979), p. 11.

31. Michael Wolff, "Walking Small at Munich," *Washington Post*, July 5, 1992, p. C3.

32. George J. W. Goodman, "Adam Smith," *Paper Money* (New York: Summit Books, 1981), pp. 290–91.

33. Stephen Baker, Elizabeth Weiner, Geri Smith, Ann Charters, and Ken Jacobson, "Latin America: The Big Move to Free Markets," *Business Week*, June 15, 1992, p. 54.

34. Steven Erlanger, "In Choppy Russian Economy, a Family Jury-Rigs a Budget," *The New York Times*, July 20, 1992, p. A7.

35. Hobart Rowen, "Dollars and Yen: Money Makes the World Go Round," review of *Changing Fortunes: The World's Money and the Threat to American Leadership*, in *Washington Post*, July 19, 1992, p. 5.
36. John Bussey, Michael Williams, and Alan Murray, "In Abrupt Shift, U.S. Intervenes to Slow Yen's Historic Rise," *Wall Street Journal*, August 20, 1993, p. A1.
37. See Ronald I. McKinnon, "Monetary and Exchange Rate Policies for International Financial Stability: A Proposal," *Journal of Economic Perspectives*, vol. 2, no. 1, winter 1988, pp. 83–103.
38. Reginald Dale, "Lisbon Notebook: Journalists' Conference," *Inside Europe*, vol. 1, no. 6, supplement in *Europe*, July–August 1992.
39. Richard M. Weintraub and Paul Blustein, "Fearing Where the Buck Stops," *Washington Post*, July 19, 1992, p. H8.
40. George Gilder, *Microcosm: The Quantum Revolution in Economics and Technology* (New York: Simon and Schuster, 1989), pp. 357–58.
41. Ibid., p. 357.
42. Ibid., p. 358.
43. Paul Volcker and Toyoo Gyohten, *Changing Fortunes: The World's Money and the Threat to American Leadership* (New York: Times Books, 1992), p. xv.
44. Kemp, "How to Fight Inflation."
45. Lehrman, "Full Employment," p. 46.
46. Friedrich A. Hayek, *The Constitution of Liberty* (Chicago: The University of Chicago Press, 1960), p. 400.
47. Ibid.
48. Ibid., pp. 402–3.
49. Ibid., p. 401.
50. Ibid., p. 403.
51. Ibid., pp. 403–4.
52. Volcker and Gyohten, *Changing Fortunes*, p. 18.
53. Ibid. pp. 78–79.
54. Ibid., p. 80.
55. Ibid., p. 11.
56. Lawrence S. Ritter and William L. Silber, *Principles of Money, Banking, and Financial Markets* (New York: Basic Books, 1974), pp. 506–7.
57. Mises, *Economic Policy*, p. 72.

Chapter 6. Agenda for a New Bretton Woods

1. Paul Farhi, "The Difficulty of Reducing the Debt," *Washington Post*, August 9, 1993, p. A4.
2. Paul A. Volcker and Toyoo Gyohten, *Changing Fortunes: The*

World's Money and the Threat to American Leadership (New York: Times Books, 1992), pp. 239–40.

3. Ludwig von Mises, *Economic Policy: Thoughts for Today and Tomorrow* (Washington, D.C.: Regnery Gateway, 1979), pp. 72–73.

4. Volcker and Gyohten, *Changing Fortunes*, p. 27.

5. Ibid., p. 177.

6. Martin C. Anderson, "The National Economic Policy: Prospects for Reaganomics," in *Champions of Freedom* (Hillsdale, Mich.: The Hillsdale College Press, 1983), vol. 10, p. 74.

7. Ibid., p. 75.

8. Philip Stephens, "Government Set to Ditch Balanced Budget Strategy," *Financial Times*, August 13, 1992, p. 1.

9. Lawrence A. Kudlow, "Back to Bretton Woods," *Wall Street Journal,* December 31, 1991.

10. Steven Greenhouse, "With Rates This Low, Where's the Boom?" *The New York Times*, August 24, 1993, p. D2.

11. Phillip Cagan, "A Compensated Dollar: Better or More Likely Than Gold?" in *The Search for Stable Money*, edited by James A. Dorn and Anna J. Schwartz (Chicago and London: University of Chicago Press, 1987), pp. 268–69.

12. Richard Timberlake, *Gold, Greenbacks, and the Constitution* (Berryville, Va.: The George Edward Durell Foundation, 1991), pp. 11–12.

13. Ludwig von Mises, *The Theory of Money and Credit* (Indianapolis, Ind.: Liberty Classics, 1980), pp. 491–92.

14. Ibid., p. 493.

15. Donald L. Kemmerer, "Why We Should Return to the Gold Standard," *Human Events*, June 30, 1979, p. 16.

16. Patrick Harverson, "Bush Says Sorry But Stocks Still Slide," *Financial Times*, August 22–23, 1992, weekend FT, p. II.

17. "D-Day for the Dollar," *Financial Times*, August 22–23, 1992, p. 22.

18. Harverson, "Bush Says Sorry."

19. I. M. Destler and C. Randall Henning, *Dollar Politics: Exchange Rate Policymaking in the United States* (Washington, D.C.: Institute for International Economics, 1989), p. 25.

20. Giulio M. Gallarotti, "The Classical Gold Standard as a Spontaneous Order (Centralized Versus Decentralized International Monetary Systems: The Lessons of the Classical Gold Standard)," preliminary draft of paper prepared for the Cato Institute Seventh Annual Monetary Conference, Washington, D.C., February 23–24, 1989, p. 5.

21. Ibid., p. 6.

22. Ibid., p. 4.

23. Ibid., p. 5. In the last line, the author is paraphrasing a statement appearing in Stanley Zucker, *Ludwig Bamberger: German Liberal Politician and Social Critic* (Pittsburgh: University of Pittsburgh Press, 1975).

24. Yoichi Funabashi, *Managing the Dollar: From the Plaza to the Louvre* (Washington, D.C.: Institute for International Economics, 1988), p. 198.

25. Rick Wartzman, "Fed Officials Show Support for Germany," *Wall Street Journal*, August 31, 1992, p. A2.

26. Jim Hoagland, "False Promises, Monetary Alibis," *Washington Post*, April 9, 1992, p. A27.

27. Ibid.

28. Volcker and Gyohten, *Changing Fortunes*, p. 294.

29. George Melloan, "Monetary Jitters: Deja Vu All Over Again," *Wall Street Journal*, August 31, 1992, p. A11.

30. Ibid.

31. Ibid.

32. Hoagland, "False Promises."

33. See Alan Greenspan, "Can the U.S. Return to a Gold Standard?" *Wall Street Journal*, September 1, 1981.

34. Mises, *The Theory of Money and Credit*, pp. 456–57.

35. Murray N. Rothbard, *The Case for a 100 Percent Gold Dollar* (Auburn, Ala.: The Ludwig von Mises Institute, 1991), p. 68.

36. Philip Shenon, "Non-Aligned Bloc Seeks a New Reason for Being," *The New York Times*, September 2, 1992, p. A9.

37. David Asman, "Wealth of Naciones: People Power Comes to Latin America," *Policy Review*, spring 1992, no. 60, p. 44.

38. Volcker and Gyohten, *Changing Fortunes*, p. 293.

39. Ibid., pp. 303–4.

40. "75%: Why Sweden Acted," interview by David Brooks, *Wall Street Journal*, September 11, 1992, p. A18.

41. Philip Stephens, "Thatcher Attacks Major on Europe," *Financial Times*, September 4, 1992, p. 1.

42. George J. W. Goodman, "Adam Smith," in *Paper Money* (New York: Summit Books, 1981), pp. 142–43.

43. "75%: Why Sweden Acted."

44. Clyde H. Farnsworth, "I.M.F. Panel Votes to Add $60 Billion to Pool for Loans," *The New York Times*, May 9, 1990, p. A1.

45. Hobart Rowen, "U.S. Rejects IMF Call for More Funds," *Washington Post*, September 25, 1989, p. A4.

46. Melanie Tammen, "How IMF Plays the Bailout Game," *Washington Times*, December 15, 1989, p. F4.

Epilogue: The Sanctity of Sound Money

1. John Maynard Keynes, *The General Theory of Employment, Interest and Money*, in *The Collected Writings of John Maynard Keynes* (London: Macmillan for the Royal Economic Society, 1971), vol. VII, pp. 383–84. Cited in Vincent Bladen, *From Adam Smith to Maynard Keynes: The Heritage of Political Economy* (Toronto and Buffalo: University of Toronto Press, 1974), p. 486.
2. Friedrich A. Hayek, *The Constitution of Liberty* (Chicago: The University of Chicago Press, 1960), pp. 338–39.
3. William Greider, *Secrets of the Temple: How the Federal Reserve Runs the Country* (New York: Touchstone/Simon & Schuster, 1987), pp. 241–42.
4. Grover Cleveland (1893), quoted in *The Freeman: Ideas on Liberty*, August 1992, vol. 42, no. 8, back cover.
5. Adam Smith, *Paper Money* (New York: Summit Books, 1981), p. 295.
6. Ludwig von Mises, *Economic Policy: Thoughts for Today and Tomorrow* (Washington, D.C.: Regnery Gateway, 1979), p. 65.
7. Ibid., pp. 65–66.
8. *Webster's Ninth New Collegiate Dictionary* (Springfield, Mass.: Merriam-Webster, 1986), p. 160.
9. "Fool's Gold," *The Economist*, January 23, 1993, p. 17.
10. "Central Bank Holdings of Gold," *World Gold Review* (London: World Gold Council, Gold Economics Service), summer 1992, p. 11.
11. Ibid.
12. Ibid., p. 5.
13. Peter T. White, "The Power of Money," *National Geographic*, vol. 183, no. 1, January 1993, p. 94.
14. "Chinese Addicts," *The Economist*, April 10, 1993, p. 84.
15. "Melting Away," *The Economist*, April 4, 1992, pp. 99–100.
16. Jack Kemp, "Is There a Political Consensus for Monetary Reform?," remarks at U.S. Congressional Summit on Exchange Rates and the Dollar, Washington, D.C., November 13, 1985.

Acknowledgments

N early a decade ago, the *Wall Street Journal* published an editorial by Robert L. Bartley entitled "Fix What Broke." I have been influenced by countless essays, articles, and events involving global monetary relations during the intervening years, but there is no doubt in my mind that the catalyst for writing this book was that editorial.

Many individuals contributed to the completion of this project by providing their analysis and advice, corroboration and correction. Others offered encouragement and enthusiasm, and displayed remarkable patience (it is rather uncomfortable to be a sounding board for lengthy discourses on international monetary reform). I am grateful for all the support, professional and personal, and happy that the lines often crossed.

The Hoover Institution continues to serve as an intellectual sanctuary and a testing ground for policy ideas. I deeply appreciate my good friends and lively colleagues at Hoover, and I am especially indebted to John Raisian for his abiding faith and assistance. Milton Friedman, always willing to provide incisive comments and scholarly direction, is more than a legend—he is an inspiration. I have the greatest respect, too for Martin Anderson, intellectual trailblazer for sound economic and monetary policies. Brenda McLean has been a friend *extraordinaire*.

No one could hope to write a book on the policy implications of international economic developments for general readers without the skills of an exceptionally gifted editor and dedicated publisher. I have both in Erwin Glikes. Thank you, Erwin—again. Thanks are also due to Marsha Finley for her diligent copy editing and to Edith Lewis at The Free Press for putting the final manuscript in apple-pie order.

Finally, I wish to acknowledge the insights provided by Paul D. Conley, a perceptive and wise gentleman who happens to be my grandfather. And I finish by merely alluding to the unwavering support I received from my husband, G. L., because words cannot possibly describe how much it has meant and how much he means.

Index

DATE DUE

Trexler Library
Muhlenberg College
Allentown, PA 18104